JOHN HENRY NEWMAN

AUTOBIOGRAPHICAL WRITINGS

John Henry Newman
Autobiographical Writings

EDITED

WITH INTRODUCTIONS BY

HENRY TRISTRAM

OF THE ORATORY

SHEED AND WARD : NEW YORK

CONTENTS

FOREWORD

Among the papers of Father Henry Tristram, when he died on February 8th, 1955, was this collection of Cardinal Newman's autobiographical writings. He selected the documents and prepared them for the press. The collection is now published, in its entirety, as he left it.[1] It should be noted that all the Introductions (except the last) are by him, and that he has contributed a long Supplement to the second Autobiographical Sketch.

The final editor has merely contributed a short Introduction to the Memorandum about the Catholic University, which Father Tristram had not provided. He has also carefully revised the texts themselves, with the aid of the autographs. A few mistakes and omissions have been corrected, the longest being an interesting passage which Newman had crossed out in the Autobiographical Memoir (p. 82). Occasional footnotes have been inserted, for the sake of greater clarity, but these are initialled C.S.D., to distinguish them. Any addition made to the text by the editors is enclosed in square brackets.

The *Autobiographical Writings* crown Father Tristram's work on Newman. His Introductions provide the information needed to understand the texts. For those who would delve deeper, there exist, besides the standard biographies, the article on Newman in which Father Tristram collaborated with Father Joseph Bacchus, in the *Dictionnaire de Théologie Catholique*, and Père Bouyer's recent Life, which often comments on the texts now printed in full.

It seems to be more and more urged that not only does Newman take his place intellectually among the early writers, to whom he was so devoted, but that in sanctity too, he is not unworthy to be named with them. Pope Pius XII has singled him out for praise, and described him as "lumen et decus eximium" of the English nation. The documents now published, most of them very private, and never meant to be scattered broadcast, enable us to follow Newman in his "hunger and thirst for holiness". His secret trials and struggles are laid bare. Newman himself has justified the "use of frankness, after the manner of Scripture, in speaking of the saints; for their lingering

[1] Father Tristram gave a copy of the collection to Père Bouyer, with a view to a French edition. The first volume appeared this year, and contains, although without the sometimes important additions of the final editor, the greater number of the documents, the rest being reserved for a second volume.

imperfections surely make us love them more, without leading us to
reverence them less, and act as a relief to the discouragement and
despondency which may come over those, who, in the midst of much
error and sin, are striving to imitate them. ... And in like manner, the
dissatisfaction of Saints, of St Basil, or again of our own St Thomas,
with the contemporary policy or conduct of the Holy See, while it is
no justification of ordinary men, bishops, clergy, or laity, in feeling
the same, is no reflection either on those Saints or on the Vicar of
Christ. ... Accidents of this nature are unavoidable in the state of
being which we are allotted here below" (Advertisement to the 1857
edition of *The Church of the Fathers*, *Historical Sketches*, vol. ii,
p. xii).

The Oratory   C. STEPHEN DESSAIN
Birmingham   of the oratory
June 1956

GENERAL INTRODUCTION

The volume which is now offered to the public contains all the autobiographical material which Cardinal Newman left behind him in his room when he died.

It comprises the following documents:

1. An Autobiography in Miniature.
2. Two autobiographical sketches—together with a continuation covering the later years of his life, contributed, as will be explained later, by the Editor.
3. The Autobiographical Memoir.
4. "My Illness in Sicily."
5. Three early journals.
6. The Journal, 1859-1879.
7. "Memorandum About my Connection with the Catholic University."

Lest a false impression should unwittingly be conveyed, it must be at once admitted that these papers cannot, strictly speaking, be assigned to the category of unpublished matter. Anne Mozley, as we shall see later, was furnished by Newman himself with all the relevant papers for her *Letters and Correspondence of J. H. Newman*; and Wilfrid Ward was allowed unrestricted access to all the sources for his *Life of J. H. Cardinal Newman*, which is significantly described on the title page, as "based on his private journals and correspondence". She incorporated the third and the fourth papers in her first volume; and he made copious extracts from the sixth and seventh. But it may be claimed without qualification that they have not hitherto been published in their original form. Ward did no more and no less than what every authorized biographer has a right to do: he selected for quotation the passages that were, in his opinion, apposite to his purpose, and he omitted those that were not; and he quoted lavishly because he loyally adhered to Newman's expressed wish, that the history of his life should be told, as far as possible, in his own words. Anne Mozley, availing herself of the permission given her by Newman, made ample use of her position as editor, and suppressed more than discretion prescribed, more even than was necessary for the due observance of the reticences held sacred by the writers of the Victorian era.

But suspicions inevitably arise in the minds of readers, when their eyes glimpse the sinister row of dots which serve to indicate that a sentence or a passage, more or less long, has been omitted; and understandably because they have no means of judging what has been left out, or why. The omission may be, and probably in most cases is, due to the feeling on the part of the biographer, that a biography should be an integrated whole, a work of art, not a litter of unco-ordinated material. Is this passage, they naturally ask themselves, or that, omitted for reasons of prudence, because, if quoted, it would strike a jarring note, and mar the prevailing harmony of the biographer's treatment of his theme? An editor, as distinct from a biographer, lies under no such inner compulsion: he has his documents to reproduce, and he acquits himself of his duty if he reproduces them. The present editor may claim to be in a position to assert without reservation that in this respect, at least, Newman presents no problem; he has never found in his papers a single sentence, or in fact a single word that would detract from his reputation, if broadcast to the world. Hence it seems to him the obvious course to reproduce all the documents, exactly as they came from the pen of their author. In one or two instances he has even included passages which Newman himself deleted. They have all, with the exception of the first and second parts of the fifth, only copies of which have been found, been transcribed from the autographs, precisely as they stand there. Hence readers may be confident that nothing has, for any reason whatsoever, been withheld from them.

This may seem to some, whose standards of judgment may differ from those of the editor, an overbold course to adopt, but it is at least honest. Moreover he may claim Newman's sanction, as is clear from a note, dated 5 July, 1876, which reads: "But it must be fully understood, that I leave this *Sketch*,[1] as I leave all my papers as *materials* and *documents* only, to be used simply at the discretion (for publication or not, in whole or in part) of the parties who after my death come into possession of my papers. J H N".

The question may reasonably be asked, what precise object has the editor in view in publishing these papers now? The answer is simple and not far to seek. Even those of them that have already been published in part, are not at present easily accessible to large circles of readers. Presented in a single convenient volume, they should reach a far more numerous public, and stimulate a more widespread

[1] Referring to III, The Autobiographical Memoir. C.S.D.

and deeper interest in Newman. Some—a goodly number, perhaps—
may be encouraged to pursue their reading further, and take up the
study of his many works, of which new editions will in course
of time, it is hoped, be available. If they do, they will reap a rich
reward. From their own experience they will find it an untold advantage to have been brought into immediate contact, and not through
the medium of another person's mind, with one who, in a passage in
the Preface to the *Apologia*, too often overlooked, describes himself
as "a man who has been so long before the eyes of the world; who
has so many to speak of him from personal knowledge; whose
natural impulse it has ever been to speak out; who has ever spoken
too much rather than too little; who would have saved himself many
a scrape, if he had been wise enough to hold his tongue; who has
ever been fair to the doctrines and arguments of his opponents; who
has never slurred over facts and reasonings which told against himself; who has never given his name or authority to proofs which he
thought unsound, or to testimony which he did not think at least
plausible; who has never shrunk from confessing a fault when he felt
that he had committed one; who has ever consulted for others more
than for himself; who has given up much that he loved and prized
and could have retained, but that he loved honesty better than name,
and Truth better than dear friends ..."

I
AN AUTOBIOGRAPHY
IN MINIATURE

INTRODUCTION

This document is a curious survival from the past, and it is inexplicable how it should happen to have been preserved. Its composition, from the first word to the last, extended over a period of no less than seventy-two years, from 1812, when Newman was eleven years of age, to 1884, when he was eighty-three, surely a record for so meagre a manuscript. It is written on the back cover of an ordinary school exercise book, the first and last two entries in ink, the intervening four in pencil. The outside of the cover is pale blue in colour, and in moments of distraction its owner has covered it all over with scrawls and scribbles and numbers, in the middle of which his surname stands out. At some time or other, perhaps about the year 1875, when he had become worried by the prospect of a biography, or biographies, he destroyed the rest of the book, and kept only this back cover, which he inserted in a scrap-album, filled with odds-and-ends of a highly miscellaneous nature, including his first letters from school, a page torn out of a diary for 1810, "presented to him by his kind Mama", his Latin verse book, with the cross and the rosary roughly drawn on the first page, and other papers dating from his boyhood and youth.

When the small boy at Ealing School made his first entry in this record, just before presenting himself for a lesson in Greek, which he had begun two years before, the "home", of which he was dreaming, was a house in Southampton Street (then No. 17), near the British Museum, but the greater part of the summer holiday he would have spent at Norwood, where the Newmans had a cottage in rural surroundings, Vine Cottage, Knight's Hill Green, which is several times referred to in Harriett Newman's story for children (*Family Adventures*, pp. 22, 69, 76, 86, 140).

Manifestly they were then in comfortable circumstances, but on March 8th, 1816 (owing to the financial crisis after the Napoleonic Wars), the bank, in which Mr Newman was a partner, was forced by the obstinacy of a single person to close its doors. Within a month (April 2nd) the creditors were all paid in full, but Mr Newman was reduced to comparative poverty. In order to maintain his family in comfort, he undertook, although entirely without business experience, the management of a brewery at Alton, a small Hampshire town; and on October 30th, 1816 they migrated there from Norwood. Newman was then away from home at school. Shortly afterwards (December 14th) he was taken to Oxford by his father, entered at Trinity College, and matriculated by the President, who was also Vice-Chancellor, although he did not go into residence until the following June 17th. It was at Alton, as his Eclogues (not in *Verses on Various Occasions*) show, that he spent at least his Oxford Long Vacations.

Unfortunately in the fourth entry "the date" does not "speak", at least to us. Nothing out of the ordinary seems to have happened in the family circle; but the clouds of further financial disasters may have begun to gather. Probably he was thinking of his own position. His scholarship at Trinity had not yet run out; but upon his return to Oxford four days previously, he could hardly have failed to be conscious that his prospects were blighted by the fiasco in the "Schools"; for his name did not appear in the mathematical class list, and in the classical it was "below the line" in the second class—the equivalent of the future third. What hope had he of a career in the University? Later in the year another blow fell: Mr Newman's connection with the Alton Brewery ceased, and the house in Southampton Street had perforce to be given up. In a letter to his aunt on November 7th, he described his situation as one "which the world would call calamitous". The family was split up between his aunt's house in Strand-on-the-Green, near Kew, and successive houses in London, occupied by his parents, until his father's death on September 29th, 1824.

His circumstances began to change for the better at Easter 1822, when he redeemed his failure in the "Schools" by gaining a fellowship at Oriel, then the badge of intellectual eminence. Afterwards he became Curate of St Clement's, Oxford (1824), Vice-Principal of Alban Hall (1825), Tutor of Oriel (1826), Public Examiner (1827-8), and Vicar of St Mary's, the University Church (1828). At this time he was sufficiently affluent to support his younger brother, Francis, through his University course, and, in conjunction with his brother, to pay off his aunt's considerable debts. In 1829 he took a cottage for the summer at Horspath, a few miles out of Oxford, for his mother and his two sisters, Harriett and Jemima, the dearly-loved youngest sister, Mary, having died on January 5th, 1828, and he stayed with them, riding into Oxford on his horse in the morning and returning to them in the late afternoon. He must just have arrived at Oriel, when he made the fifth entry. His religious opinions were in a state of transition. Under the influence of the Oriel school he had been drifting towards theological liberalism, but the loss of his sister and his own illness "rudely" checked him in his downward course; and his growing intimacy with R. H. Froude gave a fresh orientation to his thoughts, although he was still in the dark as to what the upshot would be.

Sixteen momentous years passed over his head before he found out for certain whither God was "taking" him. Received into the Church on October 9th, 1845, he accepted Dr. Wiseman's offer of Old Oscott, re-named by him Maryvale, an old house north of Birmingham, which had then been in Catholic hands for nearly two centuries, as a refuge for himself and his fellow-converts. His residence there was interrupted by a sojourn in Rome for rather more than a year (September 1846-December 1847); but when he returned to Maryvale, he came armed with a papal brief empowering him to establish the Oratory in England, which he did on February 1st, 1848.

In 1850 Maryvale had been given up, and with half the community, the other half having migrated to London under Faber, he was settled in Alcester Street, Birmingham, where in the grimmest of surroundings he had his first experience of parochial work; but a plot of land had already been secured, in Hagley Road, as a site for the Oratory, which was to be his home from 1852 until the end of his life.

Finally, on May 12th, 1879, to crown his life in the evening of his days, Pope Leo XIII, moved by his "genius and learning", his "piety", his "zeal ... in the exercise of the Sacred Ministry", his "devotion and filial attachment to the Holy Apostolic See", and his "signal services ... for long years rendered to religion", raised him to the Sacred College; and England felt that by this honour conferred upon the most venerated of her sons she herself was honoured.

"It is not wonderful," wrote Dean Church just after the event, "that people should be impressed by the vicissitudes and surprises and dramatic completeness of Cardinal Newman's career. It is not wonderful that he should be impressed by it himself."

[AN AUTOBIOGRAPHY IN MINIATURE]

John Newman wrote this just before he was going up to Greek on Tuesday, June 10th, 1812, when it only wanted 3 days to his going home, thinking of the time (at home) when looking at this he shall recollect when he did it.

At school now back again.

And now at Alton where he never expected to be, being lately come for the Vacation from Oxford where he dared not hope to be—how quick time passes and how ignorant are we of futurity. April 8th 1819 Thursday.

And now at Oxford but with far different feelings—let the date speak —Friday February 16th 1821—

And now in my rooms at Oriel College, a Tutor, a Parish Priest and Fellow, having suffered much, slowly advancing to what is good and holy, and led on by God's hand blindly, not knowing whither He is taking me. Even so, O Lord. September 7, 1829. Monday morning. $\frac{1}{4}$ past 10.

And now a Catholic at Maryvale and expecting soon to set out for Rome. May 29, 1846.

And now a Priest and Father of the Oratory, having just received the degree of Doctor from the Holy Father. September 23, 1850.

And now a Cardinal. March 2, 1884.

II

TWO AUTOBIOGRAPHICAL
SKETCHES

INTRODUCTION

The two autobiographical sketches comprised in this section are transcripts from documents in Newman's own handwriting.

The first occupies four pages of paper. It is couched in the third person, and neatly written, with only one correction in the text, and the insertion of a single afterthought, but it is incomplete, for it breaks off suddenly at the beginning of the Tractarian Movement. There can be little doubt that it was intended for some work of reference, but it is quite impossible even to guess which. The date of composition can be fixed within narrow limits, by the reference to Sir Richard Bethell (afterwards Lord Westbury) as the Attorney-General at the time. He held that office from 1856, with an interval in 1858-9, until 1861, when he succeeded Lord Campbell as Lord Chancellor.

The second is a draft in the first person, drawn up with many corrections and erasures, in response to a request for information to furnish the basis of an article in a biographical dictionary to be published in Quebec under the title of *The Men and Women of the Nineteenth Century*. The manuscript is headed: "Oct. 26/63. Memorandum for Mr Henry J. Morgan Quebec Canada"; and at the end there is appended a brief note to the compiler:

Sir,
   I suppose the inclosed will be more than sufficient for your purpose, as the Articles in a Biographical Dictionary cannot run to any great length.
                                        J H N

The list of his works with which he concludes the notice, has been omitted, as being incomplete and irrelevant.

Since these two notices do not carry us further than the year 1863, and certain readers may like to have at hand a short conspectus of Newman's whole life, the editor has had the presumption, for their convenience, to add a third written by himself, which covers the years 1863-90.

[AUTOBIOGRAPHICAL NOTICE FOR A WORK OF REFERENCE]

John Henry Newman was born on February 21st, 1801 in Old Broad Street in the City of London. He was the eldest of six children. His father, whose family came from Cambridgeshire, was partner in a Banking House in Lombard Street. His mother was of one of the Huguenot families, who left France for England on the revocation of the Edict of Nantes. Shortly after the peace of 1815, the Banking House wound up its accounts, and paid its creditors in full, but the effort involved his father personally in difficulties, which ended in his premature decay and death.

The subject of this memoir was sent in 1808, being just turned seven years of age, to Dr Nicholas's school at Ealing, near London; where he remained above eight years, having among his contemporaries Mr Richard Westmacott, the Academician, the present Bishop of New Zealand, Sir Frederic Thesiger, and Lord Dalzell. In December 1816, being not yet sixteen, he matriculated at Trinity College, Oxford, gaining in 1818 one of the Scholarships, then lately thrown open to University competition. He passed his examination for the B.A. degree in 1820; and, though he seems to have taken up books sufficient for the first honors in classics and mathematics, his name appears only in the third class in the former order of merit.

In 1822, being then twenty-one, he stood for a fellowship at Oriel College, then at the height of its literary fame, under the Provostship of Dr Copleston, afterwards Bishop of Llandaff; and he was successful against the present Attorney General, Sir R. Bethell, and the Revd E. Coleridge of Eton, brother of the Judge. This success brought him to the knowledge of Dr Whately, Archbishop of Dublin, who at that time was resident in Oxford, previous to his succeeding to a living in Suffolk. Dr Whately employed him in turning into a synthetical form his manuscript Dialogues on Logic, and his composition became the rough draft of the celebrated Treatise, which was published some years afterwards. Dr Whately introduced him also to the late Mr Smedley, at that time Editor of the *Encyclopaedia Metropolitana*; which led to his writing for that work the articles on Cicero and Apollonius Tyanaeus, in 1824 and 1826. The former of these was written, without previous engagement, in the course of six weeks, to supply the place of an article expected from the late Archdeacon Hare.

In the course of 1824 and 1825 he successively received the orders of Deacon and Priest from the late Dr Legge, Bishop of Oxford. In the latter year he was appointed Vice-Principal of Alban Hall by his friend, Dr Whately, who had succeeded to the Headship on Professor Elmsley's death. This office he held with his fellowship, and resigned it in the following year, on his becoming one of the Tutors of his College. In 1827 and 1828 he held the office of Public Examiner. In 1828, on Dr Hawkins being elected Provost of Oriel, in the place of Dr Copleston, promoted to the see of Llandaff, he succeeded him in the Vicarage of St Mary's, which he held till 1843. In 1829 his name occurs in the list of the majority, who placed Sir Robert Inglis in the representation of the University instead of Mr Peel, in the famous contest occasioned by the conversion of the latter statesman to the cause of Catholic Emancipation. At this time he was a member of the Bible and Church Missionary Societies. From 1830 to 1832 he was one of the Select University Preachers. In 1831 he resigned his Tutorship at Oriel. In July 1833 the Tract Movement began with a Sermon preached by Mr Keble before the Judges of Assize, and afterwards published under the title of National Apostasy.

Oct. 26/63

Memorandum for Mr Henry J. Morgan Quebec Canada

I was born in London in 1801—my Father was a Banker in the city of London—my Mother was of a Huguenot Family which had settled in England after the Revocation of the Edict of Nantes. I went to school when 7 years old at Ealing near London, at the Revd George Nicholas's LL D of Wadham College Oxford. I remained there till the age of 15 when I was entered a commoner at Trinity College Oxford. When 17, I gained the Trinity Scholarship which had shortly before been thrown open to the competition of the University. When 19 I passed my examination & took my degree, failing in obtaining high honors. When 21, I was elected Fellow of Oriel College. In the course of the next ten years I was College Tutor, University Examiner, Vicar of St Mary's, Whitehall Preacher, University Preacher.

In September 1833 I began the series called *Tracts for the Times*. In 1838 I became Editor of the *British Critic*. In 1841 on occasion of the publication of No. 90 of the *Tracts*, the Board of Heads of Houses brought out a censure of the doctrine contained in it as an evasive interpretation of the Thirty-Nine Articles, and at the wish of Dr. Bagot, Bishop of Oxford, I brought the series to an end. At the same time I retired from the Editorship of the *British Critic*. In 1842 I retired from Oxford to Littlemore, a hamlet 2 miles from Oxford, which was an integral part of St. Mary's parish, where I had built a church. In 1843 I published a retractation of the strong charges I had made against the Church of Rome, and six months after resigned my living, having held it 15 years, but dwelling still in Littlemore; at the same time I announced to my intimate friends the prospect of my leaving the Anglican for the Roman Communion. In the Autumn of 1845 I was received at Littlemore into the Catholic Church by Fr. Dominic, a Passionist monk, whom I sent for by means of some friends.

In 1846 I left Littlemore for St. Mary's College, Oscott, at the wish of Dr. Wiseman, then Rector of that College and Coadjutor Bishop of the District in which I found myself on my conversion. Late in the year I went to Rome, where I was ordained Priest, remaining there through the whole of 1847. In February 1848 I founded the English Congregation of the Oratory at Maryvale, a country house four or five miles from Birmingham, which the Bishop of the District had given to me, and collected members. In February 1849 I opened an Oratorian House and Church in Birmingham, which has been my home to this time. A little later I founded the London Oratory, sending to it some of the members of the Birmingham House, the chief of whom was Revd F. W. Faber, who ultimately became head of the London Oratory, continuing in that position till a month ago when he died.

In 1850, just before the troubles occasioned by what was popularly called "the Popish Aggression", I delivered a set of Lectures in the London Oratory in consequence of which the Pope sent me a Doctor's diploma; and in 1851 another series in Birmingham, in which I made charges against Dr. Achilli, a Dominican friar, who had become a convert to the Protestant faith, which involved me in an action for libel. As I had to bring my witnesses from Italy, the expenses were very serious, approaching £9000 to £10000, which I was able to meet by the generosity of Catholics in all parts of the world. Of this sum Great Britain contributed about £6700, Ireland £2200, and France nearly £3000; but there were contributions made in North and South America, in Italy, Germany, Holland, Malta, and other places. The cause came on in June 1852, and I lost it, and was sentenced to a fine of £100. The Judges, however, took care to signify their opinion of Achilli's guilt, though I had not been able to bring sufficient legal proofs for everything that I had said. The public took the same view.

In 1851 I undertook to start the new Catholic University of Ireland, as its Rector, without relinquishing my duties at Birmingham. This work I was employed in till the end of 1858, when I resigned it. In the beginning of 1859, on my relinquishment of my Irish engagement, I undertook the editorship of the *Rambler* for a short time, in the wish to extricate it from certain ecclesiastical difficulties in which it then found itself. At the same time I began a school on the plan of the Protestant public schools, Winchester, Rugby, etc., with such modifications as Catholic discipline requires, which has up to this day met with much success and great encouragement for the future.

SUPPLEMENT
by HENRY TRISTRAM

Thus far Newman has himself carried the narrative of his life in two separate documents, one in the third, the other in the first person, the former written not later than 1861, the latter dated October 26th, 1863; but as he seems never to have been called upon to continue it, we may here so far presume, for the sake of completeness, as to do what he has left undone.

It is necessary, however, to revert to the affair of the *Rambler*, since his editorship of that outspoken and petulant review for two numbers (May and July, 1859), and his connection with its conductors, a group of what may be called "liberal Catholics", entailed for him an unfortunate chain of consequences. To the July number he contributed an article, "On Consulting the Faithful in Matters of Doctrine", which was delated to Rome by Dr Brown, Bishop of Newport; and Dr Ullathorne, his own bishop, informed him on January 13th, 1860 of what had happened. Thereupon Newman at once, in a letter to Cardinal Wiseman, undertook, within the space of a month, to accept and profess *ex animo* the dogmatic propositions thought to be infringed, to explain his argument in strict accordance with them, and to show that the English text was absolutely consistent with them. But the information which he required, before he could do this, was not forthcoming. For some mysterious reason, perhaps sheer negligence on Wiseman's part, although he was actually in Rome at the time, this letter was never brought to the notice of the authorities. Yet on April 29th, 1860 Manning, at Wiseman's request, wrote to assure him that Wiseman thought it better to wait until his return to bring the matter to a satisfactory termination. From this Newman inferred that he was not expected to take any further step to clear himself from the charge; whereas the authorities drew their own conclusions from his apparent indifference, and he remained "under a cloud", until the misunderstanding was removed in 1867.

Meanwhile, in 1864, Charles Kingsley, Rector of Eversley and Professor of Modern History at Cambridge, a popular novelist and a minor poet, anti-Tractarian and ludicrously anti-Catholic in his views, in the course of a review of Froude's *History of England* which appeared in *Macmillan's Magazine* (January 1864), rashly alleged that "truth, for its own sake, had never been a virtue with the Roman clergy", and adduced Newman as his authority for the principle, that "it need not, and on the whole ought not to be". Failing to obtain an adequate retractation of this unfounded assertion, Newman determined to refute the calumny, not by argument, but by a plain, unvarnished account of his religious development from his early years. "I will vanquish," he declared, "not my Accuser, but my judges." Like St Paul he appealed to Caesar, but in this instance Caesar was the British Protestant public, which had condemned him unheard as a traitor in 1845, and had thenceforth consigned him to an ignominious oblivion. The *Apologia pro Vita Sua*, as his defence was called, was issued in weekly parts, the first on April 21st, and the last on June 16th. It had a wide circulation, and produced a revulsion of public feeling in his favour. The aggressor let the verdict go by default; and his victim secured for himself a place in popular esteem which he never afterwards lost. The Catholic Church might be, men felt, all that it had ever been denounced as being; but Newman, at least, was an exception to the rule.

The extraordinary success of the *Apologia* encouraged Newman to take up his pen again, if an occasion should happen to occur. It was not long before a controversy arose between Manning and Pusey. The former, provoked by an allusion made by the latter to the contrast in the attitudes adopted by English Catholics towards the Church of England, addressed a letter to him entitled *The Workings of the Holy Spirit in the Church of England* (1864); and Pusey replied at great length in another letter, nominally addressed to Keble, *The Church of England a Portion of Christ's One Holy Catholic Church, and a Means of restoring Visible Unity. An Eirenicon.* Newman, thereupon, felt that there was a call upon him to intervene, partly because Pusey had alluded to him, but partly also because he seemed to regard the extremists, such as Faber and Ward, as the accepted exponents of the true Catholic teaching. His *Letter Addressed to the Rev. E. B. Pusey on Occasion of his Recent Eirenicon* (1866), apart from its ephemeral polemical interest, has taken rank as a notable treatise on our Lady and her prerogatives, which is at the same time a work of high literary excellence.

The next few years he devoted to a consideration of the question of faith and reason, and their mutual relations, not strictly in its theological aspect, but primarily as involved in the origin and growth of belief in the individual, as an individual, especially the unlearned individual. He granted that the question of the supernatural origin of Christianity ought to be submitted to the same rigorous tests as are applied in the sciences, and he did not dispute the assertion of the theologians that it had satisfied these tests. Such considerations as these did not fall within his purview; his interest lay elsewhere. What he sought to establish, was that the *motivum credibilitatis* is personal to each individual, as well as formal, public, objective; and although concurrent with, or included in, the scientific proof, is nevertheless *sui generis*, and different in different individuals. Stated in its simplest terms, the question that presented itself to him was this: since the great mass of Catholics are either ignorant of, or at best only partially acquainted with, the various forms of proof, e.g., for the existence of God, how is their faith rational? This subject he had discussed piecemeal in his *University Sermons*, but inadequately, because he was merely feeling his way through uncharted territory, and had too little confidence in his line of approach. After his conversion it occupied his mind intermittently all the time; but it was not until 1866 that he hit upon what he thought to be the key to his difficulty: viz., that he should treat certitude as one form of assent, and distinguish assent from inference. Herein lay the germ of the volume which, after three years' work, was published in 1870 under the unpretentious and disarming title, *An Essay in aid of a Grammar of Assent*.

During the decade before the Vatican Council (1869-70) Newman had to experience the humiliating consequences of being out of harmony with the dominant faction among English Catholics, which in this instance was singularly aggressive, exalting its opinions into dogmas, and intent upon suppressing every school of thought but its own. The "fierce and intolerant temper", which was its characteristic, displayed itself in the ecclesiastical policy of Manning, Archbishop of Westminster (1865), and in the writings of W. G. Ward, then editor of the *Dublin Review*. In these years three subjects came successively to the front—the temporal power, the higher education of the laity in the English universities, and above all the question of papal Infallibility—and feeling ran high. On all three Manning and Ward not only held, but expressed extreme views; and in the matter of Infallibility they did their utmost to secure a definition in unequivocal terms. Newman, on the other hand, sensitive to the distress of the "little ones of Christ", whose claims to a hearing were ruthlessly being thrust aside, took a more moderate line, and advocated a "wise and gentle minimism". Unfortunately the extremists possessed in Rome a mouthpiece in the person of Mgr. Talbot, a convert Anglican clergyman like themselves, who had the ear of Pius IX, and never let slip an opportunity of belittling Newman and turning Roman opinion against him. Newman, however, although he had always accepted the doctrine of papal infallibility on theological grounds, might justly, before the Council, have been described as a minimizer and an inopportunist in his own restrained manner; but when the definition had been promulgated, he made his submission without even a momentary hesitation; he simply accepted with the assurance of faith what he had previously held as a theological conclusion. Some years later, time, his "best friend and patron", as he said, wrote an ironical comment on the agitations of the previous decade; for when Gladstone made an ill-founded and irresponsible attack upon the Holy See in two pamphlets, it was Newman who, of all that distinguished statesman's Catholic opponents, made by far the most effective defence of the encyclical *Quanta Cura*, the *Syllabus*, and the Vatican definition in his *Letter to the Duke of Norfolk* (1875); and incidentally took advantage of the chance occasion to produce a work of permanent apologetic value, in which he soars above the temporary and the particular, and enunciates truths pertinent, not only then, but at all times. The same characteristic marks the exposition of the threefold office of the Church in the Preface to the third edition of the *Via Media* (1877). Thus in his two last substantive works he proved beyond doubt his absolute loyalty to the Church, which only a hostile partisan could have been undiscerning enough to question.

From 1868 to 1881 he devoted himself to the laborious task of preparing for the press the Uniform Edition of his writings. He began diffidently, and apparently without any definite plan before his mind, for fear of adverse criticisms from Protestants and Catholics alike, from the former, if he introduced changes into the text, from the latter, if he did not. The first volumes to be published were the *Parochial and Plain Sermons* and *Sermons on Subjects of the Day*. Since it might have been considered objectionable, if he, as a Catholic and a priest, had so far presumed as to issue a new edition of his Protestant sermons, he induced his former Littlemore curate, W. J. Copeland, still an Anglican, to undertake the editorship of them. The welcome with which they were received so far exceeded his expectations, that he took courage to publish his other works under his own name, many of them with notes corrective of the text. Whatever time remained over, he spent in the arrangement of his personal papers and letters in order to lighten the labour of his future biographer, since he realized that he could not hope to avoid the fate of prominent men; and in the composition of such autobiographical documents, as the *Memorandum of My Connection with the Catholic University*, and the *Autobiographical Memoir* included in Miss Mozley's two volumes of *Letters and Correspondence*.

Nothing is, or in fact could be, said here about his public life, for such an idea in connection with him would be entirely illusory. Nature and vocation disposed him to pursue the *fallentis semita vitae*, and circumstances inexorably closed every other path to him. He might have done a great work at Oxford, comparable to that of his Tractarian days; but the way was barred, because his residence there might have attracted young Catholics to the University. He could have gone to the Vatican Council, either as Consultor, or as theologian to Dupanloup, or even to the Bishop Brown who had delated him; but he felt that he would be out of place there, and exposed to the annoyance of ecclesiastical tactlessness. Hence he was thrown back upon his own immediate surroundings in a Birmingham suburb, and the opportunities offered by the passing days. He was indeed perpetual superior of his community, and that position of course involved certain duties; he preached in his turn, but never, with few exceptions, outside his own church; and he lovingly arranged the books in the library. The Oratory School also provided him with an interest of another kind; he helped to prepare the older boys for examinations; he coached the actors for the annual Latin play; and for some time he gave the religious instruction. How astonishing an anti-climax! that a man whose name was almost legendary, who could have served the Church in England, as no other man could, should have been imprisoned in this trivial round. But outside the narrow confines of his life there lay the world from which he had withdrawn; and the world did not forget him in his seclusion. Although he held aloof from public affairs whether political or ecclesiastical, yet he was always ready to place himself at the disposal of all, whatever their religious profession or social standing, who appealed to him in any of the mischances or difficulties of life. This apostolate to the individual soul was an apostolate entirely after his own heart; and the appeals were many, even from among those who were not, and had no thought of becoming, Catholics, so much so, that, as Fr Ryder says, "now and again one came across something which almost looked like a *cultus* of Cardinal Newman outside the Church."

At the end of 1877 the Fellows of Trinity College, Oxford, the College to which, as an undergraduate, he had belonged, and which "had never been unkind" to him, created a precedent by electing him to an Honorary Fellowship. This domestic (as it may be called) honour gave him great happiness, since it restored him to Oxford, and forged a link between his old age and his distant youth. In 1879 the new Pontiff, Leo XIII, in his first consistory, raised him to the Sacred College as Cardinal Deacon of San Giorgio in Velabro, in recognition of his signal services to the Church, and as a token of the policy he himself had determined to inaugurate. To Newman personally his unexpected elevation meant this, and this only, that the cloud which had for so long overshadowed him, had at last been lifted, and that his influence, with his writings as its instrument, would have free course to mould the future.

He was now close upon his eightieth year, and in his frail state of health could not look forward to a long span of life. In 1881 he crowned his labours on the Uniform Edition of his works by publishing his *Select Treatises of St. Athanasius*; in 1882 he edited, with an Introduction, Palmer's *Notes of a Visit to the Russian Church*: in 1884 he contributed an article on the inspiration of Scripture to the *Nineteenth Century*, which elicited severe criticisms from Dr Healy of Maynooth, afterwards Archbishop of Tuam, and he answered his critic in a pamphlet, *What is of Obligation for a Catholic to Believe Concerning the Inspiration of the Canonical Scriptures*; and in 1885 he controverted in the *Contemporary Review* the charge of "scepticism", urged against him in the same periodical by a prominent Nonconformist divine, Dr Fairbairn, to whose rejoinder he replied in a paper afterwards printed for private circulation. Then for the last time he laid down the pen, which he had wielded in the service of revealed religion for sixty years.

His bodily infirmities increased; he was unable to recite the Divine Office owing to failing sight; it became more and more difficult for him to say the Rosary, as his fingers lost their sensitiveness, although he persevered with larger and larger beads. On Christmas Day 1889 he celebrated what proved to be his last Mass; but he continued to say, whenever he was well enough, a *Missa sicca* in the hope that, if the coming of summer restored his strength, he would be prepared to resume his normal practice. This, however, was not to be. Taken ill unexpectedly, late on Saturday, August 9th, 1890, and sinking into a coma, he died, without recovering consciousness, in the evening on the following Monday, and was buried eight days later, August 19th, at Rednal, the country house of the Birmingham Oratory. In 1845 he had profoundly shocked Protestant England by his conversion, which won him the appellation of traitor; he had thrust aside as unfounded the ordinary Englishman's distrust of the Church, and defied his bitterest prejudice, the fruit of ancient and persistent calumny. Yet on his death, all Englishmen, Protestants, no less than Catholics, without thought of the gulf between him and them, united with one accord to express their respect, reverence, affection, for the man, who had been for more than a generation by universal consent the foremost representative of Catholicism in the country. Has there ever been a revolution in public opinion comparable to this?

Genius eludes definitions. It would be inappropriate to describe Newman as a "miscellaneous writer", since that convenient term is at best slightly derogatory; but we are baffled when we try to attach a label to him and to assign him to a neat and precise category. Let it be granted that he was not a theologian, nor a philosopher, nor a historian, nor a preacher, nor a poet, at least not in the front rank. For himself he disclaimed his right to any one of "these five great names", as he called them; and we may with him, from one point of view, regret that he did not "take and prosecute one line of research, one study, one science". And yet, if he had become a specialist, English literature would have been the poorer. Divergent interests, no doubt, as he was well aware, lead to, if they do not imply, superficiality. But in his case his interests had a common centre, and his writings, diverse as they may at first sight seem, are rooted in a single preoccupation, and possess a remarkable unity. If they are viewed in perspective, it becomes at once apparent that his many volumes fall into place as parts of a magnificent *Summa Apologetica*. Whatever lack of system there may be, is more than counter-balanced by the fact that they are informed by a spirit more precious than system, and that spirit the quintessence of their author's personality. In spite of his many and repeated disclaimers, he admitted that he was a "controversialist"; and his outstanding claim upon our attention, although, when we place ourselves at his feet, we acquire much mellow wisdom by the way, is that he was, as Cardinal Manning said of him after his death, perhaps in atonement, "our greatest witness for the Faith";—a witness who has survived his own death, and still lives, because, whenever he wrote, he kept in view, not so much the rank and file among his own contemporaries, but, to use his own words, "active minds and the genera-tion to come".

III

THE AUTOBIOGRAPHICAL
MEMOIR

INTRODUCTION

William Mason's *Life and Letters of Thomas Gray* (1774) and James Boswell's *Life of Samuel Johnson* (1791) mark two successive stages in the development of biography as a literary *genre* in England. Both Mason and Boswell were innovators—in so far as each allowed the subject of his biography to speak for himself, instead of making him the mouthpiece of opinions and sentiments, not his own, but foisted on him, as being such as seemed to the biographer to reveal his subject's character, as he conceived it. The former sought to attain his end by the publication of private letters; and the latter not only followed this precedent, but went beyond it by presuming to report private conversations. Both methods exposed those who adopted them to criticism, and both innovators received their due share of abuse. Boswell however suffered considerably the more, his twofold offence being considered the more flagrant. "Boswellizing" met with reprobation as a transgression against good taste; Wordsworth, and not Wordsworth alone, stigmatized his *Johnson* as an "ungentlemanly book". Lockhart was nearing the end of his *Life of Sir Walter Scott* at the time when Newman undertook, with the help of Keble, to edit Froude's papers; and Lockhart formally disclaimed any intention for his own part to "boswellize Scott". Froude, like Dr Johnson, had been a tireless conversationalist, but few of his sayings had been preserved, and Newman published without compunction the three dozen or so remarks of his that had been recorded, whether by himself or other friends.

Not having the wherewithal to "boswellize" Froude, Newman was compelled to fall back upon his correspondence to obtain biographical material; and this he saw was precious for such a purpose, as being "next best to talking with him", and exhibiting him "in a light otherwise unattainable". Yet he felt that, even if he ventured so far as to publish no more than carefully selected extracts from it, such a course demanded an apology; and this he gave in the preface, written by him, to the first two volumes of the *Remains*. It was the hope of the editors, he said, that the work, made up mainly of Froude's letters and private journal, would "present, as far as it goes, the picture of a mind"; and if this object were achieved, they were content to let "the details take their chance". Accordingly he confined the outline of Froude's life in the preface within the limits of a single page, and he supplied very little editorial matter, merely a note here or there, when the text seemed to him to call for some elucidation.

When he came to examine the remainder of Froude's papers, he was much impressed by an unfinished work on St Thomas of Canterbury, above all by the method adopted by the author, who had made it his one object "to lay before the reader a series of letters", thus placing at his service "the means of forming his own judgment" on persons and events, together with a brief "running comment", just sufficient to connect the letters with one another and to throw light on obscure points. This Newman ever afterwards proclaimed to be the ideal method in biography; and in support of his assertion he could adduce Stanley's *Life of Dr Arnold*. The ponderous Victorian "life" he dismissed as a "mistake", not only inordinately "dull", but swollen to its generous proportions with "indefinitely much padding". Hardly any man's life, he thought, was worth writing at such a length. "My own notion of writing a life," he explained to Father Coleridge on April 13th, 1866, "is the notion of Hurrell Froude, viz., to do it by letters, and to bring in as little letterpress of one's own as possible." His reason for this preference or prejudice he had already explained in a letter to his sister on May 16th, 1863: "Contemporary letters are facts, and as such they reveal the true life of a man." It may be granted that in the historical sense they are "facts"; but even so, they may reflect merely the passing mood of the writer, not his permanent disposition or attitude. Only very seldom is it practicable to publish the letters in bulk, and consequently in most instances it becomes imperative to select and to omit. Then the biographer's choice cannot but be determined by his conception of his subject's character; and however impartial or objective he may strive to be, the personal factor makes its influence felt; although he rigorously refrains from comment, yet even in the process of selection *latet dolus*. But Newman brushed this consideration aside. His quarrel with biographers in general was that they "varnish, they assign motives, they interpret Lord Burleigh's nods". The truth is lost in a maze of speculation, and few readers possess the clue to guide them through it.

As life went on, this question of literary form ceased with him to be an abstract question, and became personal. In his later years he showed an acute, even a painful, sensitiveness on the subject, whenever he chanced to see any references in the press either to himself or to his family. "I am," he told Lord Blachford, "as if my skin was torn off." All such references he abhorred as indelicate intrusions upon his privacy. As for memoir-writers, and there were several in the last decade of his life, he found it hard to forgive them. He looked forward with apprehension to the prospect of what would inevitably happen after his death, since he foresaw that he would not escape the fate of Keble, whose biography had been written, with indifferent success, by Sir J. T. Coleridge; and his fears led him to make such provision as he could in view of future contingencies, so as to forestall the attempts of unauthorized writers, all too eager to stake their claims to a promising victim for their pens.

His main concern was concentrated upon the Anglican half of his life; the Catholic period he considered to be beneath the notice of a serious biographer. The bulk of the essential material was in his own possession. He seems to have had an innate passion for hoarding; from his earliest years he or his relatives carefully kept masses of manuscript debris that most people would have destroyed as a matter of course. As far as this was a deliberate procedure, it was no doubt due to a sentimental clinging to the past. How else are we to explain the survival of his childish letters, of his school exercise-books? But from the time when he first took his place on the stage of public life as the acknowledged leader of the Tractarian Movement, he began sedulously to preserve, if not the whole, at least the major part of his correspondence, perhaps regarding it as the raw material of history. His correspondents likewise treasured his letters to them, perhaps for no other reason than their personal affection for him, perhaps too, as Anne Mozley suggests, because these letters had "a weight and distinctiveness, whether of subject or mode of treatment, which secured them from the common fate after perusal". In his diary he made a careful record day by day of the names of his correspondents, both those to whom he had written and those who had written to him. This practice, it may be here observed, stood him in good stead during the Kingsley controversy; when he wished to bring out his state of mind at successive periods from contemporary documents, he had at hand pointers to the various quarters to which application for help should be made.

In his vivid memory, the past, so far from being buried, lived on as an integral part of the present. The relics, or "mementoes", as he called them, preserved with such reverence, were not left to accumulate dust on the shelves of his cupboards, but every now and again they were taken out, read and re-read. In the decade between 1842 and 1853 they accompanied him in his moves from Oxford to Littlemore, from Littlemore to Maryvale, from Maryvale to St. Wilfrid's, from St Wilfrid's to Alcester Street, and finally from Alcester Street to Edgbaston, where they now are. From a comparatively early age he had looked forward to the task of setting his accumulated papers in order as an occupation eminently suitable for his declining years. But circumstances forced him to anticipate time's warning signal. Thus as early as 1850, when he had entered upon his fiftieth year, he was engaged in arranging his papers, so that they should be "no more of a trouble to [him] than if they did not exist". Again, on April 3rd, 1852, he recorded in his diary that he "had finished getting all [his] books and papers into [his] room at Edgbaston." And yet again on August 11th, 1859, after the severance of his connection with the Catholic University, he informed his sister that he was making another effort "to go through all [his] papers, burning, sorting, and otherwise disposing of them." And lastly on June 18th, 1870, he pleaded as an excuse for not visiting her, that he wished to "get to [his] papers and letters, and put everything in order", which, he feared, would be "a tremendous work".

It was, no doubt, the result of his preoccupation with his papers during the next few years that he was led seriously to consider the question of his own biography. It was his settled opinion, expressed not once, but frequently, not to a single individual, but to several independently of one another, that his personal history should be narrated through the medium of his letters. He envisaged, not a biographer, but an editor, whose function it would be to make a selection of these letters, to arrange them in their temporal or logical sequence, and then to furnish, in the form of a simple narrative, what was necessary to make the work a coherent and intelligible whole. He seems to have thought that the narrative contained in the *Apologia*, if rounded off by the relevant letters, would be quite adequate for the period of the Movement; but he felt that his formative years needed to be treated more fully. Accordingly in 1874 he composed a kind of proem to the *Apologia*, "written," as Anne Mozley explains, "in the third person, not to conceal the hand that penned it, but better to show the simplicity of style in which he desired that all told about himself should be composed."

It seems to have been his intention that all his papers should at his death pass into the hands of Ambrose St. John, his junior by fourteen years, his most intimate associate for more than thirty, and the one remaining "link" between his life at Littlemore and his life in the Oratory. For this reason on June 1st, 1874 he wrote the following note,[1] headed "For Father Ambrose St. John", in which he set forth his wishes on the subject of his biography:

Had I my will no Memoir should be written of me, except such a thin running notice as would suffice to hold together a series of my letters. Letters I don't mind, for they are facts, and belong, for good or bad, to the personality of the writer of them; but a Memoir, or at least a Life, is more or less the product of the imagination, a conclusion from facts, more or less theoretical and unauthoritative. Besides, for the most part, Lives are padded, or spun out, that they may give an adventitious interest, form a continuous narrative, and complete a volume.

However, I am forced to forebode that some one or other, who knows little or nothing about me, whether well or ill-disposed to me, will have something to say about my history, if my friends are silent; and, in consequence, that they who have known me well and who have been in my intimate confidence, will find it their duty to meet by some sort of biographical notice vague and random ideas and accounts of me derived from the ephemeral literature and controversy of the last forty years. This necessity, I am aware, has been in a measure obviated by myself in my "Apologia pro vitâ suâ"; nevertheless, the anticipation of it has led me to leave behind me in addition, for the inspection of my friends, large portions of my private Memoranda, by way of assisting and supplementing their recollections of me. This I have done, not exactly in order

---

[1] As a preface to The Autobiographical Memoir. C.S.D.

to the publication of such casual notes, but partly to add materials for a
Memoir, partly to furnish familiar and circumstantial knowledge of the men
and the matters which are its subject, and partly in explanation or defence, if
necessary, of what at certain times I have said or done. Among these are some
papers, which, viewed as a whole, hardly more than two or three persons in the
world ought to see, though I do not wish absolutely to forbid the publication of
passages in them. And my reason for not destroying them is hereby to give my
representatives (as I have been saying) that elbow-room in their knowledge of
me in matters of detail, which may enable them to determine what is likely to
have been my conduct or my opinion in cases in which, as they stand, it is not
quite clear; leaving it to their affection for me and their discretion to deal
tenderly with what in the first place is confidential and sacred.

Moreover, I have thus ventured on some specimens of a Memoir myself, not
so much for publication, as in order to show them what, in my own judgment,
should in a Memoir be said about me, and how, viz., in respect to matter,
manner, and length.   J.H.N.

Newman's plans, however, were frustrated, for St. John died at midnight on
May 24th, 1875 at the age of sixty. Afterwards, on June 16th, 1876, he appended a
note to the paper of instructions just quoted: "Since writing the above, I have lost
Ambrose St. John. This misfortune, together with a growing interest in my subject, has led me, on transcription, to turn my Sketch into a much fuller and more
finished composition than it was originally. J.H.N." The subject of his biography
still continued to occupy his thoughts, as is clear from a memorandum written on
October 22nd, 1876:

I don't want a panegyric written of me, which would be sickening, but a real
fair downright account of me according to the best ability and judgment of the
writer.[1] As to my Catholic life there is very little to say unless at the risk of
causing great scandal, controversy, partizanship. If my representatives in my
behalf attacked others, e.g. Barnabo or Manning, their friends would be sure to
retort upon me and this would not be edifying. [Since I am now a Cardinal,
bygones should be bygones. August 7, 1881.] I wish all statements which reflect
on others to be held from publication, unless and until reflections are published
in any quarter against me. E.g. if the friends of Manning or Faber or anyone
else were to insinuate a charge against me, as regards the Rambler or the
London Oratory, there lie the papers which I leave behind me, affording the
means of refuting it, whether as correcting facts, or as explaining my views and
my motives. And so again, was anything said disagreeable about the proposal to
make me a Bishop, I could not object to the whole series of letters (in my
Catholic University Packet) being published, especially as there is nothing (I
think) personal in them against anyone. And so again if I am accused of
wishing to found a College at Oxford.

But such publication is not to be determined on hastily or without real
necessity. Some officious writer on his own hook, implicating no one else,
might commit the offence; and it would be hard that through his impertinence
others, as Manning, should suffer. And even when a remonstrance had to be
made, it would not for certain be necessary to state what could be said, in reply
to a mere floating opinion or paragraph in a paper. Thus, before now, even
friendly writers being perplexed at seeing me so discountenanced by authorities,
or hearing unfavourable judgments passed upon me, have thought there must
be some fault or other in me at bottom, and have said in complimentary language that "great geniuses commonly had infirmities of temper", or "original
minds were hard to get on with", sometimes in the newspapers, sometimes in

[1] This sentence occurs at the end of a note in which Newman declares his
opinion that the memoir of his Anglican years should be written by an Anglican.
The sentence following is dated July 1876. The memorandum of October 22nd
begins after the sentence in square brackets. C.S.D.

letters addressed to myself. In a case like this all that need be said in my behalf
would be to demand proof, to nail down the speaker to facts, and to observe,
"If Mr So and So had recollected the "audi alteram partem", if he knew as
much as might be told on the matter of which he speaks, he would have been
slow to give expression to what he could not in that case deny was a rash
judgment. It is only on great provocation and grave reasons of expedience or
propriety that one could consent to reopen the past." (The above is still more
cogent now that I am a Cardinal. August 7, 1881.)

The determination expressed in this memorandum that, as far as he was concerned, the past should be buried in oblivion, was actually put to the proof, when
E. S. Purcell, remembered as the author of the *Life of Cardinal Manning*, submitted for his approval a biographical notice, which he had written for *Celebrities
of the Day*, and received from him an outspoken declaration of his disapproba-
tion. "My own feeling about the past," Newman wrote to him on June 11th, 1881,
"is 'Let bygones be bygones'. The change of sentiment about me is so satisfactory
that to speak about it is to interfere with it, and is to revive occurrences which are
at present in simple oblivion. Of course, you cannot help stating the circumstances which led to the *Apologia*, but I am pained to find the name of Kingsley
recalled, who by his passionate attack on me became one of my best friends,
whom I always wished to shake hands with, when living, and towards whose
memory I have much tenderness. Much less can I reconcile myself to your references to Catholic opponents as 'fanatical', and their 'suppleness'. And I would
observe that, as regards doctrine, the 'supremacy of conscience' is not an adequate
account of what I should consider safe to say on the subject. Lastly, I must, to my
great discomfort and the appearance of rude ingratitude, deprecate the pane-
gyrical language in which your memoir is written, not only on account of its
probable effect upon the reader, but of the great pain which it gives myself." His
last words on this subject have been recorded by William Neville, who succeeded
to the place at Newman's side on St. John's death. At some unspecified date, after
repeating his "distinct opinion that there could not be a biography of him, at least
not a biography comprehending the Catholic period of his life", since "that period
did not afford materials for a biography", as having been "a time of disappointments, quarrels and failures, nothing more", Newman remarked gravely, but with
a smile: "You must not suppose that these little affairs of mine will be on the
tapis in the courts of the next world."
In the summer of 1877 he left the manuscript of the Memoir, or a transcript of
it, in the hands of his sister; and when he recovered it again in the course of the
next summer, he made, apparently after having read it through once more,
another note: "August 9, 1878. I am not at all sure that this Memoir is not too
minute and trifling after the manner of 'Laudator temporis acti'."
For several years he let the subject of his biography remain in abeyance; but
then, owing to an accidental circumstance, it came to the front again. Anne
Mozley, connected with him through the marriage of two of her brothers to his
two sisters, had edited the posthumous issue of the writngs of yet another
brother, James Bowling Mozley; and intended to complete the work with a
volume of his letters. During the year 1884, as the proofs came from the press, she
sent them to Newman for his criticism. When he had read them to the end, he
wrote to her on November 20th, 1884 to express his appreciation. "I think," he
said in the course of his letter, "your book is not only singularly interesting and
valuable ... but well done as a sample of clear and careful composition, and of
good judgment as a literary work. You have fulfilled in James's case Queen
Catherine's wish: 'After my death I wish no other herald but such an honest
chronicler as Griffith'; and that because you have let him speak for himself."

Her manifest competence for such a work raised in his mind the question of his own biography, and he proceeded to take her into his confidence. Years before, he told her, he had on two separate occasions come to the conclusion that his Protestant life should be written by a Protestant, not by a Catholic; and to his surprise he found in 1876 that his friend Lord Blachford (Frederic Rogers) not only took this view, but urged that this portion should be written during his life and published immediately upon his death, so as to "anticipate all catch-pennies ... and any interference on the part of injudicious Catholic friends." It was his idea that the volume, which was, in his intention, to be brief, should consist of the Memoir amplified by his family letters, which he had arranged with this object in view some years before. All he wanted of her, was that she should read the material, and pass "a fair judgment upon the expedience of publishing" it. She, on her side, suggested the name of Lord Blachford as the ideal Protestant editor, and expressed her readiness to "help in the way of illustration and additions to the context in ... footnotes." But Newman brushed this evasive answer aside, and on January 26th, 1885 made it quite clear to her that he wanted her, and no one else, to edit his papers. As a friend, a Protestant, and (within limits) a contemporary, she fulfilled his three conditions.

But was ever a work of this kind produced in similar circumstances? Newman was in his eighty-fifth year, Anne Mozley in her seventy-sixth, and William Neville, who acted as factotum and intermediary, in his sixty-first. And further, Newman was losing the use of his right hand, Anne Mozley was suffering from a progressive disease of the eyes, which eventually resulted in total blindness, and Neville, whatever his virtues, and they were many, was far from being the most practical of men. An awkward train journey separated her from them; and Newman not only had no confidence in the reliability of the postal service, but apparently doubted her capacity to cope with the perplexities involved in railway-travelling. Moreover he lived in a perpetual fidget about the safety of his papers, unless he was assured that they were under lock and key; and even then he fretted lest, through any indiscretion on her part, the suspicions of the public should be aroused. Her unruffled patience throughout was amazing; she fell in with his every wish, and calmly equipped herself for what she considered the supreme work of her life.

Newman sent Neville's transcript of the Memoir to her on January 14th, 1885. She read the first two chapters through at a single sitting, and "found it of absorbing interest". Her first comment, if she meant what she appears to have meant, is worth noting. "It seems," she wrote, "to introduce a new form of biography." Does the history of literature furnish another example of a man, who has written, not his own autobiography, which has become common enough, but his own biography, as though the writer and his subject were distinct individuals? The illusion must have been difficult to maintain. Of course he set out to be objective and impartial, and Anne Mozley thought the Memoir "wonderful for the absolute truth and fairness of the narrative so transparent in its flow." There is apparent, however, a certain tension, as though he were striving, not always quite successfully, to suppress the feeling, *tua res agitur*, and perhaps that is why Wilfrid Ward applied to it the epithet "curious".

At one point in his correspondence with Anne Mozley, Newman raised the question whether it would not be advisable to preface the Memoir with an introductory chapter dealing with his early years and schooldays. But in the end he decided against this plan, apparently on the ground that he found it "difficult to realize or imagine the identity of the boy before and after August 1816"— the date of his conversion. She acquiesced in his ruling on this point; but on the adequacy of the narrative in the *Apologia* as an account of the years of the

Movement, she ventured to express her disagreement with him. She suggested that he should extend the Memoir at least as far as the year 1843, reminding him of his own admission that he "originally called it a specimen", as though he had the intention of continuing it. For some reason or other, which his letters do not reveal, he did not see his way to fall in with her wish; the Memoir remained as it stood in 1876, perhaps because he felt that at his age such an effort would be beyond his strength.

When he had supplied her either by post or by hand with all the requisite documents, he thought that he had done all that it was open to him to do. In fact, he made it a condition of her editorship that, during the preparation of her work, no reference should be made to him on any subject whatsoever; if she wished for guidance, she was at liberty to apply to Dean Church or Lord Blachford; and he insisted that it should be made known that he had not collaborated even in the slightest degree. This condition, as is evident from the correspondence between them, was scrupulously observed on both sides; he asked no questions, and she made no effort to keep him informed of her progress.

Newman died on August 11th, 1890, and Anne Mozley survived him for less than a year. There was a brief illness at the last, and death came not inopportunely on June 27th, 1891. During the interval between these two dates, approximately half way between them, her *magnum opus*, *Letters and Correspondence of John Henry Newman during his Life in the English Church*, made its appearance. Thus it was her good fortune to have lived long enough, not only to bring to a successful issue the concentrated efforts of six years directed to a single object, but also to savour the universal tribute of appreciation extended to her by reviewers and others, not least of all by those who had long lived in Newman's intimacy, and who would have been sensitive to the smallest blemish. Assuredly she has an outstanding claim upon the gratitude of all those who study, or will study, Newman, if for no other reason, at least for this, that with self-effacing loyalty she observed his wish that his own letters should be his biography, never taking on herself the part of interpreter, never passing judgment upon persons or events, always as sparing as possible of explanatory matter. Ever since they were published, her two volumes have been the foundation of all that has been written about Newman as an Anglican; and although much material, which she had no opportunity to examine, has since accumulated, they will never cease to be indispensable; they may be supplemented, but they will not be superseded.

Two manuscripts of the Memoir survive. The first, in Newman's writing, seems to be the original of 1874, dismembered by him in 1876, worked over, and put together again, many pages having been omitted, and others substituted for them. As it stands, deletions and corrections are numerous. The other is a copy of this in Neville's writing, probably made under Newman's supervision, with a number of excisions authorized by him. If Newman ever made a fair copy of his original, as he thought, it has disappeared; but on the whole it is unlikely that he did so. Anne Mozley transcribed for her own use Neville's copy, and this is reproduced in *Letters and Correspondence*; but availing herself of her editorial privileges, she left out a few passages which Newman allowed to remain in his manuscript. The version in this volume has been made from Newman's autograph; but some of the passages which he deleted, have been restored to the text[1]; and where alternatives remain in the autograph, the later version has been adopted. A few minor additions which Newman himself made in Neville's copy have also been inserted.

[1] A footnote indicates the deleted passages as they occur. C.S.D.

For Ambrose St John

June 13. 1874

Chapter 1

John Henry Newman, the subject of this memoir, was born in Old Broad Street in the City of London on the 21st of February, 1801, and was baptized in the Church of St. Bennet Fink on April 9th of the same year. His Father was a London Banker, whose family came from Cambridgeshire. His Mother was of a French Protestant family, who left France for this country on the revocation of the Edict of Nantes. He was the eldest of six children, three boys and three girls of whom [one son][1] survives him, Novr 9. 1884.

On the first of May, 1808, when he was seven years old, he was sent to a school of 200 boys, increasing to 300, at Ealing, near London, under the care of the Revd George Nicholas, LLD of Wadham College. As a child, he was of a studious turn, and of a quick apprehension; and Dr Nicholas, to whom he became greatly attached, was accustomed to say, that no boy had run through the school, from the bottom to the top, so rapidly as John Newman. Though in no respect a precocious boy, he attempted original compositions in prose and verse from the age of eleven, and in prose showed a great sensibility and took much pains in matters of style. He devoted to such literary exercises and to such books as came in his way, a good portion of his play-time; and his school-fellows have left on record that they never, or scarcely ever, saw him taking part in any game.

At Ealing he remained eight years and a half, his own intreaties aiding his mother and his school-master in hindering his removal to Winchester College. In the last half year of his school life, from August to December 1816, accidentally outstaying his immediate school friends, he fell under the influence of an excellent man, the Revd Walter Mayers, of Pembroke College, Oxford, one of the classical masters, from whom he received deep religious impressions, at the time Calvinistic in character, which were to him the beginning of a new life. From school he went straight to Oxford, being entered

[1] There is a space here in the MS. Francis Newman lived till 1897. C.S.D.

at Trinity College on December 14th 1816, when he was as yet two months short of sixteen.

He used to relate in illustration of the seeming accidents on which our course of life and personal history turn, that, even when the post chaise was at the door, his father was in doubt whether to direct the post boy to make for Hounslow, or for the first stage on the road to Cambridge. He seems to have been decided in favour of Oxford by the Revd John Mullens, Curate of St. James's Piccadilly, a man of ability and learning, who had for some years taken an interest in the boy's education. When they got to Oxford, Mr Mullens at first hoped to find a vacancy for him in his own College, Exeter: but, failing in this, he took the advice of his Exeter friends to introduce him to Dr Lee, President of Trinity, and at that time Vice Chancellor, by whom Newman was matriculated as a commoner of that Society. On his return to Ealing to inform his school-master of the issue of his expedition, his timid mention of a College of which he himself had never heard before, was met by Dr Nicholas's reassuring reply, "Trinity? a most gentlemanlike College; I am much pleased to hear it."

He was called into residence in the following June, in his fourth term, and, for want of the vacancy of a room, not till the Term was far advanced, the Commemoration close at hand, the College Lectures over, and the young men on the point of leaving for the Long Vacation. However, it was his good fortune, in the few days which remained before he was left to himself, to make the acquaintance of Mr John William Bowden, a freshman also, afterwards one of his Majesty's Commissioners of Stamps and Taxes. The acquaintance ripened into a friendship so intimate, though Mr Bowden was just by three years the older of the two, (the birthday of both being the 21st of February) that the two youths lived simply with and for each other all through their undergraduate time up to the term when they went into the schools for their B.A. examination, being recognised in College as inseparables—taking their meals together, reading, walking, boating together, nay, visiting each other's homes in the Vacations; and though so close a companionship could not continue, when at length they ceased to be in a state of pupillage, and had taken their several paths in life, yet the mutual attachment, thus formed at the University, was maintained between them unimpaired till Mr Bowden's premature death in 1844, receiving an additional tie, as time went on, by their cordial agreement in ecclesiastical views and academical politics, and by the interest with which they both entered into the Oxford Movement of 1833. Mr Bowden was one of the first writers in the Tracts for the Times, and it was at Mr Newman's suggestion that he wrote his history of Pope Gregory the vii, the valuable work of his leisure hours and yearly vacation when a Government Commissioner at the Stamps and Taxes. It may be added that Mr Newman's first literary attempts in print were made in partnership with Mr Bowden, when they were both of them Undergraduates.

In May 1818 Mr Newman gained one of the Trinity scholarships, then lately thrown open to University competition; but here it may be well to trace, from his own letters at the time, the steps by which he had already risen in the good opinion of his College during the year since he was called up, an unknown youth of 16, for his solitary residence of three weeks. It is hoped that the details of his progress, though seemingly trifling, will not be uninteresting.

A letter of his remains which he wrote to his Father immediately upon his being left to himself on that occasion; like a boy his first thought is about his outward appearance:—

"June 11. 1817. The minute I had parted from you, I went straight to the tailor's, who assured me that, if he made me twenty gowns, they would fit me no better. If he took it shorter, he would if I pleased, but I might grow &c &c. I then went *home* (!); and had hardly seated myself, when I heard a knock at the door, and, opening it, one of the Commoners entered, whom Mr Short (Note The Revd Thomas Short, for so many years the respected and popular Tutor of the College) had sent to me, having before come himself with this said Commoner, when I was out. He came to explain to me some of the customs of the College, and accompany me into the Hall at dinner. I have learned from him something I am much rejoiced at. "Mr Ingram" said he, "was very much liked; he was very good natured; he was presented with a piece of plate the other day by the members of the College. Mr Short on the contrary is not liked; he is strict; all wish Mr Ingram were Tutor still". Thus I think I have gained by the exchange, and that is a lucky thing. Some time after, on my remarking that Mr Short must be very clever, having been second Master at Rugby, he replied, "Do you think so?" Another proof that he is a strict Tutor.

"At dinner I was much entertained with the novelty of the thing. Fish, flesh, and fowl,—beautiful salmon, haunches of mutton, lamb &c, fine strong beer,—served up in old pewter plates and mis-shapen earthenware jugs. Tell Mama there were gooseberry, raspberry, and apricot pies. And in all this the joint did not go round, but there was such a profusion that scarcely two ate of the same. Neither do they sit according to their rank, but as they happened to come in.

"I learned from the same source, whence I learned concerning Mr Short, that there are a great many juniors to me. I hear also that there are no more lectures this term, this week being the week for examinations, and next week most of them go. I shall try to get all the information I am able respecting what books I ought to study, and hope, if my eyes are good natured to me, to fag.

"Tell Harriett (his sister) I have seen the fat cook. The wine has come; $8\frac{1}{3}$ per cent is taken off for ready money. Two things I cannot get, milk and beer; so I am obliged to put up with cream for the one and with ale for the other."

He writes again to him on the 16th

"I was very uncomfortable the first day or two, because my eyes were not well, so that I could not see to read, and, whenever my eyes are bad, I am low spirited. Besides, I did not know any one, and, after being used to a number about me, I felt very solitary. But now my eyes are better, and I can read without hurting them, and I have begun to fag pretty well.

"I am not noticed at all except by being silently stared at. I am glad, not because I wish to be apart from them and ill natured, but because I really do not think I should gain the least advantage from their company. For H. the other day asked me to take a glass of wine with two or three others, and they drank and drank all the time I was there. I was very glad that prayers came half an hour after I came to them, for I am sure I was not entertained with either their drinking or their conversation. They drank while I was there very much, and I believe intended to drink again. They sat down with the avowed determination of each making himself drunk. I really think, if any one should ask me what qualifications were necessary for Trinity College, I should say there was only one, Drink, drink, drink."

He writes again to his Father on June 19th

"Almost all have left, or are leaving. Next week I suppose it will be quite a rare sight for one to be seen in the streets. Among the rest T. goes tomorrow.

"Tell Mama the said "Commoner's" name is Bowden; that he went this morning; and that H. has squeezed through his examination.

I was in a very good place in the theatre yesterday. Mr Peel was made a Doctor of Laws, by the Vice-Chancellor."

He (Newman) was very impatient to be directed in his reading, and, as he understood he could not leave College without leave from the President, he resolved in his simplicity to "take that opportunity" as he says, "of asking him what books he ought to read" in the Vacation. On June 27th three days before his departure he tells his Father the result of his experiment:—

"I went today to the President and was shown into a parlour, the servant saying he would be ready to see me in a minute. I waited an hour and a half, and then rang the bell; when it proved to be a mistake, and he was not at home. I shall go again to-morrow morning."

He did go again, and was told by the President, who was a courteous, gentlemanlike man, and afterwards very kind to him, that he left all such questions, as Mr Newman asked, to be answered by the Tutors.

In consequence, up to Sunday the 29th, the day before his departure, he had not gained any information on the point which lay so near his heart; but he persevered, and fortune favoured him. As in the evening of that day he was returning home from a walk along the Parks, he saw one of the Tutors in top-boots on horseback on his way into the country. Thinking it his last chance, he dashed into the road, and abruptly accosting him, asked him what books he should read during the Vacation. The person addressed answered him very kindly; explained that he was leaving Oxford for the Vacation, and referred him to one of his Colleagues still in College, who would give him the information he desired. On his return home he availed himself of this reference and obtained a satisfactory answer to all his difficulties.

Such was his introduction to University Life, not of a character to make him at home with it; but the prospect of things improved immediately on his return after the Long Vacation. He writes to his Mother thus on October the 28th:

"Mr Short has not examined me; but he has appointed me some lectures." After naming them, he adds, "This is little enough, but of course they begin with little to see what I can do."

On November 13th "I have been fagging very hard, but not without benefit, and I may add, not without recompense. The first day I attended my Tutor (Mr Short) for Mathematics, I found I was in the second division of what at school is called a class. I own I was rather astonished at hearing them begin the Ass's Bridge, nor was my amazement in the least degree abated, when my turn came, to hear him say with a condescending air, "I believe, Sir, you never saw Euclid before." I answered I had. "How far?" I had been over five books. Then *he* looked surprised, but I added I could not say I knew them perfectly by any means. I am sure by his manner he then took it into his head that I was not well grounded, for he proceeded to ask me what a point was, and what a line, and what a plane angle. He concluded, however, by telling me that I might come 'in with the other gentlemen at 10 o'clock with the 4th, 5th, and 6th books.'"

"The next time I came, he was not condescending, but it was, 'Sir', very stiffly indeed.

"The next time, after I had demonstrated, I saw him peep at my paper, to see if I had any thing written down,—a good sign.

"The next time, he asked if I wanted any thing explained,—another good sign.

"And to-day, after I had demonstrated a tough one out of the fifth book, he told me I had done it very correctly.

"Nor is this all—I had a declamation to do last week, a Latin one. I took a great deal of pains with it. As I was going to Lecture to-day, I was stopped by the Fellow who looks over the Declamations (the Dean, Mr Kinsey), and to whom we recite them, and told by him that mine did me much credit."

He adds on another subject:—

"The tailor entered my room the other day, and asked me if I wanted mourning. I told him, No. 'Of course you have got some', said he. No, I answered with surprise. 'Every one will be in mourning', he returned. For whom? 'The Princess Charlotte'. You see what a hermit I am; but the Paper had been lying on my table the whole day, and I had not had time to take it up."

He continues the last subject in a letter of the 21st "The dismal figure Oxford makes from the deep mourning! Black coat, waistcoat, trowsers, gloves, ribbon, (no chain), to the watch; no white except the neck-cloth and unplaited frill. The Proctors will not suffer any one to appear except in black." Presently he goes back to his own affairs:—

"I have not mentioned the conclusion of my approximation to Mr Short. The next time I went to him, he lent me a book on Mathematics, being a Dissertation &c upon Euclid; and the next morning invited me to breakfast. As to the book, I have made some extracts from it, and I know all about multiple, superparticular, submultiple, subsuperparticular, subsuperpartient of the lesser inequality, sesquilateral, sequiquintal, supertriquartal, and subsuperbitertial. I am engaged at present in making a Dissertation on the fifth book; indeed I even dream of four magnitudes, being proportionals".

By November 28th he has risen still higher in the good opinion of Mr Short. He writes to his Mother, and, after making some remarks on "every one of his lectures being so childishly easy," he continues "These very thoughts suggested themselves to Mr Short, and the other morning he said he was sorry I should not be attending lectures which would profit me more, and that next term he should take care to give me books which would give me more trouble."

He adds that the higher class in mathematics into which he had been advanced fell off to two; in other words, that he and another went on too fast for the rest to keep up with them; then of that other he says:

"This one who remained is the one I was first introduced to last Term" (Mr Bowden); "and he is pretty assiduous. The consequence is, as he is much forwarder than myself, he spurns at the books of Euclid, and hurries to get through them. I disdain to say he goes too fast; so I am obliged to fag more." Then he adds in an exulting tone, "If any one wishes to study much, I believe there can be no College that will encourage him more than Trinity. It is wishing to rise in the University, and is rising fast. The scholarships were formerly open only to the members of the College; last year, for the first time, they were thrown open to the whole University. In discipline it has become one of the strictest of Colleges. There are lamentations in every corner of the increasing rigour; it is laughable, but it is delightful, to hear the groans of the oppressed."

Mr Short seems to have taken an increased interest in Newman during the Term which immediately followed, and at length paid him the greatest compliment which it was within his power to pay to an undergraduate. He it was who had the reputation of having led the authorities of the College to the step just mentioned of opening their scholarships to all comers, which in the event has been so great a benefit to Trinity; he was naturally anxious for the success of his important measure; and therefore it was a special token of his good opinion when he invited Mr Newman to present himself as a candidate at the competitive examination, which was to determine the election of a scholar on the ensuing Trinity Monday. This Mr Short could do without impropriety, because, as he told Newman, the Tutors had no votes in the election. As has been already said Newman stood, and was elected.

He relates the circumstances attendant on this for him happy event in a letter to his Mother of May 25:

"On Wednesday April 29 about breakfast time Mr Wilson [afterwards President] and Mr Short called for me, and asked me whether I intended to stand for the scholarship. I answered that I intended next year. However, they wished me to stand this year, because they would wish to see me on the foundation. I said I would think of it. I wrote home that day. How often was my pen going to tell the secret! but I determined to surprise you. I told you in a letter written in the midst of the examination that there were five (candidates) of our own (men); did you suspect that I was one of the five? A Worcester man was very near getting it.

"They made me first do some verses, then Latin translation; then Latin theme; then a chorus of Euripides; then an English theme; then some Plato; then some Lucretius; then some Xenophon; then some Livy. What is more distressing than suspense? At last I was called to the place, where they had been voting; the Vice chancellor" (the President) "said some Latin over me; then made me a speech. The Electors then shook hands with me, and I immediately assumed the Scholar's gown.

"First, as I was going out, before I had changed my gown, one of the candidates met me, and wanted to know if it was decided. What was I to say? 'It was'. 'And who has got it?' 'O an in-college man,' I said; and I hurried away, as fast as I could. On returning with my newly earned gown, I met the whole set going to their respective homes. I did not know what to do. I held my eyes down.

"By this I am a scholar for nine years at £60 a year. In which time, if there be no fellow of my county" (among the fellows) "I may be elected Fellow, as a regular thing, for five years without taking orders".

He adds the next day:—"I am sure I felt the tortures of suspense so much, that I wished and wished I had never attempted it. The idea of "turpis repulsa' haunted me. I tried to keep myself as cool as possible, but I could not help being sanguine. I constantly reverted to it in my thoughts, in spite of my endeavours to the contrary. Very few men thought I should get it, and my *reason* thought the same.

My age was such a stumbling block." (that is, he could stand again being only 17, others could not) "But I, when I heard the voice of the Dean summoning me before the Electors, seemed to myself to feel no surprise. I am told I turned pale."

There is one other matter which should be mentioned in connexion with this 18th of May 1818, a day which was ever so dear to the subject of this Memoir, though the matter in question is not of a very pleasant character. Trinity Monday was not only the election-day of Fellows and Scholars, but also the Gaudy of the year; and among other "vestigia ruris", then remaining, was the custom of keeping it throughout the College, with few exceptions, by a grand drinking bout. This licence was not peculiar to Trinity; such orgies, ordinary as well as extraordinary, might be called the rule of the place; so much so, that it was a standing joke, in passing Oriel College, which, as initiating a better way, was satirized as if imposing on its Undergraduates tea instead of wine, to cry out to the Porter, "Well, Porter, does the kettle boil?" To the same effect was an amusing squib against Oriel sent anonymously to the Editor of the "Undergraduate", (which is soon to be mentioned,) in 1819, professing to be a letter from an Oriel Tutor to a friend in the country; some of the lines of which run as follows;

> I communicate now, as a secret, to you,
> That we've other important improvements in view ...
> But such is our plan, and if this should succeed,
> We prohibit all wine, and shall substitute mead;
> With this we shall suffer the men to make free,
> Or that equally innocent beverage, tea.
> But wine is at Colleges often the cause
> Of gross violations of statutes and laws.

So austere a discipline certainly was not the tradition of Trinity; and, since Newman had not a grain in his composition of that temper of conviviality so natural to young men, and could not even understand the enjoyment experienced by "a number of lads drinking bad wine, smoking bad cigars, and singing bad songs far into the night," as it has sometimes been expressed, it was no merit in him that the disgust of drink which he showed in one of his first letters from Oxford quoted above, should have continued to him all through his course. For the most part he was let go his own way, as soon as it was discovered what that way was; but Trinity Monday would come once a year, and then that way of his, whether he would or not, became a protest against those who took another way. Moreover, much as he might wish to keep his feelings to himself, which he did generally, and, as he afterwards thought, on looking back, too much, he had very strong feelings on the point, as the following vehement letter, addressed to his friend Mr Mayers in the following year, manifests clearly enough. It is quite out of keeping with his letters, as they have been quoted above and as he generally wrote; but, in spite of his gentleness of manner, there were in him at all times "ignes suppositi cineri doloso", which as the sequel of his life shows, had not always so much to justify them as they may be considered to have in the instance before us.

"Trinity Sunday, 1819. To-morrow is our Gaudy. If there be one time of the year, in which the glory of our College is humbled, and all appearance of goodness fades away, it is on Trinity Monday. O how the Angels must lament over a whole Society throwing off the allegiance and service of their Maker, which they have pledged the day before at His Table, and showing themselves true sons of Belial!

"It is sickening to see what I might call the apostasies of many. This year it was supposed there would have been no such merry making. A quarrel existed among us; the College was divided into two sets; and no proposition for the usual subscription for wine was set on foot. Unhappily a day or two before the time a reconciliation takes place; the wine party is agreed upon, and this wicked union, to be sealed with drunkenness, is profanely joked upon with allusions to one of the expressions in the Athanasian Creed.

["As it is, I keep quiet, for all have pledged themselves to go; yes, all but one, a poor despised, awkward man, of unprepossessing appearance and untidy person, who, I really think, has more proper sense of religion than them all together.][1]

"To see the secret eagerness, with which many wished there would be no gaudy; to see how they took hope, as time advanced, and no mention was made of it; but they are all gone, there has been weakness and fear of ridicule. Those who resisted last year, are going this. I fear even for myself, so great a delusion seems suddenly to have come over all.

"O that the purpose of some may be changed before the time! I know not how to make myself of use. I am intimate with very few. The gaudy has done more harm to the College than the whole year

[1] This paragraph was deleted by Newman in the autograph. C.S.D.

can compensate. An habitual negligence of the awfulness of the Holy Communion is introduced. How can we prosper?"

It is necessary to observe here, that Mr Bowden was at this time away from Oxford for the vacation, having gone home a fortnight before to attend the deathbed of a sister. We will hope there were other exceptions too, though, as writing to one who had no knowledge of the Undergraduate body, he [Newman] would not give their names.

But to return:—The Trinity scholarship thus unexpectedly gained, was the only academical distinction which fell to the lot of Mr Newman during his undergraduate course; and, as he had on this occasion the trial of success, so, when the course was coming to its end, he had to undergo the trial of failure. His first University examination, the Responsions (commonly called Little-go) he passed with credit, Mr Hawkins afterwards Provost of Oriel, being his examiner; but at his final examination in November 1820, at which alone honours were given, he stood for the highest, in both classics and mathematics, and suffered an utter breakdown, and a seeming extinction of his prospects of a University career.

However, that the issue of his exertions should not, as far as the Schools are concerned, have corresponded to his expectations, looking back upon the circumstances of the case, is not on the whole surprising. He had come to Oxford too soon. Yet what else was to be done with him at the end of 1816? He was more advanced in the studies necessary for Oxford than the run of youths even two years beyond him in age; at a private Tutor's he might have simply lost his time, nay, would have gone back, unless he had been exceptionally fortunate in finding one able to take in hand his critical scholarship, which was at this time deficient;—so against the advice of his Schoolmaster, who knew the state of things at Oxford, he passed at once from school to College. Apparently he had himself been impatient to get there, but he recognized his disadvantage in consequence as soon as he began lecture[s]. He writes to his father in the first term of lectures, that term in which he was so successfully to make his way with Mr Short. "I now see the disadvantage of going so soon to Oxford, and before I have the great addition of time of two or three years more first; for there are several who know more than I do in Latin and Greek, and I do not like that." He was not 20, when he went in for the final examination; whereas the usual age was 22.

His youth was against him in another respect also. It was not only that he was short by two or three years of the full period marked out for the B.A. examination, but of course he had not that experience for shaping for himself his course of reading or that maturity of mind for digesting it, which a longer time would have given him. He read books, made ample analyses and abstracts, and entered upon collateral questions and original essays which did him no service in the Schools. In the long Vacation of 1818 he was taken up with Gibbon and Locke. At another time he wrote a critique of the plays of Aeschylus on the principles of Aristotle's Poetics, though original composition at that time had no place in School examinations, and he spent many weeks in reading and transcribing Larcher's notes on Herodotus. Moreover it must be borne in mind, that University examinations necessarily and properly proceed upon a tradition, and accordingly the Tutors of those Colleges, as Trinity, which had not as yet supplied public examiners, could not accurately know or instinctively feel, as certain other Tutors could, what particular reading and what circumstantial preparation would tell in favour of those of their pupils whom they sent in the Schools as candidates for its honours. Christ Church had ever had an examiner in the Schools since 1801 when the system of honours commenced, except in 1804 and 1819; Oriel and Brasenose for six years out of the last ten; and Balliol, and Exeter for four years during the same time; and, though the examiners were conscientiously fair and considerate in their decisions, they would understand a candidate better and follow his lead and line of thought more sympathetically, if they understood his position of mind and intellectual habits than if these were new to them.

(Note) He recollected to his old age one instance in point. When the Fellows of Trinity inquired of the Examiners, how he came so utterly to fail, it was specified as a critical instance in point his having translated in Virgil the word "proprium" by "proper" instead of "his own". But he knew the sense of the Latin word perfectly well; only, as translating a poet, he had in mind Shakespeare's use of it in "Measure for Measure" in the Duke's speech, "The mere effusion of thy *proper* loins", and foolishly copied it on purpose, not considering how he might be misunderstood.

It is also true that Mr Newman had, in union with his friend Mr Bowden, for a few months at the end of 1818 and the beginning of 1819 been tempted to dabble in matters foreign to academical objects. They had published a Poem, their joint composition, and commenced a small periodical, like Addison's Spectator; but these excursive acts cannot be urged in explanation of Mr Newman's failure. They only occupied their leisure hours, and that for a very short time and were not more than such a recreation as boating might be in the summer term. The memoranda which Mr Newman has left behind him, would show this abundantly, were it worth while to quote them.

[Thus after the Long Vacation of 1818, he gets to Oxford on a Saturday, and on the Monday he writes to his mother, "Bowden is certainly an excellent man to study with; he came to me with his Thucydides this morning and we have begun." On November 12 he says, "We began with our private Tutor in Mathematics at the beginning of this Term; we have two hours a day from him." On December 2, in mock heroics after the vein of Gibbon, whom he had lately been reading, "Though the dinner bell has rung, I must go on writing, for from 5 o'clock till 12 the classic page of the historian of Patavium must make my eyes heavy and my head dull. I think the days are shorter than usual; surely the melting of the polar ice has not abridged the old fashioned 24 hours." During the Christmas Holidays he wrote a very full analysis or abridgment of the whole of Thucydides. And in the following March he speaks of taking up for Collections, that is the College Terminal examination, three books of Thucydides, five of Livy, one of Aristotle's Rhetoric, two greater and twelve minor Prophets and the second half of Bridge's Algebra.][1]

As to the literary efforts in question, the periodical was called "the Undergraduate", and it began and ended in February 1819. It sold well, but, to his great disgust, Newman's name got out, and this was its death blow. They made it over to its publishers, who continued it with an editor of their own for some weeks, when it expired. ["Bowden came into my room on Monday morning," he writes home, "and spoke these words, "The men of Magdalen universally say that Newman of Trinity is the author of the Undergraduate." What imprudence had I committed? I had told no one. I never felt such a dreadful shock. The whole day I could hardly walk or speak. One good thing is that no one in Trinity believes it. Why my name should be known and not Bowden's is incomprehensible. What! can any one fag, fag, and be an Author? Alas! the third day has come a frost, 'a nipping frost'."

[1] Passage deleted by Newman in the autograph. C.S.D.

In a day or two he adds to his Mother, "I hope we have completely
weathered the storm. You would say we were admirable actors, if you
saw how we behaved before people, so cool, so collected, so indifferent. As to the person you suspect, 'Doubt that the stars are fire' but
never doubt his honour."]¹

His and Bowden's poem was a romance founded on the Massacre
of Sᵗ Bartholomew. The subject was the issue of the unfortunate
union of a Protestant gentleman with a Catholic lady, ending in the
tragical death of both, through the machinations of a cruel fanatical
priest, whose inappropriate name was Clement. Mʳ Bowden did the
historical and picturesque portions, Mʳ Newman the theological.
There were no love scenes, nor could there be, for, as it turned out to
the monk's surprise, the parties had been, some time before the
action, husband and wife by a clandestine marriage, known, however, to the father of the lady.

The following passages, from Mʳ Newman's pen, will give an idea
of the theology of the Poem. First, as to the Priest:—
[First, as to the Catholic Religion; he says:—

> Mistaken worship! can the outward tear
> Make clean the breast devoid of godly fear?
> Can pomp and splendour holy love supply,
> The grateful heart, the meek submissive eye?
> Mistaken worship! where the priestly plan
> In servile bondage rules degraded man,
> Proclaims on high in proud imperious tone
> Devotion springs from ignorance alone;
> And dares prefer to sorrow for the past,
> The scourge of penance or the groans of fast;
> Where every crime a price appointed brings
> To soothe the churchman's pride, the sinner's stings,
> Where righteous grief and penitence are made
> A holy market and a pious trade.

It cannot be suspected that the monk is better than his religion, nor
is he; for instance]¹

> "In silent agony she shrank to feel
> How fierce his soul, how bigotted his zeal;

¹ Passage deleted by Newman in the autograph. C.S.D.

> For he had been to her from early youth
> From vice her guardian and her guide to truth.
> Her memory told her that he once was kind,
> Ere the monk's cowl had changed his gentler mind;
> But now of late his holy call had thrown
> A haughty coldness o'er him not his own.
> Yet still she paid him reverence, tho' no more
> She told her bosom-secrets as before.
> True he was stern, but they who knew him best,
> Said fast and penance steeled that holy breast;
> She knew him harsh to avenge heaven's injured laws,
> But deemed superior sanctity the cause;
> She knew him oft mysterious, wild, and strange,
> But hoped that heavenly converse wrought the change."

As priest, so people; hence we are prepared by the above to believe further that

> "Then low before the shrine in concert bowed,
> The fierce, the wild, the crafty, and the proud.
> Infatuate men! shall He who reigns above,
> Father of all, the God of peace and love,
> Shall He be honoured by the murderer's blade?
> Shall he accept the prayers in vengeance made?
> And thou, misguided Ruler of the land,
> Weak to comply, or cruel to command,
> Hop'st thou in peace to pass a length of days,
> Happy in virtue's love and wisdom's praise?
> Lo, tho' success thy scheme of blood may gain,
> Remorse and suffering follow in its train,
> The sleepless couch, the day of wild affright,
> And spectres flitting through the shades of night."

One extract more, in which the virtuous parties are contrasted with the bad monk and his followers, and enough will have been said about this juvenile sally, "St Bartholomew's Eve."

> "Daughter of Albert," said the youth, "for thee
> Have heaven and man for ever destined me.
> And must I fly? and leave thee here alone,
> No friends to aid, midst enemies unknown;

> To crouch before a bigot's despot sway,
> To waste in tears the long, slow, burdened day,
> Thy free soul chained, compelled to frame each thought
> By the drear rules a monk's stern tongue has taught,
> To shrink from sinful memory's busy powers,
> And find a prison in thine own proud towers?—
> Think on that hour, when, to his fate resigned,
> Our trembling hands thy dying father joined;
> 'Twas twilight; we alone; 'My friend,' he said,
> 'To thee I leave this helpless orphan maid';
> And shall a priest, whom holy vestments shield,
> Cancel the bond a father's lips have sealed?
> No! fly with me, 'mid favouring shades; the while,
> Thy father's ghost upon our flight will smile."

This was in February, 1819; also in the Summer Term of the same year there may have been some relaxation of his diligence, Bowden being called away by a domestic affliction, and the Dean, Mr Kinsey, who treated Newman with the familiar kindness of an older brother, taking him off to Professor Buckland's Lectures on Geology, at that time a new and interesting Science, but in no degree subserving the interests of candidates for a first class in the examination Schools. In the Long Vacation, however, which followed he did a great deal of work, nor did a second study of Gibbon in which he then indulged himself, take him away from the classics. He writes to Bowden in October 1819 "What books had we better read this term? We settled on Sophocles and Aeschylus. We are to begin reading without let or hindrance,—on, on, like the Destroyer (Note.Thalaba) in the mysterious boat, till we arrive at the ocean of great-goes." He adds:—"You must excuse my talking on book subjects, but, having been stationary all the Vacation, I have no others to discourse upon; and Herodotus, Thucydides, and Gibbon have employed me nearly from morning to night. A second perusal of the last historian has raised him in my scale of merit. With all his faults, his want of simplicity, his affectation, and his monotony, few can be put in comparison with him; and sometimes, when I reflect on his happy choice of expressions, his vigorous compression of ideas, and the life and significance of his every word, I am prompted indignantly to exclaim that no style is left for historians of an after day. O, who is worthy to succeed our Gibbon! Exoriare aliquis! and may he be a better man!"

In the same month he writes to his mother, "I think I contemplate with brighter hopes the honours of the schools. We are reading between eleven and twelve hours a day, and have an hour for walking, and an hour for dinner." At the end of the term, December 18, he says to her, "The Fellows have been very kind: said we might stop up when we like, and go down when we like, and have offered to do any thing we [they] can for us. This is to me an important year; I heartily wish it over, though most probably I shall look back on it with regret, when past."

A grave feeling, with something of sadness and even awe in it at the prospect before him, increased as the year 1820 opened and the months moved on; as shows itself in the various letters he wrote home. In May he says to his Father, "I intend to be at home a week in the middle of June, the first week of August, and a week in October; in the intervening time, Trinity, I hope, will keep me in an uninterrupted, calm, delightful course of study." And a month afterwards to his Mother:—"The long prospect is now before me. I anticipate that soothing, quiet, unostentatious pleasure, which only an equable and unvarying time of living can give. I look forward to it with great delight. I hope it will resemble the last Long Vacation. When I first went to College, I could write long letters without effort, and lament when the full sheet refused additional matter; for every thing then was novel, and I had not any dread of approaching examinations to awe me into silence. I have often remarked that the undergraduate residence (of three years) is a picture of a whole life, of youth, of manhood, and of old age; which could not be understood or felt without actual experience."

At this time he seems to have been half conscious of some mental or moral change within him, which he fully recognized in the following year, when he took a retrospect of his undergraduate experiences. "In 1819 and the beginning of 1820," he writes in 1821, "I hoped great things for myself, not liking to go into the Church, but to the Law. I attended History Lectures (Professorial), hearing that the names were reported to the Minister." These dreams of a secular ambition, which were quite foreign to his frame of mind in 1817, when he employed himself in writing sermons and sermonets as an exercise, seem now to have departed from him, never to return.

In the Long Vacation of 1820, which he was now entering, when even Bowden was not with him, he had Trinity College, its garden and library, all to himself; and in his solitude, pleasant as he found it, he became graver and graver. At first he says to his Mother "The prospect before me looks alternately dark and bright; but, when I divest my mind of flurried fear, I think I may say I have advanced much more and much more quickly and easily than I had expected."

This was in July; in August he writes to his brother Frank, "Here at Oxford I am most comfortable. The quiet and stillness of every thing around me tends to calm and lull those emotions, which the near prospect of my grand examination and a heart too solicitous about fame and too fearful of failure, are continually striving to excite. I read very much certainly, but God enables me to praise Him with joyful lips, when I rise, and when I lie down, and when I wake in the night. For the calm happiness I enjoy, I cannot feel thankful as I ought. How in my future life, if I do live, shall I look back with a sad smile at these days! It is my daily and, I hope, heartfelt prayer, that I may not get any honours here, if they are to be the least cause of sin to me. As the time approaches, and I have laboured more at my books, the trial is greater."

At the same date he writes to one of his sisters, "I try to keep myself as cool as I can, but find it very difficult. However it is my duty not to 'take thought for the morrow'. I cannot think much of the schools without wishing much to distinguish myself in them; and that wishing much would make me discontented, if I did not succeed; and that is coveting, for then we covet, when we desire a thing so earnestly as to be discontented, if we fail in getting it. I will not therefore ask for success but for good."

Meanwhile his application to his books, which had recommenced with such vigour in the Long Vacation of 1819, was now almost an absorption into them; he gives a retrospective account of it in a letter to an Irish friend, written in 1821. "During the Long Vacation of 1819," he says, "I read nearly at the rate of nine hours a day. From that time to my examination in November 1820, it was almost a continuous mass of reading. I stayed in Oxford during the vacations, got up winter and summer at 5 or 6, hardly allowed myself time for my meals, and then ate indeed the bread of carefulness. During 20 out of the 24 weeks immediately preceding my examination, I fagged at an average of more than twelve hours a day. If one day I read only nine, I read the next fifteen."

The termination of these "laborious days" was now approaching, and he ushered it in with a long letter to his friend, Mr Mayers. In the course of it he says: "I am more happy here than I suppose I ever was yet. ... Yet in truth I am in no common situation. The very few honours that have ever been taken by men of our College, the utter absence of first classes for the last ten years, the repeated failures which have occurred, and the late spirit of reading which has shown itself among us, render those who attempt this autumn objects of wonder, curiosity, speculation, and anxiety. Five of us were going up for first classes this time; one has deferred his examination; one most likely goes up for no honours at all; one is expected to fail; one, whom I think quite certain of success, may before the examination remove to another College;—one remains. 'Unless', I am told, 'success at length attends on Trinity this examination, we have determined it is useless to read.'

"The high expectations too that are formed of me, the confidence with which those who know nothing of me put down two first classes to my name, the monstrous notions they may form of the closeness of my application, and on the other hand my consciousness of my own deficiencies—these things may create a smile to think I feared them in my future life, but they are sufficient to dismay me now. I fear much more from failure, than I hope from success."

It was not strangers only who did not know him, that felt so assured that Newman would succeed. His friend Bowden, who had read with him, had passed his own ordeal and went home before him; thence he wrote to Newman prophesying all good things of him, being confident that his examination would be brilliant. This was in November: "I shall expect," he said, "to hear in your answer, whether they put you on in any books besides those you took up." And in a second letter, "By the time you receive this, I conclude you will have completed your labours in the Schools, and covered yourself and the College with glory." Bowden did but express the expectation of his friends generally, but fortune had gone against him. He had overread himself, and, being suddenly called up a day sooner than he expected, he lost his head, utterly broke down, and after vain attempts for several days had to retire, only making sure first of his B.A. degree. When the class list came out, his name did not appear at all on the Mathematical side of the Paper, and in Classics it was found in the lower division of the second class of honours, which at that time went by the contemptuous title of the "Under-the-line", there being as yet no third and fourth classes.

Though he never was able to satisfy himself how it came about that he did so little justice on that occasion to his long and assiduous toil, it must be borne in mind that a similar affection after a severe course of reading overtook him seven years later on all but the same day (November 26th instead of November 25) when he was exercising his office of University Examiner in the very same Schools in which in 1820 he had failed as examinee, and that attack came on with greater violence, for he was obliged to leave Oxford, and for a time to relinquish his office.

During the long days of his ineffectual efforts in the Schools, he suffered severely; and again with especial keenness immediately on his having to give those efforts up; but he was not long in recovering his composure. His letters to his father & mother run as follows:—

To his father. "December 1, 1820, It is all over, and I have not succeeded. The pain it gives me to be obliged to inform you and my Mother of it, I cannot express. What I feel on my own account is indeed nothing at all, compared with the thought that I have disappointed you. And most willingly would I consent to a hundred times the sadness that now overshadows me if so doing would save my Mother and you from feeling vexation. I will not attempt to describe what I have gone through, but it is past away, and I feel quite lightened of a load. The Examining Masters were as kind as it was possible to be; but my nerves quite forsook me, and I failed. I have done every thing I could to attain my object; I have spared no labour; and my reputation in my College is as solid as before, if not so splendid. If a man falls in battle after a display of bravery, he is honoured as a hero; ought not the same glory to attend him who falls in the field of literary conflict?"

His parents answered him, as might be supposed, that they were more than satisfied with his exertions, that he must wait patiently and cheerfully the time appointed for his reaping the fruit of them. "The only sorrow we feel," they said, "is for the keenness of your feelings." By the time this letter came he had recovered himself, and in his answer to his Mother, he was unwilling to allow that his distress was so great as she implied it to be.

"Dec. 3. 1820. I am ashamed to think that any thing I have said should have led you to suppose that I am at all pained on my own account ... I am perfectly convinced that there are few men in College who do not feel for me more than I do for myself. ... A man has just left me, and his last words were, "Well, Newman, I would rather have your philosophy, than the high honours to which you have been aspiring." I say this, not in vanity, but to prove the truth of my assertion. ... I am sure that success could not have made me happier than I am at present. ... Very much I *have* gone through, but the clouds have passed away. ... Since I have done my part, I have gained what is good."

Only a few words are necessary to complete the outline of this portion of Mʳ Newman's career. He had been destined by his father's loving ambition for the bar, and with that purpose had been sent to the University; and in 1819 had entered at Lincoln's Inn; but his failure in the Schools making his prospect of rising in a difficult profession doubtful, and his religious views becoming more pronounced, he decided in the course of 1821, with his father's full acquiescence, on taking Orders. His scholarship at Trinity continuing for several years still, he was furnished with a sufficient plea for remaining at Oxford, though a B.A., and for taking private pupils as a means of support. He wished also to be of use to his youngest brother, whom he was desirous of bringing to the University, and, as the year drew to its close and just at the time when he began to take pupils, he conceived the audacious idea of standing for a fellowship at Oriel, at that time the object of ambition of all rising men in Oxford, and attainable only by those who had the highest academical pretensions. It may be called audacious for various reasons, and certainly would so seem to others; but in truth he had never himself accepted his failure in the schools as the measure of his intellectual merits, and, in proportion as the relief of mind ceased to be felt, consequent at first upon his freedom from scholastic work and its anxieties, a reaction took place within him; and he began to think about retrieving his losses, and to aspire to some honorable and permanent place in his loved University, refused tempting offers of tutorships in gentlemen's families which would take him from Oxford, and kept whispering to himself as about himself the line of Gray, "And hushed in grim repose, expects his evening prey."

This change in his state of mind took place in him in the autumn of 1821, and he has described his feelings at that time in the following passage of his "Loss and Gain."

"He recollected with what awe and transport he had at first come to the University, as to some sacred shrine; and how from time to time hopes had come over him that some day or other he should have gained a title to residence on one of its old foundations. One night, in particular, came across his memory, how a friend and he had ascended to the top of one of its many towers with the purpose of making observations on the stars; and how, while his friend was busily engaged with the pointers, he, earthly-minded youth, had been looking down into the deep, gas-lit, dark-shadowed quadrangles, and wondering if he should ever be Fellow of this or that College, which he singled out from the mass of academical buildings."

It is scarcely necessary to say here, that his attempt at Oriel, startling as it was to his friends, and hopeless as it was in his own calm judgment, was successful. It follows next to draw out the circumstances under which it was made.

APPENDIX

On Thursday, June 1st, 1854, a few days before his installation as Rector of the Catholic University on the Feast of Pentecost, Newman inaugurated a small weekly periodical, which he called the *University Gazette*. His immediate object was to provide a medium of communication through which the public might be kept informed on matters of general interest connected with the University; but he made use of it also to supplement the *Discourses on University Education*, delivered (in part) in 1852, and published complete in 1853 (*Idea*, pp. 1-239). As then he had "attempted to determine the abstract nature of University Education", so now in a series of essays, afterwards included in *Historical Sketches* under the title of "Rise and Progress of Universities" (iii, 1-251), he undertook to discuss "actual Academical Institutions, past or present, in their historical characteristics and several fortunes".

This series continued to run in the pages of the *University Gazette* until almost the end of the year, when they ceased. Then, to No. 34 (January 18th, 1855), pp. 294-6, he contributed, over the initial "E", a letter, "On Latin Composition", which appears in the *Idea of a University*, pp. 366-71, as "Old Mr Black's Confession of his search after a Latin style". He intended to follow this up with a second letter, already written, purporting to come from another hand; but eventually he decided not to insert it, because, as he explains in a note, it seemed to him, on second thoughts, to be "without point and, even more, because it reflected on the Oxford of [his] day". He had good reason to be apprehensive, for, if he had not withheld it, he would have given needless pain to several of his older contemporaries, whom he ever held in high esteem. Those under whose influence he had come at Trinity were, with one exception, still alive. The one exception was the Dean, W. M. Kinsey, who had recently died; but John Wilson, the senior of the two Tutors in his undergraduate days, had been elected President of the College in 1850, and Thomas Short, the junior, in spite of his legendary antiquity, had lost little of his vigour, and in fact survived for a quarter of a century longer; and J. A. Ogle, who had been his Private Tutor, was Regius Professor of Medicine.

But as they have all now been dead for the better part of a century, the motives of delicacy that determined Newman's decision in 1855, have completely lost their force; and consequently the suppressed letter is reproduced here, as it stands in his manuscript.

Mʳ Editor,

In the Arabian Tales there was a second Calender who told his tale after the first; and, as the first had but one eye, neither had the second. I wonder whether you will have the Caliph Haroun's patience or curiosity to let me tell a tale parallel to your correspondent E's, for, as he went to the University at a very early age, and lost time there, yet without idleness, so did I; and, as his history is useful to the student, so may mine be. Under the anticipation, that perhaps you will think so, I will proceed to give it; and, if useful it really be, I shall not trouble myself nor be annoyed at the consciousness, that I cannot even speak of my own failures without some self-complacency. Certainly it is difficult to speak about oneself in any way without some feeling of satisfaction; but if I really have a good and sufficient motive, and maintain a strict incognito, this adventitious feeling must not deter me.

I went to the University with an active mind, and with no thought but that of hard reading; but when I got there, I had as little tutorial assistance or guidance as is easy to conceive, and found myself left almost entirely to my own devices. I do not impute this inconvenience to those who were responsible for my intellectual advancement. Since my day there has been formed a supplemental system, called with you that of "grinding", by which the individual student is worked up for his examinations. But at that time the very idea of study was new, and had been carried into effect in only a few Colleges. These Colleges had the tradition of it to themselves; they alone had real Tutors; they alone really prepared their youths for the Schools; and, as they alone could supply the Examiners, they had the standard as well as the tradition of scholarship in their own hands. The teaching and the honors of the place were in the possession of a small clique; if any one of their pupils appeared for examination, a prestige went with him; the Schools were crowded with the young men of other Colleges as well as of his own, and his success was three-quarters certain before he had answered a question. In a short time he became himself a Tutor, and perpetuated the process, which had produced himself. I do not know that any one was in fault here; when there has been a declension and decay, if there is to be a revival, there must be a beginning, and a beginning will ever have a local and personal character, and will have to progress, not only in intensity, but in extent. It must have a centre, before it has a circumference; and those who are as yet external to its range will be in a worse condition than they would have been before the revival, for they will be at a disadvantage compared with those whom that revival has reached.

However, so it was, that I had little or no guidance in my studies;

and, like your late correspondent, I sought, and found not. And in consequence, like your late correspondent also, I was obliged to teach myself, and a very sorry and unsatisfactory teaching it was. Teaching indeed it hardly was at all, as you will see, except that an active mind, which does its best, cannot altogether waste its time. Yet though always busy, I spent four years with no fruit; and by the age of twenty or twenty one, I had in fact to begin my education. One attainment alone did I secure in the previous four years, that of persevering application.

It is a great thing to have a routine prescribed, in which the student is obliged to move, without choice of his own; when he is left to his own private judgment, he is determined to this or that course of study by accident or caprice, and the faster and more vigorously he proceeds along it, the greater is the distance he has ultimately to retrace. I never was tempted to give up the studies of the place; I never was without one or other classic or branch of mathematics in hand; but I needed a kind friend to keep me from taking up other pursuits at the same time, and I damaged and thwarted the real progress of my mind by dabbling in studies and occupations, good in themselves, but out of place. I attended lectures in geology and mineralogy; I studied manuals and tried experiments in chemistry; I wrote a poem, and I commenced a periodical. Meanwhile, not only in Term time, but in the long Vacations, nay, in the other Vacations also, I read furiously the books in which the candidates for academical honors were examined. I got up in winter at five, lighting my own fire; and in summer at half-past four, getting four hours reading before breakfast. A year or two afterwards I took only four hours sleep, but this was after my Undergraduate course was over. My greatest effort for the Schools was during the half-year immediately preceding my appearance in them; I was reading classics; still, however, by myself; I have still the memoranda I made day by day; I know it is no mistake; and I know that it was real reading,—I mean, my attention was alive throughout; and it was *bona fide* reading; well, for the last 20 weeks I read regularly 12 hours a day; generally, I believe, exactly that number every day, but at all events that average; if I read one day only 9 hours, another I read 15.—So it was; and then I went into the Schools for my examination;—and completely failed. Of course I got a common pass, but of honors nothing; only the record that I had tried and got them not.

When I look back upon those anxious, toilsome years and their event, I seem to myself to see a type of Protestantism;—zeal, earnestness, resolution, without a guide; effort without a result. It was a pattern instance of private judgment and its characteristics. I think of the words you have lately quoted, and apply them to myself, though it was only an Undergraduate life I lost, which is retrievable, —"Heu, vitam perdidi, operose nihil agendo!"

You will say that what I lost was, not mental advancement, but academical honors. I think I lost both.

Chapter 2

It did certainly startle Mr Newman's friends at Trinity to find him contemplating an attempt upon an Oriel Fellowship; and many of them it pained also, for they were sure it would end in a second miscarriage. They had not the shadow of a hope of his succeeding; and they would have thought him wise, if, instead of following an *ignis fatuus*, he had accepted one of the family tutorships offered for his acceptance. What would confirm them in this view was the grave fact, that he had lost almost the whole of the current year in recreations and diversions of his own, instead of devoting the time since he took his batchelor's degree in preparation for a difficult competition. What his actual occupations had been appears accidentally from a series of passages in his letters home and in his Private Memoranda, some of which shall now be given in the order, in which they were written.

To his Father he writes on his return to Oxford in February 1821 after his failure in the Schools, "I arrived here safe the day before yesterday, and have found a general welcome. D^r and Mrs Lee have been very kind. I intend attending the Lectures on Anatomy and Mineralogy."

To the same on March 20. "I have been with Mr Kinsey to Abingdon, to the house of a gentleman who has a fine collection of Minerals. We were employed in looking over them from one to four o'clock. Some of them are most beautiful. When I come home, I shall make various excursions to the British Museum, if open, for the sake of the Minerals."

During this term he attended the course of lectures on Mineralogy, given by Professor Buckland, and made a careful analysis of them, which is to be found among his papers.

To his Mother in the same month; "Thank Harriett (his sister) for her skill in steaming away the superfluous water of the nitro-sulphate of copper. The mineralogical Lectures were finished yesterday ... ...

"I am glad to be able to inform you that Signor Giovanni Enrico Neandrini has finished his first composition. The melody is light and airy, and is well supported by the harmony."

To the same in June. "I have been very much to myself this term. Buckland's lectures (on Geology) I had intended to have taken down, as I did last Term, but several things prevented me:—the time it takes; and the very desultory way in which he imparts his information. For, to tell the truth, the science is so in its infancy, that no regular system is formed. Hence the lectures are rather an enumeration of facts from which probabilities are deduced, than a consistent and luminous theory, of certainties illustrated by occasional examples. It is, however, most entertaining, and opens an amazing field to imagination and to poetry."

To these accidental notices of his employment of his time after his B.A. degree, others may be added, more complete because made on retrospect. He says in passages of his private Memoranda that he had now "more leisure for religious exercises and the study of the Scriptures than when he was a fagging drudge"; that "mineralogy and chemistry were his chief studies and the composition of music"; though, from the time he thought of standing at Oriel, he "gave considerable time to Latin composition, to logic, and to Natural Philosophy"; that, as an Undergraduate, he used to say, "When I have taken my degree, I will do many things, compose a piece of music for instruments, experimentalize in chemistry, thirdly" (on which he insisted much) "get up the Persian language &c &c." In consequence of this last design, his Mother bought him an Arabic and a Persian Vocabulary, now in the Oratory Library, but nothing came of it. It does not appear from any papers he has left how this study came into his mind. Was it suggested by Henry Martyn's history?[1]

These notices have perhaps a claim to be introduced into this Memoir for their own sake, but here they are simply meant to illustrate the surprise and discomposure with which his good friends at Trinity, nay almost he himself, in spite of himself, contemplated his resolution to engage in so forlorn a hope, as an attempt on an Oriel fellowship. None thought it possible that he could succeed in it; and, at his own suggestion, Mr Kinsey wrote to his Father, with the purpose, as far as might be, of putting before him the state of the case, and guarding against disappointment. He told him that in the competition at Oriel "the struggles of the best have failed", and, that, "knowing the many opponents which his son would have to encounter, men of celebrity for talent and reading, he, the writer, with all his eager desire for his friend's success, did not permit himself to be at all sanguine as to his beating the field."

Mr Short was as little inclined to look hopefully upon Newman's

[1] Evangelical missionary in India and Persia, 1781-1812. C.S.D.

prospects at Oriel as the rest, but he took a larger view of the matter and was not all unwilling that he should stand. He knew enough of him to expect that he would do himself and his College credit, and this expectation he had strongly expressed to friends of Newman in London, who, being sincerely interested in him, and anxious about his future, asked Short what he had to say on the subject. Short answered them that he would not succeed, but that he would show what was in him, and thereby in a certain measure retrieve his unexpected failure a year before; he wished the Oriel men to have an opportunity of passing a judgment on him. In truth it was, naturally and fairly, a matter of personal and collegiate interest with Mr Short, over and above his good-will towards Newman. The opening of the Trinity scholarships was Short's doing, and he had actually recommended him to stand in 1818; in the election formidable out-college opponents had been put aside for him, and his failure in his examination had been an untoward incident in the first start of a great reform. Mr Short had brought out these feelings to him, with the greatest delicacy, soon after his misfortune, on his asking Short in April 1821 whether he should write for one of the Chancellor's prizes, yearly given for the best English and Latin Essays. Mr Short answered in the affirmative, and went on to give the following reason for wishing it. "I have no doubt," he said, "of your producing something that either will succeed now, or train you to certain success another year. In fact the uppermost wish in my mind respecting you is that you may distinguish yourself in the Rostrum, and prove to the world, what is already well known to ourselves, that the purity of our elections is unsullied. For should your old competitor at Worcester obtain high honours in the schools, sneerers will not be wanting to amuse themselves at your and our expense. Perhaps these reasons never occurred to you." He had said in a former part of the letter, that he should himself have suggested to him to attempt the Essay, long before, but he had been anxious whether Mr Newman's health allowed it.

By a singular coincidence, Oriel College that same year and at that very time was subjecting itself, and even more directly and wittingly, to a criticism upon its impartiality in conducting its competitive examinations, fiercer and more public than that which Mr Short only feared for Trinity. Though in that day the acknowledged centre of Oxford intellectualism, it [Oriel] had never professed in its election simply to choose the candidate who passed the best examination;

and, though on its foundation were for the most part men who had taken the highest honours in the Schools, it never made the School standard its own. Religious, ethical, social considerations, as well as intellectual merits external to the *curriculum* of the Schools, all told in its decisions; the votes fell on the men whom each elector in his conscience thought best to answer to the standard of a fellow of Oriel, as Adam de Brome and King Edward's Statutes determined it. In consequence there was ever the chance of the election of a candidate of a nature to startle his competitors and the public at large, as being unexpected and unaccountable. Such an anomalous election, as many men thought it, had taken place in 1821, just three days before Newman's letter to Mr Short above spoken of. A second class man had been preferred to one whose name stood in the first class; and though the successful candidate had, as if in justification of his selection, gained the Chancellor's Latin Essay prize a few months later, yet, it so happened, his rival, whom he had beaten, was able at the annual Commemoration to hurl defiance at him in the Theatre from the opposite rostrum, as [having been] the successful competitor for the English Essay. This Essay, as being in English, gave an opportunity for vigorous, brilliant, and popular writing, which was denied to a composition written in Latin; and judgment on the rival merits of the two men was thus shifted to a public opinion external both to College and to University, and in fact that judgment was passed in certain influential quarters to the disadvantage of the successful candidate and his electors. There was a celebrated Review which had for many years been in feud with Oxford, and especially with Dr Copleston, Provost of Oriel, and his Society. An editor whoever he be, taking human nature at the best, sometimes "dormitat", however "bonus", and an article against Oriel found its way into his July number, so exceptionable, to use a mild word, that in a second edition, according to the recollection of the present writer, sentences or expressions were erased from it. The article is upon Classical Learning, and the writer, after speaking of the English Universities generally in that connexion, directs his attention to their open fellowships, to the nature of the examination usual for determining the choice between candidates, and to the proceedings and the result of the election. The allusion to Oriel, and to the election made at the preceding Easter was unmistakable. The following is a portion of the writer's invective, for such it must be called.

(N.B. Let it be observed I have concealed the really *bad* fact that the *writer* was the *unsuccessful candidate*. But Copleston has blabbed it.)

"Let a young man only abdicate the privilege of thinking,—to some no painful sacrifice,—and devote his whole body and soul to the sordid ambition of success, and the way to win with such electors is no formidable problem. ... After a dull examination in the Schools, —if a failure so much the better,—he may begin to be the butt of Common rooms, circulate Tutors' wit, and prose against the Edinburgh Review. ... (Guiltless of fame, originality, or humour,) our tyro may then approach the scene of action, secure that the judges will take good care, that 'the race shall not be to the swift, nor the battle to the strong'. Hardy professions of impartiality are indeed held forth, to attract unwary merit; and selfish mediocrity finds the most exquisite of all its gratifications in the momentary chance of harassing the talent it would tremble to confront. The candidates are locked up to write themes,—solve a Sorites,—discover the latin for an earthquake,—and perform other equally edifying tasks; and the close of this solemn farce is the annunciation of a choice that had been long before determined, in proportion to the scrapings, grins, and genuflections of the several competitors. Who can be surprised if under a system like this, genius and knowledge should so seldom strike a lasting root? or that the maturity, which succeeds to a youth so prostituted, should produce, by its most vigorous efforts, nothing better than learned drivelling or marrowless inflation?"

It is scarcely necessary to say that this tirade against Oxford and Oriel was as unjust as it was unmannerly; however "diis aliter visum". Such a spirited denunciation seems to have been considered in a high quarter just what was wanted to show the world what retribution (was to) descend, and what terrible examples would be made, if an Oxford College presumed to maintain a standard and exercise a judgment of its own, on the qualifications necessary in those who were to fill up vacant places on its foundation; and, though the Oriel Fellows were of too independent and manly a cast of mind and had too high a repute and too haughty pretensions to succumb to a self appointed and angry censor, yet in spite of their natural indignation at his language, the charge brought against them, as coming with so weighty a sanction, would necessarily tend to make them more wary of the steps they took in the ensuing election of 1822, more unwilling, if it could be helped, to run risks, and more anxious that their decisions should be justified by the event. This state of things at Oriel cannot be said to have told in Mr Newman's favour, when at length he resolved on submitting his talents and attainments, such as they were, to the inspection of Provost and Fellows. For they could not pronounce in his favour without repeating in an exaggerated form their offence of the foregoing year, that is, without passing over the first class competitors, and electing instead of them one whose place in the paper of honours was ever taken in popular estimation as the token of a mistake or misfortune,—an intimation, known and understood by all men, that there had been an attempt in the candidate in question at something higher and a failure in attaining it.

Such being the external view presented to us by Mr Newman's venturous proceeding, let us trace seriatim, from his private Memoranda, how it presented itself to his own mind.

The examination was to be in the first days of the ensuing April; it was now the middle of November; he had at least four good months before him. He notes down on November 15, "I passed this evening with the Dean", Mr Kinsey, "whose Oriel cousin was there. He said the principal thing in the examination for Fellows was writing Latin. I thought I ought to stand; and indeed, since, I have nearly decided on so doing. How active still are the evil passions of vainglory, ambition, &c within me. After my failure last November I thought that they never would be unruly again. Alas! no sooner is any mention made of my standing for a fellowship, than every barrier seems swept away, and they spread and overflow and deluge me; ὥσπερ ξὺν ἵπποις ἡνιοστροφῶ δρόμου &c. Choeph 1009 [1022].

He continues December 1:—"There is every reason for thinking I shall not succeed, and I seem to see it would not be good for me, but my heart boils over with vainglorious anticipations of success. It is not likely because I am not equal to it in abilities or attainments; it seems probable that I shall fail once or twice, and get some fellowship somewhere at last."

Two months later, February 5, 1822 he writes "Today I called on the Provost of Oriel, and asked his permission to stand at the ensuing election. I cannot help thinking I shall one time or other get a fellowship there, most probably next year. I am glad I am going to stand now; I shall make myself known, and learn the nature of the examination. The principal thing seems to be Latin Composition, and a metaphysical turn is a great advantage; general mathematics are also required....Last 5th of January (1821) I wrote to my Aunt,'I deprecate the day in which God gives me any repute or approach to wealth'; alas, how am I changed! I am perpetually praying to get into Oriel and to obtain the prize for my Essay. O Lord, dispose of me as will most promote Thy glory, but give me resignation and contentment."

On February 21 he came of age, and he writes to his Mother in answer to her congratulations, "I thought of the years that are gone, and the expanse which lies before me, and quite shed tears to think I could no longer call myself a boy." And then, after noticing his employments, he continues, "What time I have left, I am glad, and indeed obliged, to devote to my attempt at Oriel, wishing to prepare myself for that which after all will not admit of preparation."

Then he says, in corroboration of what Mr Kinsey was saying in the letter above quoted, "I was very uneasy to find by some thing in my Father's and your letter, that you thought I had a chance of getting in this time. Do not think so, I intreat. You only hear, and cannot see the difficulties. Those on the spot think there is little or no chance, and who indeed will not rightly wonder at the audacity of him, who, being an under-the-line himself, presumes to contend with some of the first men in the University for a seat by the side of names like Keble and Hawkins?"

He wished his home friends not to share his hopes, lest they should have to share his disappointment. The chances were much against him; his hopes nevertheless were high, but while an avowal of this might mislead those who did not know Oxford, it would incur the ridicule of those who did. His hopes are recorded in a memorandum made the next day:—

"I have called on Tyler to-day," the then Dean of Oriel, "I do not know how it happens, but I certainly feel very confident with respect to Oriel, and seem to myself to have a great chance of success. Hope leads me on to fancy my confidence itself has some thing of success in it, and I seem to recollect some thing of the same kind of ardour, when I stood at Trinity."

However, before many weeks were out, he was obliged to let out to his Father, what he had been so carefully concealing from him. Made anxious by the tone of his son's letter written on occasion of his birthday, he wrote to warn him, that, if he continued in the desponding temper which his letters home betokened, he certainly would not be able to do justice to his talents and attainments, and would be the cause of his own failure. This obliged him to write in answer on March 15 thus:—

"I assure you that they know very little of me and judge very superficially, who think I do not put a value on myself *relatively* to others. I think (since I am forced to speak boastfully) few have attained the facility of comprehension which I have arrived at from the regularity and constancy of my reading, and the laborious and nerve-bracing and fancy-repressing study of Mathematics, which has been my principal subject."

On the 18th he repeats in a private Memorandum, "I fear I am treasuring up for myself great disappointment, for I think I have a great chance of succeeding. I lay great stress on the attention I have given to Mathematics on account of the general strength it imparts to the mind. Besides, ever since my attempts at school, I have given great time to composition. As, when I was going up for my Degree Examination, every day made my hopes fainter, so now they seem to swell and ripen, as the time approaches."

The examination was now close at hand, and he suffered some reaction of feeling when he plunged into it. On the close of it, he thus writes:—"I have several times been much comforted yesterday and today by a motto in Oriel Hall, (in a coat of arms in a window), 'Pie repone te'. I am now going to bed, and have been very calm the whole evening. Before I look at this book again, it will be decided."

Next day, the Friday in Easter week, he writes, "I have this morning been elected Fellow of Oriel."

Some account of what passed in this to him memorable day, is introduced into his Apologia; other incidents of it are noted in his letters to members of his family, and others again he used to recount at a later date to his friends. When the examination had got as far as the third day, his papers had made that impression on Dr Copleston and other of the electors, that three of them, James, Tyler, and Dornford went over to Trinity to make inquiries of the Fellows about his antecedents and general character. This of course was done in confidence; nor did his kind Tutor, Mr Short, in any degree violate it; at the same time he was himself so excited by this visit, that he could not help sending for Mr Newman on the pretext of inquiring of him what had been his work and how he had done it; and by the encouraging tone in which he commented on his answers, he did him a great deal of good. (Note) Mr Short told him on Febr. 27, 1878 that, on sending for him, he found him intending to retire, and that he persuaded him to continue the contest.[1] Newman used to

---

[1] Marginal note by Newman. C.S.D.

relate how, when sent for, he found Mr Short at an early dinner in his rooms, being about to start from Oxford, and how Short made him sit down at table and partake of his lamb cutlets and fried parsley, a bodily refreshment which had some share in the re-assurance with which Short's words inspired him. He wrote to his Mother in retrospect some three weeks after, "Short elevated me so much, and made me fancy I had done so well, that on Wednesday I construed some part of my (*vivâ voce*) passages with very great readiness and even accuracy."

Mr Newman used also to relate the mode in which the announcement of his success was made to him. The Provost's Butler, to whom it fell by usage to take the news to the fortunate candidates, made his way to Mr Newman's lodgings in Broad Street, and found him playing the violin. This in itself disconcerted the messenger, who did not associate such an accomplishment with a candidateship for the Oriel Common Room; but his perplexity was increased, when, on his delivering what may be supposed to have been his usual form of speech on such occasions, that "he had, he feared, disagreeable news to announce, viz. that Mr Newman was elected Fellow of Oriel, and that his immediate presence was required there," the person addressed, thinking that such language savoured of impertinent familiarity, merely answered "Very well" and went on fiddling. This led the man to ask whether perhaps he had not mistaken the rooms and gone to the wrong person, to which Mr Newman replied that [it] was all right. But, as may be imagined, no sooner had the man left, than he flung down his instrument, and dashed down stairs with all speed to Oriel College. And he recollected after fifty years the eloquent faces and eager bows of the tradesmen and others whom he met on his way, who had heard the news, and well understood why he was crossing from St Mary's to the lane opposite at so extraordinary a pace.

He repeats in a letter to his Mother a circumstance in his first interview, which followed, with the Provost and Fellows, which in his "Apologia" he has quoted from his letter to Mr Bowden. "I could bear the congratulations of Copleston, but, when Keble advanced to take my hand, I quite shrank, and could have nearly sunk into the floor, ashamed at so great an honour;—however, I shall soon be used to this." He pursues his history of the day thus:—"The news spread to Trinity with great rapidity. I had hardly been in Kinsey's room a minute, when in rushed Ogle like one mad. Then I proceeded to the President's, and in rushed Ogle again. I find that Tomlinson rushed into Echalaz's room, nearly kicking down the door to communicate the news. Echalaz in turn ran down stairs; Tompson heard a noise and my name mentioned, and rushed out also, and in the room opposite found Echalaz, Ogle and Ward, leaping up and down, backwards and forwards. Men hurried from all directions to Trinity, to their acquaintance there, to congratulate them on the success of their College. The bells were set ringing from three towers (I had to pay for them). The men who were staying up at Trinity reading for their degree, accuse me of having spoilt their day's reading."

There is a letter from him to his brother Charles, in which he says "I took my seat in Chapel, and dined with a large party in the Common Room. I sat next Keble, and, as I had heard him represented, he is more like an undergraduate than the first man in Oxford, so perfectly unassuming and unaffected in his manner." And lastly, he says in his letter to his Father, "I am absolutely a member of the Common Room, am called by them "Newman", and am abashed to find I must soon learn to call them "Keble", "Hawkins", "Tyler".

So ends the eventful day.

As to Mr Newman he ever felt this twelfth of April, 1822 to be the turning point of his life, and of all days most memorable. It raised him from obscurity and need to competency and reputation. He never wished any thing better or higher than, in the words of the epitaph, "to live and die a fellow of Oriel". Henceforth his way was clear before him; and he was constant all through his life, as his intimate friends know, in his thankful remembrance year after year of this great mercy of Divine Providence, and of his electors, by whom it was brought about. Nor was it in its secular aspect only that it was so unique an event in his history; it opened upon him a theological career, placing him on the high and broad platform of University society and intelligence, and bringing him across those various influences personal and intellectual, and the teaching of those various schools of ecclesiastical thought whereby the religious sentiment in his mind, which had been his blessing from the time he left school, was gradually developed and formed and brought on to its legitimate issue.

This narrative of his attempt and its success will be most suitably closed by the account of his examination as given by the very man, to whom more than to any one the Oriel examinations owed their form and colour, and who specially on that account had to meet the stress of those Northern criticisms which in their most concentrated and least defensible shape have been exhibited above. "That defect," says Bishop Copleston in a letter to Dr Hawkins under date of May 2, 1843, "which I always saw and lamented, and in vain endeavoured to remedy, still, it seems, not only exists, but increases,—the quackery of the Schools. Every election to a fellowship which tends to discourage the narrow and almost the technical routine of public examinations, I consider as an important triumph. You remember Newman himself was an example. He was not even a good classical scholar, yet in mind and powers of composition, and in taste and knowledge, he was decidedly superior to some competitors, who were a class above him in the Schools."

As Mr Newman held the important offices of Tutor and Public Examiner in the years which followed, it may be *right* to observe here that immediately on his becoming Fellow of Oriel, he set himself to make up his deficiency in critical scholarship, and with very fair success. Whately, soon after his election, among his other kind offices, signified to him what he said "a little bird had told him".

Chapter 3

The responsibility of becoming guarantee to the University, that Newman, in spite of his ill success in the Schools, was deserving academical distinction, was now transferred from Trinity to Oriel; and, if it had required courage in him to offer himself to his electors in the latter College, it also required courage, as has been said, in them to take him. Strong as they might be in their reliance on the independence and the purity of their elections, and broad as were their shoulders, if public opinion was invoked against them, still they had, in choosing him, taken on themselves a real onus, and a real anxiety in the prospect of his future; and, had the sense of their generosity towards him, on that his introduction to them, remained at all times present with him, he might have been saved from the hard thoughts and words, and the impatient acts, to which in after times he was led at the expense of some of them. However true might be the principles and sacred the interests which on those occasions he was defending, he had no call to forget the past, no license at an after date to forget, that, if he was able to assert his own views in opposition to theirs, it was in truth they who had put him into a position, enabling him to do so.

As to their anxiety, after his election, how he would turn out, there were, certainly, on his first introduction to the Common Room, definite points about him which made him somewhat a difficulty to those who brought him there. In the first place they had to deal with his extreme shyness. It disconcerted them to find that with all their best efforts they could not draw him out or get him to converse. He shrank into himself, when his duty was to meet their advances. Easy and fluent as he was among his equals and near relatives, his very admiration of his new associates made a sudden intimacy with them impossible to him. An observant friend who even at a later date saw him accidentally among strangers, not knowing the true account of his bearing, told him he considered that he had had a near escape of being a stutterer. This untowardness in him was increased by a vivid self consciousness, which sometimes inflicted on him days of acute suffering from the recollection of solecisms, whether actual or imagined, which he recognized in his conduct in society. And then there was in addition that real isolation of thought and spiritual solitariness, which was the result of his Calvinistic beliefs. His electors, however, had not the key to the reserve which hung about him; and in default of it, accounts of another kind began to assail their ears which increased their perplexity. With a half malicious intent of frightening them, it was told them that Mr Newman had for years belonged to a club of instrumental music and had himself taken part in its public performances, a diversion, innocent indeed in itself, but scarcely in keeping or in sympathy with an intellectual Common Room or promising a satisfactory career to a nascent Fellow of Oriel.

It was under the circumstance of misgivings such as these, that Mr Tyler, Mr James, and other leading Fellows of the day took a step as successful in the event for their own relief, as it was advantageous to Mr Newman. Mr Whately, afterwards Protestant Archbishop of Dublin, who had lately relinquished his fellowship by marriage, was just at that time residing in lodgings in Oxford previously to his taking possession of a Suffolk benefice, and they determined on putting their unformed probationer into his hands. If there was a man easy for a raw bashful youth to get on with it was Whately —a great talker, who endured very readily the silence of his company, —original in his views, lively, forcible, witty in expressing them, brimful of information on a variety of subjects,—so entertaining that, logician as he was, he is said sometimes to have fixed the attention of a party of ladies to his conversation, or rather discourse, for two or three hours at a stretch,—free and easy in manners, rough indeed and dogmatic in his enunciation of opinion, but singularly gracious to undergraduates and young masters, who, if they were worth any thing, were only too happy to be knocked about in argument by such a man. And he on his part professed to be pleased at having cubs in hand whom he might lick into shape, and who, he said, like dogs of King Charles's breed, could be held up by one leg without yelling. Mr Newman brought with him the first of recommendations to Whately in being a good listener, and in his special facility of entering into ideas as soon as, or before, they were expressed. It was not long before Mr Whately succeeded in drawing him out, and he paid him the compliment of saying that he was the clearest-headed man he knew. He took him out walking and riding, and was soon able to reassure the Oriel men that they had made no great mistake in their election. Mr Newman on his part felt the warmest admiration for Whately, much gratitude, and a deep affection. If his master was now and then sharp, rude, or positive, this inflicted no pain on so young a man, when relieved by the kindness of heart, the real gentleness, and the generous spirit, which those who came near him well understood to be his characteristics. The worst that could be said of Whately was, that, in his intercourse with his friends, he was a bright June sun tempered by a March north-easter.

During these months, Whately was full of the subject of Logic,—which, in spite of the Aldrich read for his B.A. examination, was quite a novelty to Mr Newman. He lent him the MS of his "Analytical Dialogues", never printed and now very scarce, and allowed him to take copies of it, which are to be found among his (Mr Newman's) papers. At length he went so far as to propose to him to cast these dialogues into the shape of a synthetical Treatise. It was a peculiarity of Whately to compose his books by the medium of other brains. This did not detract at all from the originality of what he wrote. Others did but stimulate his intellect into the activity necessary for carrying him through the drudgery of composition. He called his hearers his anvils. He expounded his views as he walked with them; he indoctrinated them, made them repeat him, and sometimes even to put him on paper, with the purpose of making use of such sketches when he should take in hand the work which was to be given to the public. He attempted to make, at one time Mr Rickards such an anvil, at another Mr Woodgate; he succeeded best with Mr Hinds, afterwards Bishop of Norwich; and it was in some such way that he began to write his well-known Treatise upon Logic, through Mr Newman, that is, under the start he gained by revising and recomposing the rude essays of a probationer Fellow of twenty one.

This work, however, his "Elements of Logic", was not actually published till four years later, and in his Preface to it he thus graciously speaks of Mr Newman's infinitesimal share in its composition:—"I have to acknowledge assistance received from several friends, who have at various times suggested remarks and alterations. But I cannot avoid particularizing the Rev J. Newman, Fellow of Oriel College, who actually composed a considerable portion of the work as it now stands, from manuscripts not designed for publication, and who is the original author of several pages."

Newman, much gratified by this notice, thus acknowledged it to Dr Whately:

"Novr 14, 1826. I cannot tell you the surprise I felt on seeing you had thought it worth while to mention my name, as having contributed to the arrangement of the materials (of the work). Whatever I then wrote, I am conscious, was of little value &c &c. ... Yet I cannot regret that you have introduced my name in some sort of connexion with your own. There are few things which I wish more sincerely than to be known as a friend of yours, and though I may be on the verge of propriety in the earnestness with which I am expressing myself, yet you must let me give way to feelings, which never want much excitement to draw them out, and now will not be restrained. Much as I owe to Oriel in the way of mental improvement, to none, as I think, do I owe so much as to you. I know who it was that first gave me heart to look about me after my election and taught me to think correctly, and (strange office for an instructor) to rely upon myself."

It was with reference to these first Oriel experiences of Newman, his bashfulness, awkwardness and affectionate abandonment of himself to those who were so kind to him, as contrasted with his character, as it showed to outsiders in succeeding years, that B^p Copleston, after the notice of him quoted above, proceeds: "Alas, how little did we anticipate the fatal consequences!" and then applies the passage in Aeschylus to him. ἔθρεψεν δὲ λέοντα σίνιν δόμοις ἀγάλακτον, ἄμερον εὐφιλόπαιδα etc. [Agam. 717.]

Whately's formal connexion with Oriel had closed, before Mr Newman was introduced to him; and he was but an occasional visitor to the University till the year 1825, when, on the death of Dr Elmsley, he was preferred by Lord Grenville, the Chancellor, to the headship of Alban Hall. On this occasion he showed his good opinion of the subject of this Memoir by at once making him his Vice-Principal, and though to the sorrow of both parties this connexion between them lasted only for a year, Mr Newman succeeding in 1826 to the Tutor's place at Oriel vacated by Mr R. W. Jelf, Whately continued on familiar terms with him down to the promotion of the former to the Archbishopric of Dublin in 1831.

That when his great preferment came, he manifested no such desire to gain Newman's co-operation in his new sphere of action, as had led him to ask his assistance at Alban Hall, was no surprise to Mr Newman. Great changes had taken place in the interval in Mr Newman's views and position in Oxford, and he sorrowfully recognized to the full the gradual but steady diminution of intimacy and sympathy between himself and Dr Whately, which had accompanied the successive events of those five years. Accordingly it never entered into his mind that an offer would be made him to accompany the Archbishop to Ireland, which, he on his side, had it been made, must certainly have had the pain of declining. In a correspondence which passed between them in 1834, and which has been published in part by the Archbishop's executors and in full by Dᴿ Newman in his Apologia, is traced the course of this mournful alienation. At length in 1836 Mᴿ Newman incurred the Archbishop's deep displeasure on his taking part against Dᴿ Hampden's appointment to the Chair of divinity; so much so, that, on Dᴿ Whately's coming to Oxford in 1837, Mᴿ Newman felt it necessary to use the intervention of a friend before venturing to call on him; and twenty years later, when Mᴿ Newman, then a Catholic priest, was in Dublin in the years 1854-1858, on his making a like application, he was informed in answer from various quarters that his visit would not be acceptable to the Archbishop.

Dᴿ Whately honoured Mᴿ Newman with his friendship for nearly ten years. During the year in which they were in close intimacy at Alban Hall, Mᴿ Newman served him with all his heart, as his factotum, as Tutor, Chaplain, Bursar, and Dean; and he ever found in him a generous, confiding, and indulgent Superior. Never was there the faintest shadow of a quarrel or of even an accidental collision between them, though in their walks they often found themselves differing from each other on theological questions. As to theology, Mᴿ Newman was under the influence of Dᴿ Whately for four years, from 1822 to 1826, when, coincidently with his leaving Alban Hall, he began to know Mᴿ Hurrell Froude. On looking back, he found that one momentous truth of Revelation, he had learned from Dᴿ Whately, and that was the idea of the Christian Church, as a divine appointment, and as a substantive visible body, independent of the State, and endowed with rights, prerogatives, and powers of its own.

There was another person, high in position, who, on Mᴿ Newman's becoming Fellow of Oriel, had a part in bringing him out of the shyness and reserve which had at first perplexed his electors. This was Dᴿ Charles Lloyd, Canon of Christ Church, and Regius Professor of Divinity. This eminent man, who had been the Tutor and was the intimate friend of Mᴿ Peel, was in an intellectual and academical point of view diametrically opposite to Dᴿ Whately, and it was a strange chance which brought Newman under the immediate notice of divines of such contrary schools. At that time there was a not unnatural rivalry between Christ Church and Oriel; Lloyd and Whately were the respective representatives of the two Societies and of their antagonism: sharp words passed between them, they spoke scornfully of each other, and stories about them and the relation in which they stood towards [each] other were circulated in the Common Rooms. Lloyd was a scholar, and Whately was not; Whately had the reputation specially of being an original thinker, of which Lloyd was not at all ambitious; Lloyd was one of the high-and-dry school, though with far larger views than were then common, while Whately looked down on both high and low Church, calling the two parties respectively Sadducees and Pharisees. Lloyd professed to hold to theology, and laid great stress on a doctrinal standard, authoritative and traditional teaching, and ecclesiastical history; Whately called the Fathers "certain old divines", and, after Swift or some other wit, called orthodoxy "one's own doxy", and heterodoxy "another's doxy". Lloyd made much of books and reading; and, when preacher at Lincoln's Inn, considered he was to his lawyers the official expounder of the Christian Religion and the Protestant faith, just as it was the office of his Majesty's courts to lay down for him peremptorily the law of the land, whereas Whately's great satisfaction was to find a layman who had made a creed for himself, and he avowed that he was *primâ facie* well inclined to a heretic, for his heresy at least showed that he had exercised his mind upon its subject matter. It is obvious which of the two men was the more Catholic in his tone of mind; indeed at a later date Mr Newman availed himself, when accused of Catholicity, of the distinctions which Dr Lloyd in an article in a Review had introduced into the controversy with Rome, and others, who came within his influence, I believe Mr Oakeley, have testified to that influence in their case having acted in a Catholic direction; but such men attended his lectures some years later than Mr Newman, whose debt to him was of a different kind.

These lectures were an experiment, which Dr Lloyd made on becoming Regius Professor, with a view of advancing theological studies in the University. An annual set of public lectures had been usual, attendance on them being made a *sine quâ non* for ordination, but Dr Lloyd's new lectures were private and familiar. He began them in 1823, the year after Mr Newman's election at Oriel and the year of Mr Pusey's. His initial class consisted of eight: four Fellows of Oriel, Jelf, Ottley, Pusey, and Newman, and four of Christ Church. To these others were soon added, notably Mr Richard Greswell of Worcester, whose acquaintance with theological topics was for a young man wonderful. The subjects of the lectures betokened the characteristic tastes and sentiments of the lecturer. He had more liking for exegetical criticism, historical research, and controversy, than for dogma or philosophy. He employed his mind upon the grounds of Christian faith rather than on the faith itself; and, in his estimate of the grounds, he made light of the internal evidence for revealed religion, in comparison of its external proofs. During the time that Mr Newman attended his lectures, the years 1823 and 1824, when he left them on taking orders and a parochial charge, the class went through Sumner's "Records of Creation", Graves on the Pentateuch, Carpzov on the Septuagint, Prideaux's "Connexion", and other standard works, getting up the books thoroughly; for Dr Lloyd made the lecture catechetical, taking very little part in it himself, beyond asking questions, and requiring direct, full, and minutely accurate answers. It is difficult to see how into a teaching such as this purely religious questions could have found their way; but Dr Lloyd who took a personal interest in those he came across, and who always had his eyes about him, certainly did soon make out that Mr Newman held what are called evangelical views of doctrine, then greatly in disrepute in Oxford, and in consequence bestowed on him a notice, expressive of vexation and impatience on the one hand and of a liking for him personally and a good opinion of his abilities on the other. He was free and easy in his ways, and a bluff talker, with a rough lively good natured manner, and a pretended pomposity relieving itself in sudden bursts of laughter, and an indulgence in what is now called *chaffing* at the expense of his auditors; and, as he moved up and down his room, large in person beyond his years, asking them questions, gathering their answers, and taking snuff, as he went along, he would sometimes stop before Mr Newman, on his speaking in his turn, fix his eyes on him as if to look him through, with a satirical expression of countenance, and then make a feint to box his ears or kick his shins, before he went on with his march to and fro. There was nothing offensive or ungracious in all this, and the attachment which Mr Newman felt for him, was shared by his pupils generally; but he was not the man to exert an intellectual influence over Mr Newman or to leave a mark upon his mind, as Whately had done. To the last Lloyd was doubtful of Newman's outcome, and Newman felt constrained and awkward in the presence of Lloyd; but this want of sympathy between them did not interfere with a mutual kind feeling; Lloyd used to ask him over to his living at Ewelme in the vacations, and Newman retained to old age an affectionate and grateful memory of Lloyd (an excellent man). Many of his pupils rose to eminence, some of them through his helping hand. Mr Jelf was soon made preceptor to Prince George, the future King of Hanover; Mr Churton, who died prematurely, became chaplain to Howley, Bishop of London, afterwards Primate; Mr Pusey he recommended to the Minister for the Hebrew Professorship, first sending him to Germany to study that language in the Universities there. As to Mr Newman, before he had been in his Lecture Room half a year, Lloyd paid him the compliment of proposing to him, young as he was, to undertake a work for students in divinity, containing such various information as is for the most part only to be found in Latin or in folios, such as the history of the Septuagint Version, an account of the Talmud &c but nothing came of this design.

His attendance on Dr Lloyd's Lectures was at length broken off in 1824 by his accepting the curacy of St Clement's, a parish lying over Magdalen Bridge, where a new Church was needed and a younger man than the Rector to collect funds for building it. From this time he saw very little of Dr Lloyd, who in 1827 was promoted to the See of Oxford and died prematurely in 1829. At the former of these dates, the Bishop knew of his intention to give himself to the study of the Fathers and expressed a warm approval of it.

Mr Newman held the curacy of St Clement's for two years, up to the time when he became one of the public tutors of his College. He held it long enough to succeed in collecting the £5000 or £6000, which were necessary for the new Church. It was consecrated after he had relinquished his curacy, probably in the Long Vacation, when he was away from Oxford; but so it happened by a singular accident that, neither while it was building, nor after it was built, was he ever inside it. He had no part in determining its architectural character, which was in the hands of a committee. The old Church, which stood at the fork of the two London roads as they join at Magdalen Bridge, was soon afterwards removed; and it thus was Mr Newman's lot to outlive the Church, St Bennet Fink, in which he was baptized, the School House & play grounds at Ealing, where he passed between eight and nine years of his boyhood, and the Church in which he first did duty. At St Clement's he did a great deal of hard parish work, having in the poor school which he set on foot the valuable assistance of the daughters of the Rector, the Revd John Gutch, Registrar of the University, at that time an octogenarian.

It was during these years of parochial duty that Mr Newman underwent a great change in his religious opinions, a change brought about by very various influences. Of course the atmosphere of Oriel Common Room was one of these; its members, together with its distinguished Head, being as remarkable for the complexion of their theology and their union among themselves in it, as for their literary eminence. This unanimity was the more observable, inasmuch as, elected by competition, they came from various places of education, public and private, from various parts of the country, and from any whatever of the Colleges of Oxford, thus being without antecedents in common, except such as were implied in their being Oxford men, and selected by Oriel examiners. Viewed as a body, we may pronounce them to be truly conscientious men, bearing in mind their religious responsibilities, hard or at least energetic workers, liberal in their charities, correct in their lives, proud of their College rather than of themselves, and, if betraying something of habitual superciliousness towards other Societies, excusable for this at that date, considering the exceptional strictness of the then Oriel discipline and the success of the Oriel tuition in the Schools. In religion they were neither high Church nor low Church, but had become a new school, or, as their enemies would say, a *clique*, which was characterized by its spirit of moderation and comprehension, and of which the principal ornaments were Copleston, Davison, Whately, Hawkins, and Arnold. Enemies they certainly had; among these, first, were the old unspiritual high-and-dry, then in possession of the high places of Oxford, who were suspicious whither these men would go, pronounced them unsafe, and were accused of keeping Copleston from a Bishopric,—a class of men who must not be confused with such excellent persons as the Watsons, Sykes, Crawleys of the old [London] Church Societies and their surroundings, though they pulled with them;—next and especially the residents in the smaller & less distinguished Colleges, the representatives, as they may be considered, of the country party, who looked upon them as angular men, arrogant, pedantic, crotchety, and felt both envy at their reputation and took offence at the strictness of their lives. Their friends, on the other hand, as far as they had exactly friends, were of the Evangelical party, who, unused to kindness from their brethren, hailed with surprise the advances which Copleston seemed to be making towards them in his writings and by his acts, and were grateful for that liberality of mind which was in such striking contrast with the dominant high-Church; and who, in Keble again, in spite of his maintenance of baptismal regeneration, recognized, to use their own language, a spiritual man. What a large number of the Evangelical party then felt, Mr Newman, as one of them, felt also; and thus he was drawn in heart to his Oriel associates in proportion as he came to be intimate with them.

The Oriel Common Room has been above spoken of as a whole; but the influence thence exerted on Mr Newman came especially from two of its members, Mr Hawkins and Mr Pusey, of whom Pusey is external to what may be technically called the Oriel School. Though senior in age by just half a year, he was junior to Newman in both University and College standing, being elected at Oriel the year after Newman. He was a disciple of Lloyd's, not of Whately's; or perhaps it may be said, not even of Lloyd's. The son of a man conspicuous for his religious earnestness and his charities, he left Eton and Christ Church for Oriel, not only an accurate scholar and a portentous student, but endowed with a deep seriousness and a large minded, open-handed zeal in his service of God and his neighbour, which he had inherited from his home. Newman first saw him on his dining, as a stranger, at Oriel high-table, when a guest of his Eton friend Jelf, and as a future candidate, as it was reported, for a fellowship. Newman used to speak in after life of this first introduction to one with whom eventually he was so closely united, and to "the blessing of" whose "long friendship and example", as he said in the Dedication to him of his first volume of Sermons, he had owed so much. His light curly head of hair was damp with the cold water which his headaches made necessary for comfort; he walked fast with a young manner of carrying himself, and stood rather bowed, looking up from under his eye-brows, his shoulders rounded, and his bachelor's gown not buttoned at the elbow, but hanging loose over his wrists. His countenance was very sweet, and he spoke little. This chronic headache nearly lost him his election in the following year. After commencing the paper work of the examination, he found himself from the state of his head utterly unable to complete it. He deliberately tore up the exercise on which he was engaged, and withdrew from the scene of action. But this abandonment of his just expectations did not please his friends and they would not allow it; they forced him back into the examination Hall, and one of the Fellows, then a stranger to him, Dr Jenkyns afterwards Canon of Durham, gathered up the fragments of his composition as they lay scattered on the floor, and succeeded so happily in fitting and uniting them together, that they were used by his examiners as a portion of his trial. His headaches continued beyond his Oriel years, but he was always full of work. When Newman was offered the curacy of St Clement's, it was at Pusey's suggestion, and Pusey was to have taken part in its duties, when Dr Lloyd sent him off to Germany.

It is interesting to trace the course of Newman's remarks on Pusey in his Private Journal, commencing as they do in a high patronizing tone, and gradually changing into the expression of simple admiration of his new friend. April 4, 1823 he writes, speaking of the election of Fellows, "I thank God that two men have succeeded this morning" (E. B. Pusey and W. R. Churton) "who, I trust, are favorably disposed to religion, or at least moral and thinking, not worldly and careless men;" and he goes on to pray that they may be brought "into the true Church." On the 13th he notes down, "I have taken a short walk with Pusey after Church, and we have had some very pleasing conversation. He is a searching man, and seems to delight in talking on religious subjects." By May 2 Newman has advanced further in his good opinion of him. He writes, "I have had several conversations with Pusey on religion, since I last mentioned him. Thank God, how can I doubt his seriousness? His very eagerness to talk of the Scriptures seems to prove it. May I lead him forward, at the same time gaining good from him! He has told me the plan of his Essay" (for the Chancellor's prize) "and I clearly see that it is much better than mine. I cannot think I shall get it; to this day I have thought I should." And on May 17 he remarks "That Pusey is Thine, O Lord, how can I doubt? his deep views of the Pastoral Office, his high ideas of the spiritual rest of the Sabbath, his devotional spirit, his love of the Scriptures, his firmness and zeal, all testify to the operation of the Holy Ghost; yet I fear he is prejudiced against Thy children. Let me never be eager to convert him to a *party* or to a form of *opinion*. Lead us *both* on in the way of Thy commandments. What am I that I should be so blest in my near associates!"

Nothing more is said in these private notes about Pusey before the Long Vacation, but hardly is it over, when he notes down, "Have just had a most delightful walk with Pusey; our subjects all religious, all devotional and practical. At last we fell to talking of Henry Martyn and Missionaries. He spoke beautifully on the question—'Who are to go?' " ["I am conscious of horrible pride ... but still, as I think the Missionary Office the highest privilege from God I can possess, though I speak blindly, it will not be wrong to pray to God to make me a Missionary."]¹ On February 1ˢᵗ of the next year (1824) he sets down, "Have just walked with Pusey; he seems growing in the best things, in humility and love to God and man. What an active, devoted spirit! God grant he may not, like Martyn, 'burn as phosphorus' ...!" Lastly on March 15, when the year from his first acquaintance with Pusey had not yet run out, he writes, "Took a walk with Pusey; discoursed on Missionary subjects. I must bear every circumstance in continued remembrance. We went along the lower London road, crossed to Cowley; and, coming back, just before we arrived at the Magdalen Bridge turnpike, he expressed to me" ... Here is a blank in the MS. The writer has not put into writing what this special confidence was, which so affected him. He continues, "O, what words shall I use? My heart is full. How should I be humbled to the dust! What importance I think myself of! my deeds, my abilities, my writings! whereas he is humility itself, and gentleness, and love, and zeal, and self devotion. Bless him with Thy fullest gifts, and grant me to imitate him."

These extracts reach to within a few months of Mʳ Newman's ordination, which took place on June 13, 1824, at the hands of Dʳ Legge, Bishop of Oxford. It was by this important event in his life and the parochial duties which were its immediate supplement that he was thrown into a close intimacy with his other friend Mʳ Hawkins, then Vicar of Sᵗ Mary's, an intimacy not less important in the mark it left upon him, though far other, than his familiar intercourse with Pusey. Hawkins bore a very high character, and to know his various personal responsibilities and his conduct under them, was to esteem and revere him; he had an abiding sense of duty; and had far less than others of that secular spirit, which is so rife at all times in places of intellectual eminence. He was clear headed and independent in his opinions, candid in argument, tolerant of the views of others, honest as a religious inquirer, though not without something of self confidence in his enunciations. He was a good parish priest, and preached with earnestness and force, collecting about him undergraduates from various colleges for his hearers. At this date, 1824, 1825, on the ground of health he never drank wine, and was accustomed to say that he should not live beyond forty. He has already reached eighty five years, and in the full use of his faculties. On him then, as he was by his parochial charge bound to residence through

¹ This quotation was deleted by Newman in the autograph. C.S.D.

the year, Mr Newman, when Curate of St Clement's, was thrown in a special way. In the Long Vacation, when the other Fellows were away, they two had Hall and Common Room to themselves. They dined and read the Papers, they took their evening walk, and then their tea, in company; and, while Mr Newman was full of the difficulties of a young curate, he found in Mr Hawkins a kind and able adviser.

There was an interval of twelve years between their ages, but Mr Hawkins was in mind older than his years, and Mr Newman younger; and the intercourse between them was virtually that of Tutor and pupil. Up to this time the latter took for granted, if not intelligently held, the opinions called evangelical; and of an evangelical caste were his early Sermons, though mildly such. His first Sermon, on "Man goeth forth to his work and to his labour until the evening", implied in its tone a denial of baptismal regeneration; and Mr Hawkins, to whom he showed it, came down upon it at once upon this score. The sermon divided the Christian world into two classes, the one all darkness, the other all light, whereas, said Mr Hawkins, it is impossible for us in fact to draw such a line of demarcation across any body of men, large or small, because [difference in] religious and moral excellence is a matter of degree. Men are not either saints or sinners; but they are not so good as they should be, and better than they might be,—more or less converted to God, as it may happen. Preachers should follow the example of St Paul; *he* did not divide his brethren into two, the converted and unconverted, but he addressed them all as "in Christ", "sanctified in Him," as having had "the Holy Ghost in their hearts;" and this, while he was rebuking them for the irregularities and scandals which had occurred among them. Criticism such as this, which of course he did not deliver once for all, but as occasions offered, and which, when Newman dissented, he maintained and enforced, had a great though a gradual effect upon the latter, when carefully studied in the work from which it was derived, and which Hawkins gave him; this was Sumner's "Apostolical Preaching". This book was successful in the event beyond any thing else, in routing out evangelical doctrines from Mr Newman's Creed.

He observes in his Private Journal, under date of August 24, 1824, "Lately I have been thinking much on the subject of grace, regeneration &c and reading Sumner's 'Apostolical Preaching' which Hawkins has given me. Sumner's book threatens to drive me into either Calvinism or baptismal regeneration, and I wish to steer clear of both, at least in preaching. I am always slow in deciding a question; and last night I was so distressed and low about it, that the thought even struck me I must leave the Church. I have been praying about it, before I rose this morning, and I do not know what will be the end of it. I think I really desire the truth, and would embrace it, wherever I found it."

On the following January 13 he writes:—"It seems to me that the great stand is to be made, *not* against those who connect a spiritual change with baptism, but those who deny a spiritual change altogether." Here he alludes to Dr Lloyd, rightly or wrongly. "All who confess the natural corruption of the heart, and the necessity of a change (whether they connect regeneration with baptism or not) should unite against those who make regeneration a mere opening of new prospects, when the old score of offences is wiped away, and a person is for the second time put, as it were on his good behaviour." Here he had in fact got hold of the Catholic doctrine that forgiveness of sin is conveyed to us, not simply by imputation, but by the implanting of a habit of grace.

Mr Newman then, before many months of his clerical life were over, had taken the first step towards giving up the evangelical form of Christianity; however, for a long while certain shreds and tatters of that doctrine hung about his preaching, nor did he for a whole ten years altogether sever himself from those great religious societies and their meetings, which then as now were the rallying ground and the strength of the Evangelical body. Besides Sumner, Butler's celebrated work, which he studied about the year 1825, had, as was natural, an important indirect effect upon him in the same direction, as placing his doctrinal views on a broad philosophical basis, with which an emotional religion could have little sympathy.

There was another great philosophical principle which he owed to Mr Hawkins, in addition to that which Sumner's work taught him. He has already mentioned it in his "Apologia": viz. the *quasi*-Catholic doctrine of Tradition, as a main element in ascertaining and teaching the truths of Christianity. This doctrine Hawkins had, on Whately's advice, made the subject of a Sermon before the University. Whately once said of this Sermon to Newman in conversation, "Hawkins came to me and said, 'What shall I preach about?' putting into my hands at the same time some notes which he thought might supply a subject. After reading them, I said to him, 'Capital!

Make a Sermon of them by all means; I did not know till now that you had so much originality in you.' " Whately felt the doctrine as true as he considered it original.

Though the force of logic and the influence of others had so much to do with Mr Newman's change of religious opinion; it must not be supposed that the teaching of facts had no part in it. On the contrary, he notes down in memoranda made at the time, his conviction, gained by personal experience, that the religion which he had received from John Newton and Thomas Scott would not work in a parish; that it was unreal; that this he had actually found as a fact, as Mr Hawkins had told him beforehand; that Calvinism was not a key to the phenomena of human nature, as they occur in the world. And in truth, much as he owed to the evangelical teaching, so it was, he never had been a genuine evangelical. That teaching had been a great blessing for England; it had brought home to the hearts of thousands the cardinal and vital truths of Revelation, and to himself among others. The divine truths about our Lord and His Person and Offices, His grace, the regeneration of our nature in Him, the supreme duty of living, not only morally, but in His faith, fear and love, together with the study of Scripture in which these truths lay, had sheltered and protected him in his most dangerous years, had been his comfort and stay when he was forlorn, and had brought him on in habits of devotion till the time came when he was to dedicate himself to the Christian ministry, and he ever felt grateful to the good clergyman who introduced them to him, and to the books, such as Scott's "Force of Truth", Beveridge's "Private Thoughts" and Doddridge's "Rise and Progress" which insist upon them; but, after all, the evangelical teaching, considered as a system and in what was peculiar to itself, had from the first failed to find a response in his own religious experience, as afterwards in his parochial. He had indeed been converted by it to a spiritual life, and so far his experience bore witness to its truth; but he had not been converted in that special way which it laid down as imperative, but so plainly against rule, as to make it very doubtful in the eyes of normal evangelicals whether he had really been converted at all. Indeed at various times of his life, as for instance after the publication of his Apologia, letters, kindly intended, were addressed to him by strangers or anonymous writers, assuring him that he did not yet know what conversion meant, and that the all important change had still to be wrought in him, if he was to be saved.

And he himself quite agreed in the facts which were the premisses of these writers, though of course he did not feel himself obliged to follow them on to their grave conclusion. He was sensible that he had ever been wanting in those special evangelical experiences, which, like the grip of the hand or other prescribed signs of a secret society, are the sure token of a member. There is among his private papers a memorandum on the subject much to the point, which he set down originally in 1821, and then transcribed and commented on in 1826. In 1821, the date, be it observed, when he was more devoted to the evangelical creed and more strict in his religious duties than at any previous time, he had been drawing up (at great length) an account of the evangelical process of conversion in a series of Scripture texts, going through its stages of conviction of sin, terror, despair, news of the free and full salvation, apprehension of Christ, sense of pardon, assurance of salvation, joy and peace, and so on to final perseverance; and he then makes this N.B. upon his work, "I speak of conversion with great diffidence, being obliged to adopt the language of books. For my feelings, as far as I remember, were so different from any account I have ever read, that I dare not go by what may be an individual case." This was in 1821; transcribing the memorandum in 1826, he adds, "That is, I wrote *juxta praescriptum*. In the matter in question, viz. conversion, my own feelings were *not* violent, but a returning to, a renewing of, principles, under the power of the Holy Spirit, which I had already felt, and in a measure acted on, when young."[1]

He used in later years to consider the posture of his mind, early and late, relatively to the Evangelical teaching of his youth, an illustration of what he had written in his Essay on Assent upon the compatibility of the indefectibility of genuine certitude with the failure of mere beliefs which at one time of our life we took for certitudes. "We may assent", he there says, "to a certain number of propositions all together, that is, we may make a number of assents all at once; but in doing so we run the risk of putting upon one level, and treating as if of the same value, acts of the mind which are very different from each other in character and circumstance. Now a religion is not a proposition, but a system, it is a rite, a creed, a philosophy, a rule of duty, all at once; and to accept a religion is neither a simple assent to it, nor a complex, neither a conviction, nor a prejudice ... not a mere act of profession, nor of credence, nor of opinion,

[1] See the first of the Early Journals, p. 166 and p. 172 *infra*. C.S.D.

nor of speculation, but it is a collection of all these various kinds of assents, some of one description, one [some] of another; but out of all these different assents how many are of that kind, which I have called certitude? For instance, the fundamental dogma of Protestant-ism is the exclusive authority of Scripture; but, in holding this a Protestant holds a host of propositions, explicitly or implicitly, and holds them with assents of various character … Yet, if he were asked the question, he would probably answer that he was certain of the truth of Protestantism, though Protestantism means a hundred things all at once, and he believes with actual certitude only one of them all."

Applying these remarks to his own case, he used to say, that, whereas upon that great change which took place in him as a boy, there were four doctrines all of which he forthwith held, as if certain truths, viz. those of the Holy Trinity, of the Incarnation, of Pre-destination, and of the Lutheran "apprehension of Christ", the first three, which are doctrines of the Catholic Religion, and, as being such, are true, and really subjects of certitude and capable of taking indefectible possession of the mind, and therefore ought not in his case to have faded away, in fact did not fade away, but remained indelible, thro' all his changes of opinion, up to and over the date of his becoming a Catholic, whereas the fourth, which is not true, though he thought it was, and therefore not capable of being held with certitude, or with the promise of permanence, tho' he thought it was so held, did in the event, as is the nature of a mere opinion or untrue belief, take its departure from his mind in very short time, or rather was not held by him from the first. However, in his early years, he confused these four distinct doctrines together, as regards their hold upon him, and transferred that utter conviction which he had of what was revealed about the Three Persons of the Holy Trinity and the Divine Economy to his state of mind relatively to Luther's tenet of justification by faith only.

Having this confused idea of Christian doctrine and of his own apprehension of it, and considering the evangelical teaching true, because there were great truths in it, he had felt and often spoken very positively as to his certainty of its truth and the impossibility of his changing his mind about it. On one occasion in particular he has recorded his feelings when he found himself affectionately cautioned by his Father, from his own experience of the world, against the Lutheran doctrine and a headstrong acceptance of it. This was

shortly before he succeeded at Oriel and, as has been said, he takes a
note of it in his Private Journal. In the course of conversation, availing himself of some opportunity, his Father is there reported to have
said to him. "Take care; you are encouraging a morbid sensibility
and irritability of mind, which may be very serious. Religion, when
carried too far, induces a mental softness. No one's principles can
be established at twenty. Your opinions in two or three years will
certainly, certainly, change. I have seen many instances of the same
kind. You are on dangerous ground. The temper you are encouraging
may lead to something alarming. Weak minds are carried into superstition, and strong minds into infidelity; do not commit yourself, do
nothing ultra."[1] On these prudent warnings, his son observes, after
prayer against delusion, pride, and uncharitableness, "How good is
God to give me the assurance of hope! If any one had prophesied to
me confidently that I should change my opinions, and I was not convinced of the impossibility, what anguish should I feel!" Yet very few
years passed, before, against his confident expectations, his Father's
words about him came true.

[His father spoke from his general knowledge of the world; and,
had he known his son's character thoroughly, he would have had a
still greater right to anticipate a change in the religious views of the
youth whom he so much loved and was so anxious about. For, as has
been said above, the critical peculiarities of evangelical religion had
never been congenial to him, though he had fancied he held them. Its
emotional and feverish devotion and its tumultuous experiences were
foreign to his nature, which indeed was ever conspicuously faulty in
the opposite direction, as being in a way incapable, as if physically, of
enthusiasm, however legitimate and guarded.

One additional feature in Mr Newman's mind shall be noticed,
which seemed to intimate from the first that the ethical character of
Evangelical Religion could not lastingly be imprinted upon it. This
was his great attraction to what may be called the literature of
Religion, whether the writings of [the] Classics, or the works of the
Fathers. As to the Greek and Latin authors, poets and philosophers,
Aeschylus, Pindar, Herodotus, Virgil and Horace, or again Aristotle
and Cicero, he had from the first made much of them, as the Holy
Fathers did, as being in a certain sense inspired moralists and
prophets of truths greater than they knew.[; that in the familiar

---

[1] For the text of Newman's original note of this conversation, which took place
on 6th January 1822, see the second of the Early Journals, p. 179 *infra*. C.S.D.

lines, "These relics of a guilty race are forfeit to thy friends; what seemed an idol hymn now breathes of Thee, tuned by Faith's ear to some celestial meolody."][1] And as to those Fathers themselves, much more did he ever delight, and even from a date earlier than his ordination, to find himself brought into their company. What he wrote himself was mainly on such subjects as allowed him to exercise himself in one or other of these departments of literature, and, however devout might be his mood, or occupied his time, he was never unwilling to add to his work if they were to be the subjects of it.][2]

Fifty or sixty years ago the intellectual and ecclesiastical antagonist and alternative of the Evangelical creed was Arminianism. The Catholic Faith, Anglo-Catholicism, Irvingism, Infidelity, were as yet unknown to the religious inquirer. A cold Arminian doctrine, the first stage of Liberalism was the characteristic aspect, both of the high and dry Anglicans of that day and of the Oriel divines. There was great reason then to expect that on Newman's leaving the crags and precipices of Luther and Calvin, he would take refuge in the flats of Tillotson and Barrow, Jortin and Paley. It cannot be said that this was altogether a miscalculation; but the ancient Fathers saved him from the danger that threatened him. An imaginative devotion to them and to their times had been the permanent effect upon him of reading at School an account of them and extracts from their works in Joseph Milner's Church History, and even when he now and then allowed himself as in 1825 in criticisms of them, the first centuries were his *beau idéal* of Christianity. Even then what he composed, was more or less directed towards that period, and, however his time might be occupied, or his mood devotional, he never was unwilling to undertake any work, of which they were to be the staple.

Thus in 1823 he drew up an argument for the strict observance of the Christian Sabbath from the writings of S[t] Chrysostom and other Fathers; in 1825-6, when he had not only Alban Hall and S[t] Clement's on his hands, but in addition the laborious task of raising funds for his new church, he wrote a life of Apollonius and his Essay on Miracles. In 1826 he projected writing for the Encyclopaedia Metropolitana a history of the first three centuries of Christianity; and in 1827 he drew up a defence of Infant Baptism from the patristical testimonies furnished to him by Wall's well known Treatise. In the

---

[1] *The Christian Year*, 3rd Sunday of Lent. This passage was separately crossed out, before the final deletion. C.S.D.

[2] These two paragraphs were deleted by Newman in the autograph. C.S.D.

same year he gave a commission to his friend Pusey, who was then in Germany, to purchase for him as many volumes of the Fathers as came to his hand. And in 1828 he began systematically to read them.

APPENDIX

Dr Whately occupied the (Protestant) archiepiscopal See of Dublin from 1831 until 1863, when he died at the age of seventy-six on October 8th in the latter year; and two days later there appeared in *The Times* an appreciatory editorial without heading or signature. On the same day Robert Walker of the *Weekly Register*, as the mouthpiece of "every educated English Catholic", wrote to Newman, enclosing in his letter this article, to ask him to contribute to his paper something about the dead Archbishop. The following *In Memoriam* notice, written, with numerous erasures and corrections, on the unused half-sheet of a letter, postmarked February 22, 1837, and addressed The Revd J. H. Newman, Oriel College, Oxford, still remains among his papers. It is probably the draft of what he wrote in compliance with this request. It is reproduced here as a testimony to an affection that had outlived personal estrangement, the result of acute theological differences, and because the grace and charm of its style merits for it a less ephemeral fate than a single appearance in the columns of a periodical.

(From a Correspondent)

The news of the death of Archbishop Whately rouses, in the minds of Oxford men of a past generation, a host of affectionate remembrances, which have never indeed slept, but which have of late years had little opportunity for exercise. It is thirty years and more since he left the University; and not so very far from thirty since he has been even seen by some of his most attached friends; but the past is not dead to those, who, as the writer of these lines, owed much to him then, and who, amid the skirmishes of religious controversy, have loved him all along and to the end.

What he has been for good or evil in Dublin, let those speak who have a right to do so; at Oxford it was his praise to have merited in his own person the historian's eulogy, so little made account of in the world, of being high to the great, and gentle to the little. Sad to say, it is our ordinary experience in life that men are cowards to those who make fight and bullies to those who yield. So was it not with a man, who, whatever were his faults, was in generosity, in boldness of speech, and in independence of mind, a prince. Without any misgiving at all, he would in a mixed company pronounce the low church party in the Anglican Church to be Pharisees, and the High Church Sadducees; but, while such expressions of opinion were leaguing opposite camps against him as a common foe, he would in private take the young, the timid and bashful, by the hand, raise their courage, open their minds, and make them think.

And this was his mission in the University, to stir up men to inquire; and to give them a start in their inquiries. And this was his part in the Catholic movement which followed on his departure for Dublin. He was neither the originator of a creed, nor the champion of a School; he could not convert men by logic, he would not subdue them by authority; what he could do and did do with great vigour and a great relish was to break to pieces the idols which blocked out the light, and to clear a space for undertakings which he did not himself attempt. It was his to preach the simple but momentous principles, that religion need not be afraid of argument, that faith can fearlessly appeal to right reason, that inquiry does but strengthen the foundations of revelation, and that the Church is founded in the truth, and truth alone.

Every one has his place in the marvellous works of divine grace; let us trust and pray that he, to whom were committed, without his knowing it, some of the first steps of a great movement, which has not yet seen its termination, may not finally be shut out from the benefit of its issues but may "find mercy of the Lord in that day".

Chapter 4

In 1826, as has been already said, Mr Newman was appointed one of the public Tutors of Oriel College, resigning the Vice-Principalship of Alban Hall and the curacy of St Clement's. In 1827 he was appointed by Dr Howley, the then Bishop of London, one of the Preachers at Whitehall. In 1827-28 he held the University office of Public Examiner in classics for the B.A. degree and for the honour list attached to the examination. In 1828, on Mr Hawkins becoming Provost of Oriel he was presented by his College to the Vicarage of St Mary's, the University Church. In 1830 he served as Proproctor. In 1831, 1832 he was one of the University Select Preachers. This may be called his public career. He relinquished the College Tutorship in 1832, and the Vicarage of St Mary's, which was neither a University nor College office, in 1843. The other offices enumerated were of a temporary character.

As regards his Tutorship at Oriel and his incumbency, both of which were permanent appointments, his separation from each of them in turn, though not abrupt, had something of violence in its circumstances. He had accepted each of them for an indefinite term of years, or rather for life. He did not look beyond them. He desired nothing better than such a lifelong residence at Oxford, nothing higher than such an influential position, as these two offices gave him. How by his own act, slowly brought into execution, he broke off his connection with St Mary's, he has described in his Apologia; how he gradually at the end of a few years died out of his Tutorship, shall be told in the pages that follow. It is too important an event in his history to pass it over, together with the sentiments and motives which led to it; for, as the Oxford theological movement proper, (so to call it,) may be said to have ended in his resignation of St Mary's, so it dates its origin from his and Hurrell Froude's premature separation from the office of College Tutor.

The story, however, cannot be told without mention of the mournful differences which arose between Mr Newman and his dear friend, the new Provost of Oriel, Dr Hawkins, who, on Dr Copleston's promotion to the Bishopric of Llandaff at the end of 1827, succeeded to the Headship; but, in a case in which each party in the quarrel held his own ground on reasons so intelligible and so defensible, and with so honest a sense of duty, the narrative which is now to follow, will involve as little to the disparagement of Dr Hawkins as of Mr Newman.

There was a standing difference of opinion among religious men of that day, whether a College Tutorship was or was not an engagement compatible with the Ordination Vow; and Mr Newman's advisers, of different schools, had, with more or less of emphasis, answered for him the question in the negative. His friends of the Low Church party, though they might wish him to take orders early, had no thought of his doing so as the qualification, which it was then commonly considered, for holding the office of a College Tutor. He thus speaks on the point in his Private Journal of June 1823, "Scott says, as a general rule, *not* soon. Hawkins says the same:—'Why bind yourself with a vow, when there is no necessity, and which *may* mean something incompatible with staying at College and taking pupils?' " He continues "R. doubts the propriety of College Tutors being clergymen; Mr Mayers (and he has been consulting Marsh of Colchester) advises immediate entrance into the Church by all means; 'Nothing,' he says, 'does the Church want so much, as clergymen, who, without the tie of regular duty, can make progresses among their brethren and relieve them at certain seasons'."[1] So far his Private Journal; here we are principally concerned with Dr Hawkins's view, as just given. It will be observed, that, in the principle he laid down, he did not go so far as to pronounce College employments directly and formally unclerical, but it was a question with him whether they might not be so; they required an apology, and raised at first sight a reasonable scruple. The *onus probandi*, that a College Tutorship was in the instance of a clergyman allowable, lay upon its advocates, as (to take cases which some might think parallel) whether it was allowable for him to hunt, shoot, or go to the theatre. It was lawful for a time or under circumstances, but any how it was no fulfilment of the solemn vow made at ordination, nor could be consistently exercised by one who was bound by such a vow as his lifelong occupation. Just this, neither more nor less, it is here believed, was the decision of Dr Hawkins.

But far other was Mr Newman's view of the matter. He had as deep a sense of the solemnity of the ordination vow, as another could have, but he thought there were various modes of fulfilling it, and

[1] See the second of the Early Journals, p. 192 *infra*. C.S.D.

that the Tutorial office was simply one of them. As to that vow, he has recorded in his Private Journal what he calls his terror at the obligation it involved. He writes the hour after he had received the diaconate, "It is over; at first, after the hands were laid on me, my heart shuddered within me; the words 'for ever' are so terrible." The next day he says, "For ever! words never to be recalled! I have the responsibility of souls on me to the day of my death." He felt he had left the secular line once for all, that he had entered upon a divine ministry, and for the first two years of his clerical life he connected his sacred office with nothing short of the prospect of missionary work in heathen countries as the destined fulfilment of it. When then, as time went on, the direct duties of a College exerted a more urgent claim upon him and he became Tutor, it must be understood that, in his view, the Tutorial office was but another way, though not so heroic a way, as a mission to idolaters, by which he was carrying out his vow. To have considered that office to be merely secular, and yet to have engaged in it, would have been the greatest of inconsistencies. Nor is this a matter of mere inference from the sentiments and views such as those recorded in his Journal. On occasion of his Father's death, three months after his ordination, he observes, "My Mother said the other day she hoped to live to see me married, but *I* think I shall either die within College walls, or as a missionary in a foreign land," thus coupling the two lives together, dissimilar as they were in their character. A few years later we find in his Verses a like reference to College engagements, not as a clergyman's accident of life, but as his divinely appointed path of duty. He says that he is "enrolled" in a sacred warfare, and that he would not exchange it for any other employment, that he is a "prisoner" in an Oxford "cell", according to the "high dispose" of Him "who binds on each his part", that he is like the snap-dragon on the College walls, and that such a *habitat* was so high a lot that well might he "in College cloister live and die." And, when it was decided that he was to be one of the public tutors, and he was about to enter upon the duties of his new office, he says in his Journal, "May I engage in them, remembering that I am a minister of Christ, and have a commission to preach the gospel, remembering the worth of souls and that I shall have to answer for the opportunities given me of benefiting those who are under my care." It will be seen presently why it is necessary thus distinctly to bring out Mr Newman's view of the substantially religious nature of a College Tutorship.

It was in Easter term 1826 that Newman entered upon duties which he felt thus sacred, and he commenced them with an energy proverbial in the instance of "new brooms". He was one out of four Tutors, and the junior of them, and, though it would be very unjust to say of him that he intentionally departed from the received ways of the College, it cannot be denied that there was something unusual and startling in his treatment of the undergraduate members of it who came under his jurisdiction. He began by setting himself fiercely against the Gentlemen-Commoners, young men of birth, wealth or prospects, whom he considered (of course with real exceptions) to be the scandal and the ruin of the place. Oriel, he considered, was losing its high repute through them, and he behaved towards them with a haughtiness which incurred their bitter resentment. He was much annoyed at the favour shown them in high quarters, and did not scruple to manifest as much annoyance with those who favoured as with those who were favoured. He had hardly got through his first month of office, when he writes in his Private Journal, "There is much in the system which I think wrong; I think the Tutors see too little of the men, and there is not enough of direct religious instruction. It is my wish to consider myself as the minister of Christ. Unless I find that opportunities occur of doing spiritual good to those over whom I am placed, it will become a grave question, whether I ought to continue in the Tuition."

He was especially opposed to young men being compelled, or even suffered as a matter of course to go terminally to communion, and shocked at the reception he met with from those to whom he complained of so gross a profanation of a sacred rite. When he asked one high authority whether there was any obligation upon the undergraduates to communicate, he was cut short with the answer, "That question never, I believe, enters into their heads, and I beg you will not put it into them". When he told another that a certain number of them, after communion, intoxicated themselves at a champagne breakfast, he was answered, "I don't believe it, and, if it is true, I don't want to know it". Even Hawkins was against him here; and when one of the well-conducted minority[1] of the Gentlemen-Commoners, for, as has been said, it must not be supposed that there

[1] In my letter of October 1884, in answer to Lord Malmesbury's report of my conduct at that time, I say that the well conducted portion of the College was the majority; these separate statements need not be contradictory. The undergraduates were no stationary body, but continually changing in number. In the years between 1824 and 1828, what was the majority in one term, or half-year, might be the minority in another.

was none such, keenly feeling the evil of the existing rule from what he saw around him, published a pamphlet of remonstrance against it, Hawkins published an answer to him in defence of it.

In consequence, in much disgust with the state of the Undergraduates at large, Newman turned for relief to his own special pupils, and primarily to the orderly and promising among them. He offered them his sympathy and help in College work, and in this way, as time went on, he gained first their attachment and then their affection. He set himself against the system of Private Tutors, that is, as a system, and except in extraordinary cases; viz. the system, then prevailing, of young graduates, Bachelors or Masters, undertaking the work of preparing candidates for the honours of the Schools, and, by this interposition between College Tutor and pupil, inflicting an expense on the latter and a loss of legitimate influence on the former, which neither party was called upon to sustain. He laid it down as his rule, which in a great measure he was able to carry out, that on such of his pupils as wished to work for academical honours, he was bound to bestow time and trouble outside that formal lecture routine which was provided for Undergraduates generally in the Table of Lectures put forth at the beginning of each term. With such youths he cultivated relations, not only of intimacy, but of friendship, and almost of equality, putting off, as much as might be, the martinet manner then in fashion with College Tutors, and seeking their society in outdoor exercise, on evenings, and in Vacation. And, when he became Vicar of St Mary's in 1828 the hold he had acquired over them led to their following him on to sacred ground, and receiving directly religious instruction from his sermons; but from the first, independently of St Mary's he had set before himself in his Tutorial work the aim of gaining souls to God.

About the time of his entering upon his Vicarage, important changes took place in the Oriel staff of Tutors, and that in a direction favorable to his view of a Tutor's duties. The two senior retired, their places being supplied by two young Fellows, Mr Robert I. Wilberforce and Mr R. Hurrell Froude, disciples of Mr Keble, and both of them, as being such, in practical agreement with Mr Newman as to the nature of the office of College Tutor. As Mr Dornford, who was now senior of the Tutorial body, was far from indisposed to the view of his three colleagues, there ensued in consequence a sudden, though at first unobserved, antagonism in the College administration between Provost and Tutors, the former keeping to that construction

of a Tutor's duties to the young men, which he had held hitherto, and
which may be called the disciplinarian, and the four Tutors adhering
to the pastoral view of these duties. And thus, strangely enough,
Mr Newman, at the very moment of his friend Dr Hawkins's entering
upon the Provostship, became conscious for the first time of his own
congeniality of mind with Keble, of which neither Mr Keble nor he
had had hitherto any suspicion, and he understood at length how it
was that Keble's friends felt so singular an enthusiasm for their
Master.

It had been Froude's great argument in behalf of Keble, when the
election of Provost was coming on, that Keble, if Provost, would
bring in with him quite a new world, that donnishness and humbug
would be no more in the College, nor the pride of talent, nor an
ignoble secular ambition. But such vague language did not touch
Newman, who loved and admired Hawkins, and who answered with
a laugh, that if an Angel's place was vacant, he should look towards
Keble, but that they were only electing a Provost. (Note. Pusey
expresses the same feeling in his Sermon on the opening of Keble
College Chapel in 1876, when he says that "we thought Hawkins the
more practical man.") Little did Newman suspect that Froude's
meaning, when accurately brought out, was that Keble had a theory
of the duties of a College towards its alumni which substantially co-
incided with his own. Nor was it only deficiency in analysis [of
character] which caused Froude's advocacy of his Master to be thus
ineffectual with Newman; by reason of that almost fastidious modesty and shrinking from the very shadow of pomposity, which was
the characteristic of both Keble and Froude, they were in a later year
as well as now, indisposed to commit themselves in words to a theory
of a Tutor's office, which nevertheless they religiously acted on.
Newman on the contrary, when he had a clear view of a matter, was
accustomed to formulate it, and was apt to be what Isaac Williams
considered irreverent and rude in the nakedness of his analysis, and
unmeasured and even impatient in enforcing it. He held almost
fiercely that secular education could be so conducted as to become a
pastoral cure. He recollected that Origen had so treated it and had by
means of the classics effected the conversion of Gregory, the Apostle
of Pontus, and of Athenodorus his brother. He recollected that in the
Laudian statutes for Oxford a Tutor was not a mere academical
Policeman, or Constable, but a moral and religious guardian of the
youths committed to him. If a Tutor was this, he might allowably, or

rather fittingly, have received holy orders; but if the view of Hawkins was the true one, then he, Newman, felt he was taking part in a heartless system of law and form, in which the good and promising were sacrificed to the worthless or uninteresting. On this he was peremptory, but in all this he received no sympathy from the new Provost, who, as far as he mastered Newman's views, maintained that Newman was sacrificing the many to the few, and governing, not by intelligible rules and their impartial application, but by a system, if it was so to be called, of mere personal influence and favoritism.

This conflict of opinion, however, between Provost and Tutor did not affect their united action [all] at once. For a time all went on well, with the prospect of a future tinted with that rose-colour which prevails at the opening of a new reign. The Provost loyally and energetically backed up his Tutors in their measures for the enforcement of discipline and the purification of the College. He inflicted severe punishments on offenders; he showed no hesitation in ridding the place of those who were doing no good there either to themselves or to others. It began to be the fashion at Oriel to be regular in academical conduct, and admission into the Tutors' set became an object of ambition to men hitherto not remarkable for a strict deportment. First classes were once more looming in the offing. With whatever occasional rubs and disputes between Provost and Tutors, the former as a man of straightforward religious principle and severe conscientiousness, could not but be much gratified at finding himself so well served by them, and they, eager and hopeful in their work, had no anticipations that they should not get on well with him. This was on the whole the state of things in 1828, but still there was at bottom that grave, though latent, difference in principle, as has been described above, which was too likely at one time or another to issue in a serious collision between the one party and the other.

At length the cause of quarrel came, and, when it came, it was so mixed up with both academical and ecclesiastical differences between the two parties, differences which it would involve much time and trouble as well as pain to bring out intelligibly now, that a compromise was hopeless. It was immediately occasioned by a claim of the Tutors to use their own discretion in their mode of arranging their ordinary terminal Lecture Table, a claim, which, on the Provost's denying it, they based upon the special relation existing, from the nature of the case and the University Statutes, between each Tutor and his own pupils, in contrast with his accidental relation to the rest of the Undergraduates [whom he from time to time saw in Lecture]. The Provost practically made the relation very much one and the same in both cases; but at least three of the Tutors, Newman, Wilberforce, and Froude, considered that their interest in their office was absolutely at an end, and they could not continue to hold it, unless they were allowed to make a broad distinction between their duties severally to their own pupils and to those of other Tutors.

A long discussion and correspondence followed, of which nothing came, reaching through 1829 to June 1830. Then the Provost closed it, by signifying to Newman, Wilberforce, and Froude, his intention to stop their supply of pupils, as he had a right to do, thus gradually depriving them of their office, according as their existing pupils took their degrees and left the University.

After expressing, in a last letter on the subject, the reluctance which he had all along felt to allude to any course of action which might have the air of a threat, he continues:—

"And I am most reluctant to do so still; but I yield to what you seem to desire, and feel bound therefore to say that, if you cannot comply with my earnest desire, I shall not feel justified in committing any other pupils to your care."

Among Mr Newman's papers are letters written by Dornford and Froude at the very beginning and at the close of the controversy; and, as they accurately express what Newman himself felt also on the points in debate, and afford him the sanction of their concurrence in his first step and in his last, they shall here be given.

Dornford's written in December 1828, states distinctly his opinion that the arrangement of the College Lectures which was the point in duspute, lay with the Tutors and not with the Provost. Froude's insists on the practical effect upon himself and upon his view of duty, of that particular arrangement of Lectures, which alone the Provost would hear of.

1. Dornford, under date of December 26. 1828. "And now for your new plan of lecturing. There is much in it that I like, and at a first glance it seemed open to no objections; but now it appears to me that it is much better adapted to 200 men than to 50 and ... will add very much to the labour. ... However, there can be no objection, I think, if you all feel strongly about it, to make the experiment and see how it works. And I perfectly agree with you here, that we are

not at all bound to consult any one but ourselves on the adoption of it."

2. This was when the new system of lectures was first contemplated. When the Provost had finally disposed of it by depriving the Tutors who advocated it of their office, Froude wrote to him as follows:—

June 10. 1830. "I do not find that your explanation sets the system you recommend in a light in any respect different from that in which I had before considered it. I have therefore no need to deliberate long as to my answer.

"In order to comply with such a system, I should be obliged to abandon all hope of knowing my pupils in the way in which I know them at present, and consequently of retaining that influence over them which I believe I now possess.

"Of this I can be certain from my knowledge of myself, and from my present experience, slight as it may be.

"But in abandoning this hope, I should be giving up the only thing which makes my present situation satisfactory to myself, and should therefore have no inducement to retain it, except a wish to obviate the inconvenience which a sudden vacancy might occasion.

"For this reason, in the event of its being proved to me that I cannot with propriety act contrary to your wish on this point, I shall be desirous of withdrawing from my situation at the earliest time which suits your convenience, and at any rate shall resign at Christmas."

He [Froude] wrote again on June 15 to the Provost, thus: "I have never thought, as you suppose, that your view itself is necessarily at variance with the Statutes. When I appealed to them as a sanction of my conduct, it was not to show that they disallowed the *system* which you approve, but simply that they recognized *such a relation between Tutor and Pupil*, as would justify me in acting on my own views, though they should not happen to be consistent with yours.

"Unless I believed that they do recognize such a relation, I should feel bound either to acquiesce at once in the system which you approve, or to resign my situation in any manner that might best suit your convenience. But, as it is, I feel no less bound to consult to the best of my judgment for the good of those pupils that have been committed to me, and to act on this judgment, such as it is, till you think proper to revoke my authority over them.

"When I speak of acting on my own judgment, I should mention, in vindication of myself, that *in principle* it coincides with that which Keble formed, when a Tutor here, and which he still retains as strongly as possible; and that almost in detail it has been suggested by the late Bishop of Oxford" (Lloyd) "who thought [however] that the Christ Church system was carried to an injurious length, and that some modification of it might be found that would combine the advantages of both.

"And, though I see the absurdity of assuming that whatever could suit Keble and Lloyd is suitable also to me, I would remind you that, while almost every one who is put under me requires a *superintendence* which I find myself unable to give under your system, there are very few who require *instruction* beyond what any educated person is able to afford."

Mr Newman had already written to the Provost to the same effect, on June 8th, and, according to his way, more abruptly. "My chief private objection," he says, "to the system you propose is, that, in my own case, as I know from experience (whatever others may be able to effect) the mere lecturing required of me would be incompatible with due attention to that more useful private instruction which has imparted to the office of Tutor the importance of a clerical occupation."

To the same purpose he wrote afterwards to Mr James, a late Fellow of the College, a year & a half later, on December 8, 1831, on occasion of a report that he had resumed his post, as Tutor:—"Had the Tutorship been originally offered me by the late Provost on the terms interpreted by the present, I never should have accepted it; or, if so, only as a trial. I have ever considered the office pastoral, such that the Tutor was intrusted with a discretionary power over his pupils. It was on this ground that four years ago I persuaded Robert Wilberforce to undertake it. I have before now, while the Provost was a Fellow, expressed the same view to him. My decision, right or wrong, was made, not in haste or passion, but from long principle, and it is immutable, as far as any man dare use such a term of his resolves."

Mr Newman's connexion with the College Tutorship did not altogether terminate till the Summer of 1832. As has been said, the Provost declined to give him more pupils, but Newman was not disposed to surrender those whom he still had, from the great interest he took in them and in their prospective success in the Schools, and also as holding that the Tutorship was a University office, of which the

Vice Chancellor only could directly deprive him. By the Long Vacation of 1832 his pupils had, all but a few, passed their B.A. examination, and the two or three who remained he gave over into the hands of the Provost. At the end of the year he went abroad with Hurrell Froude and his Father.

Perhaps it is worth mentioning, though it does not seem to be set down in Mr Newman's memoranda, that the main practical argument which the Provost urged upon him in behalf of his continuing Tutor on the old system of lecturing, was, "You may not be doing so much good as you may wish, or think you could do, but the question is, whether you will not do some good, some real substantial good." Mr Newman used to laugh and say to his friends, "You see the good Provost actually takes for granted that there is no possible way for me to do good in my generation, except by being one of his Lecturers; with him it is that or nothing." In the year after his relinquishing his College office, on his return from abroad, the Tract movement began. Humanly speaking, that movement never would have been, had he not been deprived of his Tutorship, or had Keble, not Hawkins, been Provost.

The end

(Here follow three passages, A, B, C, originally incorporated in this Chapter, but on consideration omitted.)

[APPENDIX: EXCISIONS A, B, C]

(These passages, cut out from Chapter 4 as being severe upon Hawkins, will give elbow-room *private* information to a Memoir writer. For this reason I add them.)

A

Nor was Newman the only one among the Fellows, who thought the new Provost did not act up to the promise of his antecedents. At that time there was a keen and growing feeling in the Colleges, especially among the Tutors of them, that the Heads of Houses usurped, or at least injuriously engrossed power in University matters, and that those who did the work, the resident Fellows, not those who had no work to do, should have the power. Now Hawkins, it was alleged, when a member of the Common Room, had ever used the language of a Tribune of the people; he had been strongly on the side of Fellows and Tutors; he had prophesied that the existing state of things could not last, and that, unless concessions on a large scale proceeded from the Heads, there would before long be a serious re-action against them. Yet now, on the contrary, that he was Provost, he did not shrink from declaring that all was as it ought to be, that after all the Masters were a real and effective power in the resident body, that the Proctors efficiently represented them in the Heb-domadal Board, and that no reform was called for. This is what was said in Oriel by his friends as well as by others. They accused him also in their talk with each other, of assuming state and pomp, and of separating himself from his own Fellows, as if his membership in the Hebdomadal Board was a closer tie than his membership with his College, and moreover, of courting the society and countenance of men of rank and name, whether in the world, or in the state, or the Church. They smiled, when instead of speaking of the Provost's "lodgings", he talked about "my house". Such an imputation, even though well-founded, would not be revived here, did it not serve to account for the change of feeling and bearing towards him of New-man and others in the years which followed. Perhaps they said in their hearts, "Keble would not have so acted".

But a more tangible grievance occurred in the Spring of 1829, and illustrative of their complaint of him, and that not on private College matters, but on a great political question. Mr Peel, the representative of the University in Parliament, had declared in favour of the Catholic claims, had resigned his seat, and then, changing appar-ently his purpose, had offered himself for re-election. The Provost took his side, the four Tutors were against him. In the eyes of the latter, his re-election was far more than a question of politics and political expediency; it was a moral, an academical, an ecclesiastical, nay a religious question; at least it grew to be such with them. Their opponents were liberals, and the liberal side, little as some of those recognized it, who took their stand on it, was the anti-Church, anti-Christian side;—little, of course, as some of those as yet recognized it who took their stand on it, for Pusey, Sewell, Woodgate, and Bowden were on that side, whom it would be wild to accuse of reli-gious indifference or of heterodoxy. The Provost did not recognize it either, but then he was an eager, foremost partizan of Peel, which those men were not, nay he had the credit even of having had a chief hand in Peel's change of purpose, and of having involved the Uni-versity in this most unnecessary, wanton contest. Peel had done the right thing in resigning; but now the University was called upon to reverse his act. This was from the Provost's meddling in the high world of politics.

But he managed to make the quarrel between him and his Tutors domestic and personal as well as ecclesiastical. It was customary, as a rule, for Head and Fellows to move together on public questions; a Provost consulted the Common Room before acting. But Dr Hawkins, without letting his Fellows know of his intention, had abruptly gone to London, engaged himself to the Government party, and, when on returning he found they were against him, and were moving with the Tories, contemptuously to their face called the great Tory movement "their cabal". Such personal irritation on both sides of course gave an edge to their quarrel, and cut off the chances of reconciliation, and was much to be deplored; however, after all, the quarrel between the two parties was based on principle, and rested, as was more clearly seen in the event, on theological differences, as to which neither party was likely to surrender its own view, but rather to be more firmly rooted in it, as time went on. It is necessary to insist upon this: for when, some years afterwards, the aversion felt by Newman and his friends to the ecclesiastical attitude of Dr Hawkins showed itself in their opposition, with Convocation generally, to his friend Dr Hampden, on the appointment of the latter to the Divinity chair, Dr Hawkins was accustomed to say, in disparagement of that opposition, that the University had been seduced into taking up a mere College quarrel, meaning thereby that, whereas he had in 1830-1832 given to Hampden the Tutorship which he had taken from Newman, Newman had ever since had unfriendly feelings towards Hampden, which broke out in 1836 in an attempt to stop his preferment. But this representation will not stand examination.

The College quarrel, which is the proper subject of this chapter, and which also, as has been above said, was founded on religious principle, was brought into shape and to its issue in the course of the year which followed upon Mr Peel's matter. It arose in the following way:—at the beginning of every term the Tutors had been accustomed to meet together, and to draw up a Table of lectures which the young men were severally to attend, a difficult and tiresome task, as will be easily understood, since it involved in the case of each individual of them an exact adjustment of lectures, classes and hours. Each Undergraduate was to be in a certain number of lecture-classes, under a certain number of lecturers, on certain fixed hours *per* day;

each class must be composed of students tolerably equal in attain-ments, and must be presided over by a lecturer equal to the subject and to them. The arrangement of this Table was, in consequence, a work of many hours, and was always more or less unsatisfactory, obstinate hitches after painful efforts at removal being hopelessly left and difficulties shuffled over. Then the Table was written out fair, and sent to the Provost, who at the end of the Term presided at the examination of each youth in the subject-matter of such lectures, as according to the Table, each had attended.

Neither Mr Newman, nor the other Tutors, ever dreamed of dis-pensing with this joint publication of Terminal lectures, as hitherto in use, or of not submitting the List, when drawn up, to the Provost, or of interfering with his personal examination of the young men at the end of Term; but they attempted to draw up the List upon a principle, which they considered more direct, more intelligible, more practical than heretofore, and more in accordance with their own idea of a Tutor's office and duties. Hitherto it had been usual to draw it up without any regard to the existing relations between each Tutor and his own pupils, all the Tutors becoming Lecturers for the occasion to all the Undergraduates, whether their pupils or not, and taking this or that class by rotation, indiscriminately, whomsoever it was composed of. The principle now introduced was that each Tutor should in the first place be responsible and consult for his own pupils, should determine what subjects they ought to have lectures in, and should have the first choice as to taking those lectures themselves, and should in the second place consult for the pupils of others. Other-wise they considered the office of Tutor became that of a mere lec-turer, and that teaching was not an act of personal intercourse, but an ungenial and donnish form.

Accordingly in the beginning of 1829 they resolved on acting on their own view of the matter. They did not formally communicate to the Provost what they were doing, though he was from the first made aware of it, for several reasons. First they maintained that the Tutor-ship was in itself a University, not a mere College office, and that, although the Provost had the appointment of Tutors and the allot-ment of pupils, yet to the Vice-Chancellor, not to the Provost, were they responsible for their performance of their duties. Next, it appeared to them sufficient if the Provost saw their Table of Lectures and examined their pupils upon it at the end of Term, in order to form a judgment upon their work and its success, and that he had no concern with the principle on which they drew up their Lecture Table, which was a matter for their own discretion. And thirdly, they knew him well enough to be sure that, if, instead of acting on their right, concealing indeed, but volunteering nothing, they proceeded to consult him, he would put his veto upon it, however unnecessarily, and there would be a deadlock in the College administration. They determined then to let the matter take its course, and to leave the Provost to object, if he wished.

In a memorandum drawn up by Mr Newman in the summer of 1830, immediately after his removal from the Tutorship, he writes as follows:—"When I consulted Dornford in December 1828 on the subject of modifying the existing lecture system, it was not with the suspicion that I might be interfering with any recognized principles of College discipline. That we should be departing from the method adopted by individual Tutors, I was well aware; but, having never been informed on the subject either by the Provost (Copleston), when he appointed me, nor by the Tutors senior to myself, I had no reason to suppose, nor did I know, that peculiar principles of tuition, and much less a minute system of lecturing, was immutably established in the College. A public relation indeed I knew was recognized between the Tutors as a body and the Undergraduates as a body, and again a private relation between each Tutor and his pupils; but that the private relation was *subordinate* to the public, this is the principle which I never heard of as belonging to Oriel, and to which I have been consistently opposed. Indeed, I should never have taken the Tuition at all, at most only as an experiment for a short time, had I not fully believed that my time was primarily to be devoted to my own pupils, and only secondarily to the pupils of others. ... When I looked round at other Colleges, I found the Tutors possessed of an almost unlimited discretion, a discretionary power committed (allowed) to them by the Head of their House, when he appointed them to their situation."

He continues:—"Our plan was first adopted by us in Lent Term 1829. In the next Term, on an accidental occasion, we told the Provost what we were about, and were much surprised and disconcerted at the rude way in which he received the intelligence, without any kind of deference to us, or any enquiry into the reasons which had swayed us in making our new arrangement. On a second meeting, he told us in a pointed way that 'we must alter this next Term.' After the Long Vacation, the Provost expressed strongly his opinion in the same authoritative absolute tone. A long discussion ensued, in which I plainly told him I considered my office a University office & under University sanction, and that it was a matter of conscience with me not to give my time and exertions to the system he upheld."

B

Yet it might have been averted or remedied, had that intimacy continued which had once existed between Dr Hawkins and Mr Newman; but by 1829 their relation towards each other had become very different from what it was in 1824, when the latter had been the unpretending and grateful disciple of the former. Newman had been eager in Hawkins's behalf for years, and had sung his praises loudly, wherever he went. He had expected great things from his promotion to the Provostship, and had taken great interest in it, when it was in agitation. And then on the other hand from the first he had been deeply disappointed in the results of it. Nor was he the only one of the Fellows who thus felt.[1] Such disappointment indeed in the hopes of the prospective doings of friends entertained by those who have been instrumental in placing them in posts of influence is of very common occurrence, and often involves much injustice, and even cruelty towards the objects of it; and Mr Newman might have acted more generously towards a man to whom he owed much; but he had various grievances in regard to Dr Hawkins from the time that he became Provost, which made him very sore, and which are here referred to, though without specifying, only because it would have been unfair to him and his colleagues to leave any suspicion with the reader, that their attitude towards the Provost had any thing in it of a wanton and rude defiance, instead of being determined by a deliberate judgment which, right or wrong, they formed of him, and a motive of duty in consequence of it.

Thus matters stood at the end of the first year of the new Provostship; at the beginning of the second year, 1829, contemporaneously with the University conflict about Mr Peel's re-election (in which Provost and Tutors took opposite sides), the College quarrel took a definite shape on the question what were to be the principles and what the method of lecturing to be observed by the Tutors in relation to their Undergraduate members; that is, whether in their ordinary Lectures, as fixed in the Terminal Lecture Paper, the Tutors should each give the place of primary interest and care to his own special

[1] Vide beginning of A. (Thus a note by Newman. C.S.D.)

pupils, or to all the Undergraduates in lecture indiscriminately, his own and those of other Tutors.

The Provost took the latter view, which was in possession at Oriel, the Tutors wished to introduce the former; and while the Provost urged that the Tutors were bound by an important rule long acted upon and enforced by himself, they maintained that, though he appointed them and might virtually dismiss them, they held a University office, and, while they held it, they must fulfil its duties on their own discretion.

It is hardly too much to say that these rival views were not so opposite in practice, that a compromise between them was impossible, had their maintainers been other than they were; but there was an ever-widening theological antagonism between the two parties, and an impatience on the side of Newman, and an unsympathetic severity on the part of Dr Hawkins, who, with admirable command of temper and composure of manner, refused to retire one hair's breadth from the position which he had taken up, with a stern obstinacy which made any accommodation impossible. Nor was this all: Dr Hawkins really wished to retain Newman as Tutor, and to rid himself of Wilberforce and Froude, whom he considered Tutors by accident, and not by any true calling, and perhaps he attributed to their influence the strong line taken by Newman. Certainly they were what is called "young"; and were deficient in that gravity, which Newman felt to be indispensable for a Tutor as strongly as the Provost did himself. The Provost, on the other hand, could not endure free and easy ways and was disgusted with slang; what others only thought to be humour would instantly bring a strange rigid expression over his face; and if his Tutors sometimes acted still as boys, they might retort by asking whether he had ever been a boy himself. Whately, a free and easy man indeed, but whom Wilberforce and Froude delighted in opposing, wittily compared such boy Tutors to the bigger girls of a poor family, who before their strength was come, have to nurse and carry about their little brothers, and lose their shape in consequence; and Froude, on being told of this, with that engaging manner which was so characteristic of him, laughed with a half-consciousness and admission of its truth. It was believed by the present writer that the Provost in consequence did wish to separate the case of Newman from that of Wilberforce and Froude; however, if so, it was not judicious in him to show it. Newman knew well that the zeal, diligence and success of his two friends in their tutorial work, was as remarkable as their agreement with himself in principle was cordial and entire, and he had no wish or intention to be separated from them.

Nor did the Provost mend matters by letting it appear that he considered that a Tutor's salary was an object to Mr Newman, and not to Wilberforce and Froude. But what irritated Newman most was his imputing Newman's conduct to irritation, and refusing or not being able to see that there was a grave principle in it earnestly held, and betraying a confident expectation that what was, he considered, mere temper in Newman, would soon pass away, and that he would eventually give in. Perhaps the Provost would have acted differently, had he been got to believe Mr Newman's blunt declaration, that there was not a chance of his remaining Tutor, if his scruples were not respected; but he was unable to comprehend the intensity of Mr Newman's feeling that, unless he could make his educational engagements a fulfilment of his ordination vow, he could have no part in them, and instead of thus reading his curt and not always respectful manner and style in the conversations and correspondence which ensued, he adopted a superior tone, implied that overwork made Mr Newman look at things unhealthily, and was for ever inquiring "how he felt to-day?", so that it became a joke among the Tutors, while Mr Newman, on the other hand, became simply indignant that, with the solemn consciousness which haunted him that he was a minister of Christ and a preacher of His gospel, the Provost should venture to press on him an occupation, which, while pressing it, he himself confessed was not properly clerical, and only to be tolerated for a time as an accident, and not the end and staple of a clergyman's life.

[Before concluding this sorrowful passage in Mr Newman's life, as pregnant with important consequences as in itself sorrowful, it may be right, passing from the ethical character and personal feelings displayed on either side of the quarrel, to give in its actual documents which are among Newman's papers, the outline of its history.][1]

C

Next shall follow Mr Newman's statement of the new system given in for the Provost's inspection, with the reply which Dr Hawkins made to it:

"April 28, 1830. The Lectures on the Lecture Paper are either Public or Private." (He had better have called them "either Common or

[1] This paragraph was deleted by Newman. C.S.D.

Personal"; for they were all public, as being all on the Lecture List, all sent to the Provost on being settled, and all matter for the College examination in the Provost's presence at the end of the Term;—he continues,) "The Public Lectures are taken indiscriminately by the Tutors, and are in number from eight to ten." So far the old system remained in force. "Most of these end with the Term."

"The Private Lectures are those in which each Tutor lectures his own pupils, viz., in moral subjects, as Divinity and Ethics, or in books continued term after term, as History, or in order to prepare his pupils for the Public Lectures.

"Though the instruction of each pupil is supposed to be committed to his own Tutor, yet this rule is modified.

(1) by the Public Lectures, which are given on subjects required of all, or in those which it is usual to read, or not uncommon to read;

(2) in the Private Lectures by the interchange of pupils between Tutors, for mutual convenience-sake; though here the ultimate decision is with the Tutor lecturing."

It may be said in criticism of this account of the new system, as it was objected by Dornford, that, on the face of it, it was of a somewhat complicated character, and would require unusual men to carry it out, and a very unusual good understanding and oneness of spirit between them. On the other hand Mr Newman would plead that there was such a harmony of mind and principle between the Tutors, and that the system had had the trial of a year. It would seem to have been wiser in the Provost, had he let them have their swing, and make their experiment and experience the failure of the complications to which they had committed themselves; for the addition of a new Tutor, who would be sure to come in on Dornford's coming retirement, would have at once secured the Provost's object without his own interference.

This view, however, did not commend itself to the Provost, who answered Mr Newman's statement in the following letter, in which, it will be seen, he does not criticize or argue against it, but employs himself in drawing out the details of the received system, which from experience Newman knew as well as Hawkins could, and there peremptorily leaving the matter. His letter is dated May 15. Newman had written several letters to him in the interval, but the Provost so little understood Newman that he fancied delay would tend to allay any irritation which the Tutors might feel on the subject in debate, whereas it was the very way to increase it. He wrote as follows:—

"On the first day of Term all the Tutors met to arrange all the Lectures in common, conferring with one another upon the several Lectures, which each student ought to attend. The Classes accordingly were formed without any reference in the first instance either to the Tutor who should have any one of the Classes, or to the students, who should belong to any one of them, having been entered under this or that particular Tutor. When a sufficient number of Classes had been thus formed, and all the students placed in such a number of Classes as were sufficient for each, *then* the Tutors made their choice of these Classes. ... After this came the arrangement of these Classes as to days &c. ... The important points are, that the Classes were not formed in the first instance either *by* any particular Tutor or *for* him; and that the pupils were not arranged in the Classes with any regard to their being the *pupils of one Tutor or another*. It was not unimportant that all the students were placed in the proper number of Classes *before* the Lectures were chosen by the Tutors."

At the same date he says:—"As you have brought your system into *actual operation*, I ask nothing more than that you will, not at once, but *gradually* return to the old system. And this will be done with ease by your merely suffering your Classes, when each shall have finished whatever work it is now engaged with, to be thrown back into the common stock of Classes, and by your not forming Classes in future of your own particular pupils."

When each party had stated its own view in opposition to the other, they had arrived at the end of the controversy. There was no chance of the pleas of the one side having any effect on the other. Neither of them would give way. However, before inserting the final letters to each other of the Provost and of the Tutors, the arguments shall be set down on which they respectively relied.

(1) First the Provost. He naturally took this ground that the Lecture system, as he maintained it, was the received system, that it had been in force for many years, and had been recognized and acted on by such men as Copleston, Davison, Bishop, Marsh, Whately, Tyler, and Keble. And next, that it had worked well; that is, if it was a proof of its working well that it had fostered such a spirit of diligence in the College, that Oriel men had, in the course of the eight years before 1828, gained 15 first classes, 8 in Classics and 7 in Mathematics, which, though Oriel was not the largest of Colleges, was as much as any other College had gained except Christ Church, and which none came near except Balliol. Why then was a method of teaching which

had been framed by the men who by their reputation and exertions had made Oriel what it was, and had been justified by its results, to be put aside for an untried system by the arbitrary act of several young men, who had little experience in tutorial work, and that without asking any advice from others, and specially without the direct sanction of him who surely had the oversight of all College measures, and was moreover the very representative and living witness and guardian of that old tradition now so rudely superseded?

(2) Mr Newman replied as follows:—first he said that the method to be adopted by a Tutor in teaching his pupils could not be made a binding tradition; that the Tutorship, as far as the College was concerned, was a substantive, self-dependent office; that it was not under the jurisdiction of the College; that it necessarily involved a discretionary action and a personal responsibility; that the precedents of former Tutors were no rule for existing ones; that, while he was Tutor, he must act to the best of his judgment for the good of his pupils; that he might be put aside, or dismissed, but he could not be controlled in a matter of duty. He said all this on the notorious ground that a Tutorship was not merely a College, but a University office, that he was, as a Tutor, subject, not to the Provost, but to the Vice-Chancellor. This was what the Provost had overlooked, and it was the hinge of the whole question. He appealed to the words of the University Statute Book, in order to show what a Tutor ought to be. He was not a Lecturer to a mixed multitude of Undergraduates, with whom he had no definite relations, but, as the Latin word implies, a guardian of certain given pupils or wards. According to the Statutes he was intended to be a "vir probitate et eruditione perspectâ, religione sincerus", who "scholares tutelae suae commissos probis moribus instruat, et in probatis authoribus instituat, et maximè in rudimentis religionis et doctrinae articulis", &c.; that he had even to attend to his pupil's dress and appearance. All this was not inconsistent with his also giving Lectures to others besides his own pupils, which he was more than willing to do, but he certainly felt that his first duty was to those specially which were his and not another Tutor's.

Next, as to the system advocated by the Provost working well, Newman denied or explained the Provost's proof of it. It was true indeed, he said, that while Mr Tyler was in force, in the course of his nine years, twenty-two first classes had been gained by Oriel men, 14 in Classics and 8 in Mathematics, but they were gained really by the very system which Dr Hawkins was proscribing, by private and personal lecturing over and above those promiscuous lectures which were given without reference to the relation of Tutor and pupil. The only difference was that they were extras and paid for accordingly, that the College Tutor took upon himself the additional duties of private tuition, whereas Newman would include such duties in a College Tutor's office as such. This of course would throw upon him more work certainly, but that was his own concern, not the Provost's; but of this he was sure, that, were the Provost's system left to itself without private tuition, whether accidental and by compact, as Tyler's, or formally collegiate as his own (Newman's), honours would be scarce in Oriel.

This is what he said, while the dispute with the Provost was proceeding; and it receives an important comment by the later events, as the following comparative statement will show. Taking the four years before the new system came into full work, and the four subsequent years, which represent its effective action, we find the contrast between them stands thus:—in the first four, from Michaelmas 1825 to Easter 1829 inclusive, in which (Tyler relaxing in energy) we have the outcome of the old system, only two first classes were gained by Oriel men. But during the four following years, which represent the new system of Newman, Wilberforce and Froude, that is, from Michaelmas 1829 to Easter 1833, there were eleven gained. In the further five years from Michaelmas 1833 to Easter 1837, during which the old system was partially restored, the first classes in Oriel fell back to five.[1]

On the whole then, what was the Provost's quarrel with the dealings of the Tutors with his Undergraduates? As many subjects were lectured in as before, as many classes formed, as many lectures given; and it was in all cases the interest of the Tutors themselves that each should lecture on the subject with which he was most familiar; and the Provost might interfere in any particular instance in which this was not the case. If then they felt that their own plan satisfied their conscience better than another, which separated them from their own pupils, why might they not pursue it? why might they not at least make trial of it?

[1] Only "partially restored", as has been said, because the innovation had made its mark on the College, and Mr. Newman, though not Tutor, was Dean and Vicar of St. Mary's. [Note by Newman. C.S.D.]

IV

MY ILLNESS IN
SICILY

INTRODUCTION

On March 17th, 1885, Neville was commissioned by Newman to deliver into Anne Mozley's hands a document headed "My Illness in Sicily", which he wished her to include in her work as a supplement to the Memoir.

The experience with which this document is concerned, must be placed in its biographical setting, if its significance for Newman personally is to be fully realized; and at the same time it should be borne in mind that at the time at which it occurred the Church of England was passing through a grave political crisis which, it was thought, threatened its very existence. Relieved of his duties at Oriel, as were also his fellow-tutors, R. H. Froude and R. I. Wilberforce, in consequence of a difference of opinion between them and the Provost as to the scope of the tutorial office, Newman felt himself free to accept an invitation to accompany Froude on a tour of the Mediterranean, which the latter, for reasons of health, proposed to make with his father, Archdeacon Froude. The travellers set out from Falmouth on December 8th, 1832 on board the packet *Hermes*. The voyage proved to be entirely uneventful, and Newman "experienced none of that largeness and expansion of mind", which should have been the fruit of foreign travel. His thoughts were fixed on England and what was happening there, and "the news from England came rarely and imperfectly". After calling at Cadiz, Gibraltar and Algiers they reached Malta on December 24th, and spent Christmas Day in quarantine. Leaving again for Corfu on December 26th they put in at Zante and Patras, which was the furthest point they reached in their itinerary, and arrived at their destination on December 30th. In Corfu they spent a week, and then returned to Malta, where they lingered a whole month, from January 10th to February 7th, in quarantine for part of the time. On the latter date, since the *Hermes* had returned to England, they took another steamship to Naples by way of Messina and Palermo, spending a day or two at each of these ports. Arriving at Naples on February 14th, they remained there until the end of the month, and then set out for Rome, which they reached on March 2nd. Rome was to have been the climax of their wanderings; but while they were there, Newman, on his own initiative and against the advice of friends, "for the gratification of an imagination, for the idea of a warm fancy, drawn by a strange love of Sicily to gaze upon its cities and mountains", made up his mind, and could not be shaken in his resolution, to return to the island of his dreams and thence, after exploring the interior, to make his way home by Palermo. In consequence he parted company with the Froudes on April 9th, they setting out to Città Vecchia en route to France and home, and he to Naples with Sicily as his objective. There he made his preparations for the journey, his equipment consisting of "a set of cooking utensils and tea service—curry powder, spice, pepper, salt, sugar, tea, and ham; cold cream, a straw hat, and a map of Sicily." He also engaged a servant to accompany him, Gennaro by name, a "trustyman", a veteran of the Peninsular War, who had spent sixteen years in the service of an English family; and he either hired or bought three mules for purposes of transport. After a delay of nine days he secured a passage in a sailing vessel, the *Serapis* of Yarmouth, and on Friday, April 19th, he left Naples. A "brisk breeze" was blowing, with the result that he fell victim to a severe bout of sea-sickness. The next day, Saturday, April 20th, the ship lay becalmed off Stromboli, but it reached Messina on Sunday, April 21st, between 6 and 7 a.m. After he had found accommodation at the "Leon d'Oro", he tried to get into touch with Mr Morrison, presumably the English Chaplain, in order to find out the time of the Church of England service, but he failed to find him. Detained there against his will until he could obtain passports and the other necessary papers, he did not begin his journey down the coast until noon on Monday, April 22nd. As he set out, he "felt amused and almost ashamed of the figure [he] was cutting". "I was," he explained to his sister Harriett, "chief of a cavalcade consisting of a servant, two mules [what had become of the third?], and several muleteers (though the latter were soon reduced to one, who was to go with us through), and when I happened to catch a sight of my shadow, the thought of my personal equipments, at least as regards my hat and my coat, was still more perplexing. My neckcloth was the only black thing about me, yet black without being clerical. Nor had I any such exuberance of spirits as would bear me up against the ridiculousness of my exterior. I was setting out on an expedition which would be pleasant in memory rather than in performance." He seems, in spite of the mules, to have walked, not ridden, the twenty miles through Ali to a place which he thought was called San Paolo, and found for the night in the inn a better room and bed, though verminous, than he anticipated. The next day, Tuesday, April 23rd, he described as a "great success". Starting out between 5 and 6 a.m., with twelve miles to cover to Taormina, he left the road two miles from his destination, and proceeded "up a steep path" to Taurominium to be enraptured by the "superb view" from the theatre, "the most wonderful I can ever see". Thence he made his way on to Giarre, where he spent the night, having accomplished about twenty-two miles in the day. The next morning, Wednesday, April 24th, making an early start he climbed to the "Chestnut Trees", no doubt near Trecastagne, but they were disappointing, "being nothing but roots, cut level with the ground", breakfasted in a house where there was a sick man, an ominous circumstance, and continued the ascent to Nicolosi, through fields of lava. He found accommodation in a "so-called inn ... the most forlorn place I ever was in", hungry, exhausted and "altogether out of sorts"; but in the morning after a night's rest he woke up feeling "quite strong". Nonetheless he decided against making any attempt to climb Etna. Instead he continued on his way to Catania, finding the walk of twelve miles an exhilarating experience. There he spent the day and the night at the Corona d'Oro, making the acquaintance of Signor C. Gemellaro, Froude's friend. The following morning, Friday, April 26th, he set out for Syracuse, a distance of forty miles, by *speronara*, a large boat, about thirty-five feet long, with an awning four feet high at the stern, the rest being open. That night he slept on board with thirteen other passengers, and reached his destination between 3 and 4 a.m. on Saturday, April 27th. Then he occupied his time in reading Thucydides in order to refresh his memory and in visiting places of historical interest. Later in the day he dined with three English officers on their way home from India by the overland route; and in the evening attended a party to celebrate the wedding of a judge's son to the Russian consul's daughter, arrayed in his "traveller's dress, thinking, goose as I was, to be incognito, and merely a sight-seer", but to his great embarrassment finding himself treated as a "lion". On Sunday, April 28th, after a glimpse at the amphitheatre, he embarked on a *speronara* once again for the return journey to Catania; but he had an unfortunate experience, for the wind changed, and they were forced to put back. They sheltered for the night in a cove five miles north of Syracuse, and when day dawned they made for Agosto. Disembarking there, he rode the rest of the way on the back of his mule to Catania, reaching his destination, after a "toilsome journey", about 11 p.m. After being jolted by the mule over a distance of thirty-two miles, sometimes at a speed of five or six miles an hour, he was "more dead than alive" on his arrival. However, he had a "remarkably good night"; but the following day, Tuesday, April 30th, "some feverishness" came on, and so he rested there for the day, visiting the theatre and other places, and the following night.

Restored by his brief respite from travelling, and reassured by Signor Gemellaro, who told him that he would have no roads as bad as those he had already experienced, he resolved to strike into the middle of the island and make for Girgenti on the south coast, which he rather optimistically hoped to reach in four days. The morning, Wednesday, May 1st, turned out to be very wet, but in spite of that discouraging circumstance he set out in a north-westerly direction, and traversed the twenty miles to Adernò without mishap, except that he was obliged to lie down once to rest. The next day, Thursday, May 2nd, with the help of an additional mule from Regalbuto, he struggled on to Leonforte, "very weak and ill"; and there he remained, "unable to go on", until the following Monday, May 6th. The seriousness of his condition, at least in the opinion of an interested observer, may be gauged from a note written on the inside of the cover of a notebook, which is still preserved:

To the Revd R H Froude
Oriel College
Oxford
England

Revd J H Newman
When I lay ill for 3 days at Leonforte & my servant thought I was dying, I wrote for him the above direction, wishing Froude to break [the news of] my death to my mother and sisters

J H N Sept 22 1850

Instead of dying, however, after a "little airing on mule" on the Saturday evening, and a short walk on the Sunday afternoon, he felt well enough to resume his journey on Monday, May 6th. But he soon found that he had over-estimated his strength. After setting out at dawn on mule-back, he completely broke down about seven miles from Leonforte, and was installed by his servant in a hut beside the road to rest for a while. It was his good fortune that a competent doctor chanced to be in the neighbourhood; and he was able to afford him some relief in his immediate necessities. After lying down for some hours he was placed once more on the back of his mule, and eventually arrived at Castro Giovanni, where a lodging was found for him, and he was put to bed.

Providentially, as he found out by experience, he had fallen into good hands. His host, whose name was Luigi Vestivo, and those about him, spent themselves to the utmost on behalf of the stranger whom chance had placed under their care. Before Newman left for Palermo some weeks later, Vestivo asked him for some record of the time of his involuntary sojourn among them, and he wrote the following note in a book or on a sheet of paper: "Joannes Henricus Newman, Anglus, in his aedibus libentissimo hospitio exceptus est, curatus, sanatus. Mens. Maii 24, 1833." On his return to England, he also sent him, in response to his request, a Bible, presumably in the Authorized Version, accompanied by a letter, which must have puzzled its recipient:

Aloisio Vestivo Ennensi—Haud tui sum immemor, Vir Benevolentissime, et beneficiorum tuorum, cum ex difficultatibus meis tandem, Deo opitulantè, tutus evaserim; haud tui profecto immemor, chari capitis, in dulcissimâ hac nostrâ sede, et domicilio omnium bonarum artium et praeclararum religionum, Universitate Oxoniensi.

Vellem equidem, sicut me recordatio tui, ita Ecclesias nostras, Siciliensem & Anglicanam, mutua charitatis officia tenerent! nec vos eâ lege Romam diligeretis, ut nos suspicaremini! Enimvero ego Romam veneror, ut matrem nostram; et libenter obedirem, ni daret praecepta ejusmodi, quae S. Scriptura non patitur.

Tu verò, Vir Optime, preces pro me offeras, quoties sanctissimam Missam

audias; a me autem accipies vicissim, quam possum dare, Presbyteri bene-
dictionem.

Mitto ad te &c

Vale, Vir Benevolentissime, Fortis sis, et abundes in fide, in veritate, in
bonis operibus—et credas &c

What impressed Newman deeply, apart from their kindness, was the absolute
honesty of his host and of all who looked after him. Of this the following note is
a memorial:

(This bit of paper went down to Palermo by a carrier or the like (I think, 150
miles from Castro Giovanni) and returned with the money, in dollars. And
my money, watch &c were in the hands of others, I lost *nothing*)

> Gentlemen,
> Pray honor my letter of Credit
> with £20 English
> Yours
> John H Newman
> Deliver it to the
> bearer

Newman had picked up a certain smattering of Italian during his travels; but
with the oncoming of his illness, as he tells us, his limited knowledge of the
language vanished completely from his mind. Since the doctor who attended him
did not command even a smattering of English, it became a problem how they
could make contact with each other. They hit upon a way out of the *impasse* by
having recourse to Latin, which Newman had not forgotten, and of which the
doctor still retained his early memories, relying, however, not on the spoken, but
on the written word, as the channel of communication. The paper on which they
jotted down their questions and answers, Newman brought back with him to
England, and preserved to the end of his life; and it may be of interest to certain
classes of readers, if it is reproduced here:

This paper contains my intercourse for some days with my doctor at Castro
Giovanni when I was abed with the fever, and had taken a violent antipathy to
my domestic for altering the doctor's prescriptions &c J H N. Sept. 22, 1850.

N.   Te, Doctor, enixe oro, ut non me linquas domestico meo, qui mutet tua
praecepta circa me impudentissimo modo. Scribe tua praecepta Lingua
Latina, ut ego sim judex.

D.   Praecepta mea sunt, quum vos abetis unam febbrem gastricam cum dolore
puntorio pectorali, ut sic medela sunt omnia refrigerantia, et sicut odie
prendeste unum purgantem salis anglais, et nullum effectum abuisti, ideo
cras eget replicetur salis aglais, adeo ut possunt abere excreata faecis.
Odie eget refrige corpus idem acidum limoneum et aqua, dosis unum
buccalem ipsum istantem, et alter in altra ora, et nihil per cibbum solius
pasta in aqua quocta, o ovum solutum in aqua calida, et nihil aliud. Cras
facit magis resolutio.

N.   Multas grates: Hoc addas beneficio tuo. Mitte mihi *immediate* aliquam
fidelem mulierem quae me protegat juxta tua praecepta. Ne recusas!

D.   Dicite mihi se voluisti mulierem de hoc loco, quod ego omnia facio, et
ullum timorem abere debetis.

N.   Ego ero sine timore?

N.   Fac illam mulierem scire quod meus domesticus se subjiciet illi.

D.   Dicite mihi se caput dolet.
Ego praescripsi brodum cum macheron ipsa sera.
Odie dic replicetur salis anglais, solutum in aqua.

N.   Hoc ipso tempore non—sed *timeo*.

D.   Nullum timore abetis.

N.   Quando rursus venies? Nam tu es mea sola lux.

D. Ego veniam odie, protracta ora. Nullum remedium opportet facere odie.
N. Quando equitor, infima pars Recti (quod vocant) solet irritari et inflam-
    mari—quod *nunc* malo casu evenit. *Hinc* tarditas, quae invenies, opera-
    tionis Medicinae. *Ego* soleo vincere hanc per minutissimas portiones
    sulphuris et lactis conjunctim. Habeo illam in hac ipsa Camerâ: aut si
    lac sit fortior, cur non, vice lactis, mixtura aquae et ovi? Meus egregius
    domesticus se hodie cohonestavit novis erroribus! Ut res se habent,
    Patior sub suppressione urinae, molesto dolore!
D. Cras dabbo te sulphure; Opportet subpressioni urinae quatuor sanguis
    sughe, quod difficile est invenire in hoc loco. Vos habetis meteborismum in
    abdomine, opportet facere chlisterem cum decoctum malve et olio olivae.
    Facite chlisterem usque veriphicetur excreatum faecis, et opportet multi-
    plicare.
D. Opportet refrigere corpus cum decoctum radicis graminea et salsa pariglia
    conjunctis minutissimas partes sulphure et lactis.
N. Precor, substituas in servitio meo illum probrum hominem, qui nuper
    camerâ excessit, pro domestico meo, quem timeo.
N. Nonne est officium nutricis meae pernoctare mecum aut saltem dividere
    noctem cum Gennaro?

Newman relates that the doctor dismissed his Latin as "nonsense"; but anyone
who compares their respective contributions to the questions and answers
recorded above, will have no hesitation in agreeing with him that his Latin was
"very good", considering his desperate state of health, and that the doctor was
not a "deep Latin Scholar".

His pupil, Frederic Rogers (afterwards Lord Blachford), who had gained a
double First in the previous year, stood for an Oriel Fellowship at Easter 1833,
and was elected. The news of his success he sent to Newman on April 12th, but
his letter did not reach Newman until long afterwards. The latter consequently did
not know of it, until he saw the announcement in *Galignani's Messenger* on
June 4th at Palermo. Writing to congratulate him the next day, he gave him a long
account of his illness, the first he wrote, which, in combination with a somewhat
later one to Henry Wilberforce, will serve admirably to introduce, or to supplement, his own narrative. Its recipient described it as "particularly interesting".
But the reader must be warned that, since the original is not forthcoming, nor in
fact any transcript in Newman's writing, the copy which follows has been taken
from Mozley's *Letters and Correspondence*, vol. I, pp. 404-8.

Palermo; June 5, 1833.

...And now I suppose you are wondering what I do now at Palermo; and
perhaps my friends at Oxford have been wondering, unless they have sat down
in the comfortable conclusion that I am imprisoned here for want of a vessel.
I only hope the Rose Hill[1] people are not uneasy. I have *not* been weather-
bound or shipless, taken by Barbary pirates, or seized as a propagandist for
Liberalism. No; but, you will be sorry to hear, confined with a very dangerous
fever in the very centre of Sicily for three weeks. I will give you an account of
it, if my hand and my head let me. Only do not mention it till you hear I am at
home, which I trust will be in about a fortnight or three weeks. I sail, please
God, in a Marseilles vessel on Saturday next, the 8th, whence I shall despatch
this to you.

This season has been remarkable for rain in this part of the world, as Froude,
if he is returned, has perhaps told you. At Catania, Dr Gemellaro told me that
there sometimes fell only seven inches of rain in the wet months, but that this
year there had fallen thirty-four. In consequence, a bad fever, of the nature of
the scarlet, was epidemic; which I did not know, nor should have thought of
perhaps, if I had. The immediate cause of my illness seems to have been my

---

[1] The home of Newman's mother and sisters, at Littlemore. C.S.D.

expedition from Catania to Syracuse; but doubtless I was predisposed to take injury from any bad state of the atmosphere, by the sleepless nights and famished days (though few) which I had had immediately before. Sicilian couches abound in the most inveterate enemies of slumber, and my provisions —for you get none at the inns—though they ought not, were affected by the weather, or were in themselves bad. (I bought them at Naples.) And about Etna the transitions from heat to cold are very rapid and severe—in the same day I was almost cut in two, and exhausted with the scorching and dust of lava, though I believe I never got chilled. And in many places they have no glass in the windows, and the shutters do not fit tight, which is bad of a night. Now you will say, how was it *I* alone suffered all this of all Sicilian travellers? Why, to tell the truth, *the* way to avoid it would have been to have taken a Sicilian regular lioniser and purveyor, who would have avoided all difficulties; but this for *one* person is very expensive, and it falls light on several. I had a Neapolitan servant, a good cook (I had bought my provisions before I took him, and they *seemed* good), but knowing nothing of Sicily. I knew a great deal of Sicily from others, everyone was giving me advice to do things *they had not tried themselves*. It was from one of these plans I suffered. Now all this, that I have put down in the last half-page, sounds so *gauche*, that I beg you would keep it to yourself; for it is a gratuitous exposure on my part, and only takes up room in my letter, as you will see from what follows.

Everyone recommended me to go from Catania to Syracuse in a speronaro (by water). The distance by land and sea is forty miles—by land the road is indescribably bad, especially after rain—and the distance too long for mules in one day, and there is no inn on the road. The time by sea was unanimously declared by different persons to be seven hours—the boatmen said five. Dr. Gemellaro so fully acquiesced in these statements as to allow of my making an engagement with him for the middle of the day on which I was to set out from Syracuse on my return. I set out for Syracuse by 7 or 8 a.m. Well, when we were about half-way, a scirocco sprang up, and by degrees it became evident we could not reach Syracuse that night. We made for *Thapsus*, and slept in the boat off the peninsula. On my return, which I made by sea from the probability of the scirocco continuing, and the probable state of the road, the same ill luck attended me. The wind changed, and I slept in the boat. Next morning we made for Agosta (all we could do), the ancient Hybla. (Megara Hyblaea— whence the honey.)—We arrived by 8 a.m. at Agosta. Delays of obtaining pratique, passport, &c. &c., kept us till 3 p.m., when we set forward on mules for Catania with the belief that the distance was twenty-two miles. By the time it grew dusk we had gone fourteen miles, and descended to the water's side; when to our dismay we learned we had eighteen miles before us, three rivers to ford or ferry, a deep sand to traverse for half the way, and the danger of being plundered. To complete the whole, when we got to the most suspicious part of our journey our guide lost his way. However, he found it again, and alarms are nothing when they are over, but half an hour was a substantial loss. We got to Catania between eleven and twelve at night. The sun had been broiling during the day—the night was damp. I must add, that the first day I was in the speronaro I had had no food for twenty-four hours—having of course taken no provision with me—that at Syracuse I had eaten very little, and only a break- fast on the day of this fatiguing journey; and, out of the three nights, I had slept only one, and that but a little. I am ashamed of the minuteness with which I am telling all this—but my head is not yet entirely my own.

From my return to Catania I sickened. When the idea of illness first came upon me I do not know, but I was obliged on May 1 to lie down for some time when I had got half through my day's journey; and the next morning I could not proceed. This was at Leonforte, above one hundred miles from Palermo. Three days I remained at the inn there with the fever increasing, and no medical aid. On the night of the third day I had a strange (but providential) notion that I was quite well. So on the next morning I ordered the mules, and set off to Girgenti, my destination. I had not gone far when a distressing chok- ing feeling (constriction?) of the throat and chest came on; and at the end of seven miles I lay down exhausted in a cabin near the road. Here, as I lay on the ground, after a time, I felt a hand at my pulse; it was a medical man who by chance was at hand, and he prescribed for me, and enabled me by the evening to get to Castro Giovanni (the ancient Enna). At first I had difficulty in getting a lodging—had it been known I had the fever I suppose it would have been impossible, for numbers were dying of it there, at Girgenti, and, I believe, everywhere. However, at last I got most comfortably housed. I did not then know what was the matter with me, I believe, but at Leonforte I had thought myself so bad that I gave my servant directions how to convey news of my death (should it be so) to England, at the same time expressing to him a clear and confident conviction that I should *not* die. The reason I gave was that "I thought God had work for me." I do not think there was anything wrong in this, on consideration.

At Castro Giovanni I was immediately bled—an essential service—but with this exception it seems as if nature recovered herself; but not till the eleventh day, during which time the fever was increasing, and my attendants thought I could not get over it. Since, I have gained strength in the most wonderful manner. My strength was so prostrated, I could not raise myself in bed or feed myself. The eighth after the crisis I began to walk about (with help). On the twelfth I began a journey of three days to Palermo, going one day sixty-two miles; and here, where I have been these ten days, I have surprised everyone by my improvement (though I cannot run yet; the weather is very relaxing). When I came here I could not read nor write, nor talk nor think. I had no memory, and very little of the reasoning faculty. My head had been quite clear (at least at intervals) during the early part of my illness, and I had all through the fever corresponded with the doctor in (really very good) Latin; but a letter from home was brought me, containing letters from five persons, and I pored through it to find news of your election, you unworthy fellow, which it did not contain. This threw the blood into my head, which I have not yet quite recovered.

And now you will say my expedition to Sicily has been a failure. By no means. Do I repent of coming? Why, certainly I should not have come had I known that it was at the danger of my life. I had two objects in coming—to see the antiquities and to see the country. In the former I have failed. I have lost Girgenti and Selinunti, and I have lost the series of perfumed gardens through which the mule track near Selinunti is carried. But I have seen Taormini, and the country from Adernò to Palermo, and can only say that I did not know before nature could be so beautiful. It *is* a country. It passes belief. It is like the Garden of Eden, and though it ran in the *line* of my anticipations (as I say), it far exceeded them.

I continually say *En unquam*, being *very* homesick.

June 17.—At last our vessel is nearing Marseilles. I hope to send you a newspaper from London or Oxford to announce my arrival.

At the head of Newman's manuscript there is a note, written in his own hand on February 27th, 1876, referring to a letter addressed by him to H. W. Wilberforce on August 4th, 1833. The collection of correspondence to which this belongs, ignored by Anne Mozley in her volumes, was lent to Newman by Mrs Wilberforce in 1876, after her husband's death, and he transcribed it himself, omitting the more ephemeral passages. As this particular letter is, with the exception of that to Rogers, just quoted, the only one that contains a contemporary account of the illness, it is given here in full from his transcript, together with an earlier one, which will serve as an introduction to it. It should be observed that Wilberforce having heard indirectly that he had been "dangerously ill in the heart of a nearly barbarous country", wrote to him on July 13th to express his joy on his safe return, and thus elicited from him these two letters.

July 16, 1833. I was tired from my journey, having been up six nights out of the last seven. All sorts of evils came upon me in Sicily; the fever, of which many were dying on all sides of me, was but one, though perhaps the greatest of the complaints, before strange to me, which, in connexion with it, suddenly fell upon me. For a week and more my nurses &c. thought I could not recover. No medicine was given me; they bled me, but took so little blood away, that both Mr Babington and Dr Ogle say it could be of no use to me. In fact the fever ran its course, and, when the crisis came, I was spared. I was so reduced that I could not lift my hand to my mouth to feed myself, but in ten days I was able to travel to Palermo, performing one day a journey of sixty miles over a rough country. A determination of blood to my head came on, as I was getting well.

August 4, 1833. The only remaining signs of my illness now are my hair falling off and a slight cough. I was taken ill first at Catania, after spending two nights (unwillingly) in the open air. When I got to Leonforte in the very heart of the country, I broke down. For three days I lay without any medical assistance. On the morning of the fourth a notion seized me that my illness was all fancy; so I set out on my mule. After seven miles in great distress from a sort of suffocating feeling, I was forced to betake myself to a hut by the wayside, where I lay the greater part of the day. On a sudden I found fingers at my pulse; a medical man happened by chance to be in a neighbouring cottage, and they called him in. On that evening I got to Castro Giovanni, the ancient Enna, where I was laid up three weeks.

Not till I got home could I persuade myself I was not in a dream; so strange has every thing been to me.

I hope it was not presumptuous, but from the beginning of my illness I had so strong a feeling on my mind that I should recover, that, whatever I did in the way of preparation for death (I mean, as giving my servant directions &c.) was done as a mere matter of duty. I could not help saying, "I must act as if I were to die, but I think God has work for me yet." Thus I cannot answer your question, never having realized eternity as about to break upon me. Yet I had many serious thoughts. It was a lonely situation at Leonforte, a miserable inn. I am not sure my mind was quite clear at all times, so as to be sensible of its desolateness; yet I had once, doubtless when I felt myself lonely, quite a revelation come upon me of God's love to His elect, and felt as if I were one; but of course I mention this, not as laying stress upon it, but as an instance of God's mercy to me; not that I can describe the feeling in words. Then I was much relieved next day, by being able to discover, as I thought, sins in my conduct, which had led God thus to fight against me. This He had been doing ever since I left Rome, and I had been impatient from time to time at the obstacles He put in my way, and had (as it were) asked why He did so. But now I came to think that there was something of wilfulness in my coming to Sicily, as I did; and, though no one had advised me against it, yet I fancied I ought to have discovered others thought it an over-venturous thing. And then I felt more than I had done the wilfulness of my character generally, and I reflected that I was lying there the very day on which three years before I had sent in my resignation of the Tutorship (or something like it) and, though I could not (and do not) at all repent doing so, yet I began to understand that the *manner* was hasty and impatient. And then I recollected that the very day before I left Oxford, I had preached a (University) Sermon against Wilfulness, so that I seemed to be predicting my own condemnation. And I went on to ask myself whether I had not cherished resentment against the Provost, and whether in me was not fulfilled the text 1 Cor. xi. 29-32 (as I still think it has been). But after all I was comforted by the thought that, in bringing myself into my present situation, I had not (as I have just said) run counter to any advice given me, and I said, "I have not sinned against light", and repeated this often. And then I thought I would try to obey God's will as far as I could, and with a dreamy confused notion which the fever (I suppose) occasioned I thought that in setting off the fourth day from Leonforte, I was, as long as I could, *walking* in the way of God's commandments and putting myself in the *way* of His mercy, as if He would meet me (Isai. xxvi. 8). And surely so He did, as I lay in the hut; and, though I have no distinct remembrance of the whole matter, yet it certainly seems like some instinct which He put within me, and made me follow, to get me to Castro Giovanni, where I had a comfortable room, and was attended to most hospitably and kindly.

On May 20 or 21 he was able to leave his bed for the first time; and during the few days before he left Castro Giovanni, he went into the open air every day for exercise. At length, on the 25th he set out for Palermo in a carriage, and after covering about twenty miles slept at a village, the name of which he could not recall. The next day, so he records in his Diary, he travelled about sixty miles to another village, called either Villalunga or Villafrati, almost certainly the latter, where he passed the night; and on the third day, the 27th, after a drive of twenty-five miles he reached his destination before noon.

At Palermo he was forced by circumstances to mark time, sorely against his will, until June 13th. The hours and days hung heavy on his hands. His rapidly returning strength, coupled with the urgent sense of a mission to be fulfilled in England, made the delay well nigh intolerable. The mental tension under which he laboured, even when recalled after the lapse of thirty years, makes itself felt in the nervous staccato sentences, in which he refers to these wearisome days and nights in the *Apologia*:

> I was aching to get home; yet for want of a vessel I was kept at Palermo for three weeks. I began to visit the Churches, and they calmed my impatience, though I did not attend any services. I knew nothing of the Presence of the Blessed Sacrament there. At last I got off in an orange boat [the *Conte Ruggiero*], bound for Marseilles. Then it was that I wrote the lines, "Lead kindly light", which have since become well known. We were becalmed a whole week in the Straits of Bonifacio. I was writing verses the whole time of my passage. At length I got to Marseilles, and set off for England. The fatigue of travelling was too much for me, and I was laid up for several days at Lyons. At last I got off again, and did not stop night or day, (except a compulsory delay at Paris,) till I reached England, and my mother's house. My brother had arrived from Persia only a few hours before. This was on the Tuesday. The following Sunday, July 14th, Mr Keble preached the Assize Sermon in the University Pulpit. It was published under the title of "National Apostasy". I have ever considered and kept the day, as the start of the religious movement of 1833.

Thus Newman, without a thought of self, resigned the credit to another. But by others an earlier date has been assigned as the birthday of the Movement,—January 22nd, 1832, the day on which, in his turn as Select Preacher, he delivered the sermon, "Personal Influence, the Means of Propagating the Truth". These two views are not irreconcilable with each other: Newman's sermon was an appeal for volunteers in the spiritual combat; Keble's a call to action in the political crisis that seemed to menace the Church of England. It was only after the Whig Government had furnished the occasion by its Bill for the suppression of the Irish Sees, as Newman terms it, that the Movement began to take shape and to gather momentum.

In his Journal on June 25th, 1869, in order to illustrate the wonderful dealings of Divine Providence with him throughout his life, Newman wrote as follows:

> Another thought has come on me, that I have had three great illnesses in my life, and how have they turned out! The first keen, terrible one, when I was a boy of fifteen, and it made me a Christian—with experiences before and after, awful and known only to God. My second, not painful, but tedious and

shattering, was that which I had in 1827, when I was one of the Examining Masters, and it too broke me off from an incipient liberalism, and determined my religious course. The third was in 1833, when I was in Sicily, before the commencement of the Oxford Movement.

Although he does not say so in so many words, yet he clearly implies that he regarded the third illness as the opening of the third stage in his religious development; it seemed to him to have been a period of probation, a kind of enforced retreat, which God had designed for him in preparation for the part he was to play in the Movement about to be initiated. When he left England in December 1832, he was in a state of perplexity about his future course; when he returned in July 1833, he appeared in Oxford as a man charged with a mission,—a mission to save the Church of England from the perils that encompassed her. His first reflections on the ways of Providence are contained in the letters to H. W. Wilberforce already quoted; but it is easy to discern the reasons that impelled him, as time went on, and the Movement gathered strength, to draw up an account of his Sicilian experience as a decisive episode in his life.

As the dates attached to the successive sections indicate, the narrative was begun on August 31st, 1834, and continued at intervals on December 28th, 1834, March 1st, 1835, September 6th, 1835, March 8th, 1840, and completed on March 25th, 1840. From the notes subsequently inserted it is evident that on occasion he returned to it and read it, wholly or in part, in 1842, 1855, 1874, and 1876. It is written on sheets, now loose, placed within a flexible mottled cover, with the date 1821 outside, which once contained a "Collection of Scripture passages", no doubt the "account of the Evangelical process of conversion in a series of Scripture texts", to which he refers in the Memoir. This he tore out and destroyed, but kept the narrative of his illness, which apparently had been written on unused pages in the same book. The first page of the autograph is, for some unexplained reason, missing, but, before disposing of it, he had transcribed it on the inside of the cover on July 24th, 1874. The label on the outside reads "Original Memorandum concerning my illness in 1833. Personal and most private. (written 1834-1840)."

Neville, as Newman noted on the first page, copied the original in March 1885; and it was this copy that he took to Anne Mozley on March 17th. She consulted a friend, almost certainly Dean Church, on the propriety of publishing it. He replied favourably. "He so plainly always looked on the fever in all its features," he wrote, "as a *crisis in his life*, partly judgment on past self-will, partly a sign of special electing and directing favour, that the prominence given to it is quite accounted for by those who knew him, and explains why all these strange pictures of fever are given." Fortified by his approval, she published the narrative; but on her own responsibility she omitted a number of passages, which she considered "too private for print or scrutiny of strange eyes". In this transcript these passages have been restored to the text in their proper places, as Newman himself passed them for publication, and expressly allowed the editor, whoever he might be, to exercise his discretion.

(Feb. 27. 1876. on the subject of this illness, see my letter to H. W. Wilberforce of August 4. 1833)[1]

MY ILLNESS IN SICILY.

August 31. 1834
(This page is a copy from the original of Aug. 31. 1834. The pages following this are the original itself.)

"I have wished for some time to write in this book an account of my illness in Sicily (in May 1833); for the remembrance is pleasant and profitable. I shall not be able to recollect every thing in due order—so my account may be confused, running to and fro.

"I seem to see, and I saw, a strange providence in it. At the time I was deeply impressed with a feeling that it was a judgment for profaning the Lord's Supper, in having cherished some resentment against the Provost for putting me out of the Tutorship; though this impression has now faded away. Again I felt it was a punishment for my wilfulness in going to Sicily by myself. What is here to be noticed is its remarkable bearing on my history, so to call it. I had been released from College business, and written a book which I felt was on the whole worth publishing. Suddenly I am led to go abroad, the work being still in MS. When out, I could not but feel that some thing of service was in store for me. I recollect writing to (John F.) Christie to this effect, that, nevertheless, if God willed me a private life, the happier for me; and I think I do feel this, O my God: so that, if Thou wilt give me retirement, Thou wilt give me what I shall rejoice and prefer to receive, except that I should be vexed to see *no one* else doing what I could in a measure do myself. Well, in an unlooked for way I come to Sicily, and the devil thinks his time is come. (This and all that follows is the *original autograph.* J H N. note July 24. 1874) I was given over into his hands. From that time every thing went wrong; I could almost fancy it was on that day I caught my fever—certainly I was weak & low from that time forward, & had so many little troubles to bear that I kept asking almost impatiently why God so fought against me. Towards the end of the next day I was quite knocked up, and laid down at Nicolosi on the bed with the feeling

[1] Printed above, p. 118. C.S.D.

that my reason perchance might fail me. Then followed my voyage
from Catania to Syracuse & back, and then to Adernò—where the
insects for the first time ceased to plague me, I having noticed feverish symptoms in me the foregoing day, (e.g. I could not eat at
Catania on April 30) & that night being almost choked with a feeling,
which at the time I attributed to having taken some ginger with my
supper. However I have got into the narrative here, without meaning
it. What I wanted first to speak of was the Providence & strange
meaning of it. I could almost think the devil saw I am to be a means
of usefulness, & tried to destroy me. The fever was most dangerous;
for a week my attendants gave me up, & people were dying of it on
all sides; yet all through I had a confident feeling *I should recover*.
I told my Servt so, & gave as a reason (even when semi-delirious &
engaged in giving him my friends' direction at home & so preparing
externally for death,) that "I thought God had some work for me"—
these I believe were exactly my words. And when, after the fever, I
was on the road to Palermo, so weak I could not walk by myself, I
sat on the bed in the morning May 26 or May 27 profusely weeping,
& only able to say that I could not help thinking God had something
for me to do at home. This I repeated to my servant to whom the
words were unintelligible of course. Now it certainly is remarkable
that a new & large sphere of action has opened upon me from the
very moment I returned. My book (Arians) indeed was not published
for some months; but long before (that), I was busy. Immediately
on my return I heard that Keble was going to preach an Assize
Sermon on the times—and it was preached on the very first Sunday
after my return—then it was printed. Close upon this, I suppose
within a fortnight of my return, I suggested to Palmer, Keble, &
Froude an association for Tracts. In August I wrote & printed four—
then followed the Address to the Archb^p—which with the Tracts
quite occupied me during the Mich: Term, in the course of which
(Nov. 5) my work was published. Then followed my Sermons
(published) in February (or March) of this (present) year. Then, in
Easter Term, the resistance of the Dissenters' Univ: Admission Bill,
in which I was much concerned. Lastly has happened this disturbance (Jubber) about the Marriage;[1] (& now I have just preached a
Visitation Sermon.) Besides this I have ever since I returned been a
frequent correspondence [i.e. correspondent] in the British Magazine

---

[1] Newman refused to perform the marriage of Miss Jubber, a Dissenter, who
had not been baptized. C.S.D.

—& altogether my name, which was not known out of Oxford circles before I went abroad, is now known pretty generally. My Sermons have sold very well. Now in all this there seems something remarkable & providential. O my God, keep me still from being the sport & victim of Satan. By Thy Mercies in Thy Son's Holy Table which I have this day partaken, be to me a Savior.

Now for the particulars of my illness. On Thursday May 2 I started from Adernò—the scene was most beautiful—hills thrown about on all sides, & covered with green corn, in all variety of shades, relieving [-ed] by the light (raw sienna) stone of the hills. The whole day the scene was like the Garden of Eden most exquisitely beautiful, though varying, sometimes with deep valleys on the side, & many trees, high hills with towns on the top as S. Filippo d'Argyro— Etna behind us, & Castro Juan [Giovanni] before in the distance. On the whole I suppose I went 42 miles that day on my mule—but with great pain. I set out walking, the mules coming after—& fell to tears thinking of dear Mary as I looked at the beautiful prospect. When I got to Reganbuto,[1] I was obliged to lie down for an hour or so. I cannot tell whether I thought myself ill or not. With much distress I proceeded, taking some wine at S. Filippo &, I believe, elsewhere; (I recollect with difficulty dismounting & crawling with my servant's help to a wine shop—& sitting on a stone.) till in the evening I got to Leonforte. In the course of the day I thought whether or not I sh^d go aside to see Castro G. wh was about four miles out of the way. I walked some little way, instead of on mule back, towards the close of the day. When I got to Leonforte, the inn wh is a fair one, was pre-occupied by some Sicilian Duke (an old man whom I fell in with at Reganbuto, led about by a consequential looking high domestic) and I was forced to wander about for a lodging for the night. I got one at a miserable place, tho' not (I believe) so bad as some I had slept in. It was a room of a second rate inn, opening into another room in which was a sick man. His illness, I believe, was in consequence of some accident. Yet it was not the first sick house I had been in—viz where I breakfasted at the Chestnut Trees—but that too was not a catching illness, as my servant protested both before & after—yet it struck me afterwards as strange. Here (at Leonforte) I lay, I believe without sleep—and next morning, when I attempted to get up, I fell back & was too ill to do so. (This to the best of my recollection.)

[1] Regalbuto. C.S.D.

Dec 28. 1834. I believe I must have been somewhat, (not light headed, but) scarcely myself, the day before on my journey—else surely my indisposition would have been forced upon my mind by my frequent stoppings and restings. I fancy I had but one wish, to *get on*—that my troubles at Syracuse had quite taken away my present enjoyment of what I saw—& that I looked on every thing but as the matter for future retrospective pleasure, which indeed was my original view in coming here. Well, after some time, the great Personage having gone from the other inn, I managed to dress and get down there, where I went to bed in what was considered a sumptuous, & certainly was a comfortable & gaily ornamented room. This was on Friday May 3. When I got to bed or before (I cannot recollect which, only there certainly was a change on going to bed—I think for the better—I think I fancied the warmth did me good.) (But I recollect too that the clothes on the bed seemed to oppress me.) I had some pain, I forget where—I believe in the bowels—yet somehow or other I seem to fancy my legs or my feet were in pain—but I suspect this *is* a fancy. I think it was today (not the next) that I began to think what I could take to do me good. I had some rhubarb & ginger pills with me, & I took half a one—(i.e. I know I broke one in half) next I thought & thought, till it struck me camomile would do me good (as being a tonic & stomachic. March 8 1840). I had seen some growing wild at Corfu, & remembering this, bade my servant inquire. There were no shops in the place, much less a chemist's—but it so happened that camomile *was* a familiar medicine with the common people, & each house had it—so he got some. At first he made me some tea of the leaves, which was very rough & I had some comparison for it, I believe at the time, but forget what. Next he made me some with the flowers wh I thought beautiful & was certainly most refreshing. I consider it was owing to this (under Providence) that I was enabled ultimately to proceed on my journey. I recollect thinking at last I had found out what was the matter with me, flatulency[1]—& the whole night I passed in that distressing way (a pain in my stomach) which I used often to do at home, before I went abroad. I told my servant so, & bade him feel my pulse—he said it was fever. I said, oh no—I knew myself better. As I lay in bed the first day many thoughts came over me. I felt God was fighting agst me—& felt at last I knew *why*—it was for self will. I felt I had been very self willed

---

[1] This word was later deleted, and those in the following line, in brackets, seem to have been meant to take its place. C.S.D.

—that the Froudes had been ag[st] my coming, so also (at Naples) the Wilberforces—perhaps the Neales & Andersons—I said to myself Why did no one speak out? say half a word? Why was I left now to interpret their meaning? Then I tried to fancy where the Froudes were, & how happy I should have been with them—in France, or perhaps in England. Yet I felt & kept saying to myself "I have not sinned against light." And at one time I had a most consoling overpowering thought of God's electing love, & seemed to feel I was His. But I believe all my feelings, painful & pleasant, were heightened by somewhat of delirium, tho' they still are from God in the way of Providence. Next day the self reproaching feelings increased. I seemed to see more & more my utter hollowness. I began to think of all my professed[1] principles, & felt they were mere intellectual deductions from one or two admitted truths. I compared myself with Keble, and felt that I was merely developing his, not my convictions. I know I had *very* clear thoughts about this then; &, I believe in the main true ones. Indeed this is how I look on myself; very much (as the illustration goes) as a pane of glass, which transmit[s] heat being cold itself. I have a vivid perception of the consequences of certain admitted principles, have a considerable intellectual capacity of drawing them out, have the refinement to admire them, & a rhetorical or histrionic power to represent them; and, having no great (i.e. no vivid) love of this world, whether riches, honors, or any thing else, and some firmness and natural dignity of character, take the profession of them upon me, as I might sing a tune which I liked—loving the Truth, but not possessing it—for I believe myself at heart to be nearly hollow—i.e. with little love, little self denial. I believe I have some faith, that is all—& as to my sins, they need my possessing no little amount of faith to set against them & gain their remission. By the bye, this statement will account for it how I can preach the Truth without thinking much of myself. Arnold in his letter to Grant about me, accuses me among others of identifying high excellence with certain peculiarities of my own—i.e. preaching myself. But to return. Still more serious thoughts came over me. I thought I had been very self willed about the Tutorship affair—and now I viewed my whole course as of one of presumption. It struck me that the 5th of May was just at hand, which was a memorable day, as being that on which (what we called) my Ultimatum was sent in to the Provost. On the 3rd anniversary I sh[d] be lying on a sick bed in a strange country.

---

[1] Newman first wrote "apparent". C.S.D.

Then I bitterly blamed myself, as disrespectful & insulting to the Provost, my superior. So keenly did I feel this, that I dictated to myself (as it were) a letter which I was to send to (I fixed upon) James (the late fellow), on my getting to England, stating in strong terms my self reproach; & I was not to preach at St Mary's or any where for a length of time as a penitent unworthy to show himself. I recollected too that my last act on leaving Oxford was to preach a University Sermon on the character of Saul agst self will. Yet still I said to myself "I have not sinned against light." (Now, or at Palermo I thought strongly & retained the thought that my illness came upon me as having come to the Sacr^t in malice and resentment.) I cannot describe my full misery on this Saturday May 4. My door only *locked* (i.e. no mere clasp, but with a key)—my servant was a good deal away, & thus locked me in. My feelings were acute & nervous in a high degree. I forced myself up to keep my mind from thinking of itself, & from leading to that distressing bodily affection which in such cases follow[s] in my case;[1]—I kept counting the number of stars, flowers &c. in the pattern of the paper on the walls to occupy me. Just at this time, (before or after) the miserable whine of Sicilian beggars was heard outside my door, the staircase communicating with the street. Who can describe the wretchedness of that low feeble monotonous cry, which went on I cannot say how long, (I unable to do any thing) till my servant released me after a time. Now in my lowest distress I was relieved, first by some music from some travelling performers who were passing on (I believe) to Palermo. (N.B. I had seen a *bagpipe* to my surprise between Catania & Paternò.) The music was (I believe) such as harp & clarionet—And now I think it was that my servant proposed a walk. He had talked much of some handsome fountain at the end of the Town—but I put off seeing it, I believe now—& we walked out on the St Filippo road, & then turned up a lane on the south (i.e. the left hand) There I sat down on a bank upon (under?) a fig tree—the leaves I believe were out—& wondered how it s^{hd} be that I was there—it was the evening. I forget what else I thought of or saw. (I think this walk was on this day; yet some how have some times a notion that the ride on the Mule wh is to come presently was today.) My servant wished to get me on (I believe) naturally enough—(Febr 6. 1843. We had a speculation about having a *litter* made, on which I might be carried to Palermo.)—he thought me dying; & told me a story about a sick

---

[1] These three words were added later. C.S.D.

officer he had attended on in Spain, who left him all his baggage & then got well. I did not see the drift of the story at the time. I gave him a direction to write to, if I died (Froude's) but I said "I do not think I shall"—"I have not sinned against light" or "God has still work for me to do." I think the latter.

Sunday March 1. 1835. (continuation): During the Friday May 3 & Saturday May 4, I had eaten nothing or very little. I could not swallow. On the Sunday May 5, I was eating every half hour all through the day. A fancy came upon me, either the Saturday or Sunday night, that I was quite well, & only wanted food—& I quite laughed with myself through the night at the news I sh^d have to tell in England, how ridiculous & shameful, that I had missed seeing Girgenti from such a neglect. One of these nights, Saturday (I think) I was awake all night—(My servant slept in the room—I forget when first—) I recollect asking him, whether he said prayers—he said, yes —I had had a plan of reading to him on Sundays—& had hoped to do it on the Sunday I supposed I sh^d pass at Girgenti. I recollect (on the Saturday) the dreamy view I had of the room, with the wretched lamp. I dreamed of the buildings of Catania. Well, on the Sunday I kept eating all day. I do not think I knew it was Sunday. However, in the evening, (if not on the Saturday) we went out on our mules, towards Palermo for a ride—It was very fine scenery. As we came back there was a Sicilian family of the upper rank, with servants &c. lounging outside the Town, near the steep parapet of the cliff. I recollect asking some questions about them, and somehow so strongly connecting them with the notion of its being Sunday, that I certainly thought it was Sunday, whether it was or no. That evening I determined to set off next Morning for Palermo. I had a strange feeling on my mind that God meets those who go on in *His way*, who remember Him in His way, in the paths of the Lord, that I must put myself in His path, His way, that I must do my part & that He met those who rejoiced & worked righteousness & remembered Him in His ways—some texts of this kind kept haunting me, & I determined to set out by daybreak.

Before setting out (on Monday the 6th) I drank some toast & water which my servant made—We set off almost before Sunrise— Scarcely had we got half a mile, when I felt very *weak* (I believe) and said I must have something to eat. I said I must have some chicken (on wh I had lived the days before . My serv^t remonstrated—the things were just packed up. I was peremptory & he was obliged to undo the baggage & get it. I forget what was on my mind. As I went on again, a great thirst came on. I began sucking some most delicious oranges which were on the way side—very large & fine. I kept thinking what I sh^d be able to say to my Mother & Sisters about the fineness of these oranges—not sweet or tart, but a fine aromatic bitter. (I believe they *were* very fine. My serv^t said so; they were very large.) It was not thirst I felt, but a convulsive feeling of suffocation almost in my throat—very distressing—at last I took to eating the leaves of the trees, as I went on. I said I must have *water*. I imputed it to the toast & water, wh I was sure was bad. The bread had been harsh for some time(?) and I said it was very *rough* bread. This I think was the notion which the feeling in my throat gave me. Several miles past & no water—no house. At last a cottage to the right—but no means of getting any thing. We were going through a level (high, I suppose) with Castro Giovanni before us. I recollect (then, I believe) debating whether it was worth while to turn aside thither—it was 4 miles out of the way. We saw the outline of the buildings—and a temple or castle. My serv^t was told by the muleteer(?) it was Roman work, I think. There were few trees, or beauty of scenery *near* the road. Caltacibetta on the other side (the right) (I forget whether I saw it now, or in the afternoon, in my further progress.) At length I was taken some little way to the right to a hut, where I got some water, & rested.

This was seven miles from Leonforte. It might be between 6 and 7 o'clock? I set off before 5, and we went about 3 or 4 miles an hour. I *think* it was a tent. There was no floor, only the ground. Under Etna, where we lost ourselves, I noticed high biack cones, like collections of hop-poles; and I think shepherds were in them—we heard dogs. This might be something of the same kind. My blue travelling cloke was spread under me—and I lay down at length. How long I lay, hours probably, I do not know. (In the course of the day I recollect a man came in to the good people there, who were of different ages & sexes, & (as far as I understood him) asked for money to pray souls out of purgatory. How in my then state I could understand his Sicilian, I do not know. I recollect asking my Servt whether a bad man had not come in; & he said, no, a very good man.) As I lay, when I opened my eyes, I saw the men & women, young & old, hanging over me, with great interest—& apparently much rejoiced to see me a little better. At length, as I lay, I felt fingers at my pulse.

Sunday September 6. 1835. It was a medical man, who was visiting persons ill of the fever (I believe) near, & some one had told him there was a sick person a foreigner close by, & he came. I forget what he said—I was almost stupid or at times, I think. He recommended to give me a drink of *Camomile*, lemon, & sugar, every now & then & to get on to Castro Giovanni. It was most refreshing. After a time, I do not know the time of day, some one said an English party was passing. It turned out to be a diligence on the way to Palermo. A thought came across me, that, if I were dying, I might let my friends know the last of me, & I insisted on speaking to them. My servant remonstrated. I was very earnest—commanded him—& could almost fancy rose, or opened my travelling bag, or bade him carry it, or something or other. At length I got my way, & one of the party made his appearance. They were not English, but this man, a German, could speak English. I gave him the letter of introduction I had to Mr Thomas (?) at Palermo, and begged him to say I forget what— & I thanked him most fervently, & felt much relieved—tho' it was not much which I did or he promised. After a time, I supposed towards the evening, I managed to be put sideways & held on the mule, & so set off for Castro G. (Giovanni or Juan). The parting with the poor people in the tent was very affectionate. I asked their name & said I would mention it in England. (I have forgotten it.) My servant burst into tears, tho' I shd not have thought him especially tender. It was (I suppose) 4 miles to Castro G, & up hill—very steep. When we got there, we could get no place; nothing appeared possible but some damp & dark place, which my servant wd not consent to. Some friars (in brown?) passed by, & I intreated my servant to ask them to take me in to a monastery. At length he got me a very nice comfortable room in a house of a man of some property who let lodgings.

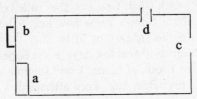

(a) the bed. (b) the window looking out into the street. (c) the door leading down a stone staircase out a doors (?). d a double (?) door leading to another room. I was put to bed—the medical man (who had felt my pulse & was (they say) the chief in the place was out of the way) & they brought in another, who was said to be inferior, but I made much of him. He had moustaches & a harsh voice.

Now I do not know how to relate what comes; I shall recollect so irregularly and medical & other circumstances so mingle together, & there were some things I do not like to put on paper. First they determined to take blood from me. I preferred my instep to my arm, thinking they might not be skilful. They struck once and (I think) again, & no blood came—I thought myself going. (I cannot quite tell whether or not I am colouring this—so let me say once for all that any descriptions of my feelings should be attended all through with "I believe"—for I have half recollections, glimpses which vanish when I look right at them.) My servant was so distressed, he fainted away—at last the blood came. I had three incisions. It was like cupping. They took away 4 ounces, little enough. Mr Babington, to whom I told it afterwards, said it could do me no good, but they said they were afraid to do more, I seemed so weak. I cannot tell whether I was myself the next morning. I have vague recollections of "English Salts" (Epsom) being given me more than once. This was given the second day (?) with an injunction to dose me with cold lemonade. My servant was for warm tea. I insisted on the lemonade, & made a formal complaint to the doctor that he (Gennaro) changed the prescriptions. (I w^d not see him for a while). I corresponded with him the doctor in Latin—I have the papers still with me. He, I suppose, was no deep Latin scholar, & pretended my Latin was nonsense—but it is very good, particularly considering I was so ill. I was light headed these days, & barely recollect things. I was not still a moment, my serv^t said afterwards & was flushed in the face. They called it a gastric fever—it was very destructive there. Persons were dying daily —& at Girgenti & Drepani (?) as I learned afterwards. It was attended commonly with what, I believe, they called cholera but not in my case. I am afraid I don't know how long it lasted.[1] Perhaps from Catania or Adernò (May 1 or 2) to May 11?—I have some notion the other complaint[2] was five days. I was in pain. The doctor asked what medicine I took at home, I said sulphur, & he gave me some of mine from my carpet bag. Then afterwards I had castor oil

---

[1] Newman originally wrote: "It was attended commonly with diarrhoea, I believe (and they called it the cholera) but not in my case. I had an obstinate costiveness (with pains in my bowels continually, but I forget *when* exactly). I was much swelled up, and I had retention of urine. I am afraid to say how long my costiveness lasted." C.S.D.

[2] Originally "the retention". C.S.D.

every two hours. (I fancy I thought I was taking Dover's Powders for which I asked.) They gave me over, for a week—but my serv^t said he thought I sh^d get well from the avidity with wh I always took my medicine. The fever came to a crisis in 7, 9, or 11 days—mine (I believe) in eleven.—I doubt whether all these measures relieved me. Certain others were adopted—And these did relieve me of the retention. I had some miserable nights—the dreamy confusion of delirium—sitting on a staircase, wanting something, or with some difficulty—very wretched—& something about my Mother & Sisters. —How I dreaded the long nights—lying without sleep, as it seemed, all through the darkness. I wanted to get some one to sit up with me but did not succeed. Indeed it was with difficulty I got nurses—the principal one said to Gennaro (as he told me afterwards—July 23 1855) & he to her, "well we must go through it, and if we catch the fever, we catch it—" Gennaro slept in the room—I got the muleteer to sit up with me—the heat too was miserable. I suspect I ought to have been kept quite cool. I was reduced to the lowest conceivable weakness, not being able to raise my hand to my head, nor to swallow. I had maccaroni &c—but nothing agreed—biscuits—some I liked. (When I first got there, there were some camomile flowers on the table near the bed, which were most refreshing and I begged they might not be removed.) I had continually most oppressive almost faintings. I suspect the heat had much to do with it. They had nothing but vinegar to relieve me, which the muleteer with his great bullet tips of fingers (so I recollect I called them, while he administered it with them) applied to my nose in the middle of night. When I got better, I used to watch for the day—and when light appeared thro' the shutter, for there was no blind or curtain, I used to soliloquize "O sweet light, God's best gift &c."—By the bye I discharged the muleteer after some days with a quarrel, (he going before the magistrates) between him & me by Gennaro about wages, depending on working & stopping days; in which I got somewhat the worse, as might be expected.—My continual faintness was most distressing by day afterward. A continual snuffing up in vinegar was the only thing which kept me up. I wanted cold water to my head, but this was long afterwards—the D^r and Gennaro w^d not let me—I managed to outwit Gennaro by pretending to dab my temples with vinegar—and so held a cold cloth to them. He used to bathe with vinegar temples, ears, nose, face, & neck (?)—A fair was held in Castro G. after a few days—and

March 8. 1840 (Littlemore)—I think I was much annoyed with the great noise which this fair caused—it was under my window. It was a great fair, I believe—and there were, to the best of my recollection, lodgers in consequence or guests, in the next room (through the folding doors)—three, according to my impression, who talked. What distressed me most was the daily mass bell (I suppose it was in a neighbouring Church.) I used quite to writhe about, and put my head under the bed clothes—and asked Gennaro if it could not be stopped. He answered with a laugh of surprise that it should not annoy me, & of encouragement, as if making light of it. I have since thought they might suppose it was a heretic's misery under a holy bell. Gennaro ruled me most entirely—I was very submissive, & he authoritative. The master of the house was very civil—he heard I liked music, & he got some performers to play to me in the next room. It was very beautiful, but too much for me. What strange dreamy reminiscences of feeling does this attempt at relation raise! So the music was left off. When I was getting well, all sorts of maladies came upon me. One which came, or which I fancied, was determination of blood to the head. I had a notion it was mounting, mounting, that it had got as high as my ears &c. I got an idea that sleep would bring it on; that I ought not to sleep, & I did all I could to resist it.—A cough came on—a wearisome continual cough, for some hours every day in the evening—I spit a good deal—at length they would not let me—saying it would hurt me. They made an issue in my arm for it—which took it off, I think. Even at Lyons I had profuse cold sweats at night.—I got a notion I had got inflammation of the chest—and, recollecting that in 1829 at Brighton Dr Price had said he would not leave my mother till she could draw a deep breath without pain, I was ever drawing deep breaths, and felt pain at the bottom of my chest.[1] I almost could fancy my servant said it was indigestion.—I had piles too, and was obliged to have leeches & burning hot steam—& then a preparation of herbs very cooling. I was given the prescription, but lost it. Mallows, I think, was one ingredient.[2]

When the doctor came in the early part of my illness, he used to

---

[1] The rest of this paragraph was crossed out by Newman. C.S.D.

[2] March 14, 1885. Saturday. The Cardinal told me just now that in travelling to Lyons his feet became most terribly swollen, and in consequence two of his fellow passengers when they got to Lyons lifted him out of the diligence and then placing their hands under his shoulders supported him till he got to the Inn which was some little distance off. [Note by W. P. Neville. C.S.D.]

shake his head on feeling my pulse, and say "A—ah, A—ah, debil, debil"—He gave me syrup for my cough. I was miserably sore from lying on my side, and had something soft, I forget what, put under my hips. At a certain time, I began to itch very much. Since I have thought that it was the return of insects to feed on me. I had remarked they did not touch me the miserable night I passed at Adernò; and I suspect that during the whole interval, i.e. of my illness they kept clear of me. After the crisis my lips peeled, and (I think) my hands, which (I think) were quite yellow. And (I think) I kept picking something about my nose, but cannot tell what. When I got home, my hair all came off, and I was forced to put on a wig—my hair being darker, when it came again—And I observed a curious effect about my nails—there was a darker colour which gradually rose, or as it were grew up, all across them till it possessed the whole nail—as if the old nail had been loosened, or otherwise affected.

When I was getting better, I walked about the room to gain my feet—first leaning on my servant & a stick—then going alone with a stick. But even when I was come to Palermo, I could not get out of the carriage by myself—and for some time walked with a stick; improving rapidly, so that one of the servants about the inn, said, I think in English, "Come, Sir, cheer up: you will get quite young again."—After walking about the room a little of a day, my servant got me to walk a little in the next room, through the folding doors, partly to amuse me, for it was at the time I thought I had inflammation of the chest. And at length he got me with great difficulty down stairs, (down the stone steps) and took me out and seated me on a chair, I think under my windows—looking out across somewhat of a space, so I seem to think, to a pillar which he said was Roman. As I sat in the chair, I could not command myself, but cried profusely, the sight of the sky was so piercing. A number of poor collected about me to see me; I had made them a present already at my servant's suggestion as a thank offering. The chief Lady Bountiful of the place had died of my fever during my illness. I heard of her state from day to day, and at last of her death. The bell at length went for her funeral. One day I was able with Gennaro's help to get as far as the Cathedral. I suppose it could not be far. I walked up the aisles. It was Norman to the best of my recollection. I remembered nothing but thick heavy pillars with square capitals. The day before setting off for Palermo, for which I was very impatient, we went out a little way in a close carriage.

When I was getting well, and lay in bed thinking, the events of my life came thick before me, I believe—but I could not recollect the state of things. E.g. I could not tell if Dr Nicholas was alive or not. I had all sorts of schemes how I was to make money, to pay my extra expences from my illness. And I thought a good deal of my book on the Arians, and how it might be improved—& re-arranged parts— and I almost think I eventually adopted some of these suggestions. I think it was on one of the early days of my illness,—no it rather must be when I was getting well, for I fancy it connected with the rush of blood to my head, that I called for pencil & paper, and, as it were, composed the verses (since in the L.A.) beginning "Mid Balak's magic fires &c". When I got to Palermo (I think it was) I found to my surprise that I had already composed them at Messina. The immediate cause of the rush of blood to my head was receiving a letter from home—it came up from Palermo—& I think was from five correspondents—My Mother & sisters, (J.F.) Christie, & another. I pored over it, small writing, without my glasses with great avidity, hoping to see the news of the Oriel election—but it was not there. All I recollect of the letter was an account of Christie being robbed of his portmanteau as he was going to Cambridge to examine Ridley's papers or books. It seemed like a strange dream—I did not know whether to believe it or not. It seemed like a dream or absurdity how I ever should get to England again. As to the Oriel election, I first saw the news of it in a Galignani at Palermo —and on seeing that Rogers was elected, I kissed the paper rapturously.

March 25. 1840. (Littlemore) I think I have forgotten to say that I had continual pain in the early part of my illness, in a way w^h was very uncommon with me.[1] Also I should mention some fantastic dreams I had when I was getting well, which I barely recollect now. One, that I was introduced to the Russian Court, and that I began talking to the Empress—and then I bethought myself "How ill-manneredly! in the case of great people, one should not speak, but be spoken to." Another, that one army from Rheggio was crossing the Strait to another at Messina, & taking a tower—I was in the one or the other, French or English I think. Another was of an army coming up heights to Castro Giovanni. These dreams about armies

[1] Newman originally wrote: "... in my bowels in the early part of my illness, in a way which was very uncommon ..." C.S.D.

might be partly suggested by a visit of three magistrates to me who talked about the quartering of the English at Castro Giuan. The occasion of their coming was a quarrel I had with my doctor. When I found myself getting well, I was greatly impressed with his skill and very grateful. I wished to make him presents over and above his pay. I gave him or the Master of the House a pocket compass, thermometer, a Virgil, and I *think* some other Latin Book, and perhaps some other things. The doctor took a fancy to something which Gennaro thought was too expensive to part with, or, as I fancy from the event, wished the Master of the House to have. He took it away with him, and my Servant took the matter before the Magistracy, who accordingly, partly perhaps from curiosity, payed me a visit. I did not understand a word they said, though Gennaro interpreted some things. By the bye, on my falling ill, *all* my knowledge of Italian, such as it was, went—while Latin remained. One of the three was an ecclesiastical—& I do not know why, but I stared at him in a strange way, till my servant, thinking it would hurt me, forbade me briskly. I got my property back, and then Gennaro wished me to give it to Aloysio the Master of the House, but I would not. I was visited at the beginning of my illness by a priest, and told my servant, when half light headed, I wished to dispute with him. I was also visited by the brother of my Landlord, who asked & obtained of me a yellow wash leather, such as they rub plate with. There was some one else in the early part of my illness, whom, in my Latin with the D^r, I call probus homo. He might have been the husband of my inferior nurse.

And now I have said every thing pretty nearly that I can recollect of this illness. I set off from Castro Juan May 25 Whitsun eve. I mistook by the bye, and calculated it a week wrong, for I fancied at Palermo next Sunday after to be Whitsunday whereas it was Trinity. On the Sunday before I was well enough to know it was Jemima's birthday, and fancy that I revived about the 17th, but the crisis must have been earlier. By the bye, I should have acknowledged the great honesty of all my attendants. Gennaro had charge of clothes, money, every thing. I lost nothing. A large sum of money came to me from Palermo in dollars safe. He paid nothing without asking my leave; and though he had coveted all my effects, if I died, yet even then he wished them formally bequeathed to him—and, as it was, when I got to England, I had lost after all only one common (3/6) shirt in all, &

something else, perhaps a pair of stockings or a towel. My watch, &
indeed every thing I had was at the mercy of a number of persons. No
English Consul was nearer, I suppose, than Girgenti. To proceed—
I set off the 25th and had great compunction about travelling through
the Sunday (next day) but at last overcame it. I travelled through an
exquisitely beautiful country, part of it, however, by night. My joy,
however, was too great for me at first. I never saw such a country.
The Spring in its greatest luxuriance. All sorts of strange trees—very
steep and high hills over which the road went; mountains in the
distance—a profusion of aloes along the road—Such bright colouring
—all in tune too with my reviving life. I had a great appetite and was
always coaxing (as I may call it) Gennaro for cakes. Here by the bye
I should record my feelings of returning appetite after the illness. As
I got better at Castro G. he used to give me an egg baked in wood
ashes and some tea for breakfast & cakes. How I longed for it!
and when I took the tea, I could not help crying out from delight.
I used to say "It is life from the dead!" I never had such feelings. All
through my illness I had depended on Gennaro so much I could not
bear him from the room five minutes. I used always to be crying out
for I don't know how long together "Gen-na-roooooo." They fed me
on chicken broth. I did not take beef broth or beef tea till I got to
Palermo—& that gave me something of the ecstatic feelings which
the tea had given. I got to Palermo the third day, May 27, having
(I think) on the 26th rested at a sort of inn where the landlord came
& looked at me, sitting opposite to me, for some time till he frightened me. I was very weak. When I got up the morning of the 26th or
27th, I sat some time by the bed side, crying bitterly and all I could
say was, that I was sure God had some work for me to do in England.
This indeed I had said to Dr Wiseman at Rome, but, though sincerely said, they were not deeply pointedly? said, but in answer to
the question how long we stayed there, I said that we had work at
home. I wish I could see my letter to Christie; I must ask him for it.
But now my feeling was intense and overpowering—and my servant
of course could not understand me at all. But to proceed to Palermo
—I was lodged at Page's Hotel—the hostess Ann Page, who had
married, I think, an Italian or Sicilian. She was very eager to please
me and begged me to recommend her house at home. She was a
motherly sort of person—& made me sago and tapioca &c. The beef
was unpleasant. They do not drain out the blood. I had no mutton,
I think—I think there is none. The merchants (wine merchants) were

very civil. At first they thought me dying—I was so weak & could not speak except by drawling. I used to go on the water every day and that set me up. I revived day by day wonderfully. I was there nearly three weeks, till June 13. It was a very trying time; yet perhaps I should not have been strong enough before that time—to go by myself! I composed a Lyra a day, I think, from the day I got there. Hay making was going on while I was there. I went up to the Monte Pellegrino; I went to the Hydra cave—&c. but I made very little real use of my time, expecting to sail almost daily, & homesick & much disappointed at the delay. I went a great deal into the public gardens called (I think) the Villa Reale, and along the beach outside them, sitting in the seats. However, they told me I must not go out in the middle of the day, though in the shade. Sometimes there were sciròcs and very trying; the wind like a furnace. And the clouds were blue, the tawny mountains looking wondrous. I dined, beside at the merchants, at Mr Thomas's, a merchant living 2 or 3 miles out on the Monreale Road—a married man. The day before we sailed, I met there Mr Page of Ch Ch.[1] I called on the German who had passed & come out to me when I lay in the cabin on the road under Castro Juan. My conveyance in which I had come to Palermo came from Palermo. All this time I knew my friends in England were in a state of anxiety, but had no means of communicating with them. My "private Diary" for 1833 gives many daily details through—

The thought keeps pressing on me, while I write this, what am I writing it for? For myself, I may look at it once or twice in my whole life, and what sympathy is there in *my* looking at it? Whom have I, whom can I have, who would take interest in it? I was going to say, I only have found one who even took that sort of affectionate interest in me as to be pleased with such details—and that is H. Wilberforce and what shall I ever see of him? This is the sort of interest which a wife takes and none but she—it is a woman's interest—and that interest, so be it, shall never be taken in me. Never, so be it, will I be other than God has found me. All my habits for years, my tendencies, are towards celibacy. I could not take that interest in this world which marriage requires. I am too disgusted with this world— And, above all, call it what one will, I have a repugnance to a clergyman's marrying. I do not say it is not lawful—I cannot deny the right—but, whether a prejudice or not, it shocks me. And therefore I willingly give up the possession of that sympathy, which I feel is not,

[1] Christ Church, Oxford. C.S.D.

cannot be, granted to me. Yet, not the less do I feel the need of it. Who will care to be told such details as I have put down above? Shall I ever have in my old age spiritual children who will take an interest such as a wife does? How time is getting on! I seem to be reconciling myself to the idea of being old. It seems but yesterday that the Whigs came into power—another such tomorrow will make me almost fifty, an elderly man. What a dream is life. I used to regret festival days going quick. They are come and they are gone; but, so it is, time is nothing except as the seed of eternity.

I left Gennaro at Palermo; he was to go back to Naples to his wife and family. Since, I have heard he is in Ld Carrington's family in England. He was humanly speaking the preserver of my life, I think. What I should have done without him, I cannot think. He nursed me as a child. An English servant never could do what he did. He had once been deranged; and was easily overset by liquor. I found him so at Palermo, though he denied it. He once or twice left me a whole day, or a long while. When we parted I fancy I gave him about £10 over and above his wages and a character written (?) Before I had given him any thing, he began to spell for something, but what he thought of was an old blue cloke of mine which I had since 1823; a little thing for him to set his services at—at the same time a great thing for me to give for I had an affection for it. It had nursed me all through my illness; had even been put on my bed, put on me when I rose to have my bed made &c. I had nearly lost it at Corfu—it was stolen by a soldier but recovered. I have it still. I have brought it up here to Littlemore, & on some cold nights I have had it on my bed. I have so few things to sympathize with me, that I take to clokes.

March 25. 1840

(April 24. 1874. I wonder I have not mentioned how I simply lost my memory as to *how* I came to be ill and in bed—and how strangely by little and little first one fact came back to me, then another, till at length I realized my journey and my illness in continuity.)

V

THE JOURNALS

GENERAL INTRODUCTION

In a sermon preached early in 1835 on the subject of "Self-Contemplation"[1] John Henry Newman, then Fellow of Oriel College, and Vicar of St Mary the Virgin, Oxford, drew a sharp distinction between "two views of doctrine": "the ancient and universal teaching of the Church, which insists on the Objects and fruits of faith, and considers the spiritual character of that faith itself sufficiently secured, if these are as they should be; and the method, now in esteem, of attempting instead to secure directly and primarily that 'mind of the spirit', which may savingly receive the truths, and fulfil the obedience of the Gospel."[2] An Irish peer, Lord Lifford, who read the sermon when it was published, submitted to him certain questions it had raised in his mind, and Newman replied at great length.

Now, I do not at all deny that the modern system does insist on the fruits and Objects of faith, which you clearly show it does by your quotations from Mr Scott;[3] but I say it does not *directly* or *primarily*. If an awakened sinner asked an ancient believer what he must do to be saved, he would answer (I consider): 'Look to the Word Incarnate, look to the Holy Trinity, look to the Sacraments, God's instruments, and break off your sins, do good whereas you have done evil.' But I conceive one of the modern school, without denying this, would for the most part drop it, and say instead: 'Your heart must be changed; till you have faith, you have nothing; you must have a spiritual apprehension of Christ; you must utterly renounce yourself and your merits and throw yourself at the foot of the Cross, etc.' Now the question is not whether this is not *true*; (I have said expressly; 'That such a spiritual temper is indispensable, is agreed on all hands'.)[4] but whether it is *the way to make a man a Christian*. I would maintain that if we take care of the Objects and works of faith, faith will almost take care of itself. This modern view says: 'Take care of the state of heart, and the Objects and works of faith will almost take care of themselves.' But I have been stating this modern view as judicious, pious, and moderate men put it forward abstractedly. But the mass of men develop it, and then what is in itself (as I conceive) a mistake, becomes a mischief. One says: '*Examine* yourselves whether you have this spiritual temper. Without it you are nothing; though you abound in good works, are orthodox in creed, you are but a moral man. Do you love Christ? Do you hate sin? Do you feel that he is the pearl of great price?' And so on. Now such questions are either mere generalisms meaning nothing at all, or they lead to a direct contemplation of our feelings as *the* means, *the* evidence of justification.[5]

The date of this letter should be noted—September 12th, 1837. A little more than three months before, on Tuesday, June 1st, in a concluding lecture of a series on the doctrine of justification, delivered in Adam de Brome's Chapel in St Mary's, Oxford, Newman had discussed this precise subject *ex professo* with considerable fulness, viz., the system of doctrine, in which "faith or spiritual-mindedness is contemplated and rested on as the end of religion instead of Christ"; in which "stress is laid rather on the believing than on the Object of belief, on the comfort and persuasiveness of the doctrine rather than on the doctrine itself"; and which thus makes religion "to consist in contemplating ourselves instead of Christ; not simply in looking to Christ, but in ascertaining that we look to Christ, not in His Divinity and Atonement, but in our conversion and our faith in those truths."[6] The results of such a system must be given in Newman's own words, which cannot be abridged without loss:

[1] *Parochial and Plain Sermons*, vol. ii, xv. [2] Op. cit., pp. 165-6.
[3] Cf. *Apologia*, p. 5. [4] *Parochial and Plain Sermons*, vol. ii, p. 166.
[5] Draft of unpublished letter. [6] *Lectures on Justification*, pp. 324-5.

Poor miserable captives, to whom such doctrine is preached as the Gospel! What! is *this* the liberty wherewith Christ has made us free, and wherein we stand, the home of our own thoughts, the prison of our own sensations, the province of self, a monotonous confession of what we are by nature, not what Christ is in us, and a resting at best not on His love towards us, but in our faith towards Him! This is nothing but a specious idolatry; a man thus minded does not simply think of God when he prays to Him, but is observing whether he feels properly or not; does not believe and obey, but considers it enough to be conscious that he is what he calls warm and spiritual; does not consider the grace of the Blessed Eucharist, the Body and Blood of his Saviour Jesus Christ, except—O shameful and fearful error!—except as a quality of his own mind.[1]

The system which he was here attempting to describe, was known as Evangelicalism, not however in its earliest phases, but at the stage of development, which it had reached in the second and third decades of the century. Its adherents were what might now be called spiritual introverts. In his eyes their most glaring fault was their subjectivism; and this was becoming more and more pronounced among them. He feared that, if the thought of self was allowed to occupy the focus of the spiritual life, the great dogmas of the faith would fade into the margin, and ultimately vanish altogether. Of this tendency, which would, unless checked, attain, though by a different path, the same goal as the more or less contemporary liberalism, of which he was the avowed opponent, he saw abundant signs in the writings of the Evangelicals. His cherished "principle of dogma" was in danger, and with it revealed religion, since "religion cannot but be dogmatic".[2] In an essay entitled "Victorian History", Mr G. M. Young says of the passage in the *Lectures on Justification*, from which the above quotation is taken, that "every word deserves to be weighed by anyone who would understand the malady of early-Victorian society, introspection with a circle of experience artificially closed."[3] The revolutionary spirit engendered by the movement for reform threatened, or was thought to threaten, the existence of the Church of England; and the Evangelicals, instead of taking their stand with the Tractarians in a counter-movement, yielded before the storm and found consolation in a non-institutional religion of the spirit.

It has been asserted, first by Thomas Mozley, and the assertion has been repeated time and again, that Newman was brought up under Evangelical influences in an Evangelical home. Nothing could be further from the truth. His parents certainly belonged to the Church of England; they were baptized, married, and buried in it; but just as certainly they did not adhere to any party in it. Their religion was "the national religion of England", which he has described in the *Grammar of Assent*[4] under the appellation of "Bible Religion"; and dogmatically that meant no more than the acceptance of the Church Catechism interpreted according to the whim of the individual. Evangelicalism was simply a phase through which he passed in the course of his development, due to the influence exerted on him by an Evangelical master, Walter Mayers, at Ealing School; and it lasted for no more than six years, from the autumn of 1816, when he was converted, until the Easter of 1822, when his success at Oriel introduced him into the "noetic" circle of the Common Room. That moment marked, imperceptibly at first, the opening of another phase, which culminated, after a slight deviation in the direction of the "liberalism of the day", in his reception into the Catholic Church on October 9th, 1845.

It does not fall within our scope here to estimate what permanent effects his

---

[1] *Lectures on Justification*, p. 330.   [2] *Discussions and Arguments*, p. 134.
[3] *Selected Modern English Essays*, Second Series, The World's Classics, p. 269.
[4] pp. 56-8.

Evangelical phase had upon him. The chief, of course, was the realization of himself and his Creator as the "two only absolute and luminously self-evident beings"[1] in the universe; and then the knowledge of certain "great and burning truths" of Revelation, impressed upon his mind by his early teachers, which reached their full flowering under the influence of Catholicism.[2] But our interest here is psychological rather than doctrinal, in the effects upon his character rather than upon his beliefs; and here we may allow that his Evangelicalism did in fact intensify in him a certain natural tendency to introspection. The boy "full of thought", as his sister Harriett pictured him in her little book, *Family Adventures*, grew into the introspective youth, isolated by his conversion from the world of things and the world of men, and driven in upon himself. Bremond is surely justified in insisting upon his *autocentrisme*, and in describing him as *le plus autobiographique des hommes*.[3] As early as 1833 the great Dr Arnold accused him of "identifying high excellence with certain peculiarities" of his own, i.e., of preaching himself; but it is not clear whether he admitted the truth of the impeachment or not.[4] His own maxim, "egotism is true modesty",[5] dominates all his writings, which are intensely personal and revelatory. His father detected in him this tendency to concentration upon self, and warned him of the danger of yielding to it, just before he attained the age of twenty-one. They had attended together a service at Kentish Town Chapel on January 6th, 1822, and the father took the opportunity to open his mind to the son. "You are encouraging," he said, "a nervous and morbid sensibility and irritability of mind, which may be very serious. I know what it is myself perfectly well. I know it is a disease of mind. Religion, when carried too far, induces a softness of mind. ... Take care, I repeat. You are on dangerous ground."[6] The circumstances of his life, however, neutralized this sensible piece of advice, and reinforced his natural disposition. In a mood of depression after his mother's death in 1836 he indulged in a ferment of self-examination, and his conclusions about himself are revealing. "God intended me," he wrote to his younger sister, Jemima, "to be lonely; He has so framed my mind that I am in a great measure beyond the sympathies of other people and thrown upon Himself"; and to his elder, Harriett, with reference to his early years at Oriel before the advent of R. H. Froude, "Ever since that time I have learnt to throw myself on myself."[7]

It is thus that we may best account for the fact that from quite early in life he developed into a confirmed hoarder of books, papers, letters, and other odds and ends, every kind of article that had a personal bearing. As material for biography, such things may be suspect. But can it seriously be maintained that one so young would have thought that he would have any claim upon the memory of posterity? No, he treasured these possessions, just because they formed, as it were, an extension of his personality, and from time to time he jotted down notes on them to explain their significance. After 1850 there begin to occur in his letters at various successive dates allusions to the fact that he was engaged upon the burdensome task of sorting and arranging his papers; and gradually there grew up in his mind an anticipation that he would eventually fall victim to a biographer whether friendly or hostile. The ideal biography in his opinion would consist of a collection of documents and letters linked together by a brief connecting narrative. He

---

[1] *Apologia*, p. 4, cf. p. 195.
[2] Letter of Feb. 26th, 1887, in Ward, *Newman*, vol. ii, p. 526.
[3] *Newman*, pp. 42, xvi.
[4] *Letters and Correspondence of J. H. Newman*, vol. i, p. 417.
[5] *Grammar of Assent*, p. 384.
[6] *Letters and Correspondence*, vol. i, p. 126. (cf. p. 82 supra. C.S.D.)
[7] *Letters and Correspondence*, vol. ii, p. 197.

wanted his story to be told from first-hand, original sources, so that the "life" might be autobiographical rather than biographical. Such a volume confined to the Anglican period (1801-45) he seemed disposed to welcome; and this, he felt, only one who had been, or still was, an Anglican, was qualified to write; but as for the history of the Catholic period (1845-90) he personally would have preferred that it should remain untold. His fellow-Oratorian, "dear Ambrose St. John ... the link between my old life and my new",[1] was the biographer of his choice, and in the final arrangement of his papers, as his guiding principle he adopted the rule that every thing should be preserved that would provide him with appropriate material, or serve, as he put it, "to give dear Ambrose elbow-room in his knowledge of me." St. John, however, died in 1875, and in the event, at Newman's request, Anne Mozley, the sister of his two brothers-in-law, John and Thomas Mozley, undertook the Anglican period,[2] while the Catholic period was left to the chances of the future. In his penultimate note relating to the biography then inevitable, Newman expressed his final wish: "I leave all my papers, as materials and documents only, to be used simply at the discretion (for publication or not, in whole or in part) of the parties who, after my death, come into possession of my papers. J.H.N."

One of the common features that marked the introspectiveness of the age, which, as we have already said, Mr Young describes as "the malady of early Victorian society", was that the keeping of journals or diaries was in the fashion. Most young ladies, and many others who were not young ladies, kept them. In *The Importance of Being Earnest* which dates from a period at least half a century later, Cecily says: "I keep a diary in order to enter the wonderful secrets of my life. If I didn't write them down, I should probably forget all about them." And a little later, refusing to let Algernon Moncrieff see it, she says: "You see, it is simply a very young girl's record of her own thoughts and impressions, and consequently meant for publication." The custom was not unusual in Evangelical circles; but in these circles they were more serious. Since the adherents of this school regarded an inner sense of God's love as the decisive proof of conversion, it was their common practice, as we have seen, to exercise an anxious watch over their feelings as the criteria of their spiritual state; and the more ardent among them even kept, or began to keep, since often enough they fell short of their good resolutions, journals, in which they recorded their spiritual progress and their lapses, and chronicled such events as had, or were thought to have, a bearing upon it.

R. H. Froude, although brought up in an atmosphere far from Evangelical, is a case in point. His journal extends from January 2nd, 1826 to May 31st, 1828. It is subjective and self-revealing to an extraordinary degree, and Newman, when it fell into his hands, entertained some qualms about the propriety of publishing it, and felt that such a course needed some justification; but in the end he overcame his scruples and gave it pride of place in the *Remains*.[3] Miss Giberne kept a journal, partly religious, but mainly secular, which is preserved at the Birmingham Oratory, and her sister Mrs B. Pearson did so too. Perhaps her other sisters followed the same custom, for they were members of an Evangelical family. So also did Manning—a relic of his Evangelical days. He lost the bag containing, among other things, his journals and letters on Wednesday, November 12th, 1851 during his journey to Rome, but he consoled himself for his loss by thinking that it might teach him to be less self-contemplative.[4]

The discretion upon which Newman relied on the part of his representatives, is

[1] *Apologia*, p. 283.
[2] *Letters and Correspondence*, by Anne Mozley, London, 1891.
[3] Vol. i, pp. 5-69, 441-97.   [4] Purcell, *Manning*, vol. i, p. 640.

more especially requisite in the instance of a series of school exercise books, which are labelled "Personal and most Private". To them he applies the terms, "Private Journal", "Private Notes", "Memoranda"; and he refers to them in the *Apologia*: "After I was grown up, I put on paper my recollections of the thoughts and feelings on religious subjects, which I had at the time that I was a child and a boy,— such as had remained on my mind with sufficient prominence to make me then consider them worth recording."[1] Newman, then, when he had attained an adult age, began to write his "recollections of [his] thoughts and feelings on religious subjects." He did this in a book with a stiff mottled cover, dated "Oriel College, Oxf., 1822". It contained his original journal, and covered the years 1805-28. It has on the outside of the cover a note "Most private, October 16, 1874." He afterwards destroyed the contents, transcribing some in another book, but he preserved the cover. On the inside there is written the following note: "If on my death this book gets into the hands of another, not having been destroyed, I charge him to burn it without reading, as he would desire in the fulfilment of any wish of his own, concerning earthly matters after his death:—as he hopes at the day of judgment he wishes to stand acquitted of breaking the command of 'doing as he would be done by'. Even so—Lord Jesus." Lower down in pencil there is written: "I revoke all this. It is lawful to read it. J.H.N."; and beside this, in ink "I revoke this. December 1, 1851. J.H.N." The inside of his book having now disappeared, the covers now hold loose sheets filled with prayers and lists of persons to be prayed for inserted instead of it.

The ultimate fate of this journal after his death seems to have worried Newman at intervals all through his life. It was written first in 1820-1, then transcribed with additions in 1823, and carried on so as to cover the years until 1828, and re-transcribed with omissions in the Lent of 1840. At last on December 31st, 1872 he began to copy it into two similar exercise books with flexible maroon covers, $7\frac{1}{4} \times 9\frac{1}{4}$ inches in size, of seventy-four pages each. The second book has the date July 22nd, 1855, on the first page, but this was only the date of the previous transcription, and the note: "I have altered nothing, only omitted". Now in 1872-3, when they were finally recopied, he made "great omissions". The copies which were then superseded, were "all burned carefully" afterwards in 1874. Even after that he had second thoughts, and destroyed the pages from 7 to 22 inclusive.[2]

Miss Maisie Ward, who was the first writer to use these journals for biographical purposes, thought at first that "a private diary of Newman's youth" would prove to be "the most priceless of discoveries"; but she was soon undeceived. She saw on reading it that it was "interesting mainly as a literary and psychological curiosity"; and she suspected that it was "as such that he preserved part of it". She could not square the picture of the "young monster", as he appears in these pages, with what we know of him from elsewhere. The opinion of the present writer is that Newman always regarded it as a perfectly truthful record of his spiritual state at the time, written in an unpleasant style, and with many evidences of bad taste, but, apart from those flaws, beyond reproach. It is the ordinary puzzle in the lives of the saints that they wrote of themselves in similar terms; and that the nearer they approached to the infinite holiness of God, the stronger became their language of self-depreciation. He would not have considered it in the slightest degree exaggerated. She explains it by the fact that he wrote more naturally than he talked, and that he chronicled all his passing moods and thoughts. Hence you have "a document as strange as anything in biography", and consequently she gave up "as impossible the effort I at first made to take it seriously as self-revelation."[3] But is not this the conclusion to which spiritual

[1] p. 1. [2] Of the first exercise book. C.S.D.
[3] *Young Mr Newman*, pp. 57-9.

biographers are all ultimately forced? Yet Newman's words of himself can be paralleled in others of his writings, even in the *Meditations and Devotions*.

The next volume of his journal is contained in a volume similar in appearance to the first and empty volume. It is labelled "Original Memoranda [in pencil "Notes"] Personal and Most Private 1838-1847." It will be noticed that it is the original book, and not a copy. But he has marked it with a note on the outside, "Most Private—October 16, 1874." It opens with an account of the circumstances of the first confession he heard as an Anglican on March 18th, 1838; then it contains a few Latin prayers, the Lenten rules observed by him from 1839, and notes made during retreats at Littlemore, Holy Week and Advent 1843, at Maryvale for Minor Orders, June 3rd-5th, 1846, and at Sant' Eusebio, Rome, for Sacred Orders, April 8-17th, 1847. At the other end there is an alphabetical list of some of the people attended by him in sickness as Curate of St Clements in 1824 and later years; but these have not been reproduced here.

The fifth and last manuscript occupies an exercise book, $7\frac{1}{2} \times 9\frac{1}{4}$ in size, bound in a yellow flexible cover, mottled in red and blue. The pages are numbered from 1 to 44 in pencil, probably by another hand, but Newman has also written on the inner side of the back cover, so that he has filled, with a few gaps, forty-five pages in all. The cover bears a label on which some one has written in pencil, "Journal of J.H.N."; and "journal" is the name by which Wilfred Ward refers to it. But it is hardly a journal in the proper sense of the term; it is rather a book in which Newman has written down various considerations at different times and at long intervals. The entries succeed one another in their due order, except that the entry dated November 27th, 1866, was inserted on a page left blank after that of January 8th, 1860; but since it narrates what happened immediately after that date, it has been thought well not to change the order. The first entry is dated December 15th, 1859; the last after he had been made Cardinal.

At the end Newman says of this book that he is "dissatisfied with the whole of it," since "it is more or less a complaint from one end to the other." But if one examines it, it becomes evident that there is really only one subject of complaint, that he, a man conscious of his great gifts and talents, and of his ability to do great things for God's Church, things that needed to be done, and that no one else could do, was thrust aside and condemned to idleness, whereas lesser men were brought forward, and played havoc with the most delicate and exacting matters of policy, which time has now set right. Newman was content to leave things to time for his justification. It was a favourite quotation of his from Crabbe:

> "Leaving the case to Time, who solves all doubt,
> By bringing Truth, his glorious daughter, out."

In the same spirit he wrote to Miss Bowles on January 8th, 1867: "I consider that Time is the great remedy and Avenger of all wrongs, as far as this world goes. If only we are patient, God works for us. He works for those who do not work for themselves. Of course an inward brooding over injuries is not patience, but a recollecting with a view to the future is prudence."

THREE EARLY JOURNALS

INTRODUCTION [1]

The following three manuscripts are contained in three school exercise books, the first two in books of identical appearance and size, 7¼ by 9¼ inches, the third in a book with a mottled cover backed with red leather, and slightly smaller, 7 by 8¼ inches, but containing a far larger number of pages.

1. From the first the gummed label is missing, but a fragment which remains, has written on it in pencil, "Copies of Private Memoranda, part 1", and below this "Part 1" in ink. It extends from 1804 to 1826, and occupies pp. 1-69, but pp. 7-22 inclusive, together with an appendix of prayers, have been torn out and burnt, it is impossible to guess why. His remembrances of his life until August, 1816 were written first in 1821, 1822, transcribed faithfully with additions in 1823, re-transcribed faithfully in Lent, 1840, and finally on December 31st, 1872, but with great omissions. Fr. Ambrose St. John, whom Newman intended to be his biographer, if there should be a demand for a biography, was still alive, and seemed likely to survive him, and Newman retained so much in order to give him elbow-room in his knowledge. The superseded copies were then carefully burnt.

2. On this volume the gummed label survives entire. It reads:

> *Misericordias Domini in aeternum cantabo.*
> Edgbaston. July 22, 1855.
> Extracts from my Private Journal of 1821-1828.
> I have altered nothing, only omitted.[2]

Newman had crossed from Ireland after his first year there on July 19th. So he must have sat down to the work of copying almost immediately after his arrival.

3. The third volume has two gummed labels upon the cover. The upper one reads:

> Pidgeon Hole 4
> No. 5
> Most private—Oct. 16, 1874.

And the lower:

> (with parish deaths beds at the other end.)
> Original Notes
> Personal and most private
> 1838-1847

[1] This Introduction repeats some of the information contained in the General Introduction to the Journals, but it has been thought best not to alter what Father Tristram wrote. It will be noted that his only explanation of the fourth Journal, 1859-79, is to be found in the concluding paragraphs of the above-mentioned General Introduction. C.S.D.

[2] Actually this is the heading inside the book. The gummed label reads:
Copies of Memoranda part 2
Personal and *most* Private
1821-1828   C.S.D.

This originally read Originals of Memoranda, but Newman has crossed out the final "s" of Originals and the following "of".[1] This volume opens with an account of the circumstances of the first confession that he heard, dated March 18th, 1838. Then it gives a record of the austerities he practised during Lent at Littlemore. Afterwards it contains his notes of the Retreats at Littlemore during Lent and Advent, 1843, and a dozen prayers drawn up *in usum Dilecti filii mei Henrici*. This was probably Henry Walsh, who joined them at Littlemore on November 2nd, 1842, and remained with them until August 23rd, 1845, when he left for Stanley Grove. He afterwards became a clergyman in the diocese of Hereford. Then there follow notes of his Retreat for Minor Orders in 1846, and of a longer one, April 8th-17th, 1847, at Sant' Eusebio, Rome; and finally a copy of a Minute Journal, August 1st-9th, 1843.

At the other end of the book there is an alphabetical record of some of the persons he attended in sickness, principally in St Clement's, during his curacy there, 1824-6.

This volume differs from the other two in that it is not a copy, but contains the original notes made by Newman at the time.

Newman has been careful to mark these volumes as personal and private, and he had no thought that they would ever be published. But they illustrate the attempts he made to lead a spiritual life in unpropitious surroundings, and so throw a certain light upon his character as a young man; and after the passage of the years the reasons why he withheld them have ceased to exist, and there remains no reason now why they should be kept back.

[1] Later he crossed out, in pencil, the word "Memoranda", and substituted "Notes". C.S.D.

BOOK or PART 1 (running from p. 1 to p.—69

December 31. 1872.   with an omission of from p. 7
The first part taken   to p. 22 inclusive and an appen-
is from A.D. 1804 to 1826.   dix of prayers)

Misericordias Domini in aeternum cantabo. I am loth to destroy altogether the record of God's great mercies to me, of the wonderful things He has done for my soul, and of my early moral and spiritual history. Yet on the other hand I know the difficulty of keeping it, and the delicacy and danger of making selection.

If I have decided on not destroying it all, that does not imply that it is in whole or in part fit for publication, so far as preserved. *CERTAINLY NOT!* I retained so much, in order to give dear Ambrose elbow room in his knowledge of me, if he was to make a memoir of me.

The following remembrances of my life up to August 1816 were written first in 1820, 1821. Then faithfully transcribed with additions in 1823. Then faithfully transcribed with omissions in the Lent of 1840. Now to be partially and finally re-transcribed with great omissions, and put aside for good. The copies which were superseded were all burned carefully.

The unpleasant style in which it is written arises from my habit from a boy to *compose*. I seldom wrote without an eye to style, and since my taste was bad, my style was bad. I wrote in style, as another might write in verse, or sing instead of speaking, or dance instead of walking. Also my Evangelical tone contributed to its bad taste.

J H N

I was born on February 21, 1801, baptized April 3, 1801. I left my Grandmother's at Fulham together with her, for home, as I recollect, not later than 1805. (I say this, "not later" because I recollect seeing my Grandmother go up from *Ham* to see my brother Frank on his birth in London in June 1805.) I left Ham, as I recollect well, in September 1807. I went to school May 1. 1808. I was entered at Trinity College Oxford on December 14. 1816.

(from p. 7 to p. 22 inclusive are omitted)

May 15. 1874.

On finally looking through and burning my papers, I have found the rough notes from which the original of the above (1820-21 memoranda) was made. The following notes are not crossed out, and have not been used in that original.

1. "On my conversion. How the wisdom and goodness of God is discerned—I was going from school half a year sooner (than I did)—my staying arose from 8th of March (1816. vid. "Copies of Letters" No 1 first leaf) Thereby I was left at school by myself, my friends gone away—" ("That is, it was a time of reflection, and when the influences of Mr Mayers would have room to act upon me. Also, I was terrified at the heavy hand of God which came down upon me.) Also this:—

2. "The reality of conversion:—as cutting at the root of doubt, providing a chain between God and the soul. (i.e. with every link complete) I know I am right. How do you know it? I know I know. How? I know I know I know &c &c.

(vide Grammar of Assent p 195—197 ed 4.)

"Again, every action tells, has weight and meaning. No shadows—consistency. The unconverted man changes his end with his time of life, or goes on changing about—but here it is all reality."

Two Hymns of Dr Watts's formed part of my prayers as a child, perhaps more than two. I have never seen them since. The evening one began "And now another day is gone"; the Sunday hymn had in it "I have been there and fain would go 'Tis like a little heaven below." (Sept 4 1881 J H N)

Again:—

3. "In 1819 and the beginning of 1820, I hoped great things for myself, not liking to go into the Church, but to the Law. I attended History Lectures (Modern History, University not College) hearing that the names were reported to the Minister."

Transcripts of unconnected papers.

1.

(The end of 1816 I was quite aware *then* that these were doggerel—but they were in fact extempore prayers)

Let me always, my God & king
In Thy dear Name rejoice
And daily to Thy praises sing
With ever grateful voice
I am a worm, and Thou art good
To save a wretch like me,
Who always has Thy grace withstood,
And turned his back on Thee.

O grant that I may persevere
And finally obtain
A glorious crown, purchased for dear,
That ever may remain
Purchased for dear, for by the Blood,
Of Jesus it is given
Who suffered death, the Just & Good,
That we may live in heaven.
O may I scorn each mundane joy,
And meditate on Thee.
May heaven all my thoughts employ,
Then happy shall I be.

End of 1816.   2.

For Jesus' sake, my God, bestow
Thy grace on helpless me
&c &c.

(I wrote in Latin, I believe, for two reasons 1. that servants and
scouts might not read. 2. to practise myself in Latin. When I went to
Oxford, Bowden made it a rule always to talk together in Latin.)

1816. Ante Calend. Decembr III
Deus. Optime Maxime, qui nobis cunctis imperas, qui mundi res
dirigis, qui nobis piis vel impiis praemium vel paenam inferes in
futuro, preces humiliter tibi offero, ut mihi Χαριν tuam praebeas, sine
quâ nequeo rectum facere. Paucis diebus mihi domum ibitur. Tunc
Satanas me novis, quamvis notis illecebris assiliet. Tu mihi vires
suppedita, ut mundum, ut carnem, ut diabolum superem. Fidei
clypeo armato mihi liceat ignea του πονηρου tela extinguere.
Inprimis, serva me ne cedam mundi illecebris; ne coetibus, choreis,
oblectationibus nimiis attractus, ea Deo meo praeferam; ne tui
obliviscam. Serva me, obsecro.
Dein, serva me carnis a [sic] illecebris. Heu miser ego! peccavi.
Aeternam damnationem mereor propter portentosa facinora mea.
Mentem revigora; fortem redde in tentationem; defende me,
Domine, immergor, dexteram porrige. Et quoque nimiâ luxuriâ
(gluttony) me serva. Fac me temperatum, sobrium, castum.
Heu (ab) omnibus peccatis me defende.

(Transcribed from original copy. Sept 18. 1850.
J H.N.)

To Revd Walter Mayers, on his giving me Beveridge's Private Thoughts, January 1817. (N B Mr Milman was at the time Curate of Ealing. J H N.)

I am very much obliged to you for your kind present, and the letter which accompanied it. May it profit me, and be a means of keeping me in the right path. For indeed I find I have very great need of some monitor to direct me, and I sincerely trust that my conscience, enlightened by the Bible, through the influence of the Holy Spirit, may prove a faithful & vigilant guardian of the true principles of religion. I have not yet finished reading B^p Beveridge, but it seems to me, as far as I *have* read it, an excellent work; & indeed I know it must be so, else you would not have given it me.

There is one passage in the first chapter of the second part, that I do not quite comprehend; it is on the Sacrament of Baptism. I had, before I read it, debated with myself how it could be that baptized infants, dying in their infancy, could be saved, unless the Spirit of God was given them; which seems to contradict the opinion that Baptism is not accompanied by the Holy Ghost. B^p Beveridge's opinion seems to be that the seeds of grace are sown in Baptism although they often do not spring up; that Baptism is the mean whereby we receive the Holy Spirit, although not the only mean; that infants, when baptized, receive the inward & spiritual grace without the requisite repentance & faith. If this be his opinion, the sermon Mr Milman preached on grace last year was exactly consonant with his sentiments, & he agrees with Dr Mant.

I was deceived in my expectations of being in Town a few weeks after I left Ealing and then calling for the book. I have had my eyes very uncomfortable, but now they are getting well. The weeks run round swiftly, and, before I shall be aware of it, the time will come for my going to College. I hope I shall continue firm in the principles, in which you, Sir, have instructed me, and may that Holy Spirit by whom B^p Beveridge was enabled to establish his articles of faith, to form resolutions upon them, & to put those resolutions in practice, by whom also you were made the instrument of good to me, and by whom my heart was softened to receive your instructions, may he steer me safe through the dangers, to which I may be exposed at College, or afterwards in my course through life, till the home of death arrive, and find me not unprepared to leave this world. (I have

fastened Mr Mayers's letter to which this is an answer, in the copy
of Beveridge. Oct. 14. 1874)

End of 1816

Si de choreis et omnibus ejusmodi coetibus mihi opinionem dare
necesse est, en! dabo. Ea condemno.

Inprimis mihi visum est ut Apostolus Paulus talia significavit,
cùm gaudia mundi prava vitare jussit; et quoque Joannes, cùm
libidinem oculi, libidinem carnis, superbiam vitae similiter effugere
nos docuit.

... "Sic agendo tu alios qui choreis favent, condemnas." Mη
γενοιτο. Procul a me sit illud. Cuique suus mos—et si quis studet
rectè agere, benè illi est. Nec ille me, nec ego quemquam condem-
nabo. Et obedientia erga parentes (observanda est.) ...

"Sed tu teipsum proponis exemplum sanctum." Ne fiat. Non puto
aliquid virtutis inesse hac abstinentiâ, sed quasi defensionem illam
aestimo contra diaboli impetus insidiosos. Haud aliter jejunia, preces,
mihi videntur praepositi modi bonam vitam ducendi. Abstinentia
sit clypeo, preces mihi gladio sint.

Et nunc obsecro ut me sinas (vitare) quod mihi est mali instru-
mentum. Si mihi oblectationi esse aestimas, me respice et cito
mentem mutabis. Nonne omnia mihi injucunda videbuntur? Nonne
musica clamor mihi foret? Nonne saltantes apparerent, haud dico
essent, sed meae menti apparerent, του πονηρου ministri, extrà
nitidi et speciosi, intrà foedi. Et quo vultu possum ego dormiturus
exclamare Deo, "Ne duc nos in tentationem?" Te obsecro, me sinas
domi manere. ...

... Although it is far from pleasant to give my reasons, inasmuch as
I shall appear to set myself up, and to be condemning recreations
and those who indulge in them, yet, when I am urged to give them,
I hope I shall never be ashamed of them, presenting my scruples with
humility and a due obedience to my parents, open to conviction, and
ready to obey in a matter so dubious as this is, and to act against my
own (judgment), if they command, thus satisfying at once my own
conscience and them ...

... I have too much sense of my own weakness to answer for myself. The beginnings of sin are small—and is it not better, say, to be
too cautious than to be negligent? Besides, I know myself in some
things better than you do; I have hidden faults, and, if you knew
them, so serious a protest would not seem to you strange.

... I think these things of importance to myself, but I hope I am not so enthusiastical as to treat it as a matter of high religious importance. You may think this contradicts (what I said just now) about the beginnings of sin; if so, I am sorry I cannot express myself with greater exactness and propriety.

(end of 1816)

Subjects on which I wrote reflections or sermonets in the Spring of 1817. (after May 20)

1 He that eateth and drinketh unworthily &c
2 Great things doeth He, which we cannot comprehend
3 These shall go into everlasting punishment.
4 Man is like to vanity; his days are &c
5 May 22. Let no one despise thy youth &c
6 July 9. Let not sin therefore reign in your mortal body &c
7 Novr 29. 1818.   But we preach Christ crucified &c
8 August 8. 1819   All Scripture is given by inspiration of God &c
9 December 25   The Athanasian Creed.
10 Also two others, apparently of 1817. One on "Thou when thou
11 fastest &c. Matt vi. The other on "Whom we did foreknow &c Rom viii. 29.30.

(N. B. November 29. 1851 I was very fond of Beveridge's "Private Thoughts" at this time, and the above quasi Sermons are, I think, in his style. J H N)

(I have now burned them. 1874)

October 1817. My second term of residence at Oxford (in effect it was my first, for the men were nearly all gone down in June preceding, when I was called into residence.)

Coll. Trin. Oxon.

Ante Calend. Novembr, XVI. Hora 4ª Pater meus modo decessit, me invito, necessitate autem urgente. Solus sum, amicum habeo neminem, Patronum verò qui me immeritum protegit, (et O usque protecturus sit!) Summum ... Coelum serenum, imbris nonnullis, ventus vehemens.

Ant. Cal. Nov. XIV. die primo. Ecclesiam adii. Thresher video, appello, comitor; quidam nomine Bird comitatur quoque. Ward (Hibernicus) me invisit de supellectili. Ecclesiam revisante (me, quidem) concionatur; sermo egregius.

A.C.N. XIII. Me invitat Hollis villum compotare secum. Heu! nunc

omni curâ et diligentiâ opus est mihi, ne in insidias hasce του
πονηρου casurus sim. Tu, Deus O.M. gressus meos dirige. Tu es
Patronus, Tu Parens; si deseris Tu, perii.

A.C.N. XII. Hollis adeo: nihil est συμποσεως, spe gravi jucundis-
simè frustratus sum.

£   s.   d.

A.C.N. X. Debitam pecuniam pro supellectili solvo,   44   19   0
A.C.N. VIII. Plateas spatientem quidam alloquitur, nomen meum
vocat. Gambiar fuit, scholae Eliensis mihi condiscipulus.
A.C.N. VII. Hodie, dum in S. Mariae Eccles. Praepositum Coll.
Oriel concionantem audio, animo deficio, et per diem reliquum
aegrotus sum.

Pridie ant. C.N. Domum redeunti inopinato apparet nomen chartâ
inscriptum "Fletcher;" convenio, ut ibi Derby, alium condiscipulum
Eliensem video.

* Oct 30. 1884   *Edward* Fletcher's Father lived in Ealing, and
Edward was at our School. He was no *especial* friend of mine, but
a schoolfellow

Ant Non. Nov III. Ad Coll. Nov. Capellam cum Bowden feror.

Ant. Id Nov VII Quieto sedenti adest W. circiter horam primam
nocturnam (7 o'clock P M) nuntium ferens de compotatione ... . Eo.
Me vino inebriare conantur. Haud voti sunt compotes. Horâ prae-
teritâ abeo invitis lubens.

Ant. Id. VI Bowden me invitat ad se. Ipse jucundissimus, et alii
quidem aliqui jucundi quoque. Sunt tamen, qui, sermonis integri
impatientes, nihil nisi turbas amant.

Ant. Id. Nov. V. Balneo me immergor: antea quoque, quamvis id
non memoravi. Eccles. S. M. Pembrok. Coll. Magister concionatur.
Ep. 2 ad Tim. iii, 14.

Ant Id. Nov IV Phillips* me combibitum et concoenatum invitat.
Tempus jucundè teritur, et utiliter simul. Sunt qui de artibus, scient-
iis loqui non recusant. (* Mr Biddulph Phillips afterwards a
Catholic.)

A.I.N.III Balneo* me immergo. (* the cold plunging bath at
Holywell)

Id. Nov. Me decanus laudat per declamationem meam, mihi decus
afferentem. Me Tutor meus laudat propter Euclidi propositionem ad
unguem demonstratam

Ant. Calend. Decembr. XVII Balneo me immergo.

A.C.D. XVI.   Balneo utor. Jentaculum cum Tutore meo capio.

Bowden quoque, Ward (Harroensis)—(uncle to W. G. Ward) Eccles. Æd. Christ. adeo—Doct^r Barnes concionatur. Actor iv. Eccles. S. M. adeo. Doct. Lloyd Aed. Christ. concionatur.

A.C.D. XIV. Balneo utor. Me vespere in libris incubantem turbant Ward (alter) et Newton: illius antiqui Neutoni nomine indignissimus.

A.C.D XIII Me veniam poscit W. suppliciter.

A.C.D Prid. Eccles. B.M. adeo. Dom. Heber Omn. Animar. concionatur. Eph vi, 12, 13. Mane Eucharist. Sacr. accipio.* Deus faxit, ut &c &c (* this was my first communion in the Anglican Church)

A. Non. Dec. III. Orchestram* adeo. (* the Music Room)

A. Id. D. VII B. Mar. Eccl. adeo. Coll. Oriel Praepos. concion. Joann ii.

(There is more of the same kind. I seem to have bathed very frequently thro' this winter. It was a plunging bath. It is close to Holywell Church)

Friday November 7. 1817 9 o'clock P.M.

I am about an hour and a half returned from the rooms of one of this College by name E. At about ½ past 6 W[ard] came to me and said that he had been desired by E. to send me his compliments and he would be very happy to see me at his wine party, and that I should be so much the more acceptable, if I brought my violin. I supposed it consisted of one or two, and they had their flutes, (for I heard flutes at the time,) and wished me to join them. I took my violin and went.

The first thing that surprised me on entering the room was to see a long table; the next to hear a smothered laugh on my conductor's announcing "Mr Newman and his fiddle." I was offered a chair, a glass, and a decanter. I took my time in drinking the glass of wine. In the meantime a fresh bottle had been decanted, and my entertainer assured me he was waiting for me to finish the glass before passing the bottle. The bottle waited—those below called out to pass it. I offered to pass it. Oh no—he could not think of my passing it without filling; there was no hurry—he would wait. At last I passed it without filling. The bottle came round. I sometimes filled my glass, sometimes passed without filling. Toasts were given—the King— I am sure I wished him well, but I would not fill, when the bottle went round with the earth's rapid circlet round the sun.

All this time I was intreated to play. I refused. An hour had passed, and I determined to go. I looked at my watch. I finished my third glass, and begged E's leave to depart. E. requested silence, and asked me to speak (my wishes). I did so. "No" assailed me on every side. My voice was drowned, but they could not prevent my moving. Then they spoke separately—I ought not to disgrace myself. I was going too soon. I said I had told W. I would go for half an hour. I got up and went. τω θεω δοξα

Tuesday 18th November 1817.

Is it gentlemanly conduct to rush into my room, and to strut up to the further end of it, and ask me in a laughing tone how I do; and then, after my remaining some time in silent wonder, to run and bolt the door, and say they are hiding from some one?

Then, to tell me they have come to invite me to wine, and, when I answer in the negative, to ask me why, pressing and pressing me to come, and asking me in a gay manner if I do not mean to take a first class, telling me I read too much, and overdo it, and then to turn from me suddenly and to hollow out "Let him alone, come along," and to throw open the door?

I said such conduct was not the conduct of gentlemen—and ordered them to leave the room. One then said he would knock me down, if I were not too contemptible a fellow. (He was 6 feet 3 or 4 inches high, and stout in proportion. He was a known figure in Oxford in his undergraduate's gown.)

Wednesday 19 November 1817

The One has been here just now, and said he was very sorry for his conduct, that a sudden gust of passion had overset him—that I had acted very well, that he had seldom or never seen any one act more firmly. I told him not to think more about it. He shook hands and went.

Tuesday.   May 19. 1818.

On Wednesday, the 29th of April I determined to stand for the scholarship in consequence of the advice of my Tutor, who thought I might be likely to attain it. And my heart beat within me, and I was sanguine that I should gain it, and I was fearful that I should be too much set upon it.

I therefore said, "O God of heaven and earth, Thou hast been pleased of Thine infinite goodness to impart Thy Holy Spirit to me and to enlighten my soul with the knowledge of the truth. Therefore, O Lord, for our Blessed Saviour's sake, hearken to the supplication which I make before Thee. Let me not rely too much upon getting this scholarship—let me not be lead [sic] away from Thee by the hopes of it. So let me order my spirit, that, if I get it not, I may not be disappointed, but may praise and bless Thy name, as knowing better than myself what is good for me. O Lord God of hosts, grant it not to me, if it is likely to be a snare to me, to turn me away from Thee. May I so dispose myself that I may praise Thy name, whether I receive what I pray for, or whether I receive it not."

Thus I prayed, and He was pleased to hear my petition, and yesterday, out of his infinite lovingkindness He gave me the scholarship. O praised be the Lord God of Israel who only doth wondrous things! Give me grace, make me holy, for Thou alone canst. Save me and bring me to those realms where Thou shinest in unclouded majesty, & make me praise Thee (then) to all eternity.

(It was on the 18th, Trinity Monday, the Gaudy, that I was obliged to leave the Scholars' wine party, to avoid being made drunk. I never went to it in the years which followed.)

1818 or 1819

Memini me tum cùm jam Rhedycinâ relictâ, domum paternam subiissem declarasse, nihil mihi fore tàm miserum et grave quàm domi uno tenore continuos menses terere; idem verò, cùm jam limina chara linquerem, ita aegrè linquebam, ut credo, si animo obsecutus essem meo, procrastinans in dies singulos moras traxissem, et quam priùs timui monotoniam, prudens sciensque elegissem. Nunc tamen, libris circumdato, est quod cogitationes meas occupet, quod prohibeat ne domi imago mentem invadat, quod ambitionis stimulos in pectore suscitet, et efficiat, ut, praeteritis neglectis, futura solum prospiciam. (Copied from the original, in which it occurs, which I then destroyed as being shabby and scarcely legible. November 29. 1851. J H N)

(I can't understand this—what the occasion of it was—whether a fragment—nor exactly why in Latin. It is in too good Latin to be a mere private paper. Is it addressed to my brother Charles? We used to write to each other in Latin. 1874 J H N)

September 17. 1820   vid p. 6

I have just read what I wrote above on May 19. 1818. Lord, I tremble. Could I thus so earnestly pray that obtaining the object of my prayers might be no snare to me, and could I faint after a time, and, on gaining the scholarship, grow cold and remiss and ungrateful? Could I be so lowly and resigned beforehand, so thankful on succeeding, and yet in a few short weeks become so vain, so puffed up, so proud, so quarrelsome, so very wicked?

What a lesson for me! Now, before my examination, I feel, by the grace of God, warm, resigned and teachable; I pray Him not to let me succeed, if success would cause me to commit the least sin; I pray for grace to enable me to bear the event with thanksgiving and humility; and yet, yet, if I *am* successful, what may happen! may I not fall as before? is it not likely? what a heart is mine! So trifling a good fortune, and it must stop my prayers, lull my watchfulness, blind me, lead me back to wallow in the mire! what *would* happen were I to get this greater success? my mouth is stopped ... How probable then, since I have prayed the Lord that I may *not* succeed if sin must follow, how probable I shall fail!

O this spirit of mine, which keeps without intermission flattering me with the certainty of gaining honours, what need have I of resignation to the will of God! how disappointed without His mighty Spirit will be the proud soul within me!

Lord, give me content and confidence in Thee, and, above all, grant me not my heart's desire by any means, if the price be transgression in consequence. On the high ground will I stand by Thy grace. No. I will say, give me not fame, or learning. I will accept of none of these, without bargaining that sin is not included in the gift. Those bales of perishable ware oftentimes convey the infection of sin, (unfinished)

Long Vacation, 1820.
To Francis W. Newman

... It is my daily and I hope heartfelt prayer, that I may not get any honours here, if they are to be the least cause of sin to me. As the time approaches, and I have laboured more at my books, the trial is greater. May God give me the strength still to say "let me get no honours, if they are to be the least cause of sin to me"!

And do you, my dear Francis, pray for me too in the same way. "If it be possible, O Lord, let me succeed in the object of my studies— but Thou knowest all things, and I am a fool before Thee. Therefore Thy will, not mine, be done—only give me strength to bear the event with calmness—and, if Thou hast decreed that I should fail, let me adore Thy great love and wisdom, and bless Thee for not leaving to me the choice ..."

November 5. 1820

The time draws near. I have had anguish in my mind. Yes, and all owing to my former sins. My soul would have been light and cheerful; I could have rested in the lovingkindness of the Lord, I should have been of good courage, but He seems to be threatening retribution, and my enemy takes occasion to exult over his prey.

Yet, through the thick cloud of heaviness which is on my heart, the gracious Lord at intervals darts His beams and shows that he has not forsaken me. He makes me lie down at night with fervent thankfulness to Him and love and submission, though cheerfulness be absent. He supports my bodily strength through the day, and enables me to say "Thy will be done" and "Give me *good*." But I am in a state of sad suspense. I now hope, and now fear, and I am rocked with doubt, and I deserve it. I am confused in mind, and am now writing incoherently.

This, however, is my sure hold,—it was my duty to try for honours. And this is my grief,—I have not tried for success, I have not studied (as religiously) as *I ought*. I have quenched the good Spirit of God, I have grieved Him. Almighty and most merciful God, give me Thy peace. Calm me, make me contented—make me joyful. I deserve it not, and this my conscience tells me, and in this Satan triumphs over me, and laughs at his victory, and suggests I am too bad to pray. But to Thee I come. I do not ask for success, but for peace of mind. Shield me from the cruel foe—hide me under the shadow of Thy wings. Lift up Thy countenance upon me. I am strong in Jesus. Out of the depths have I cried unto Thee, O Lord. Look down and visit me...Lord comfort me.

(One of my favourite Psalms at this time was "Exaudiat te Dominus." "The Lord hear thee in the day of trouble" &c)

(Transcripts)
Casual Thoughts set down as they occurred
1817 - 1826

(There are many more, but I am burning them all. These are specimens.)

(None of them are worth much, except as showing the progress of my mind.)

1819.   March 21.   Sunday Evening.
Bells pealing. The pleasure of hearing them. It leads the mind to

a longing after some thing I know not what. It does not bring past
years to remembrance. It does not bring any thing. What does it do?
We have a kind of longing after something dear to us and well known
to us, very soothing. Such is my feeling at this minute, as I hear them.

(Why do the Germans excel in Music?)

April 29 or 30. I dreamt some one asked what o'clock it was. I
answered $\frac{1}{2}$ past 5. I directly woke & looked at my watch. It was just
$\frac{1}{2}$ past 5. I had not been accustomed to wake at that hour.

It is remarkable that no notice (or such slight notice) is taken in
the Scriptures of apparitions, the belief of which is so prevalent in
the world in every nation.

Make a poem on Faith. Bring in the plague of Athens as one of
the examples; a maid dying over her cursing and blaspheming lover.
The eastern Philosopher. To end with a faint imagination of the soul
just freed from the bonds of the mortal body.

1820 January. (Out of place.) Many religions have produced fanatics
who have figured for a time & then vanished; but where else will
you find the doctrine, which in every age and clime has made thousands fanatics, unabatedly, unextinguishably.

1819   October 10. 1819
Hints to be arranged for an Essay ... (1) prove that in vain is it
pleaded that the Epistles are a different religion from the Gospels ...
(2) The doctrine of the Atonement the key stone of Christianity—of
which we should be particularly jealous at the present time, when we
have reason to believe from the prophecies that the days of a general
apostasy are at hand, when believers will be derided and persecuted.
"How could the doctrine of the Atonement enter into any man's
head?" Thou sayest well—it never could. Thinkest thou that so many
multitudes in every age could have held fast & been supported by the
doctrine, unless &c ... (3) Yes, and as you see more of life, you will
find many kind, liberal, upright men who disclaim this doctrine, &
it will grieve you &c ... (4) I should like to know what the Socinians
understand by *faith*. As I understand the Bible, faith is *a* (perhaps
the) most difficult Christian grace, viz the believing of something
which is beyond our powers of reason and contradictory to the
imaginations of our sinful nature ... *They* walk by sight.

1819. October

Hints on the Athanasian Creed. (1) The presumption must be in favour of that, which has been approved by such pious (men) as our Reformers. (2) Would it be uncharitable to pronounce the drunkard, the extortioner, the covetous in a state of perdition? (3) As a man's faith, so is his practice. That it matters what a man's faith is we learn from Jude verse 3. (4) To us who believe the divinity of Jesus, is it credible that the Son of God, the Everlasting Jehovah, should descend to agonies & death, yet it matters not whether men believe Him as such, or not?

1819. October 10

In the enumeration of crimes by our Saviour, doctrinal and practical are mentioned indiscriminately. Matt xv. 18, 19. Mark vii, 21-23. And by St Paul Rom i, 21, 22, 1 Cor vi, 9, 10, Col iii, 5-8, 1 Tim. i, 9 & 10. And by St Peter 1 Pet iv, 3, 4. And by St John Rev. xxi, 8, xxii, 15.

1817 June 29 (this was my first solitary term of three weeks.) (out of place) On a Sermon preached at St Mary's by the Rev. W. Crowe. You say that the grace of God is always everywhere present. Now this constant grace must either be efficacious or not. You cannot mean it to be *not* efficacious; for, if so, it is no advantage to men, and indeed grace implies an efficacious aid from God. Well then, it *is* efficacious, that is to say, it is able to convert a person; then I ask, Has it ever converted any one? Yes—since then it has converted one man, how is it that it has not converted all?

You must answer, either that it is more powerful at some times and in some places, than at and in others, or that the heart of the person is not always disposed to it. 1. According to the first reason, it is only efficacious when powerful, and that in particular cases; what profits then the constant omnipresent grace you affirm to be, if *that* is not efficacious, but a more powerful kind of grace? besides, why is it and at what times more powerful? You are introducing predestination. 2. "The heart of the person is not always disposed to it:"—and who pray makes the heart disposed, who gives a flesh one instead of a stony one? is it not God? Well then, the heart which is disposed must receive grace in order to that good disposition; now *this* grace you cannot say every one has, for every one is *not* disposed—consequently to the heart that is disposed a greater share of grace must be given, a grace preventing as well as converting.

Therefore, whichever way you take it, the constant grace which you mention is of no effect without a preventing grace, and, consequently, why should there be an omnipresent constant grace, when it can only be serviceable on certain occasions? Wherefore it appears to me that the idea of a grace without effect does not exist, as being derogatory to the wisdom of God.

Corollary 1. It may also be shown that the idea of a constant grace without effect seems to affect the *goodness* of God, from which Arminians say the Calvinists so much detract. For then every one that dies impenitent has continually through his life been refusing the grace which God has continually offered to him, at the same [time] *knowing* the man could not receive it, and thereby will deserve greater punishment. This is a difficulty quite as great as any Calvinistic.

Cor[ollary]. 2 By this I may be shown that the explanation the Arminians give to "As many as were ordained, τεταγμενοι etc" is futile. They render it "disposed"; but God disposes the heart, and why should He dispose one more than another, unless He ordained?

(This is a clearly expressed illustration of the famous words in Catholic controversy, "A gratiâ sufficienti libera nos, Domine." It is remarkable that at that date I should have hit on the word "efficacious", unless it came into Mr Crowe's Sermon. [Note added in] 1874)

1820.   April 30.
It is wisely ordained that the sublimity of the Bible consists in the ideas and not in the words, and coincides with the notion of a revelation from realms where there is no language or speech, but every thing spiritual and mental. Thus the Scriptures are rendered universal objects of admiration. No translation materially affects them, as it does the Koran.

1820.   April 30
Grant for an instant that the Apocalypse is to be a sealed book till the last days, and then, when we believe infidelity will corrupt and persecution depopulate the globe, to have its meaning displayed, to sustain the fainting souls of the then martyrs. This is hypothesis, but it shows there may be reasons of which we know nothing.

1820   May 14.
As there are beings, who, being created in time are to live to eternity
à parte post, analogy would lead us to conclude that there may be
beings who, having lived from eternity a parte ante, are to die in
time. But this is absurd.

1820   August 20
It may be supposed that the greatest agony Christ endured was, not
what He suffered in His body, but that inward horror and darkness
which caused the drops of blood in the garden, and the mysterious
exclamation upon the Cross. May not this be stated in such a manner
as to repel the objection that His corporeal sufferings could not
cleanse us from sin, which is spiritual?

1820   August 20.
If we once suppose that each individual man fell in Adam, it is no
imputation on the justice of God to say that the impenitent have
neither the power nor the will to turn to God. They have forfeited
both by their own act.

1820   August 20
A poem on the death of Sisera, or a series of Poems on the Judges,
suitable to throw light upon the obscure conciseness of the history.

1820   August 27
In answer to the objection brought against the Deluge, "that no
bones of men have been discovered," it may be supposed that the
countries of the Antediluvians were drowned in the sea, (as Sodom
and Gomorrah;) in the Indian and Pacific Oceans. Or it may be
supposed that the immense expanse of interior Africa was their
country, and that God in anger since the deluge cursed it with
barrenness and drought.

1820   September 17
You say you think it very improbable that God appeared clothed in
human shape, because it is making our earth, which is so insignifi-
cant a portion of the Universe, of too much consequence. But our
earth is *visibly* in a peculiar state; sin and misery we *see* abound in it,
and in the same strain of argument I might assure myself that I never
sinned & never was miserable. À priori arguments seem to me the

most fallacious of the fallacious. You surely will not take refuge in the corner of asserting that every globe we see in the sky and every invisible sphere we conjecture is fraught with crime and wretchedness as we are. This is in the highest degree improbable. (Is not *this* an à priori argument?) *Our* small planet vanishes before a rejoicing universe, but if you make ours the common lot, it may be said that it is incompatible with the idea of a good Creator. (Does not this rescue the argument from being à priori?)

But many think how singular *we* should be in that globe! but the inhabitants of any earth thus situated might think the same. To him who pitches on the lucky number in a lottery, his good fortune must seem singular, whoever he be, but *some one must* get it.

1820 September 29

I will not *directly* assert that regeneration is not the usual attendant on baptism, if you object to it; but I will put it in this way, and if that tenet does not follow as a consequence, I will not press it. I say then, that it is *absolutely necessary* for *every* one to undergo a *total change* in his heart and affections, *before* he can enter into the kingdom of heaven. This you will agree with me is a scriptural doctrine; the question *then* is, Do we, when children receive this change in baptism? For myself I can answer that I did not; and that, when God afterwards in His mercy created me anew, no one can say it was only *reforming*. I know and am sure that before I was blind, but now I see.

1821 March 4

The second Person of the Blessed Trinity is called the Son of the Father, the Only-begotten, not in a literal sense, but as the nearest analogy in human language to convey the idea of an incomprehensible relation between the Father and the Son. Nothing can show this more clearly than the other titles given to Him in Scripture. If He were in every respect a Lamb, He could not be the Shepherd. If he were in every respect the Husband of the Church, He could not be the Father. &c.

1821 May 13

I can read religious books, the most spiritual, with great pleasure, and, when so engaged feel myself warmed to prayer and thanksgiving; but let the appointed hour of devotion arrive, and I am cold and dead. My head is full of God during the day, and particularly of the salvation of others, and I can offer up heartfelt prayers in my solitary walk, but this dreadful listlessness comes on me morning after morning and evening after evening.

1821   May 16
It is most strange that so philosophical a sect as the Socinians should believe Christ to be a mere man, yet to be exalted "far above all principality and power &c, *not only* of this world, *but also* &c" and to have "all things put under his feet". For, according to their Creed, sin is a venial, trivial matter, nor is this world extraordinarily circumstanced. How then is it to be believed that the Almighty should have distinguished this little globe &c.

1821   June 1
When I have heard or read that Horsley, Milner &c were adverse to the introduction of the doctrines of election, final perseverance &c into the pulpit, I have wondered at and been sorry for such an opinion. However, when I come to examine my own ideas on the subject, I have much the same sentiments. Do we See St Paul or St Peter in the Acts addressing the unconverted in this manner?

1821   June or July
I speak of (the process of) conversion with great diffidence, being obliged to adopt the language of books. For my own feelings, as far as I remember, were so different from any account I have ever read, that I dare not go by what *may* be an individual case. (p 58 and p 65 below)[1]

1821   June 1
About a week ago I dreamed a spirit came to me, and discoursed about the other world. I had several meetings with it. Dreams address themselves so immediately to the mind, that to express in any form of words the feelings produced by the speeches, or the speeches themselves of my mysterious visitant were a fruitless endeavour. Among other things it said that it was absolutely impossible for the reason of man to understand the mystery (I think) of the Holy Trinity, and in vain to argue about it; but that every thing in another world was so *very, very plain*, that there was not the slightest difficulty about it. I cannot put into any sufficiently strong form of words the ideas which

---

[1] pp. 167 and 172 respectively. C.S.D.

were conveyed to me. I thought I instantly fell on my knees, over-come with gratitude to God for so kind a message. It is not idle to make a memorandum of this, for out of dreams often much good can be extracted.

1821.   June 5

Buckland has just noticed in his geological lecture the extraordinary fact, that, among all the hosts of animals which are found and are proved to have existed prior to 6000 years ago, *not one* is there which would be at all serviceable to man; *but* that directly you get within that period, horses, bulls, goats, deer, asses &c are at once discovered. How strong a presumptive proof from the face of nature of what the Bible asserts to be the case.

1821   September 7

It is more than three months since my last note. I have in this interval been principally engaged in collections of texts from Scrip-ture (vid supr. p 57. "June or July." It was a collection of texts on a large scale, illustrative of the process of conversion. vid infr. p. 65, July 6. 1826. Great portions of it are among my papers.)[1]

1821   September 7

Except on the orthodox scheme, how is the *need* of a Mediator explained. If he made no atonement, what need of a creature praying his Creator to be merciful (to man)? What an empty, unmeaning formality, to make a being who would be without authority, influence &c requisite to induce God to pardon sinners!

Again, if God pardons without any atonement, why did he make the law so strict as to be an occasion of stumbling on Adam's part? It was nothing else, if it was of that accommodating nature, that it might, consistently with the holiness of God be raised or lowered in standard. But, in *our* view, the law is immutable like its Divine Author, and must be observed; therefore, when man falls, the Son of God must become incarnate. How does the Socinian scheme "magnify the law, and make it honorable?" These two thoughts are suggested by Scott's Essays.

1821.   October 15

If there were the least merit in works, why should a man (as we

---

[1] pp. 167 and 172 respectively. C.S.D.

find from Ezekiel xviii, 26) lose his hope of heaven, who, the last years of his life spent in good works, falls into sin and dies in it? His end does not in *justice* obliterate the merit of what he did before it. Some, however, will say, "We do not allow, strictly speaking, that works have merit to save—in reality a perfect life has only the *negative* power of saving from hell; but God's *mercy* has appointed that works shall be of avail to carry him to heaven. Consequently God may impose what conditions He pleases to an *act of grace*; and He is pleased to appoint that the good works of him only shall be efficacious, who does not fall away & die in sin." (This is pretty nearly the Catholic's answer.)

1821 October 15
When the Apostles &c speak of our "working out our salvation," their meaning seems to have the same relation to strict doctrinal exactness, that popular language in astronomy has to philosophical truth. Thus I say "the sun rises", instead of "the earth has rolled round so much that we come in sight of the sun."

1821 October 15   (scribbled partly in pencil)
Reasons in behalf of the Mosaic length of the world (earth) (6000 years).
1   from the shape of the earth—density, width at the equator
2   from useful (to man) beasts being created about (6000) years ago
3   from no skeleton of man older than that date
4   from the localization still of plants, trees, fruits, vegetables &c.
5   from the comparatively still scanty population of the world
6   from the absence of remains of man's works of very high antiquity.

1822.   August 20
I know well what a painful and ridiculous sense of shame I have on light occasions. It affects me like bodily pain, and makes me cry out. It is like a sword running through me. Will not this give force to such texts as Dan. xii, 2? To (bodily) torment, to evil passions &c &c. in the miserable damned is to be added shame and everlasting contempt. (After my first University Sermon, July 2, 1826, I lay on my sofa writhing, at the thought what a fool I had made of myself. May 25. 1874)

1822   August 25
Did Moses conceive the vast design of Scripture prophecy? how precise, definite and univocal are his words! And then the prophets have taken it up and on from generation to generation. The one same plan—no room for the supposition of chance. They *resolutely* pursue the one line of prophecy. Take the Protestant Church in the course of 300 years, what a striking variation of sentiment and faith is visible! Why too did they form the plan of prophesying events which were not to happen for ages after their own death? ... N.B. May it not be said, in objection, that there was less danger of confutation in prophesying distant events? ... How too were they preserved? Bad priests & priests of Baal were of frequent occurrence. The Scriptures are full of writings against *them*, and not only so, but against the whole nation. Yet no teaching more indulgent was introduced, nor the unpopular books destroyed. If not divine, their books and their plan are the most wonderful phenomenon the world has seen. Men praise and wonder at the continuous policy of the Popes— but that was for their own interest. The course taken by the Jewish prophets was just contrary to their worldly interests.

1822.   September 29
The doctrines of grace are like objects placed on one side of us, which we see indirectly with the corner of our eye, if we look straight (before us), but which we cannot *look at*.

1822.   December 13
Analyze the character of Saul, & show how naturally he is drawn. Were the history from an uninspired pen, the enemy of the reigning family would have been drawn in very dark colours—but how many are there with less dignity of soul and magnanimity (vid. Cincinnatus) than the apostate monarch of Israel.

1823   January 19
I recollect (in 1815 I believe) thinking I should like to be virtuous, but not religious. There was something in the latter idea I did not like. Nor did I see the *meaning* of loving God. I recollect (in 1815) contending against Mr Mayers in favour of Pope's "Essay on Man". What, I said, can be more free from objection than it? does it not expressly inculcate, "Virtue alone is happiness below"?

1823   January 26

Even supposing there were something in the notion of a vicarious sacrifice quite at variance with man's ideas of justice, and little evidence for it, yet had we a deep and humbling view of our extreme sinfulness and peril, terror itself and interest would induce us to cling to this gospel which offers peace. Men are easily enough persuaded to what they desire on the most insufficient reasons, and with the most striking inconsistency of principle.

1823   February 2

It may be said "There is something so inconsistent in your view of religion. God the sole worker, yet man co-operator. These statements cannot be reconciled; it is a needless mystery. How much more simple is our belief! viz that this is a scene of *probation*, that God sent His Son with offers of pardon and peace for any who call upon Him; that He gives preventing grace *by suggesting to the mind good thoughts;* and then, if we accept and cherish them, we shall have more grace given &c." I allow it. The Christian's belief certainly seems to himself inconsistent. It is a trial of his faith. The question is not, "which is the more natural scheme?" but "which is the Bible scheme?" Now the Bible expressly calls it a mystery, and glories in that mystery. And it seems to delight in setting the two doctrines in direct opposition to each other. Vid. Phil ii, "Work out your own salvation &c *for* &c"

1823.   April 6.

We may perhaps fancy that creations had been, and been annihilated, beings of every perfection had sprung into life, variations of existence of which [we] can have no conception, yet all of them, through the series of innumerable years, had been good, and holy and rejoicing, when all of a sudden, in one corner of the infinite dominion, a newly created being sets up the standard of rebellion, an idea which never before could have even entered into the conception of God's creatures. How must have all nature shrunk in horror and awe at the unnatural event! To perceive one little spot in the eternal atmosphere infected and fevered with sin! and what can be more exquisite presumption than for that guilty being himself to pretend to measure his own transgression, to call it mere imperfection, to assign it its due punishment, to treat with anger the idea of its meriting eternal vengeance, and to scoff at the doctrine which teaches the necessity of a Saviour, and Him, the Eternal Son of God!

1823   April 6.

If a man speaks incoherently, as I think, on regeneration, if he speaks of the merit of works, if he speaks of man's natural free-will, I may suppose I do not understand him, and that we differ in *terms*. But, when he talks of our natural sin as an *infirmity*, and I as a *disease*, he as an imperfection, and I as a poison, he as making man imperfect as the Angels may be, I as making him the foe of God and an object of God's wrath, here we can come to no agreement with each other, but one or other of us must fearfully mistake the Scriptures.

1823   April 13

We are apt to get censorious with respect to others, as soon as we ourselves have adopted any new strictness. At least, that is the case with me. For a long time after God had vouchsafed His grace to me, I saw no harm in going to the play[1]; directly I changed, I grew uncharitable towards those who went. While I was an undergraduate, I profaned Sunday, for instance, I made no objection to reading Newspapers on Sunday: yet the minute I leave off this practice, I can hardly bring myself to believe any one to have a renewed mind who does so. Humility is the root of charity. Charity hopeth all things, even as regards those who outwardly appear offending.

1823   August 3

Why may not females employ themselves in needle work on the sabbath? Having been used to it all through the week, they cannot attend so well to (hearing) reading without it. Having nothing to do, they become drowsy. Sunday becomes a weariness. Supposing needle work be for a charitable pursuit, it is as good as cooking. It may in particular families be inexpedient, but the question is, Is it in itself wrong?

1823   August 10

Moses, the meekest of men! What other (book) thus describes a victorious leader and a sagacious legislator? and he was excluded from the promised land for *one* defect in meekness.

1823   October 19

[Lee] has just told us in the University Sermon that we have "the

---

[1] (Till 1821 but I don't suppose I can have gone more than once or twice in between 1816 and 1820.)

word of the *Omniscient* that the earth shall be filled with the knowledge of the Lord". These are your free willers! I should have spoken
of "the word of the *Almighty*."

1824   September 16

Those who make comfort the great subject of their preaching seem to
mistake the end of their ministry. *Holiness* is the great end. There
must be a struggle and a trial here. Comfort is a cordial, but no one
drinks cordials from morning to night.

1826   July 26

Is it possible that nearly two years are gone since I wrote in this book?
My parish engagements will account for this. In that time I have
greatly changed my views on many points. I transcribe the following
from loose notes which I find among my papers. It is written in 1821
and appended to a *description* of the ordinary *process* of conversion,
(i.e. the hopes, fears, despair, joy &c &c of the person under conversion,) which I then thought almost necessary to a true Christian.
"I speak of conversion with great diffidence, being obliged to adopt
the language of books. For my own feelings, as far as I remember,
were so different from any account I have ever read, that I dare not
go by what *may* be an individual case." (vid above p 57).[1] That is, I
wrote *juxta praescriptum*. I am persuaded that very many of my most
positive and dogmatical notions were taken *from books*. In the matter
in question (conversion) my feelings were not *violent*, but a returning
to, a renewing of, principles, under the power of the Holy Spirit,
which I had *already* felt, and in a measure acted on, when young.

I have found a number of Sketches of Sermons, experimental, of
the date of 1823. I am burning them. (May 26, 1874).

1.	September 5. 1823 on	John xiv, 21-23
2	October 10	Acts xv, 9
3	October 11	Prov. xviii, 14
4	October 11	2 Tim. iii, 7
5	October 12	Isai. i, 6
6	October 12	Phil. iii, 12-14 from Simeon's skeleton
7.	October 13	Gal. ii, 20
8		Acts xxi, 13
9	October 16?	Eph. v, 19

[1] p. 166. C.S.D.

10   October 19   Ps. ix, 17 Consult Whately for arrange-
                                       ment of arguments.

11   October 26   Luke viii, 5
then one of 1824
12   May 2   Luke xxii, 25-27

about 1826

Mauvais honte arises from the sense of the ridiculous in oneself; hence those who are at once self contemplative and humorous are bashful.

Humour is of fancy, wit of wisdom;—humour of sentiment, wit of intellect. Humour raises laughter, wit admiration. Humour extends to actions, (e.g. practical jokes) wit is in words

Literary fancy, ingenuity, powers of illustration, go together.

Fancy is not imaginative, for ridicule is a wet blanket on imagination, but is fuel to fancy. Fancy is the orator's, imagination the poet's.

Mathematical power depends on the strength & *steadiness* of the abstractive faculty—so does metaphysics—so a talent for chess—so tracing out genealogies & relationships. (*My* power of thought is not *steady*, my mind wanders.)

Dornford has elegance without taste, and is in consequence fine; Rickards has taste without elegance, and is in consequence homely & prosaic.

Hawkins and Newman are both acute; but Hawkins from quickness of sight, Newman from quickness of logic. H. is slow in investigation, but so clear-sighted that he has no need of it; N. evolves so quickly that he cannot recollect what his first sight was.

N. is cautious from fear of turning out wrong; H. from coolness of head and dispassionateness.

Hawkins is so clear, that he cannot enter into difficulties, or sympathize with those who have them.

Whately writes for those who are below him in intellect; Hawkins for those who are above him.

In 1820 about, a schoolfellow to get out of debt, asked me and Owen of Ch Ch, his friend, to advise and to act for him with Harley, the acting Manager at Drury Lane Theatre, of whom I knew *nothing*. I was stupid enough to comply, and more stupid, that, at his request, I wrote two songs for him

    Nothing came of it

Jany 2 1888   J H N

Miserecordias Domini in aeternum cantabo (re-copied)

Edgbaston.   July 22. 1855.   *Book or Part 2*
Extracts from my Private Journal of 1821-1828. I have altered nothing, only omitted.

The year 1821

August 4.   1821.

I have this week been preparing myself for the Sacrament, which, God willing, I hope to take with my brother Francis once a fortnight during the Long Vacation. These are my answers to Doddridge's Questions in his Rise and Progress.

... Praised be God, I think I am much more resigned to Him than I was, more contented, less careful of the morrow, less desirous of the things of the world. ...

... I am very deficient in spirituality in prayer, in brotherly love, meekness, humility, forgiveness of injuries, charity, benevolence, purity, truth, and patience.

I am very bad-tempered, vain, proud, arrogant, prone to anger, and vehement.

But I principally wish to attain a strength of faith, of which at present I feel the want very much. Every now and then momentary clouds of doubt cross my mind, ... but though thus afflicted, I have, what may God in his mercy continue, a "full assurance of hope", concerning my final perseverance, and have had it from the time of my conversion. I am also in great want of a fervent love towards Christ...

August 8. , Wednesday
The Queen is dead. O that I had prayed more earnestly for her life! when she was getting better, I was wicked enough to feel somewhat disappointed. I know not why. Poor Princess!

August 10.
My Father noticed that Charles was not so much with Francis and me as he could wish. We had in the morning been debating how Charles might be more with us. Thank God, who, without effort, has opened a way to introduce Charles to our readings from Scripture.

August 13.   Monday
In consequence of my informing my Mother of our intention of taking the Sacrament once a fortnight, she seemed to think I began to be righteous overmuch, and was verging upon enthusiasm. I was also leading Francis with me.

August 18.   Saturday
The time has come round for the celebration of the death of my dear Saviour ... how deficient am I in any good thing: ...
... I find my pride, vanity, haughtiness, know no bounds ... I am inclosed in a net ... I look down on others whom I do not know, and those I meet in the streets, who appear of an inferior rank to myself, with ineffable contempt, and look up with meanness, I may say, and awe to those who seem above me. I am horribly vain of my attainments, abilities, and performances. And, as to pride, it is leading me every minute into ill nature, anger, lying, and uncharitableness ...
   I bought Haweis's Spiritual Communicant yesterday, and shall examine myself by that.
   ... I am still very dead on the side of gratitude (to Christ)

September 1.
I have this fortnight been secured from temptation more than former weeks; I have not had so many opportunities of being proud, contentious, and ill tempered.
   About last Tuesday week, on the recollection and self reproach of hastiness and heat in conversation, I requested Francis always to look at me, as a hint against the danger.
   I have also behaved, I trust, more kindly to Charles than before.
   But I have sinned against truth not seldom; and have been constantly impatient at Francis.
   I trust I have prayed more frequently ... and have felt the peace and love of God diffused on my heart. I have interceded more frequently for others.
   So cold a veil does not seem to separate me from my Father. I am not so distant from Charles, and he, thank God, expressed himself pleased yesterday, when reading with us, with Scott's Commentary.
   O God, grant me to grow in grace daily, and continually to examine myself, that I may always know how my accounts stand, whenever called upon to reckon for my stewardship.

Septr 3   Monday.
Went to Ealing, and had some very profitable conversation, as I trust, with Mr Mayers.

Septr 20.   Thursday
We have been at Brighton about ten days.

Septr 23.   Sunday
Today and last Sunday I heard Dr Pearson at St James's Chapel. Ever since there was an idea of our coming out of town, I have prayed God that, when absent from home, we might have faithful preachers of His word, wherever we went. And see how graciously he has answered my prayer.

Septr 28.   Friday
Is it possible that ... Today I have come ... How entirely ought I to rely on the grace of God! [Portions either obliterated or cut out.]

Septr 30.   Sunday
After dinner today I was suddenly called down stairs to give my opinion whether I thought it a sin to write a letter on a Sunday. I found dear Francis had refused to copy one. A scene ensued more painful than any I have experienced.

... I have been sadly deficient in meekness, long suffering, patience, and filial obedience. With God's assistance, I will redeem my character.

Octr 1.   Monday
My Father was reconciled to us today. When I think of the utter persuasion he must entertain of the justice of his views of our apparent disobedience, the seeming folly of our opinions, and the way in which he is harassed by worldly cares, I think his forgiveness of us an example of very striking candour, forbearance, and generosity.

[Part torn out]

Oxford   October 7.   Sunday
I had some conversation with T. on religion. He has read Wilson's Sermons on Scott, and thinks Scott a fine character. However, I fear there is too much of the head, and too little of the heart.

Oct. 9.   Tuesday

D. called on me today. He is come up to enter at Wadham. Today I have paid him some attention, but I feel as if I had done him an injury, poor boy. I have been so much actuated by pride, vanity, and insincerity, and shame of knowing him from some peculiarities of his appearance, that I am cut to the heart to think of the earnestness and simplicity of his thanks to me.

Octr 10.   Wednesday

I felt at one time today more ardent affection towards my dear Saviour than I recollect feeling before, and a more eager desire to depart and be with Christ which is far better.

October 23

It is now eight weeks since I partook of the Lord's Supper, and I ought to have cast up accounts before this.

I think I have behaved more dutifully to my Father, though I am still very deficient.

[A paragraph cut out, and the following substituted.]

... I have many times fed my pride and vanity upon empty imaginations of my own importance.

As to ill temper, hastiness of spirit, cruelty, harshness of speech, I have not advanced an inch. I pray against it every morning, & when I am entering into it, but my hard heart will have its own way.

November 15.   Thursday.

I passed this evening with the Dean, whose Oriel cousin was there. He said the principal thing at the examination for Fellows was writing Latin. I thought I ought to stand; and indeed, since, I have nearly decided on so doing. How active still are the evil passions of vain glory, ambition &c in my soul! After my failure last November, I thought that they never would be unruly again, for I felt so resigned through God's grace that it seemed as if the honours of the world had no longer any charm in themselves to tempt me with. Alas! no sooner is any mention made of my standing for a fellowship, than every mound and barrier seems swept away, and the tides of passion spread and overflow and deluge me in every direction, and without thy help, O Lord, what will be the end of this? ὥσπερ ξὺν ἵπποις ἡνιοστροφῶ δρόμου &c.

[A passage cut out here.]

December 1 Saturday

Tomorrow I am to take the Sacrament. It will be five weeks since I last examined myself.

... I have had hardly anything of those clouds of momentary doubt, of which I used to complain. O grant the mercy yet till death!

For about a week I was wonderfully preserved from ill humour— but then it returned, and I am nearly, or quite, as bad as before.

How desirous I am of worldly honour! There is every reason for thinking I shall not succeed in my object, and I seem to see it would not be good for me—but my evil heart boils over with vain-glorious anticipations of success. It is not likely, first, because I am not equal to it in abilities or attainments—2ⁿᵈ because &c.

It seems probable, if I may dare to conjecture, that I shall fail once or twice, and get some fellowship somewhere at last. But all this is a digression.

My mind wanders so in prayer, it is quite shocking. ... I used to be afraid of breaking with the world; this I do not feel so much now. O that I were known to hold those opinions I *do* hold! how intolerable is the constraint which is now upon me!

December 3.   Monday

At the Music Room I sat by R. the whole of the second act. As I collect from him, Francis will not go to concerts from religious motives. This accounts for his backwardness, when I proposed to go with him tonight.

Decʳ 6.   Thursday

R. was drowned yesterday. O what are we better that we should be spared!

Decʳ 12.   Wednesday

I have gone on day after day so grievously sinning in ill temper, that I have come to the resolution through God's grace to make an open confession to Francis, the first time I do so again.

Decʳ 14.   Friday

I have such dreadfully vain thoughts, am so conceited, and am becoming so self-dependent, that I have resolved through God's grace not to allow any thoughts to arise in my mind about any excellence I seem to myself to possess.

Decr 15. Saturday. Wined with the Dean (Kinsey), and told him I meant to stand at Oriel. He showed me Plumer's Essay, and it threw me into such a fever,[1] I do not know when I shall recover it. If the distant and improbable shadow of success affects me so, what would the reality!

1822

Sunday. January 6.

At Kentish Town Chapel Mr Grant gave a very good discourse. It was on the year gone by, and two of his remarks deserve remembering. One, that we should mark the days or seasons of mercy, and commemorate them in succeeding years by some act of charity— Ebenezer. The other as follows:—"to come out of an affliction is an awful thing, for calamity either leaves us better or worse."

After Church my Father began to speak to me as follows:—"I fear you are becoming &c ... Take care. It is very proper to quote Scripture, but you poured out texts in such quantities. Have a guard. You are encouraging a nervousness and morbid sensibility, and irritability, which may be very serious. I know what it is myself, perfectly well. I know it is a disease of mind. Religion, when carried too far, induces a softness of mind. You must *exert* yourself and do every thing you can. Depend upon it, no one's principles can be established at twenty. You opinions in two or three years will certainly, *certainly* change. I have seen many instances of the same kind. Take care, I repeat. You are on dangerous ground. The temper you are encouraging may lead to something alarming. Weak minds are carried into superstition, and strong ones into infidelity. Do not commit yourself. Do nothing ultra. Many men say and do things, when young, which they would fain retract when older, but for shame they cannot. I know you write for the Christian Observer. My opinion of the Christian Observer is this, that it is a humbug. You must use exertions. That letter was more like the composition of an old man, than of a youth just entering life with energy and aspirations."

Many of the expressions here used are the real ones. Of many reflections, which ought to suggest themselves, these occur:—1. O God, grant me to pray earnestly against any delusive heat, or fanatic fancy, or proud imagination of fancied superiority, or uncharitable zeal. Make me and keep me humble and teachable, modest and cautious. I have sadly neglected till lately to pray against fanaticism, spiritual pride &c. 2 How good is God to give me the assurance of

[1] (I thought to myself I could do as well or better.)

hope. If any one had prophesied to me confidently that I should change my opinions, and I was not convinced of the impossibility, what anguish should I feel! still however, let me not be unguarded and incautious.

Jany 11.   Friday
My Father this morning said I ought to make up my mind what I was to be. ... So I chose; and determined on the Church. Thank God, this is what I. have prayed for.

Jany 12.   Saturday
I left this day for Oxford. My Father's last words were, "Do not show any ultraism in any thing."
... My Grandmother does not seem well. "We may never meet again on earth," she said. "I trust we shall in heaven."
   Now I ought to ask myself how I have spent the Vacation, and whether to the glory of God. ... Once particularly I was very undutiful to my Father—once to my Mother. I have been generally hot and violent, showing great want of meekness and gentleness. Towards Francis I have been very violent and ill tempered[1] and perverse. On the whole I really think I have done more harm than good. I could see how surprised they were at my want of temper. I apologized for both the instances I mentioned, but what little good does that do!

January 22.   Tuesday
My Mother informs me that it is likely Francis does not return to Oxford. This is a severe stroke. Give me grace, Lord, to bear it. It is a just rebuke and punishment to me for the wicked ill nature and moroseness with which I treated him last term.
Ogle has just been here to offer me a pupil. My present precarious situation with regard to money is a just punishment for the way I sometimes wasted it, when I had it, and the little I gave away in charity.

Jany 23.   Wednesday
Yesterday I noted down Ogle's kind proposition of a pupil; today I have to register an equally kind one of Kinsey's. I have not yet looked back on the year past—let me do so now.

---

[1] Corrected by Newman from "ill natured". C.S.D.

The year 1821 begins just after my most happy failure in the schools. And, on surveying the commencement of it, though I am conscious I am now too very blind, and shall perhaps next year wonder I could be now what I am now, still I am surprised at the irresolute state of mind and wavering purpose I then manifested. For I went once or twice to the theatre in the Christmas Vacation (1820-1821) and seemed so little to feel the impropriety of so doing, that I not only went of my own accord, but mentioned it in the company of religious persons. On coming to Oxford H. Withy lent me Wilberforce's "Practical Christianity", and a most delightful book I found it. It seemed to settle me and fix me against going to the play again of my own accord.

Now that I was a batchelor, I had more time for religious exercises, than when I was a fagging drudge. Mineralogy was my principal pursuit, (as Chemistry had been in the Christmas Vacation)—and musical composition. (vid. Copies of Letters Nᵒ. 2, fly leaf p. 21)

Now that I have Pupils,[1] have very little time to myself, am writing for the Latin Essay, and have thought of standing for Oriel, I lament I did not devote time to the composition of Latin, or the reading of the higher Greek classics, or modern History ...

At the end of the (Easter) vacation 1821, I was seized with an attack of my besetting sin in an incredible manner ...

Easter or Act Term I devoted nearly entirely to religion; for about six weeks, and July in the vacation, I was employed on that collection of texts, which I have not yet finished ...

Francis and I endeavoured to take the Sacrament regularly once a fortnight during the (Long) vacation. On coming to Oxford (after it) I undertook my first pupil. I commenced a practice of carrying Tracts about with me for distribution ... In the course of the Term my temper was continually put to the test, as I have said. [Passage obliterated.] (vid. "Copies of family Letters" No 2 pp 137, 138)

... N.B. I have determined to reduce Mʳ Grant's hint, (Janʸ 6, 1822) to practice—and have selected the following days. 1. My birthday Febr. 21, 1801. 2. the day of my baptism, April 9, 1801. 3. the first or last days of the half year of my conversion, Aug. 1. and Decʳ 21, 1816. 4. The day I was matriculated at Oxford, Decʳ 14, 1816. 5. The day I got the Trinity Scholarship, May 18, 1818. 6. The day I got my Testamur & lost my class, Novʳ 27. 1820. 7. The day when our prospects so changed, Novʳ 3. 1821. ...

[1] Newman first wrote "am a Tutor." C.S.D.

Jany 24. Thursday.
A letter from home this morning informs me that Francis is coming
to Oxford after all. Besides, I have another pupil. Three things I have
been praying for lately, and all three Thou hast granted me—that I
might be in the Church, that Francis might come to Oxford, and
that I might have another pupil.

Jany 27. Sunday.
Kinsey spoke to me about Francis today, and I mentioned to him
the Worcester scholarships ...
    Pope (S. L. Pope) was with us this evening—he was startled at the
idea, when I said that drunkenness, or rather getting drunk, was, in
the sight of God, nearly as great a crime as murder.

Jany 28. Monday
Today Phillips proposed to me to be Tutor in a gentleman's family at
Paris at £200 a year. This, principally for religious reasons, I refused.
How good God is, to give me friends who wish me well. How deficient
I am in praying for them.

Jany 29 Tuesday
I had a letter from Thresher this morning, in which he proposes a
pupil for me in the Long Vacation.

Febr^y 5 Tuesday
Today I called on the Provost of Oriel, and asked his permission to
stand at the ensuing election. I cannot help thinking I shall one time
or other get a fellowship there, most probably next year. I am glad I
am going to stand *now*, but have *very* little chance of succeeding. I
hear there are some very clever men going to stand; however, I shall
make myself known, and learn the nature of the examination. The
principal thing seems to be Latin Composition, and a metaphysical
turn is a great advantage. General Mathematics is also required. I
mean to attend Rigaud's Lectures (in Experimental Philosophy).
    Hope will arise, do what I will; but it is instantly beaten down by
some very weighty reflections. 1. I am not humble or spiritual enough
to bear success yet. 2. It will make me too independent in money
matters—at present God is trying me, and feeding me by the ravens.
I have need of a severe discipline in this respect. Independence would
make me secure. 3. Provision seems to be made for me for some time.
Last 5th of January I wrote to my Aunt, and said, "I deprecate that

day in which God gives me any repute, or approach to wealth." Alas, how I am changed! I am perpetually praying to get into Oriel, and to obtain the prize for my Essay. O Lord, dispose of me as will best promote Thy glory—and, after that, as will best advance my sanctification—but give me resignation and contentment. O Lord Jesus, in all thy dispositions concerning me, to rise or to fall, give me that heavenly peace which passeth understanding.

Febr. 21. 1822

My birthday. Today I am of age. It is an awful crisis. I say "awful", for it seems to leave me to myself, and I have been as yet used to depend on others. ... May this be a point, from which I may date more decision and firmness in my profession of religion! Lord, take any thing, every thing away, if I may not purchase grace without the sacrifice. Thou knowest my heart—I am in Thy Presence. Thou seeest how fondly, and I fear idolatrously, my affections are set on succeeding at Oriel. Take all hope away, stop not an instant, O my God, if so doing will gain me Thy Spirit.

Have I grown in grace this year past? ... how very proud and bitter I am in spirit! how unforgiving—how unclean—how timid—how lukewarm in prayer. It is dreadful to go through the list ...

... I am now entering upon a new stage of life. Lord go with me: make me Thy true soldier.

... Today we dined with Wilson. Symons was there, to whom we were introduced. (He had been one of my Examiners in the Schools)

March 7. Tuesday

I have called on Tyler of Oriel today, to signify my intention. I do not know how it happens—but I certainly feel very confident with respect to Oriel, and seem to myself to have a great chance of success. God keep me from setting my heart upon it, and feeling any disappointment, if I fail ... Hope leads me on to fancy my confidence itself has something of success in it, and I seem to recollect something of the same kind of ardour, when I stood at Trinity ...
God give grace! that alone I will implore. Thou alone, Almighty Guardian, art present—and Thou overrulest the hand and the tongue, when the votes decide the contest—the *whole* disposing of the lot is Thine. And wilt Thou not give me that which is *truly* good?

W. has written to Short, offering me a situation in a **gentleman's** family (I think Sir R. Simeon's) which Short declined for me.

March 17. Sunday

When I look back on my continual conduct to Francis, [a few words obliterated.] Not a day, I may say, passes without disturbance.

... As to faith, I have been harassed with doubts ... I am very proud, easily provoked, and have not, I fear, any part in St Paul's or St James's descriptions of love.

March 18. Monday

I sent in today my Letter to the Provost of Oriel, requesting permission to stand. I fear I am treasuring up for myself great disappointment, for I think I have a great chance of succeeding. ... I lay great stress on the attention I have given to mathematics ... on account of the general strength it imparts to the mind. ... Besides, ever since my School attempts, I have given great time to composition. I have never been, since that time, without frequent exercises in argument &c. As, when I was going up for my Degree Examination, every day made my hopes fainter, so now they seem to swell and ripen, as the time approaches. ... I have sinned most horribly as to ill humour.[1] I repent and pray, and the very next minute, on the slightest temptation, sin again, and so on.

March 23.   Saturday

Yesterday and today I find I cannot write Latin at all. See, God can take away the fruit of my labour at a stroke. Surely I have been setting my heart on success.

March 30.   Saturday

I have felt very little sanguine this last week about Oriel. I think most certainly I shall fail, and therefore have cause to look forward for some great trials this next year; for how am I to live? The Lord is my Shepherd; I shall not want. I am obliged to spend every day; but, whether from being unused to want, or from my natural temper, I feel no anxiety. Certain it is, I have no present means or prospects. "The Lord will provide."

I blush to say, I have been still very ill humoured[2] with Francis. I think I am rather better, but every now and then I have a sad burst, and it draws a cloud between me and God.

---

[1] Newman first wrote "nature". C.S.D.
[2] Newman first wrote "natured". C.S.D.

April 6.   Saturday
I have not felt sanguine about Oriel this week. Today was the first
day of our examination, and I am uncommonly tired with the continual exertion of between 8 and 9 hours of composition. Why, if I
were to get in, I should have no cross at all, for my only want is
that of *means*.

April 7.   Sunday.
Today being Easter Day, I took the Sacrament. I think I am rather
better in temper than I was. I fear I am sadly attached to the world,
for I am very much cast down and harassed by this Oriel business—
but not so much perhaps from fear of failing, as from mortification
at having given the Fellows a bad opinion of me by some careless
blunders.

April 8   Monday
The past night I have been in a sad state. I thought I had something
the matter with me. My back seemed quite inflamed, and I resolved
to go to some medical man in the morning. However, I afterwards
got some rest very calmly and refreshingly, and in the morning was at
least tolerable. We do not discover the blessing of health, till something promises illness. In the middle of the day, (and I was kept in
9 hours and more,) I was so ill I could do nothing, and was obliged
to walk about. (i.e. up and down the Oriel hall.)
(It was the same nervous affection which tormented me in 1833, at
the commencement of my fever at Leonforte in Sicily. Then I was
obliged to occupy myself in counting the figures on the pattern of the
room-paper.   Aug. 1. 1856)

April 9   Tuesday
This morning I was very, very nervous, and I prayed earnestly for
strength, and God gave it to me most wonderfully. (vid. "copies of
Family letters No 1 pp. 105, 6.)

April 10.   Wednesday
This morning I felt quite myself, and acquitted myself with very little
nervousness

April 11.   Thursday
I was more nervous this morning. I have several times been much

comforted yesterday and today, by a motto in Oriel Hall, "Pie repone te." Thank God. I am now going to bed, and have been very calm the whole evening. How can I sufficiently praise Him! Before I look at this book again, it will be decided. God grant grace!

Friday.   April 12.
I have this morning been elected Fellow of Oriel. Thank God, thank God.

May 13.   Monday
For some time past I have [Rest of sentence obliterated.]

June 2. Sunday
Weeks go on, and I am not a bit better, or rather I am worse; and this morning I have to take the Sacrament. O good God, I am unmerciful, hard hearted, unforgiving, pitiless. Thy blessings are infinite. I pray and bless Thee that this temptation, into which I have been gradually sinking this last half year, is not one of painful and perplexing doubts and fits of unbelief. I praise and bless Thee that it is not a fiery attack from my besetting sin. What will become of me? I am rolling down a precipice, and there is no arm in the universe that can save me but that of Jesus.

... 1st I will read the form of social prayer with Francis three times a week, by God's grace. 2nd I will try to repress every injurious word, though I think I am in the right. 3rd I will study my Bible at least an hour a day. 4th I will strive to drive away every wandering thought during my prayers.

June 30.   Sunday
I have been miserably beset (with bad thoughts) this last week. I trust that, though still very defective, I have not been so cruel to Francis since June 2, when I took the Sacrament.

Monday   July 1
Whately has proposed to me to undertake part of an Article on Logic in the Encyclopedia Metropolitana.

Friday July 12
What a mercy I succeeded this time; besides other reasons, there seem such formidable names about to stand next time, that I fear I should

have failed the second time; and now I have a home, and every comfort about me. It is God's gift.

July 15

I give an hour a day to the Apocalypse. My idea is to interpret its symbols &c by other Scriptures, and *then* to compare it with actual events. I find it most delightful.

Friday   July 19

I have shown petulance and ill nature towards my pupil. I find it very irksome to be so tied down as I am. I am too very solitary. ... Pound me, Lord, into small bits grind me down, anything for a meek and quiet spirit.

Wednesday, July 24.

God has given me all worldly goods in great abundance, and at the same time in discrete measure; giving me a perfection of health and domestic comfort, a very great share of mental activity and powers of exertion, and, more sparingly, yet quite sufficiently, the luxuries of life. He had done all things well. I am fully of opinion, that hardly a person can be found to equal me in favours received from God.

Sunday   Aug. 18

I have generally, since my last writing in this book, given the first hour of the day to reading the Bible ... I have, thank God, gone on very well with my pupil; not but that I am conscious of very great perverseness and ill humour in heart, but I have seldom shown it in my words.

Sunday.   Septr 15

There are very few occurrences in the Long Vacation to record. Since I wrote last, I have sometimes shown a most ungovernable spirit towards my pupil; still however, on the whole, I think, thank God, I am meeker than I was; at least I do not show it so much[1] ... I am glad to say that in my solitary walks, that is, my daily, I have had nearly always my mind disposed for secret prayers, and have generally made use of that interval from study, or a good part of it, in interceding for all friends, and for all mankind.

[1] (I was at Oxford through the Vacation. How I longed for it to be over! My pupil was a little wretch, aged 17. Aug. 3. 1856.) [Note crossed out in pencil. C.S.D.]

Sunday   Septr 22
I sent by this night's post a paper to the Christian Observer, on the snares to which religious students are exposed in the University.

Sunday   Septr 29
I have had much trouble the last few days with my pupil.
...It is humbling to find how little I know in Latin and Greek, and this my pupil forces me to find out.

Thursday   Octr 10
My pupil left me this morning, and thus our intercourse ends. ... He paid me £90.

Saturday Octr 26
I was afraid I should go on with but one pupil this term; today, however, a Merton man I knew nothing of called on me and said he wished to become my pupil.

Sunday Novr 17
This morning I received the Sacrament ... I am so little serious in prayer. I cannot attend ... I read the Bible so carelessly ... I have so sinned in ill temper towards Francis; thank God, I trust I am better. ... And then I have such a habit of saying things not strictly true. And then, instead of a humble reliance on Providence for temporal things, I have either a hard unconcern, or a presumptuous defiance, as if God must give them to those whom He has chosen. And then I have proud thoughts of myself, and I do not thirst after usefulness.

Sunday   Decr 1
I have just come from hearing Hawkins preach a most beautiful sermon. I trust, and hardly can doubt, God is leading him. Lord, Thou has blessed me with all goods, but make me Thine. Melt me down, mould me into the Divine Image. Let me be spent for Thee. Let me go through sickness, pain, poverty, affliction, reproach, persecution, any thing of worldly evil, if it is to promote Thy glory. O save me from a useless life, keep me from burying my talent in the earth.

Tuesday, Decr 31
... "Ah", I answered (my Mother) "I have felt while with Francis at

Oxford, a spirit of desperate ill temper and sullen anger rush on me, so that I was ready to reply and act in the most cruel manner to intentions of the greatest kindness and affection. So violent has this sometimes proved, that I have quite trembled from head to foot, and thought I should fall down under excess of agitation" ...

1823

Tuesday, Febr. 21

My birthday. ... First, let me notice the most wonderful and most parental manner in which the Lord has supported Francis and myself in temporal things. Michaelmas year we began with hardly any thing; nor was any channel perceptible by which we were to gain any thing. I had indeed one pupil, but there did not seem any great possibility of my having more. However, by God's grace, I was enabled to trust in Him, and I entertained, I may say, no apprehension of want or difficulty. How He has answered that trust! The Terms came, and the supply was always ready. I have been enabled nearly entirely to support Francis ... to enter him at Worcester ...and it seems as if I should have the requisite sum to pay for him, when he comes to reside.

The year past (1822) has been a scene of laborious study from the commencement to the close. Let me praise that excessive Mercy which has blessed me with so strong a frame. I have sometimes quite trembled, on retiring to rest, at my own exertions. (In the Long Vacation of 1822, I took, for I do not know how long, only four hours sleep. Aug. 3 1856) Quite well indeed am I, free from headache and every pain ... I cannot but think God intends to bring me forward in some way soon ...

Two great courses of sin stain the past year, ill temper and self conceit. My vanity is an excessive, and of late a growing evil. In the beginning of this Term, I had to speak an Oration in Hall—the Provost said it was spirited. Well, I have been brooding on this, and repeating the composition again and again to myself. Wherever I go, I think people are looking at me and thinking of me ...

Again, I am a great liar, a mean liar ... from pride, lest I should confess myself wrong.

[A sentence obliterated] each time of my going home in summer and in winter I was assaulted (by bad thoughts). I fear I can hardly call myself a bit stronger. ...

Friday April 4

I was admitted actual Fellow of Oriel today. When I think of the numberless, what the world would call, chances it is indeed wonderful I succeeded last year. Gracious God, let me in this so favoured station, in which Thy Mercy has lodged me, do every thing for Thy glory. I thank Thee, that two men (E. B. Pusey, W. R. Churton. July 23 1857) have succeeded this morning, who, I trust, are favorably disposed to religion, or at least moral and thinking, not worldly and careless men. Bless them both, dear Saviour, and bring them into Thy true Church.

Sunday, April 6.

Praised be Thy Name for the temporal blessings in which for the last year and a half, Thou hast sustained Francis and myself. How wonderfully hast Thou brought us through, beginning with nothing. Keep me from disquiet now that I do not see how Francis is to be *at first* supplied on his setting out at Worcester in May. By some mistake my pupil has not paid me yet—so that at present I have hardly more than a sovereign: ...

Sunday, April 13

I must explain myself in some way to the Fellows about my wish to keep Sunday holy. Last Sunday I dined with the Provost; this morning I breakfasted with the Dean. I did not know what excuse to make ...

I have taken a short walk with Pusey after Church, and we have had some very pleasing conversation. He is a searching man, and seems to delight in talking on religious subjects.

Thursday May 1

Today H. paid me £70. How could I expect so much! How little thankful I feel to Thee!

Friday May 2

I walked with Pusey today; indeed, I have had several conversations with him on religion, since I last mentioned him. Thank God, how can I doubt his seriousness? His very eagerness to talk of the Scriptures seems to prove it. Lord, give him[1] the abundance of Thy grace and wisdom, that I may lead him forward, at the same time gaining

---

[1] Newman has written above this "me?". C.S.D.

good from him. ... He has told me the plan of his Essay, and I clearly see it is much better than mine. Thou wilt give me good—I asked for good. I cannot think I shall get it, to this day I have thought I should

Saturday. May 10.
I have begun (Henry) Martyn's Life. What an improving book! how deficient it makes me feel.

Friday May 16
Francis's approaching residence has troubled me for some time past, as well as some debts I owe. I took courage to apply to T. today (Tyler lent me £60), and now I am quite rosy and joyful.

Saturday May 17
That Pusey is Thine, O Lord, how can I doubt? his deep views of the Pastoral Office, his high ideas of the spiritual rest of the Sabbath, his devotional spirit, his love of the Scriptures, his firmness and zeal, all testify the operation of the Holy Ghost. ... Yet I fear he is prejudiced against Thy children. Let me never be eager to convert him to a *party*, or to a form of *opinion*. Increase my humility, patience, charity, meekness, gentleness. Merciful God, lead us *both* on in the way of Thy commandments. What am I, that I should be so blest in my near associates?

Tuesday May 20
The Essay has been decided, and I have been unsuccessful. I thought I should not have been hurt at this; but, so far from it, I feel convinced I set my heart very much on succeeding.

Thursday May 22
I heard today that Pusey had got an Accessit. I had thought I should have wished him to succeed, supposing I did not, but the bad feelings and lowness of spirits which I felt convinced me I knew very little of myself.

Sunday, May 25
Within the last three months three pupils have been offered me. About one of them application has been made to me three times ...
     The Provost sent for me this evening to know whether I would accept the situation of Tutor in Lord Lansdown's family. I declined.

Sunday June 8

I have lately been reading several works about the Bible Society. My mind is nearly made up to become a regular subscriber.

I have been lately considering whether I had better take orders soon or not. Scott, as a general rule, says Not soon. Hawkins says the same—"Why bind yourself with a vow, when there is no necessity, and which *may* mean some thing incompatible with staying at College and taking pupils." R. doubts the propriety of College Tutors being clergymen. Mr Mayers, and he has been consulting Marsh of Colchester, advises immediate entrance into the Church by all means. "Nothing does the Church want so much, as clergymen, who, without the tie of regular duty, can make progresses among their brethren and relieve them at certain seasons."

Sunday July 13. I have just partaken of Holy Communion at Kew Church. How wonderful that we, guilty creatures, should be made *one* with Him who is purity itself! I have been looking at several texts relative to the ministerial office, and have been much struck and humbled by 1 Tim iv, 12.

Saturday Augst 9

In walking home this evening with Charles I took occasion to speak with him on the subject of religion. Our conversation lasted from Turnham Green to Knightsbridge; ... I shall put down a few of his remarks:—"The antecedent improbability of eternal punishment is so great that it is absurd to believe it. The argument about the word αἰώνιος is an absurdity; to be so nice as to make a doctrine depend on the meaning of a word! It is a point not to be thought about, and, if I must, how do I know even that the word is in the Bible, but by my eyes? but suppose I choose to say that transcribers put the word in? Well then, that leads me into a long argument which I do not choose to follow; so the shortest and best way is not to inquire about it. A woman murdered her four infants that they might not go to hell—now, if punishment were eternal, she was very wise ... Newton in his Cardiphonia mixes his own weakness with the Bible; so do many others; he had a vulgar mind. Scott is very inconclusive and weak. Now I do not find that in Butler's Analogy, which you recommended me. So it does not depend on me. ... Many presume on the aid of supernatural assistance, who have no such assistance. They weaken and soften their minds. All those arguments you produce about our being like prisoners, and thus bad judges of our guilt, and that we ought to feel love &c to God, &c &c seem to me absurd. People are not in earnest, when they call themselves the vilest of sinners. In gratitude to God! I do not see we have so many calls for gratitude. Man is not so bad; your way of asking for grace is very roundabout; so much machinery; why not read the Bible, and employ reason at once? I acknowledge that the Bible is full of declarations that the frame of our minds must be changed." I repeated my strong conviction that no one could understand the Scriptures fruitfully, unless it were given him from above, however orthodox his creed &c. that I did not confine salvation to one sect— that in any communion whoever sought truth sincerely would not fail of heaven; that three things were incumbent on every one, before he could pretend to judge of the Scripture doctrines,—to read the Bible constantly and attentively, to pray for grace to understand it incessantly, and to strive to live up to the dictates of conscience and what the mind acknowledges to be right.

Sunday Augst 10
Heard a most pelagian discourse from St Martin (in the Fields) pulpit in the afternoon,—that we were born pure, and that original sin did not mean what we were born with, but what we acquired by habit; all the passages such as "I was shapen in wickedness" &c, "by nature the children of wrath" were figuratively only; to talk of original sin was blasphemy, for whatever God created was "very good" &c.

Saturday Aug. 16
This evening I argued with my father with very unbecoming violence. I was not, I believe, at all warm, but I have got into a way of asserting things very strongly—"so & so is most *unjust*", another thing "most illogical" &c Not that I give hazardous opinions or hasty judgments, but my manner is hasty and authoritative. This manner proceeds from pride. But he thinks it worse than it is. I have accustomed my-self to laughing sometimes when I argue to prevent my engaging too seriously in a dispute, becoming angry &c, but this may certainly degenerate into a contemptuous manner &c and as such he takes it.

Saturday Septr 27
I intend taking the Sacrament tomorrow.—I am still very vain, cold

in prayer, proud, ill tempered, insincere, implacable. The other day I was very much out of temper with Francis, and it lasted till the next morning.

Friday October 10
I have left Worton—during the three weeks I was there, I trust I have grown in grace. ... I have just received a letter to say that the £50 which I relied being paid me now, cannot be yet paid. I have but a few shillings in my pocket, and owe many bills. I have forgotten to say I have near £2 in the Bank, and probably Ch. (Chamb.) will send me his £50 or part of it by a friend.

Sunday October 19
Last week or two I have been learning Scripture by heart, and have just finished the Epistle to the Ephesians.

Friday, Octr 24
Have just had a most delightful walk with Pusey—our subjects all religious—all devotional and practical. At last we fell to talking of Henry Martyn and Missionaries; he spoke beautifully of the question, "Who are to go"? Lord, I am conscious of horrible pride. I delight myself with the idea that he must think me very spiritual and very eloquent. In many things I am not fitted for a Missionary; my eyesight is short; my voice is weak, my whole frame is very nervous; my constitution is very susceptible of cold—what is more my present circumstances and my abilities point another way. I have not a solid mind, a sound judgment, an acute understanding, power of mastering languages, arguing (perhaps I have reasoning) powers, a mathematical and rigidly demonstrative mode of thinking; but still, as I think the Missionary office the highest privilege from God I can possess, though I speak blindly, it will not be wrong to pray to God to make me a Missionary—therefore in future I purpose to do so.

Sunday Octr 26
I have the past week learned by heart the xii, xxv, & xxvi chapters of Isaiah. This morning I have begun to rise at half past five, taking care to be in bed by eleven.

Tuesday Novr 4
I am so straitened for money—and I prayed more earnestly than usual for relief. The post has brought a letter from Ch. inclosing £25.

Sunday Novr 9
Received the Sacrament at St Mary's

Sunday Novr 16
Received the Sacrament in chapel; but my thoughts wander, and my
heart is cold—and I have just returned home (to my lodgings) sad.
yet this morning from 6 to 7 God granted me to pray fervently

Thursday Novr 20.
I am at present too much engaged. Today, for instance, from 6½ to
8 prepared my lecture for Dr Lloyd, breakfasting at the same time;
from 8 to a quarter to 9 chapel—from a quarter to 9 to a quarter to
11 lectures (private pupils); from ¼ to 11 to ¼ past 12 at Lloyds, from
¼ past 12 to ¼ past 2 Lectures (private pupils). Then I had to compose
a letter for D. on his standing at Corpus. From ¼ to 3 to 4 walked
with P. to cram him—from half after 4 to 7 dinner and chapel; from
7 to 9 Lectures (private pupils), and here I write at 10, tired with the
day, and ready, God willing, for rest.

Wednesday Novr 25
I have learned 8 ch^s of Isaiah by heart, from 50th to 57th inclusive.
May they be imprinted on my heart as well as on my memory.

Friday Decr 19
Tomorrow I leave Oxford. I have been much straitened for money.
My Pupils delay to settle with me: If all that is owed me were paid, I
should have nearly £100 in hand. Writing to Mr Mayers a year back
I said, "If we were landed in Michaelmas 1823, I should be without
fear". God is graciously teaching me not to trust in myself.

1824

Monday January 26
Left for Oxford. When I got home, Francis, who arrived from
Worton soon after, relieved me with seven guineas—and now I am
again reduced.
    The principal thing I have done, while at home, is a Review of
Duncan's Travels in America for the British Review.

Sunday Febr 1.
Have just walked with Pusey. He seems growing in the best things, in

humility and love to God and man. What an active, devoted spirit! God grant he may not, like Martyn, "burn as phosphorus."

Monday Febr^y 9

O Lord, Thou doest all things well. I owe much; many bills should have been paid long ago; the very forbearance of the persons concerned in asking their money distresses me. Francis too is coming up. Yet I am fully confident Thou wilt relieve me—how mercifully I have been delivered hitherto! ...

(Same date Febr 9)

... O gracious Father, how could I for one instant mistrust Thee? On entering my room, I see a letter, containing £35!

Saturday Febr^y 21

I have just received a letter from my dear sisters on my birthday. ... What am I that I should be loved and looked up to! I quite tremble to think the age is now come, when, as far as years go, the ministry is open to me. Is it possible? have 23 years gone over my head! The days and months fly past me, and I seem as if I would cling hold of them, and hinder them from escaping. There they lie, entombed in the grave of Time, buried with faults and failings and deeds of all sorts, never to appear till the sounding of the last Trump. ... Keep me from squandering them—it is irrevocable. Lord, Thou knowest me and, sinner as I am, this is a great consolation.

Praised be Thy Name, Thou surely art drawing up my mind to heavenly things—Glory to Thee, who hast chosen a poor wretch such as me!

At Lloyd's lectures I feel very conceited, he having kindly taken notice of me—yet, with gratitude to God I say it, He has enabled me several times to wrestle with my solitary thoughts, and to drive from me the devilish imaginations of my superiority of intellect. I trust I am beginning to learn not to exalt myself, not to push forward, not to catch at applause.

But as to pride—at home how I discover it, and here also! violence in speech, shame of being thought ignorant &c.

I trust my heart is purer than it was; this year I certainly have not been attacked, as before, by my besetting sin—particularly the last half—yet I am not what I ought to be.

It is painful to think how unsettled my principles are. On hardly a point have I made up my mind. Hawkins, however, has been declaring his opinions on some points, as appears to me, very erroneously, and feeling I am as a poor child without sense or strength, I trust God will enlighten me, and tell me what is the truth

It may be well to watch myself whether I am not very selfish ... what is most absurd, I am so in eating, not that I eat much, (tho' this is sometimes the case) but that I am dainty, greedy, indulge my palate &c.

Since October, I have, I may say uniformly declined invitations for Sunday evening among the Fellows—and, though I have sometimes dined with the Provost on Sunday, still, by intimating I wish to be alone, my friends have less perplexed me.

Besides the Paper on the Sabbath,...I have written little in any way during the year. ... Besides these, and some mathematical & grammatical papers, I have done nothing but some loose observations in answer to Herbert Marsh on the Bible Society.

Sunday Febr. 29
As the small pox is much about, and seems to attack the vaccinated without discrimination, and has at length seized my fellow lodger, I have thought it advisable to be re-vaccinated this morning. ... Tuckwell, on seeing the mark of the former vaccination, said it was 20.000 to 1 I should not catch the small-pox, even if I went into the sick man's room. ... It will not be over for a week to come ... (It did not take)

Saturday March 13
Lloyd stopped me after lecture today, and proposed to me to compose a work for him for the use of students in divinity, containing such miscellaneous information as is only to be found in Latin, such as that respecting the Talmuds, the Septuagint Version &c &c ... I am reading the Homilies, Apocrypha, and Mant's Prayer book, and searching the Bible, with reference to the question of Regeneration. With Lloyds we are reading Prideaux's Connection—last Term we did Sumner's Records of Creation, Graves on the Pentateuch, ... and Carpzov on the Septuagint.

Monday March 15.
Took a walk with Pusey—discoursed on Missionary subjects. I must bear every circumstance in continual remembrance. We went along the Lower London road, crossed to Cowley, and coming back just

before we arrived at Magdalen Bridge turnpike, he confessed to me,
... O Almighty Spirit, what words shall I use? My heart is full. How
should I be humbled to the dust! what importance I think myself of!
my deeds, my abilities, my writings! whereas he is humility itself,
and gentleness, and love, and zeal, and self devotion. Bless him with
Thy fullest gifts, and grant me to imitate him.

Tuesday March 16
Lloyd invited me to come and see him at Ewelme in the course of
the ensuing Vacation.

Wednesday March 17
Have been attempting the last fortnight to fast, but could not get
myself through the most childish greediness. ... At last I have today.
God grant it may be a means of grace.

Wednesday March 24
Fasted. (This fasting, I believe, was with reference to my approaching
ordination in June.)

Saturday April 17
Have been very ill tempered with Francis of late, but certainly much
better than I used to be;—*in fact I see him less.* ... Pusey is so good
and conscientious, he quite frightens me, and I wish him not to see
what I do. ... Tomorrow is Easter Day—Pusey and I went over and
dined at Ewelme on Wednesday last.

Tuesday May 6
Since I wrote, I have been very ill tempered to Francis.

Sunday May 9
I must have mentioned before this my dread that I was becoming
vain and flippant in my talk with the Fellows. The Dean has at length
expressed his feeling that the other day I spoke sharply to him.

Sunday May 16
    To day I have come to a most important determination. St Clem-
ent's Church is to be rebuilt—but, before beginning the subscriptions,
it is proposed, Gutch the Rector being incapacited through age, to
provide a Curate, who shall be a kind of guarantee to the subscribers

that every exertion will be made, when the Church is built, to recover the parish from meeting houses, and on the other hand alehouses, into which they have been driven for want of convenient Sunday worship. The curacy has been offered to me, and, after several days consideration, I have accepted it. The parish consisting of 1500 souls, is increasing, and likely to give much trouble. The only good objection against my taking it is my weakness of voice. Mr Mayers advises me to take it; so does Tyler, Hawkins, Jelf, Pusey, Ottley; through Pusey indeed it was offered me. When I think on the arduousness, I quite shudder. O that I could draw back, but I am Christ's soldier. Every text on the ministerial duty and my ordination vows, within this last day or two, come home to me with tenfold force.

Yesterday I went and subscribed to the Bible Society, thinking it better to do so before engaging in this undertaking.

Sunday May 30
I have finished *at last* my article on Cicero, after immense trouble; shall finish correcting it tomorrow, and hope to send it off.

Thursday June 3.
Pusey and Churton have today gained the prize-essays. Do I feel any thing of regret? do I feel sad that *I* have done nothing, as far as *University* distinctions go? I think not; certainly my calm deliberate opinion is entirely in favour of that which God has willed. "I am small and of no reputation."—and I thank my God for it most heartily. But are my affections in the same direction? would that I could satisfactorily answer this, as I think I can truly say that I deliberately prefer obscurity. I smile when others seem, as sometimes happens, to undervalue me for want of University honors. God has reserved some better thing for me, and in that I will rejoice.

Sunday June 6.
Last Friday I fasted and humbled myself. Last night walked with Pusey, and had some conversation with him about Scott's Force of Truth.

Wednesday June 9
Yesterday I fasted.
    I had resolved to apply to the Treasurer for a certain sum. Having to bathe this morning, and not waking early enough to do so and go

to Chapel, I missed the opportunity of seeing him; and before dinner comes, when I certainly should see and speak to him, I received £40. The joy shed over my mind at this great deliverance is such, that I could willingly undergo the same anxiety for the same delightful surprise. I seem to take on me the vows of the ministry with tenfold rejoicing of heart.

Friday June 11
As the time approaches for my ordination, thank God, I feel more and more happy. Make me Thy instrument ... make use of me, when Thou wilt, and dash me to pieces when Thou wilt. Let me, living or dying, in fortune and misfortune, in joy and sadness, in health & Sickness, in honour and dishonour, be Thine.

Saturday June 12
Now, on returning home, how hard my heart is, how dead my faith. I seem to have an unwillingness to take the vows, a dread of so irreparable a step, a doubting whether the office is so blessed, the Christian religion so true. I am fasting today. I am licensed after the Ordination tomorrow, I believe. The salary £45 besides surplice fees.

Sunday June 13
It is over. I am thine, O Lord; I seem quite dizzy, and cannot altogether believe and understand it. At first, after the hands were laid on me, my heart shuddered within me; the words "for ever" are so terrible. It was hardly a godly feeling which made me feel melancholy at the idea of giving up all for God. At times indeed my heart burnt within me, particularly during the singing of the Veni Creator. Yet, Lord, I ask not for comfort in comparison of sanctification. ... I feel as a man thrown suddenly into deep water.

Monday June 14.
Just now, as we were on the point of beginning our prayers, I asked Francis whether he was present at the whole Ordination yesterday. He replied, Yes, except that he went out for a short time after my ordination. Of course I perceived this was for the purpose of praying for me, *me* who at the time was so hard and miserable. This thought affected me so much that I got very little way in the form of prayer, before I found a difficulty of proceeding; and when I came to read Deut. xxxiii I was obliged to give up the book to him, my tears

burst out so violently. I made one more attempt to read and could
not. I went on sobbing, while he read, to the end. O the evil of my
heart, so vile, and so proud. How I behave to *him*! "For ever," words
never to be recalled. I have the responsibility of souls on me to the
day of my death. ... What a blessed day was yesterday. I was not
sensible of it at the time—it will never come again.

Tuesday June 15
What blessed days are these! how, in after life, shall I look back with
a mournful pleasure on the time of my espousals! O God grant it
may not be with grief. I read Hall (the Dissenter) on a Minister's
encouragements and discouragements, last Saturday and Sunday ...
Alas, before the Ordination, from a most absurd feeling of shame,
from pride, from other bad motives I wished it over.

Friday June 18
I have been reading B^p Wilson's Sacra Privata, how beautiful. Am I
in Thy ministry indeed? all is mysterious. Would I were a missionary
—but I am most vile and unworthy, and do not feel what I say.

Saturday July 3
On Thursday I called at the Church Missionary House, relative to
the questions I asked them by anonymous letter last March. They
say weakness of voice, shortness of sight, want of eloquence, are not
sufficient impediments. Indeed the Stations most deficiently filled are
such as, requiring scholastic attainments, do not require bodily
vigour &c.

Wednesday July 21
Had a conversation with Hawkins on real and nominal Christianity
in fact on conversion. He admitted there was a line, but he put it
much lower than I should. The majority, he said, of my congregation
would not be touched by my preaching; for they would be conscious
to themselves of not doing *enough*, not of doing *nothing*. May I get
light, as I proceed.

Sunday Aug. 15
Two Sermons a week are very exhausting. This is only the third
week, and I am already running dry. ... The question of regeneration
perplexes me very much.

Tuesday   Aug. 24.
Lately I have been thinking much on the subject of grace, regeneration &c. and reading Sumner's Apostolical Preaching, which
Hawkins has given me. Sumner's book threatens to drive me either
into Calvinism, or baptismal regeneration, and I wish to steer clear
of both, at least in preaching. I am always slow in deciding a question; last night I was so distressed and low about it, that a slight
roughness from someone nearly brought me to tears, and the thought
even struck me I must leave the Church. I have been praying about it
before I rose this morning, & I do not know what will be the end of
it. I think I really desire the truth, and would embrace it wherever I
found it.

Such was my state, when I have just received letters signifying that
my Sermons which I sent to my Mother have wrought a surprising
change in her. The fourth, on "The Wounded Spirit", seems to have
done her most good.

Saturday   August 28.
The following are extracts from Francis's letters. ... "She said, Your
words were like a sharp sword, but brought after them the most
delightful consolation" ... "She says she parts with some of the
Sermons as with dear friends."

Friday, Septr 3
Took tea with Mr Shepherd. He and Mrs S. seem to wish me to be
more calvinistic. What shall I do? I really *desire* the truth.

Sunday Septr 19
Alas, my Father is very ill—two physicians are in attendance.
Francis says he fancies he shall never get well.

Saturday   Septr 25
Summoned to Town by my Father's illness. What will be the end of
this? What may have happened, before I open this book again!

Sunday Octr 3
That dread event has happened. Is it possible! O my Father, where
art Thou? I got to Town Sunday morning. He knew me, tried to put
out his hand and said "God bless you." Towards the evening of
Monday he said his last words. He seemed in great peace of mind.
He could, however, only articulate, "God bless you, thank my God,

thank my God["]—and lastly "my dear." Dr C. came on Wednesday, and pronounced him dying; he might live 12 hours. Towards evening we joined in prayer, commending his soul to God. Of late he had thought his end approaching. One day on the river, he told my Mother, "I shall never see another summer." On Thursday he looked beautiful, such calmness, sweetness, composure, and majesty were in this countenance. Can a man be a materialist who sees a dead body? I had never seen one before. (His last words to me, or all but his last, were to bid me to read to him the 33 chapter of Isaiah. "Who hath believed" &c.)

Wednesday Octr 6
Performed the last sad duties to my dear Father. When I die, shall I be followed to the grave by my children? my Mother said the other day she hoped to live to see me married, but *I* think I shall either die within a College walls, or a Missionary in a foreign land—no matter where, so that I die in Christ.

Thursday Dec. 16.
I am lodged in the same house with Pusey, and we have had many conversations on the subject of religion, I arguing for imputed righteousness, he against it, I inclining to separate regeneration from baptism, he doubting its separation &c. He talks of assisting me in St Clement's, when he has taken orders.

1825
January 13.
I think, I am not certain, I must give up the doctrine of imputed righteousness and that of regeneration as apart from baptism. Let me, however, explain myself on the latter subject. It seems to me the great stand is to be made, *not* against those who connect a spiritual change with baptism, but those who deny a spiritual change altogether. (This refers to Dr Lloyd. Decr 14. 1857) All who confess the natural corruption of the heart, and the necessity of a change (whether they connect regeneration with baptism or not) should unite against those who make it (regeneration) a mere opening of new prospects, when the old score of offences is wiped away, and a person is for the second time put, as it were, on his good behaviour.

First, unless God is likely to vouchsafe grace in baptism, why ordain it for infants? 2. I will not think so well of human nature, as to suppose it capable of originating the good thoughts which careless men often have—why then may not baptism place a person in a state of favour such, that God is henceforth bound by covenant to favour him with His Spirit, as they can bear it? 3 And I confess it seems more agreeable to the analogy of God's works, that there should be no harsh line, but degrees of holiness indefinitely small. And it is presumptious to attempt to decide confidently concerning the spiritual state of others; and surely I have seen instances in which even excellent men have grievously erred against charity by judging others. 4 What did our Lord mean by bidding children to come to Him, if not for spiritual blessings? But these are a few of many things which have struck me. Vid. also Luk. iii, 16. I still rather hesitate— at least I do not like to apply the term "regeneration" to the privileges of baptism, though I do not use it on the other side.

Thursday Febr. 10
I have today engaged myself again to the Encycl. Metropolitana. ... Today I have had a letter from Smedley, enclosing £14 for my last? late? (Cicero) article.

Monday Febr 21
Received letters from my Mother & Sisters. ... What am I, a sinner to be so loved!

As yet the Church Subscription flourishes greatly, and my Sunday School is, I trust, in a good train for success. I find I am called a Methodist.

The necessity of composing sermons has obliged me to systematize and complete my ideas on many subjects—on several questions, however, (those connected with regeneration) though I have thought much, and (I hope) prayed much, yet I hardly dare say confidently that my change of opinion has brought me nearer to the truth. At least, however, I may say that I have taken many doctrines almost on trust from Scott &c and on serious examination hardly find them confirmed by Scripture. I have come to no decision of the doctrines of election &c, but the predestination of individuals seems to me hardly a scriptural doctrine.

These advantages of composing sermons are greatly counterbalanced by the empty vanity of mind, to which they have given rise. Many gownsmen frequent the Church—several of our College sometimes go, and all this puffs me up. My parish occupies my time so much, that I have little opportunity for devotion or private study of the Scriptures, and, though they come before me in writing sermons, and I am constantly praying in my walks, business &c, yet I am by no means satisfied with myself. Of late too I have neglected stated self examination. It would be a great comfort to me to give up my pupils—and a great one, if I were not to have, at least for some time, the public tutorship at Oriel.

I have not so much opportunity of displaying pride, yet I am very proud.

I do trust I am not so ill tempered as I was.

I seem more pure in heart than I was. I say it with trembling, but this year past God has been most gracious. I do not recollect one grievous attack—one or two momentary temptations I have had, but I have been able to turn my back upon them. Doubtless my incessant engagements is one advantage; besides I am getting older. What an age I seem to be! It is quite dreadful.

As to the observance of the Sabbath, I confess I waver very much, but to a clergyman, whose hands are full of business on Sunday it is personally a question of comparatively small importance.

God has been most gracious to me this year (1824) in relieving me from debt ... I have borrowed enough to pay off many tiresome accounts, among others that of Lincoln's Inn. How Thou hast supported Francis and myself now above three years!

I have lately become acquainted with Woodgate. (N.B. I knew him *generally* from 1819)

Saturday March 26
I have today accepted the offer Whately made me yesterday, of being Vice Principal of Alban Hall ... I have all along thought it was more my duty to engage in College offices than in parochial duty. On this principle I have acted.

Saturday May 28.
I returned last night ... I had gone to pay the last sad duties to my dearest grandmother, who died last Sunday morning, quite suddenly (aged 92) Thou hast made her my earliest benefactor, and how she loved me!

Sunday May 29.
I have this day been ordained priest. What a divine service is that of Ordination! The whole has a fragrance in it; and to think of it is soothing and delightful.

My feelings as to those ordained with me were somewhat different from those I had this time year. I hope I was not exactly uncharitable then; still I certainly thought that there might be some among them who were coming to the Bishop out of their own heads, and without the Spirit of God. But when I looked round today, I could hope and trust that none were altogether destitute of divine influence, and, tho' there was difference of spirituality, yet all might be in some degree spiritual. Then, I thought there were many in the visible Church of Christ, who have never been visited by the Holy Ghost; now, I think there are none but probably, nay almost certainly, have been visited by Him. Who then will dare to say that any certain individual has completely emptied his soul of divine grace, and that not a drop remains at the bottom or on the sides of the vessel? Then, I thought the *onus probandi* lay with those who asserted an individual to be a real Christian; and now I think it lies with those who deny it. Yet I do not even now actually maintain that the Spirit always or generally accompanies the very act of baptism, only that the sacrament brings them into the kingdom of grace, where the Spirit will constantly meet them with His influences, nor did I then judge uncharitably of individuals or pronounce hastily, though I certainly think I did not "hope all things."

Sunday July 17

I may add to my above remarks on my change of sentiment as to Regeneration, that I have been principally or in a great measure led to this change by the fact that in my parochial duties I found many, who in most important points were inconsistent, but whom yet I could not say were altogether without grace. Most indeed were in that condition as if they had some spiritual feelings, but weak and uncertain.

It is now the Long Vacation—still I am much engaged; the remains of my duties as Junior Treasurer and Vice-Principal take up much time; and, besides my Parish, I have to write an Essay on Miracles by Michaelmas.

Lately, last Term for instance, I have been sometimes reduced to neglect morning prayer, either from forgetfulness or excess of work.

Tuesday Octr 30

What a time has elapsed since I opened this book. My Mother and Sisters came down to Oxford the beginning of August, and stayed till the end of September. Jemima and Mary partook the Sacrament for the first time, the first Sunday after their arrival here, I administering it as priest for the first time. We all partook of it also the last Sunday they were in Oxford.

O how I love them. So much I love them, that I cannot help thinking. Thou wilt either take them hence, or take me from them, because I am too set on them. It is a shocking thought.

For my business today, e.g. Sunday, I first read morning Service at Alban Hall. Then came my duty and Sermons at St Clement's. Then the Sunday School for a while. Then churched and baptized. Then baptized privately, and visited a sick person, and, having a bad cold, I am tired. (I suppose I have left out the Sunday afternoon service by mistake.)

My views continue to change. I must beware of a contrary extreme in subordinate points

I spoke about five weeks back at Deddington in behalf of the Church Missionary Society—a first speech.

I had a dispute with the singers in May, which ended in their leaving the Church, and we now sing en masse.

I have been grievously pursued with vain self conceited thoughts, and my old temptation has been sometimes troublesome.

For about a fortnight at the beginning of this month I was stopping with Bowden, who was with his family at Southampton. Bowden meets with many infidels in the Law. He has been reading this summer at my recommendation, Graves, Davison, and Butler; and he is to read Sumner and Erskine.

1826

Sunday January 22

Jelf has left Oxford, being appointed Tutor to the Prince of Cumberland, and I succeed (as I believe) to the Tuition (at Oriel). My yearly income will now be between £600 and £700. Charles too is in a way provided for; and Frank too is coming on for his degree, with the prospect of a high class and a scholarship at Worcester, perhaps a fellowship at Balliol.

Tuesday Febr^y 21

The age I am getting quite frightens me. Life seems passing away, and what is done? Teach me, Lord, the value of time, and let me not have lived in vain.

The death of my dear Father has from time to time come across my mind in a most cutting way; and I have sometimes thought with much bitterness that I might have softened his afflictions much by kind attentions which I neglected. I was cold, stiff, reserved. I know I hurt him much. ... When ... he noticed to me his pain that ... I hardly said a word. Why could I not have said how much I owed to him, his kindness in sending me to Oxford &c &c. It is over, irrevocable. O for a moment to ask his forgiveness ...

... The succeeding to the Tutorship at Oriel has occasioned my relinquishing my curacy to Mr Simcox of Wadham at Easter (next).

I have been involved (in 1825) in work against my will. This time year Smedley asked me to write an article in the Encycl. After undertaking it, Whately offered me the Vice Principalship. The Hall accounts &c being in disorder, have haunted me incessantly. Hence my parish has suffered. I have had a continual wear on my mind, forgetting, mislaying memoranda, names &c.

I am almost convinced against predestination and election in the Calvinistic sense, that is, I see no proof of them in Scripture. Pusey accused me the other day of becoming more High Church. I have doubts about the propriety of the Bible Society.

I trust I have done good at Alban Hall. I have had a divinity lecture three times a week. Whately wanted me much to remain with him, and offered to increase my salary to the amount of the Oriel tuition. Mr Hinds of Queen's is my successor. I am very good friends with the men. They saw, I think, they had hurt me (last Michaelmas Term) On my part I think myself much more culpable than I did.

Lately I have been ill tempered towards Francis.

[A line deleted]

I have been very vain this year, inordinately vain of my acuteness, clearness of mind &c despising others.

I trust I am more careful of my time than I was. My very much business has made me hoard it as a miser. I have (I hope) more serious views of the nothingness of the world. I have a great dread of having lived in vain, and life is wearing on.

How is it I think so little, to what I did, about going as a Missionary? I fear thoughts of theological fame, desire of rising in the Church &c counteract my desire for missionary employment. What I want is a humble, simple, upright, sincere, straightforward mind. I am full of art and deceit, double dealing, display.

During the last year I have become more intimate with Whately.

I think him an excellent man. I quite love him. Hawkins is getting deeper and more spiritual views.

We are to have two new Fellows at Easter. May we choose aright, and may the chosen be holy and humble men, laborious, active, and self denying. (N.B. They were R.I. Wilberforce & R. H. Froude)

The article on Apollonius and Miracles is now finishing. I think I have improved in judgment of late, being more cautious, less fanciful &c.

And now, O Lord, I am entering with the new year into a fresh course of duties (viz the Tutorship). May I engage in them in the strength of Christ, remembering I am a minister of God, and have a commission to preach the gospel, remembering the worth of souls, and that I shall have to answer for the opportunities given me of benefitting those who are under my care. May God be with me, according to the prayer of my dear grandmother, "as He was with Joseph", and may I see the fruit of my labour.

Sunday May 7
I have now been engaged in the Oriel Tuition four weeks. The College is filled principally with men of family, in many cases, of fortune. I fear there exists very considerable profligacy among them. There is much too in the system which I think wrong. I hardly acquiesce in the general reception of the Sacrament, which is expected, or even in the practice of having evening chapel. I think the Tutors see too little of the men, and that there is not enough of direct religious instruction. It is my wish to consider myself as the minister of Christ. May I most seriously reflect, that, *unless* I find that opportunities occur of doing spiritual good to those over whom I am placed, it will become a grave question, whether I *ought* to continue in the Tuition. (N.B. This illustrates my view in dispute with the Provost (Hawkins) about the Tutorship.)

My article on Miracles was sent off yesterday week.

Monday June 5. 1826
The class list came out on Friday last, and Frank was in both first classes. How I have been led on! how prospered! from time to time it seemed impossible he could continue at Oxford. I went before, failing in the schools, to punish and humble me. Then, by gaining a fellowship here, I was enabled to take him by the hand. And now he is my τιμωρὸς φόνου.

1827

Wednesday Febr. 21.

Much has happened in the past year (1826) to make me conceited and vain. My pupils have, or I take care to fancy they have, a high opinion of me. I do not actually desire men's good opinion; I am not quite disappointed when I am overlooked; but "mihi plaudo ipse domi." It is self esteem. I am not straight forward in speech, I exaggerate, misrepresent. I am becoming somewhat worldly; thoughts about livings, the Provostship, promotions &c come before my mind. I am remiss in private prayer, and reading the Scriptures. I *do* struggle against this, but *how* difficult it is! At home at Christmas I was very self willed, harsh, proud, ill tempered.

I am not aware of any Christian grace I have grown in, except it be that I have a conviction of the value of time, and the necessity of working while it is yet day.

In the course of the past year (1826) I have begun Hebrew in the Long Vacation, and advanced to the end of Exodus. My circumstances improve, but I am still in debt. Frank is off my hands, but the rest are now heavier.

Blanco White has joined our common room party. He is a very well-read, ardent, ingenious, warm hearted, simple minded, pious man. I like him much.

My present duties I see; what I shall be, I know not. This, thank God, I have, viz a recklessness of tomorrow, an utter thoughtlessness how I am to live and to be supported years hence. I beg He may employ me as may best subserve His purposes of good to mankind.

Lloyd is the new Bishop of Oxford. He is very kind, and takes great interest in my plan of reading the Fathers; but he says that our theological systems do not agree. They agree more than when I was in class with him, but I do not tell him so. I deeply feel his kindness.

1828

Thursday   Febr. 21. 1828 and following days

Oh Lord, what a year this (1827) has been! What has happened, since I wrote in this book! My heart sinks within me. I am in Thy hands, O my God, and, though my body is weak, and my head will not bear the fulness of my thoughts, and my mind is heavily weighed down, yet I will strive in Thy strength to give some account of the year past, but, if I find it too much for me, I will leave off.

O my dearest sister Mary, O my sister, my sister, I do feel from the bottom of my heart that it is all right—I see, I know it to be, in God's good Providence, the best thing for all of us; I do not, I have not in the least repined—I would not have it otherwise—but I feel sick, I must cease writing.

... I do not recollect any thing worth writing down, that took place between Lent and Easter last year (1827), during that time my health improved vastly.

When I gave my birthday account last year, I was engaged in some researches into the history of Infant Baptism, which I sent home to Harriett and Jemima.

At Easter I had to preach the usual sermon in the College chapel, and got into some little controversy about it. The Provost Copleston liking it, recommended it to Whately (part of it was on the divinity of Christ) who accused it of Arianism. Hawkins thought it dangerous, and Blanco White thought it systematized more than Scripture does. So it must have been faulty more or less.* *(It took, without knowing it, Bull's doctrine of the "Subordinatio Filii." Whately, Hawkins, and Blanco White, were all verging then towards Sabellianism themselves.)

Till August my Mother remained at Eastern Terrace, Brighton, having in the meantime taken No 11 Marine Square, which *was* to have been ready by Midsummer day, but Mr P. disappointed us. Harriet & Jemima went to Ulcombe about the middle of July, and my Mother, dearest Mary, and I went together to Hampstead at the beginning of August, where I had agreed to take Marsh's duty for six weeks. Our stay there was, to me at least, full of vexation and anxiety ...

I had been engaged in a course of reading since the beginning of the Vacation, in preparation for the Schools, which I was to enter as Examiner in Michaelmas. I was three weeks alone (almost) with (my Mother and) dear Mary, my other sisters being at Ulcombe.

Golightly read with me for ten weeks, partly at Brighton, the rest of the time at Hampstead.

R. Wilberforce came from the North in September and with him I went to Rickards's (Ulcombe), where we stayed a fortnight, and then I accompanied him home to Highwood, where for the first time I saw his Father. My Mother and Harriet came over for two days during the week I was there. We all left together, and Henry Wilberforce and I came down to Oxford.

And now for an eventful time. I had been much and incessantly harassed during the Long Vacation. I had read moreover too hard; my mind had been too much on the stretch, and had suffered from too intensely dwelling on the object, for which I was preparing myself. When at Ulcombe, I had been very weak, and showed symptoms of low fever. The term had not long begun, when the crisis in A's[1] affairs took place, which we had so long expected. The feeling that A. was in great distress, and that a large sum of money was to be raised, sooner or later, distressed me. The Schools too at once excited and fatigued me. I was very weak, when they began, several examinations of difficulty fell to me. ... My dreams were full of the Schools and of examinations. To complete it, the news came of the promotion of the Provost to a Bishoprick, and we had the prospect of an immediate vacancy in the headship of Oriel.

This completed my incapacity. I heard of it on the Friday (Novr 23), when I was in the Schools—dreamed of it that night, and (I believe) the next—drooped during the Saturday, which was my leisure day—and on Sunday felt the blood collect in my head; on Monday found my memory and mind gone, when examining a candidate for the first class, (viz. Johnson of Queen's, now Dean of Wells) and was obliged to leave the Schools in the middle of the day.

At Dr Kidd's advice I was leached on my temples. On Wednesday I set off with kind Robert Wilberforce for Highwood for two days holidays. I got worse, consulted Mr Babington, who said it was a determination of blood to the head arising from over exertion of the brain, with a disordered stomach, and could not return to Oxford. After a week's stay at Highwood, I went down home to Brighton.

I add as a curious coincidence, that this attack took [place] exactly? on the anniversary of my failure when examined myself seven years before. (On the same day in November, 1851 the Judge decided that the Achilli case must go to a jury).

Now I must give some account of the mode in which this attack manifested itself. I was not in pain exactly; nothing acute, nothing like a rheumatic headache; but a confusion, an inability to think or recollect. Once or twice indeed, when my head was on my pillow, I felt a throbbing so distressing, though it was not violent, to make me sensible I had never experienced a real headache. It was not pain, but a twisting of the brain, of the eyes. I felt my head inside was made up of parts. I could write verses pretty well, but I could not *count*. I once

---

[1] i.e., Aunt Elizabeth Newman. C.S.D.

or twice tried to count my pulse, but found it quite impossible; before I had got to 30, my eyes turned round and inside out, all of a sudden.

And now how can I summon strength to recount the particulars of the heaviest affliction with which the good hand of God has ever visited me. ... Here every thing reminds me of her. She was with us at Oxford, and I took a delight in showing her the place—and every building, every tree, seems to speak of her. I cannot realize that I shall never see her again.

It is thirteen weeks tomorrow since we lost her. She was taken ill at dinner this day thirteen weeks, Jany 4. Spasms came on in the night, the next morning she was dying—she died at 20 minutes past 9 P M on Saturday the 5th.

Hawkins was elected Provost Jany 31, went up to Town Febr^y 1, and celebrated the great day of the College on the 2nd. Keble stood a good chance of being Provost.

I am just entering upon St Mary's as Vicar; thus am I taken from literary work to Parochial.

Pusey is to be married after Easter—he has been very ill, and some months at Brighton for his health.

Keble published his Christian Year last summer. Dear Mary learned many of them by heart. They were a comfort to her in her acute pain. Mr Mayers has died suddenly.

For some time I had a presentiment more or less strong that we should lose dear Mary. I was led to this by her extreme loveliness of character, and by the circumstance of my great affection for her. I thought I loved her too well, and hardly ever dared to take my full swing of enjoyment in her dear society. It must have been in October 1826 that, as I looked at her, beautiful as she was, I seemed to say to myself, not so much "will you live?" as "how strange that you are still alive!"

I have much to try me in the way of money matters. A's debts are not far short of £500 (I think in the event £700) Frank and I paid this sum between us.[1]

----

[1] This last sentence is added in pencil. C.S.D.

Oriel College.   March 18. 1838.

(This is the first instance of my hearing a confession)
March 18.—On Wednesday Evening March 15, as I was sitting in
my rooms, a young (person) man came in, and (in the course of conversation) by degrees said he wished to confess to me previously to
receiving the Sacrament of the Holy Eucharist on Sunday next
(today) and asked if I should object to receive his Confession. I said
I should feel it painful, both from the responsibility and the distressing trial of hearing it; and that I would think of it. He said he should
go elsewhere, if I would not—yet he wished me rather, and yet should
be sorry to pain me. I saw him again the next day, when he said his
reason was to gain peace of mind & that he had thought of it for two
years & more, & latterly from reading Bishop Taylor.—and when I
reminded him that if he began he must tell me *all*, he (assented as
being) said he was aware of it. Then I told him that I felt that Confession could not be separated from Absolution, referring to the
Exhortation to the Communion—and while I thought it would be
well for many of us at least in certain seasons of our lives, if we were
in the practice of *Confession*, that I was thus far decided as to the use
of *Absolution*, that it was a removal of the disabilities & bar which sin
put in the way of our profiting by the Ordinances of the Church—that
I did not see it was more than this, though I had not a clear view on
the subject, that if it was more I trusted I should be guided to see it—
but that any how the act was *God's*, & He could as really use me as
His instrument, though ignorant, as He could the inanimate element
in Baptism. This was the *substance* of what I said, and I added I
should be ready to receive him at seven o'clock on Saturday morning
in the Chancel of St Mary's.

So yesterday the 17th at the time appointed I was there, and sat
down against the rails at the Altar at the North end to get out of
view from chance intrusion—I sat in my Surplice—and he came and
knelt before me. Then I stood up and said over him the Collect, "O
Lord we beseech Thee mercifully hear our prayers and spare all those
who confess &c." On sitting down again I said "What you are to say,

is said not to me but to God" & he began his Confession—when it was ended, I asked, if he had told me all. Then I tried to make some remarks for his direction & comfort. Then I repeated the last answer in the Catechism "To examine themselves &c" and asked him if he could sincerely concur in what was there set down; he said he could. Then I stood up, and holding my hands over his head, pronounced the Absolution from the Visitation Service. Then when he had done praying, I took hold of his hands, raised him up and dismissed him.

Mart. 15. 1838

Domine dirige nos, et me praesentem, in plenam cognitionem Evangelii tui, ut omni ex parte tutus sim, neu in ullâ offendam; id vero prae caeteris assequar, in quo maximè haereo, quid velis sacerdotes tuos et docere et agere de absolutione peccatorum in Nomine Tuo. Qui vivis &c.

Domine Jesu Christe; misericors et longanimis, propitius esto mihi et G. ———— ut confessoris partes ego, ille confitentis rite et religiose agamus in gloriam Tuam, Qui vivis &c.

Concedas nobis, Salvator mundi, ut ego, sine culpâ in cogitationibus meis, audiam et loquar, et ille recipiat illam quam enixe petit absolutionem. Qui vivis &c.

March 1. 1839

Domine Jesu Christe, qui dixisti credenti omnia esse possibilia, subveni incredulitati meae. Fac ut vivat, Misericors Deus, Joannes G. Bowden, quem olim mihi dedisti contubernalem cùm adolescens essem, post autem fecisti, qui nunc est, maritum et patrem. Fiat voluntas Tua, clementissime Jesu; sed, si vis, miserere mei. Amen. Per pretiosum sanguinem tuum. Amen.

Ant. Reddam tibi vota mea, quae distinxerunt labia mea, et locutum est os meum in tribulatione meâ.

    V.   Respice in me et miserere mei,
    R.   Et salvum fac filium ancillae tuae.

Oremus

Agimus tibi gratias, Omnipotens Deus, pro nuperâ bonitate tuâ erga Joannem G. Bowden, quem aegrotantem in precibus habuimus, tu autem misericorditer ad sanitatem revocasti Per Dominum.

March 28. 1839. Good Friday

During this Lent I have observed the following rules, Sundays being altogether excepted.

I have used no sugar—I have eaten no pastry fish fowl or toast—and my rule has been not to be helped a second time to meat at dinner. I have eaten no meat at any other time. I have not dined out.

Exceptions have been, dining out three times—with Iffley Trustees, at the Provost's, & once in hall with Williams when I came away early—And the first two of these I ate pastry. I was frequently helped twice to meat as time went on. I have not abstained from wine.

On Wednesdays and Fridays I abstained from any food whatever till 5 P M. when I ate a biscuit—I ate no breakfast or dinner, but generally an egg at tea—sometimes barley water at 5 o'clock. Twice or three times I ate a biscuit in midday.

The Tempus Passionis, the week before this and this week, I left off butter and milk, besides. Several times, however, I took milk.

The Hebdomada Magna, (Passion week) I have abstained hitherto from breakfast and dinner every day, breaking fast on a biscuit at midday; yesterday (Thursday) & today I have abstained, & mean to abstain, from tea also & egg; tasting nothing either day but bread & biscuit & water. This I purpose to continue till evening tomorrow, when the fast being over, I may perhaps eat some meat.—This I *did* observe to the end—but I sh^d say that on Wednesday I took a glass of port wine. The only great inconvenience I have found has been face ache—for which I have used sulphate of quinine pills successfully.

St Matthew's Day.   1839.   Saturday.   Ember day.
To my surprise I found that on Wednesday & yesterday (Ember) I could fast till the evening without any inconvenience. I cannot account for it. I took a pill of sulphate of quinine in the morning, and again at noon. And at three o'clock P.M. I had some barley water. But I did not taste bread, biscuit, or any food whatever either day till 8 o'clock in the evening. And I went about my business as usual, not feeling weak, nor the day after (the Thursday)—as for today I cannot tell what will be. I write this in the morning. I do not intend to keep this so strict. Gratias tibi Domine—whither art Thou leading me?

July 8. 1841
O Almighty and Most Holy Lord, the God of the spirit of all flesh, who hast said, Vengeance is Mine, I will repay, and hast commanded us to judge not lest we be judged, we devoutly beseech Thee mercifully to pardon us, if we have erred in our dealings towards G[odfrey]

F[aussett] M[argaret] P[rofessor] of Divinity in this University. Thou savest, O Lord, those who sit still, and avengest those who suffer silently; grant that no mischief befall us for that we have done, and keep us ever from taking into our own hands the things which belong to Thee, through Jesus Christ our Lord.

Littlemore   1840
Feriâ 4ᵗᵃ Hebdom Maj.   April 15.

I have this Lent abstained from fish, fowl, all meat but bacon at dinner; from butter, vegetables of all sorts, fruit, pastry, sugar, tea, wine, and beer and toast. I have never dined out. I have not worn gloves.

I breakfasted on bread & hot milk with an egg; dined on cold bacon, bread, cheese, and water; supped on barley water, bread, and an egg.

On Wednesday and Friday I abstained from all food whatever to 6 P.M. when I added a second egg to my usual supper. I sometimes drank a glass of cold water in the morning for a particular reason.

During the Hebdomada Passionis I abstained from milk also, beakfasting on bread & water, except when I took nothing, i.e. Wednesday & Friday.

During the Hebdomada Major I have taken or mean to take nothing any day till 6 P.M., making then on the three first days the same supper as on Wednesday & Friday. Tomorrow & next day (Maunday Thursday & Good Friday) I mean to restrict my supper (my only time of eating) to bread and water. This I did to the end. Easter Eve.

On Holy Saturday I shall end the Lent fast at 6 P.M., and mean to take for supper, tea, sugar, bread, butter, & two eggs.

On Sundays and the Annunciation I departed from the above just so much as this,—to take tea morning and evening, and butter, to have my bacon hot, a glass of port wine (except Palm Sunday by accident) and dry toast at tea. On Sundays & the Annunc. I wore gloves.

On St Gregory's, being not well, I took some wine & water.

Exceptions were on the first four days of Lent, before I came up to Littlemore, when I took tea and butter in the *evening*, and on Wednesday & Friday had barley water and eat a biscuit at 5 P.M. and on Thursday hot meat & on Saturday cold meat with vegetables.

On the whole then I have lived on bacon, eggs, bread, milk, barley water and water; with a glass of wine six times, and tea & butter seven mornings and eight evenings. I have felt rather weak in limbs, but especially strong in voice; have felt very little fatigue, very little pain, and no languor or lowness of spirits. I have been able to think, write and read as usual. I have hardly for five minutes felt a wish to do nothing; & the time has not hung at all heavy on my hands. I have been up continually till midnight by choice. I have slept well. I have indeed often dropped asleep for $\frac{1}{2}$ an hour or an hour of an evening, but not more than usual. I have happened to see two newspapers, not more; I have seen my friends who now & then called, & Bloxam and Rogers once or twice stayed a while.

I was tried much by the *Service* on Good Friday; and today, having some extra duty. But rallied surprisingly. This morning I did not *miss* my breakfast. I could have fancied I had had it. *Easter Eve.*

I have had quinine pills by me, & have taken them from time to time, when I felt the need of them. I have had no face or teeth ache.

I have used the full Breviary Service from Ash Wednesday; the only omission being the Vespers pro defunctis on the first Sunday in Lent by accident.

I have made no attempts to curtail my sleep, or sleep on the ground, or to endure cold.

Oxford   1841   In Dominica Palmarum. April 4
I have this Lent abstained, except on Sundays from flesh (except fish), butter, vegetables except potatoes, wine, tea, toast, pastry, fruit, sugar, and beer; have never dined out, or taken a meal with any one, or gone to wine in C[ommon]. R[oom]. or worn gloves, or (except now & then) looked at Newspapers (though in Oxford).

On Sunday I have observed no rule except abstaining from sugar. On the Annunciation I allowed myself in butter and tea.

I have breakfasted on bread, an egg (or two some times) milk & hot water, or barley water—and supped in like manner; and dined on potatoes, bread & cheese; and generally fish, if there was any in hall, or a suet pudding at Littlemore.

On Wednesday and Friday I took no food whatever, except sometimes a glass of water, till 5 or 6 P.M.

During the Hebdomada Passionis I took no milk, and hot water, at breakfast—but only cold water and bread.

During the Hebdomada Major I mean to keep the first three days as the Wednesdays and Fridays (so I did.)—On Maundy Thursday and Friday to restrict my evening (my only) meal to bread and water. (So I did.)

On Holy Saturday I shall end the fast in the evening, and then sup on tea, sugar, milk, bread, butter and eggs. (So I did.)

I have made no attempt to curtail sleep, sleep on the ground, or to endure cold.

Exceptions a glass of wine on Friday post cineres, & Tuesday in 2nd week, and wine and water on Maundy Thursday, tea at breakfast on Monday in 3rd w[eek], when a stranger to breakfast, & on Monday in 5th, when writing my letter to the Bp.

I have used all the services of the Breviary throughout, except 9, 12, & 3 on Monday, & Compline on Tuesday in 5th when writing &c letter to Bp, and nones on Palm Sunday. MUCH tried at times, owing perhaps to Oxford air & talking. Quinine pills rarely. No face ache, except Passion week (Hebd. maj.)

Febr. 20. 1842. Dominica Secunda in Quadrages. I think it worth while stating, for future examination, that I have doubts of the safety of abstaining from all oleaginous substances during Lent. In 1840 I kept a strict fast, abstaining even on Sundays (as above described) but I had bread and milk every morning till Passiontide, and till the Hebdomada Major I had bacon for dinner. I had no *other* meat throughout. In 1841 I abstained from milk (except the weakest possible milk and water) and bacon also as well as all other meat—and at the end of the time, when Mr Babington saw my throat, he said it was in a state of such serious relaxation as to put me in some danger, and this though I had eaten freely of meat on Sundays which I did not do in 1840, and with more eggs on week days. This Lent I began abstaining from milk, & bacon on Sundays? (as well as other meat) and though I took tea freely, the stimulus of which I have much missed in the former two Lents, I felt so weak, that I took to bread and milk as in 1840; and though I am now abstaining from all dinner whatever, whereas in 1841 last year I took potatoes, or suet pudding, or often fish, and bread & cheese, yet I feel very little inconvenience, & (as far as I have gone yet) am much stronger than I was on the plan with which I began or on that of last Lent. Then indeed being in Oxford, I was *talking* a good deal—but still have I been many hours (even on Wedn. & Frid.) working hard at sorting and placing my books, till my thumbs are quite stiff with the weight of the folios.

It should be recollected that in the South and East where they abstain from all animal food, even milk, they have *olives* abundantly. I heard at Corfu from two officers who had gone round the Morea during one of the strict fasts and could get nothing to eat but olives, that their friends complimented them on their return on their singularly good looks. Olives, I suppose, are far more nutritious than milk.

I throw it out then as a question whether, when one abstains from meat, it is not right to take milk and butter, as the substitute for olives in the south.

March 6. 1842. Dominica Quarta in Quadragesima. For whatever reason, whether I have been much fagged with arranging my books, or been overworked with Athanasius, or for a reason presently to be mentioned, any how I have been very much tried, and have relaxed somewhat from my rules. My chief difference from former years in point of strictness has been that I have eaten nothing between breakfast & tea, besides eating no meat except on Sundays, but on the other hand I have eaten more eggs & taken tea. However my relaxations have been these, & for these reasons. The addition of milk (*not* in tea) I have already mentioned. I have lately added butter, because it enabled me to eat more bread, because it seems to contribute to relieve the more inconvenient effect of (eggs), because it enables me to take powdered rhubarb with my meal, which seems to succeed better than anything else. Also they have sometimes sent me up either salt fish (twice), or pancakes (once), or suet pudding (twice) at tea, batter &c pudding several times, & since they came I did not refuse them. Moreover there being a fever in the place, & I having to visit, I have sometimes (for one week) in midday taken a glass of wine & a bit of bread. And on Sunday I have lived pretty much as usual, except that [I have taken] either bacon or cold meat—not hot meat. However still I am very much exhausted—& from exhaustion have not been regular sometimes in the Breviary Offices.

Good Friday. March 25

I have not been *regular* in the Breviary Office, till this week. I have not used quinine except once or twice this Lent—[Two words obliterated] was wrong the last two Lents, hardly at all this;—I have taken to *tea* this Lent, and did not the two last.

Littlemore   1842.   Good Friday.   March 25.

I have not been quite so strict this Lent as last. I have been stricter in one point, that I have eaten nothing between breakfast & tea & in not eating even fish—but I have relaxed, in having tea and butter, and hot milk, and in taking breakfast the first three days of this week, and in not using all the Offices every day till Passion (this) week.

I have done as follows.

I have abstained on week days (except St Matthias) from flesh of all kinds (exept salt fish twice) cheese, vegetables, toast, pastry, (except some times a plain pudding) fruit, sugar, milk in tea, fermented liquors (except principally in one week a glass of wine for a reason given on page opposite.) I have been much tried the earlier weeks and by an acute face ache—little tried the latter.

I have taken only two meals, breakfast 8 AM & tea 6 PM—when I have commonly taken bread, butter, eggs, and tea without milk, or hot bread & milk.

On Wednesday and Friday I have eaten nothing all day till 6 PM, sometimes drank a glass of water

On Sundays and St Matthias I dined on eggs & bacon, or cold meat, and cheese—and allowed also a glass of wine or beer, milk in tea, & toast.

I did not dine out, I did not wear gloves—I eat rhubarb commonly with my butter. I have not seen the Oxford or London (except once) Papers, (except the Record)

I did not make any alteration, as I had done the last Lents, in the Tempus Passionis. And the first three days of this I took breakfast—and yesterday and today though no breakfast (& so tomorrow. Sabbat. Sanct.) yet tea as other evenings.

I mean to end the fast as usual at 6 PM on Saturday.

I tried in Long Vac^n, & so now, not sleeping in bed, but found it [did] not succeed. I cannot get to sleep without being warm & then I am too warm. In Long Vac^n I slept always on straw mattress here.

Littlemore   1843   Good Friday April 14
This on the whole has been my strictest Lent*—(except in the three last days) though now & then (not this week) I have taken some wine & water. *Very* little quinine—none this week. I have felt less inconvenience perhaps than any year; hardly any languor; no headache. I have taken less sleep (at least in bed) than ever; lately certainly little more than 4 or than 5 hours. Besides the Breviary Offices, we have had Meditations of an hour or an hour & a half every morning—& this last week, when we have been (for 6 days, this the last) in

retreat, as much as three hours. *(observe, I have eaten freely of *butter*. Vid above Febr 20. 1842)

Our rule has been as follows, & I have observed the stricter alternatives, not those in brackets.

1. Abstaining from all food (not from liquids e.g. tea—) till 5 P.M. every day (or if taking anything, bread or eggs)

exceptions, Sundays and the Annunciation, when breakfast, as usual upon Feasts.

Nine black letter days, when breakfast at noon as usual upon Ferias.

2. Abstaining from all flesh meat, even on Sundays—salt fish on Sunday, Monday, Tuesday, & Thursday (of this I ate very little, finding it disagree with me) and besides butter, cheese, tea, milk, sugar, treacle, puddings. Wine on Sundays, & at other times if necessary. (Abstinence from tea, if not from flesh meat.) The three Days in Coena Domini &c we are taking only bread & tea.

N.B. One reason for the black letter exceptions was our not eating on Sundays till after the H. S. which on two Sundays was administered in midday.

Littlemore.   Good Friday   April 14. 1843.

With this night we have finished our first retreat, which lasted seven days, beginning with Saturday the 8th and omitting Palm Sunday. Persons engaged in it, besides myself, were Bowles, Bridges, Dalgairns, Lockhart, and John Morris, (who has been here since Passion Sunday.) We fixed on Stone's Spiritual Retreat as our manual, omitting the eighth day.

Since the beginning of the First Week in Lent we have had an hour's Meditation together in the Morning before Matins—using for the first four weeks the Dialogues in the Paradisus Animae, and during Passion Week (5th Lent) Salazar's Sinner's Conversion, by way of teaching us how to proceed by ourselves. I subjoin my own Memoranda, marking with figures the Resolutions or Desires occurring in the course of them.

i Day. Saturday April 8. On the end of man.

Exercise 1. ½ past 4—5½ .A.M. The hour has gone so wonderfully quick that I thought it was only the ½ hour, when the clock (which I had put on to accomodate my commencement) struck the end of it. I thought it was not half over, and have been puzzled, & for a moment disconcerted thinking I must have been wrong—but I certainly was not. Yet I have not been able to realize God's Presence duly the whole time. Yet it has been very pleasant to me; and especially, when the hour was gone, I felt joyful and grateful that it had seemed so short against my fears beforehand.

The main subject of the Meditation, that we are created to serve God, is rather abstract. My thoughts wandered (as I think, for a moment,) now and then. That dreadful thought about D. hurried me off. And I got troubled how God could be bearing so many of us at once; it seemed to make His Presence more unreal to me. I hardly could frame the scene at all. (Nor could I to keep it up in scarcely any that followed.)

The thoughts that struck me most were,—that God put it into my heart, when 5 or 6 years old, to ask *what* and *why* I was, yet now I am forty two, and have never answered it in *my conduct*; that if disobedience is *against nature*, I am, in the sight of Angels, like some odious *monster* which people put out of sight; that I have acted hardly ever for God's glory, that my motive in all my exertions during the last 10 years, has been the pleasure of energizing intellectually, as if my talents were given me to play a game with, (and hence I care as little about the event as one does about a game); that it is fearful to think how little I have used my gifts in God's service; that I have used them for myself. Hence that Selflove in one shape or another, e.g. vanity, desire of the good opinion of friends, &c. have been my motive; and that possibly it is *the* sovereign sin in my heart; and that therefore it will be well (1) to make it the subject of the Particular Examen.

At the end I solemnly gave myself up to God to do what He would with me—to make me what He would—to put what He would upon me.

Exercise 2. $\frac{1}{2}$ past 1 P.M. I have from time to time had wandering thoughts; that misery about D. has come in again. For a moment now and then I have almost dozed. My matter failed; at least I could not make it last any time; and then I was fidgetted waiting for the clock to strike, and this discomposed and unsettled me much. I could for most of the time do little more than make ejaculations, with the fear of these being unmeaning, and the uncomfortable feeling that it was a mode of killing time; I remained some minutes over the hour to conquer myself.

The thoughts which interested me most were, the view of the Saints moving heavenwards, one after another, up the ladder; and that I might at least be a great penitent, if not a great Saint. Also the need of my being strenuous, as my dear friend Hurrell who has gone before me; I having wasted my time in languid insincere efforts. I thought too that two thirds of my life are now gone. Also I renewed my surrender of myself in all things to God, to do what He would with me at any cost. Various great trials struck me: 1. the having to make a General Confession to some one in our Church, I not having full faith that our Church has the power of Absolution. 2. having to join the Church of Rome. 3. having to give up my Library. 4. bodily pain and hardship. I considered that God is used to accept offers, but I trust He will not exact such.

Exercise 3. ½ past 8 P.M. Whether from the subject of this Exercise (the end of the Religious Life) or because I was tired with the day, I seemed to have no ideas whatever, and could only repeat over, sometimes almost in a doze, such words as "Enable me to follow Thee" &c. I could very little, or not at all, realize, that I was in the Lord's Presence; and now I am so sleepy that I can hardly write this.

ii Day. Monday. April 10. On Sin.
Exercise 1. ½ past 4—5½ A.M. I have had every now and then wandering thoughts; but, as on Saturday, the time has gone surprisingly fast. I seemed to have done very little in it.

What struck me most was the unknown horribleness of deliberate (or mortal) sin, as an infringement of the order of nature and the will of God, which may be or is, of untold awfulness and sacredness, and as a worship of the creature, which is a matter quite incomprehensible and overwhelming. Also, what a dreadful effect one deliberate sin may have on the character, (on which I tried to conceive when was my first mortal sin,)—and if one such sin, what the effect of a number! Further, what my state may be, with good feelings not incorporated into my soul and expulsive of sin and its guilt, but merely indications of God's continued mercy, and guides, helps, means, towards expiations and pardons. Hence how do I know, but, if I were to die, all these would suddenly vanish, as a gleam on a landskip [sic]? I begged God to keep me from ever committing mortal sin again at any cost; and I cautioned myself against acts of wilful impetuosity or obstinacy in small or indifferent matters, which if not of the nature, are a sort of imitation, and from the suggestive example, of mortal sin.

Exercise 2. ½ past 9 to 10½. Every now and then a momentary dozing or rather dreaming has come over me.

I cannot tell how I have gone through it. The hour seemed slower than in the morning; and, though the subject was so full of topics ("my sins") yet I seemed unable to interest or engage my mind. Every thing fell flat, and I had to begin again. I went through time past, and thought how dreadful it would be to confess to this person or that. But various miserable feelings came over me, and I found I dared not go through some of my sins. One reason of my want of spirit, as on Saturday, may be want of *novelty* in the subject; yet those are just the circumstances under which St. Ignatius says that the affections ought to have most exercise. I suspect I do not proceed in the way of Colloquy enough, though I do not know how to do it. My prayers are very short, and the same things repeated, and with very little realization of God's presence. I must add that I made a resolution to read some part of Scripture for a quarter of an hour every day, i.e. ordinarily, and unless I were thrown out of my usual course of going on.

Exercise 3. ½ past 7-8½. I think I have had fewer wandering thoughts and very little dozing or dreaming, (which is a kind of momentary illusion or scene.) But I feel very much the want of matter; though the subject is venial sin, I was obliged to go over the Points a second time. I could but repeat my own prayers for light, pardon, & strength in case of such sins. I put before me, as very frequent ones in my case, distraction in prayer, self complacency, inaccuracy or lying, greediness, and want of self control in little things. And I resolved at once to confess to L. that I just now, in excuse for omitting to read out loud something from Stone, said that I thought it came after Compline, whereas in fact I forgot it.

iii Day. April 11. on Death and Judgment.
Exercise 1. (½ past) 4-5½ A.M. Have overslept myself, and lost half an hour by the clock stopping. This is the more provoking, because my morning exercise seems the best.

Had a feeling of disgust at having confessed to L. last night my fault. This suggested to me, in the course of the Meditation, though the thought was an intrusion, whether it would not be a good thing to confess for a time the result of a particular examen on selfcomplacency to D. L. or Bowles, if no other way will do to repress the sin. This thought to be pursued. Also, I prayed that I might have grace always to look at things, and at my actions upon them, as I would wish I had looked at them, and shall look at them, on my death bed. E.g. the mode in which I ought to behave to Rogers.

Exercise 2. ½ past 9-10 A.M. This exercise has been more impressive than any of the foregoing,—on Tepidity.

What struck me most was, 1. that, alas, I have not attended perhaps to one daily service at St Mary's for the almost 9 years I have established it. There is no doubt that I attend to the Prayers worse now, than I did twenty years ago. 2. that, though I may do isolated good actions on good motives, yet taking the ecclesiastical movement of the last 10 years as a whole, it has not in any sense been performed (on my part) with a pure intention towards God; and therefore, as far as His approval goes, and its availableness at the Last Day, is *lost*. 3. that there are persons, who, being destined by Providence to a high path, have no medium between it and hell; so that, if I do not pursue the former, I may be falling into the latter.

Exercise 3. ½ past 7-8 P.M. I had some sleep before dinner, and that I suppose made me more lively now. For in the beginning of the Exercise I felt more earnest, and could pray more fluently than in any of all the former. But this eagerness led me off to other subjects, & thus dissipated my mind. I even fell for a little while into some thoughts about my own position or some circumstances about me, which had somewhat of complacency in them. And I ended, thinking the hour long, and having nothing to pray or meditate about; so as to repeat what I had said before. But on the whole it was a great improvement on the foregoing evenings. I considered & prayed agst my present great aversion to the very name of penance.

iv Day. Wednesday April 12. On the Incarnation, Kingdom, & Obedience of Christ.

Exercise 1. ½ past 4-½ past 5 A.M. Nothing is more surprising to me than the different lengths these Exercises seem. This one passed very quickly; "on the Incarnation." It may be worth noticing one strange instance of inconsistency, as a specimen of myself. Thinking of the wonderful truth, which seems an axiom, that humiliation &c. must be pleasing to God since Christ's humiliation, it struck me what a good subject it w^d be to preach before the Houses of Parliament or the Queen upon! The Preacher, I suppose, was the only person who was not to be humbled! The only thought worth setting down is, that it is quite an absurdity to give *praise* for humility, since the Word's condescension; it is unmeaning. Humility is the very *condition* of *being* a Christian; it comes into the idea of it, & is nothing superadded. It seems quite impertinent & offensive to praise a man for a little instance of what Christ exemplifies so wonderfully. It may be said that this applies to every virtue, God being infinitely more holy, just, good, true &c than [men] are, but somehow the case does not seem quite the same.

Exercise 2. $\frac{1}{2}$ past 9-$\frac{1}{2}$ past 10. A.M. This exercise was so long that it passed through my mind that the Clock had struck. Being on the Kingdom of Christ, I was led on to meditate on the fortunes of the Church at present, and especially in England, and on my own duties regarding it, & to beg a blessing on particular schemes I have in view, & on particular persons. I cannot tell whether this is wrong or not.

I am no declaimer or fluent speaker, & therefore am not under the temptation, but *may* not an exercise become a languid piece of talk? Reverence is our requisite (as St Ignatius puts it) to guard agst this.

Exercise 3. $\frac{1}{2}$ past 7-$\frac{1}{2}$ past 8. P.M. I thought the Exercise long, yet when it had gone, wondered that it *was* gone, & that so quickly. I prayed that in all I did, I might have before my eyes the example of Christ's subjection to His parents. This picture of Christ's subjection seemed to me a very striking one, and likely to be affecting.

v Day. Thursday (Maundy) April 13. On the two Standards &c. Exercise 1. $\frac{1}{2}$ past 4-$\frac{1}{2}$ past 5 A.M. This has, I think, been far better than any other. Perhaps the subject, (the Two Standards) interested me. But I seemed fresher too in mind. Perhaps it was the bracing effect of the cold, for the ground this morning is covered with snow.

I have only to observe that I seem unwilling to say, "Give me utter obscurity"; partly from a hankering after posthumous fame, partly from a dislike that others should do the work of God in the world, & not I.

Exercise 2. $\frac{1}{2}$ past 9-$\frac{1}{2}$ past 10. A.M. This has been as long, or the longest of any. My matter fell very short, and I could do nothing but repeat addresses, till I was afraid of vain repetitions, go through the Beatitudes, and the like.

I was most impressed by a horror of sinning again mortally, and of these exercises proving a mere excitement.

I was frightened to think that it was not at all impossible that I might be betrayed into deliberate, obstinate lying. Also I asked myself some questions about my care of my Parish. My answer, I hope sufficient, is that I do what I can, & what is to be done at St Mary's; and that Copeland manages it far better than I could, here.

Exercise 3. ½ past 7-½ past 8. P.M. The time has not seemed short, yet this has been the most satisfactory Exercise of any to me, if power of fixing the mind, freedom from wandering, & vigour in thinking, be grounds for saying so.

I resolved, that is, I prayed, to practice daily mental prayer, according to the rule of St Alphonso, or the like.

vi Day. Good Friday. April 14. On the Passion of Christ.
Exercise 1. ½ past 4-½ past 5. This Exercise has neither been long or short. I have for a moment had wandering thoughts. I have had no efforts to find and to make acts of the will.

It struck me to bear in mind how much I hurt my *faith* (and hence my power of realizing & feeling grateful for our Lord's passion) by *entering into* infidel thoughts, views, arguments &c. E.g. principally of the Pantheist, & those who treat the gospels as myths.

Exercise 2. ½ past 9-½ past 10. I almost think this has seemed the longest of any. I fear my mind has got dissipated or negligent from the notion that it is the last day of Exercise. I prayed God that I might learn from our Saviour's perseverance in prayer under heaviness, ever to do the like, not to neglect Exercise or Office &c.

Exercise 3. ½ past 7-½ past 8. No wanderings, but deficiency of matter, so that, although I did keep on, & with fervour to the end, I was obliged to seek what to say. It has come upon me yesterday & today, that I cannot bear contempt, when it comes in palpable instances.

Littlemore. Advent Retreat. 1843.
From Tuesday Dec 19 to Saturday Dec. 23. both inclusive.
Persons engaged in it—St John, Dalgairns, Bowles, Bridges, & myself.
Meditations used were from the "Journal of Meditations" for Nov & Dec."

i Day. Tuesday. Dec. 19. On the end of man.
Exercise 1. ¼ to 5-¼ to 6. A.M. On the whole this med^n fair, especially in beginning—though towards the end it seemed long.

My thoughts sometimes wandered as long as a sentence or so, but were at once recovered.

Three or four vain thoughts about myself, e.g. things said in my sermons, apropos of the Meditation;—I turned from them at once.

I have been observing myself narrowly, as I went on; I cannot tell whether or not improperly so. Such watching seems to make religious thoughts a sort of art or game.

At the end I begged that Christ w^d make of me what He would.

Chief thoughts—1. that I am created *here* and *now*, in England in the 19 cent. surely not for myself. 2. how God in time past has chastened me & guided me. E.g. in 1816, 1827-8. Is it to be for nothing? 3. How little, or not at all, I have been in the habit of acting for & towards His glory. 4. How the Angels are serving, so methodically & perfectly it seems like some material contrivance, like machinery. 5. If an hour tries me, what will serving & adoring for ever in heaven?

These texts struck me. 1. What doest thou here, Elijah? 2. Starting aside like a broken bow. 3. The Lord hath been mindful of us, He will bless us. 4. Prosper then the work of our hands upon us. 5. Whom shall I send, & who will go for us? 6. Who knoweth whether thou art come to the Kingdom for such a time as this? (Esth. IV) 7. The time past of our life may suffice us &c. 8. What? couldest thou not watch with Me one hour?

Exercise 2. 1-2 P.M. Very tired. I cannot account for it. Sleepy, not drowsy, but with lightheaded flitting dreaminess. The hour was very long at the end—I could but read over & over again the med^n. I fixed my mind earnestly upon Christ as present, but fancied I was hurting my head. Had I had ten minutes sleep first, I think it w^d have been different.

I tried to give up to Him, if for His greater glory, my fellowship, my Library, the respect of friends, my health, my talent, my reason—but added "Lord, be merciful." Texts struck me. 1. who stand in the Presence of God. 2. who I am, and whom I serve. 3. the case of Jonah, who for God's greater glory was cast to the waves, & became a type of Christ.

Exercise 3. $\frac{1}{4}$ past 7-$\frac{1}{4}$ past 8. I had gone to sleep that I might be fresh for this Med^n but unluckily slept till near the time, & was quite confused & stupid when I began. I could not conceive *how* I was to get through the hour, & felt quite dismayed & reluctant. And I cannot tell how I *have* got though it. I think I certainly had my mind upon the subject of med^n without wandering, yet I was very confused. The thought which principally struck me was this, the duty, the absolute necessity of avoiding little sins, if we would be real Christians. If our sole end is to live to God, not to the world, or (as the Med^n spoke) to be soldiers of Christ fighting agst the world, we are engaged in ridding ourselves of the shadows of this world, emancipating ourselves from the meshes of time & sense—that is, resisting the daily little compliances with them in which consists our slavery. I thought of my three sins, & prayed to be able to get rid of them, indulgence of the appetite, self conceited thoughts, & wanderings in prayer.

ii Day. Wednesday. Dec. 20. On sin.
Exercise 1. $\frac{1}{4}$ to 5-$\frac{1}{4}$ to 6. The time was not long, but then I did not make so great an effort to attend & be alive. I had several wanderings, *one* for *more* than an instant; I do not suppose long, but still it betokened languor & relaxation of mind. I fear it has been a luke warm exercise. I kept thinking intellectually on the sin of the Angels. I found it difficult, from intellectual difficulties, to argue from their sin to my sin. One thought impressed me, that "I have been all but damned"—just as when you saw a man fall from a horse, you might say that he had been all but killed, & had a very narrow escape indeed. And then this image came on me, but I could not help beginning to think how it w^d dress for a composition of some kind. "Suppose their footing giving way, when persons were on some high ground, & they rolled down with the swiftness of lightning down, down, a steep descent towards a chasm; let them fall in it, & let one be caught by a projecting rock. That was I, but this was not all. I clamber up a little, but the sides are slippery, whether with snow or other cause—& the footing scarcely possible, & the greatest care is necessary to hinder destruction after all—that is I now."
Exercise 2. 1-2 P.M. Wandering at times, I fear more than any—and a little dreaminess, as yesterday. Not so tedious as some, but I suspect the more I try really to fix my mind, the more tedious it seems. The thought that struck me most, was, that Adam, as also Lucifer, sh^d suffer, & such a punishment, for a first offence—and that his sin sh^d be apparently not a mortal, but a venial one, as being in materia levi. And I prayed that, if it w^d not be too much for me, I might know the real state of my soul, as laden with so many sins, before I died.

Exercise 3. ¼ past 7-¼ past 8 P.M. I have been exceedingly tired. My limbs have ached so much from the frost, that I could hardly kneel, & was obliged to keep more or less in motion. I believe I have not been sleepy: yet what I have been thinking about I do not know. I do not think thoughts have wandered, nor did the time seem very long,— yet I fear it has passed unprofitably. I fear that at first my thoughts were not very clear, but dreamy. And this is pretty much all I have to say. I considered whether I had ever really repented of many of my mortal sins. I prayed that I now was not adding to my sins.

iii Day. Thursday Dec. 21—On Sin.
Exercise 1. ¼ to 5-¼ to 6. I was from 5 to 10 minutes past the time, from oversleeping. Far too intellectual—all I can say is that my head was achy and almost swimming—& then to urge myself actively to feel affection &c is to hurt it. But under such circumstances I can go on in a passive indolent train of thought, without such a strong control over myself as to be secure from wanderings. This, I fear, was pretty nearly my state. These thoughts struck me chiefly. 1. sin as bringing under the power of the devil—conceive even the power of a wicked man & being in his clutches—how plain that nothing but the extraordinary grace of God can rescue a soul once given over to the devil. 2. sin as separating hereafter from holy creatures. Man is formed for society, for sympathy. God is his happiness, but as the sun's light comes to us reflected & refracted, so God's saints are the means under which His glory comes to us. 3. on sin as a poison or cause of malady in the soul, from the parallel of the effects of some sins in the body. There are sins, which you see in the young, which enfeeble them indefinitely—making their nerves irritable—bringing extreme languor, making them exposed to catch cold, unable to resist external bad influences &c &c. Now if this be *seen* in the body, and if it lasts for years, many years, & after repentance, what must be the permanent parallel effect on the soul? A man may thus most fearfully carry the sins of his youth to his dying day.

Exercise 2. 1-2 P.M. My matter (on Venial Sins) failed—and I was obliged to go off to pray ag^st my three special instances of such— greediness, self conceit, and wandering in prayer. I remained some time saying "Unto Thee lift I up mine eyes &c"—and I thought whether periodical Confession, and formal though momentary prayer at intervals through the day, might not help me ag^st the last mentioned.

Exercise 3. ¼ past 7-¼ past 8. P.M. The latter part of the time has gone so quick, that I much fear I must have been asleep some part of it. I do not know what has come to me—I seem to have less & less matter, & less & less to think about. For want of what to think of I turned to my own venial sins, e.g. impatience, impetuosity, rudeness, inaccuracy in speech sometimes approaching to lying, which I have not as yet mentioned. All this is very unsatisfactory.

iv. Day. Friday Dec. 22. On Death and Judgment.
Exercise 1. ¼ to 5-¼ to 6 A.M. This is the only Exercise hitherto which has gone quick. Once or twice a wandering. I fear it was an intellectual meditation—very little raising up the heart to Christ. When I attempt, I repeat the same thing again & again, and grow tired & inattentive. What a great defect! The thought that most struck me was that death, the greatest trial, has no room for repentance of what is ill done in it. I pray that He who appointed time, place, & manner, & who hid them from me, would also give me grace to overcome—I prayed for the grace of perseverance.

Exercise 2. 1-2 P.M. It went quick, but with some wanderings, & far too little lifting up of my heart. With reference to its subject, the Particular Judgment, I thought with fear that the sins I recollected were doubtless but a very small portion, & only in fact a sample, of those I did not recollect. It struck me again that even those I knew, when all added together, were indefinitely more than I suspected— just as in accounts when we put together different items, the sum total far exceeds our previous idea. Further, I questioned whether I ought not to resolve, having now got free from the Lives of the Saints, not to engage in any *new* work, i.e. undertaking; so as to keep myself open for any thing,—e.g. office of charity or the like.

Exercise 3. ¼ past 7-¼ past 8. P.M. I fear I was asleep some considerable time, but I do not know. The first point I was alive. The thought which principally struck me was the horror of a lost soul being stripped of the graces which were (only) lent it, not made its own— e.g. becoming cruel, desperate &c &c parallel to the countenance becoming deformed. What seems to throw light on this, is my apparently great *inconsistency* of character, so that persons who know me well w^d be puzzled, saying I was reverent yet profane, considerate yet cruel, gentle yet violent &c all showing that I have *gifts* contrary to my real nature.

Saturday Dec 23. On the Two Standards; on the Nativity.

Exercise 1. ¼ to 5 A.M.-¼ to 6 A.M. Matter too much, did not get through it—used Stone's book—qu. is it better than "the Journal" for the purpose? Yet some wanderings—these I think I scarcely had at all last Lent, & not in my first Meditation this time—does not this show that the beginnings are every thing? *since* I had them, I have always had them. The time passed quickly, yet feeling I did not get thro' the matter, I have been much dissatisfied about my wanderings, as being so simply my own fault & depriving me of what I might otherwise have enjoyed. I have reflected among other things 1. on there being *but* two visible companies, & the question for all is, Are we on the side of the Saints or not? There are not many parties to judge between, but two only. 2. I felt I ought to renounce & abjure Satan, yet how it wᵈ anger him, & how sure he wᵈ be to turn on me, & how able & certain to destroy me, if I were by myself—therefore how mad to do it except as a simple act of obedience to Christ & a reliance on His power & grace to bring me through.

Exercise 2. 1-2 P.M. This has been the most pleasant of any (on the Expectation of Xt) though not particularly short in my feelings. I was led to reflect whether I ought not to be far more circumspect after receiving the H.C. than I am, that "the day may dawn & the day star arise in my heart". Some wandering.

Exercise 3. ¼ past 7-¼ past 8 P.M. Great want of matter: took to repeating the Great Antiphons of Advent.

April 1843

Posuisti, Domine, iniquitates nostras, in conspectu tuo, saeculum nostrum in illuminatione vultûs tui.

> Quia omnes dies nostri defecerunt
> Et in irâ tuâ defecimus.

> Oremus

Deus, apud quem non est impossibile omne verbum, quaesumus clementiam tuam, ut conservum nostrum, S. F. Wood, nunc gravi valetudine laborantem, et ab omnibus peccatis suis liberes, et in terreno servitio tuo retineas, et ad vitam perducas aeternam. Per Dominum.

In Festo Ss. Innocentium 1843

In usum Dilecti Filii mei Henrici ———

1. Unigenite Fili Dei, Deus de Deo, qui cum tribus pueris ambulasti

in ardenti camino, ut odor ignis non transiret per eos, à contagione mundi, carnis, et diaboli libera me, Domine.

2. Ure igne Sancti Spiritûs renes nostros et cor nostrum, Domine; Ut Tibi casto corpore serviamus, et mundo corde placeamus, per Jesum Christum Dominum nostrum.

3. Domini Jesu Christi, libera me de perturbationibus cordis et corporis, ut jugiter Tibi placeam et tranquillitate fruar omnibus diebus vitae meae.

4. Cor mundum crea in me, Deus, et spiritum rectum innova in visceribus meis. (Ps. LI   )

5. Da mihi, Domine, carnem subditam et tranquillam, et animum pace Tuâ gaudentem per Jesum Christum Dominum nostrum.

6. Confige timore Tuo carnes meas, Domine, ut neque malitiae meae nec venturi judicii Tui ignibus ardeant per Jesum Christum Dominum nostrum.

7. Noctem quietam, et honesta somnia, et impollutam mentem concedat nobis Dominus Omnipotens.

8. Deus, caritatis amator, libera me de passionibus peccati et de stimulis carnis per Dominum nostrum Jesum Christum.

9. Omnipotens Deus, precor majestatem Tuam, ut hostem meum à me arceas et omnes inordinatos motus in me comprimas per Jesum Christum Dominum nostrum.

10. Domine Jesu Christe, qui natus es de Virgine, da mihi sanctitatem oculorum et puritatem manuum et pacem cordis, ut tandem merear cum Angelis videre faciem Tuam in caelis, Tu Salutaris Vultûs mei et Deus meus.

11. Deus, Pater misericordiae, qui lux es et sol justitiae, protege me in velamento alarum Tuarum, et fac ut opera tenebrarum nec videndo neque audiendo cognoscam, per Dominum nostrum Jesum Christum.

12. Miserere, Domine adolescentiae meae, et aufer à me calorem noxiam cordis et corporis, ut habeam pacem tuam, quae exuperat omnem sensum, et veram libertatem filiorum Dei, per Jesum Christum Dominum nostrum.

Good Friday.   April 5. 1844.

Our Lent rule has been lighter this year.

1. We have eaten no flesh meat, Sundays or week days. (including suet)

2. We have not broken fast till 12.

3. At 12 we have taken a slice of bread. The full meal at 5—but we had the choice, (which perhaps we never used) of taking the full meal at 12 & the bread at 5.

4. There was no restriction on tea at any hour—early or late.

5. Nor on butter, sugar, salt fish &c. Wine on Sundays.

I have not felt any rule so light, since I have attempted any thing. This I attributed to drinking very freely of tea, as early as 8 or 9 A.M. and with sugar in it. I am told I do not look ill.

Quinquagesima.   Febr 6. 1842[1]

I propose as follows for Lent.

To abstain on all weekdays, from flesh of all kinds including fish, cheese, (butter) vegetables, toast, pastry, fruit, sugar, milk in tea, fermented liquors.

To take only two meals in the day, the first two eggs, bread, and tea ad libitum, or hot milk. At six P.M. eggs—bread,—and tea.

On Wednesday & Friday to eat nothing till the evening, and then to sup as usual.

On Sunday to abstain as on weekdays, except as regards milk, toast, butter, fermented? liquors and meat.

Not to dine out, or take meal with any, or wear gloves.

Not regular in services on the Friday post cineres nor on the First Sunday not having my book nor thro' the first week—nor on Sunday in second

Shrove Tuesday.   1843
Febr 28

1. We are to abstain (if possible) from all food till 5 P.M. every day—or if we take any thing bread or eggs. Tea does not break fast.

Exceptions—Sundays & the Annunc, when we shall breakfast as usual on Feasts.

Nine black letter days when we breakfast at noon & as usual (in food) on a common feria.

2. We are to abstain from all meat—eating instead salt fish (viz on Sunday, Monday, Tuesday, & Thursday) or Macaroni—& besides from butter, cheese, tea, sugar, treacle puddings &c. Or if not from meat, from tea altogether.

[1] These resolutions for Lent in 1842, 1843 and 1844 are written on two sheets, which have been gummed into the exercise book at this point. C.S.D.

3. We are to keep together till Low Sunday.
4. Meditation.

Shrove Tuesday.   Febr. 20. 1844

To breakfast at 12

To have one full meal in the day, and besides a collation of a bit of bread; with the choice of having the meal at 12 or 5, the collation being at the other hour.

Liquids, e.g. tea, no breach of the rule.

No flesh meat, week days or Sundays.

Maryvale 1846.   Retreat for minor orders.

June 3.6-6.55. P.M. Small frequent wanderings, growing out of the subject, into collateral subjects. Subject, *de Vocat. Apost.* I can say I am *willing* to follow Christ in poverty & reproach. I can *pray* that "He would do with me whatever He will"—but I find it hard to pray that "absolutely I may have poverty & reproach, since He had them," wh is the third stage of humility. Without being able to analyze my feelings, I think I approached nearer to our Lord in this meditation than I am usually.

June 4. 6 to 7 A.M. (1ˢᵗ Med.) *Subject. Fundamentum.*

For 5 minutes drowsy—and now & then my mind wandering off as last night. I reflected that, though from youth I had been so wonderfully dealt with by God, I have never felt that desire to praise & recommend Him to others which is expressed in "Venite et videte quanta fecit animae meae." One feel a pride in human friends and benefactors, why not in Divine?—This arises in me from want of *faith.* I cannot believe that really & after all God has dealt with me—it must be my fancy—a mock humility comes in. I thought also that the notion which men of the world have is, that they are answering the *end of life* & praising & serving God, if merely they fulfil (as they consider it) their calling—the question, *whether they thought of their* calling, being quite put aside—they might be merely taking their pleasure, but if they *happened* (granting it) to be doing God's work, it was (they think) enough—and if the thought ever came across them that they were pursuing their own pleasure not God's, they got over it by saying that "it was a cause of thankfulness that He made our duties so pleasant, or our own happiness promote His glory"—and that this was very inconsistent in the sort of men in whom it is found —for, if there is one τόπος more than another on which educated men in this country insist more than another it is on "Christianity being a matter of the *heart*, not external—religion being a private matter—that it is a great *evidence* for Xtianity that our Lord directed us to purify our motives, not our mere outward actions, like Jews, or heathen, or Mahomedans, or R.Cath[s.]"—I thought also of the horror, at the judgment, of Xt's saying of me, "Here is the end he was made for—look at it—this was the end and this has been his life—he was made for this end & he has not fulfilled it."

10.15-11.15 (2nd Med.) Subject de triplici peccato.
Momentary drowsiness, & wanderings now & then, one at least *not* from, or in consequence of the subject. The punishment of the Angels' sin shows that the Essence of sin deserves eternal damnation. I can well believe, if a number of sins incur eternal punishment, that one does, for there is no proportion between any finite number and infinity. I thought that there was *a* time when I committed my first mortal sin, & that I do not know *when* that was. It must have been preceded by a period of indifference & carelessness unless this itself be mortal. What a mystery, *what put it* into the souls of the Angels to sin! Sin, or aversion to God, is a violation of their *nature*, a sin ag[st] nature, & answers thus to what we call unnatural sin, as women eating their children. For what we know (considering how much character lies in little things, e.g. handwriting,) any one act concentrates the man, in any one act as in any one member or nerve is the whole *soul or spirit*, any one sin is the expression of the whole character—so that one sin may damn as effectually as a hundred. Again what an awful thought that in 1000 acts we are putting forth (as it were) our sinful self 1000 times, we are breathing, perspiring a continual, whole, integral, death; each sin is the reiterated expression of a whole soul at enmity with God. At the end I felt much, here am I, send me. I have not served Thee yet (this was, I think, in the former meditation.) I have acted (like men of the world) from liking. I have spoken & written & worked towards religion, but not for it,—but from liking of the work, as an intellectual exercise, to please friends, to employ time,—but now let me do some work for Thee before I die—here am I, send me.

3.30 to 4.30 (3rd Med.) *de Incarnatione.* I have nothing to remark upon it. I did not find the time heavy—& could have gone on longer, with no great variety, however, of ideas—my mind wandered a little, from time to time, but I trust not much.

5.45 to 6.45 (4th Med,) *de Vita Privat. Xti.* I found I could go on meditating or rather dwelling on the *idea* itself of the Med. without tiring—so much so that I did not know whether to go on from point to point—yet with very little of thought or fruit—It being easy to dwell on the thought, I have no *effort* to make, & thus wandering thoughts came in and went out. The whole was rather passive than active.

June 5. 6 to 7. A.M. 1st Med. *de Duobus Vexillis.* Perhaps the least satisfactory—I do not think my mind wandered much, but I was very languid, could think of nothing, and every now & then was drowsy & almost dropping into sleep. The only thought that came into my mind was when addressing the B.V. at the end to enable me to choose reproach, viz the thought of the reproach she had to undergo at the Incarnation, the suspicion of infidelity. Also Satan & his spirits seemed to me more detestable & odious than they commonly do.

10.15 to 11.15. (2nd Med.) *de Missione Apost.* I have long prayed that I might never be rich, but I found it hard to say, "Let me be poor." I got perplexed what poverty meant. The circumstance that a title of benefice or patrimony is required for orders (except of regulars) seemed inconsistent with praying for strict poverty. I had some wanderings, & was not in an orderly, collected, strictly subdued state, as much as I ought to have been—but some things came home very forcibly to me, and I suppose I prayed earnestly. I found myself able to think better falling back on my bed—but afterwards it has struck me that perhaps it led to some laxity of mind, & has given me the unpleasant feeling that I have not been so strict in the medn. as I should have been. I went through my life, & it came upon me that from 1824 to 1839 or 1840, I could not be said to cultivate carefully interior reln. [religion] or what the Exercise called the Prudentia Serpentis. (My *strict* periods have been from middle of 1816 to end of 1817—from spring of 1821 to 1824 and from 1840 about to 1846— i.e. hardly 10 or 11 years in the last 30. Some strictness may be added about 1828, & 1833 & 1836.) Also it forcibly touched me that I was to receive the tonsure this evening—which I dread.

3.30 to 4.30. Subject *the Coena Domini.* Interrupted all through with knockings &c about a letter from the Bp—waited the full hour, attended pretty well. Nothing particular to observe. Our Lord's desire that we sh^d *remember* him struck me, as being so condescendingly human.

Sent for to Oscott to be examined—the tonsure not given tonight, but tomorrow morning.

St Eusebio.   Rome [1]
April 8-17, 1847.

Vulnus quoddam vel fungum habeo in mente meâ, quo praesente Oratorianus bonus esse non possum. Nec paucis verbis potest describi, habet enim res multas partes.

In eo sum statu, ut officium meum exequar probè in definito quodam tramite, sed non possim surgere supra illum in excelsiorem locum; humi repo, vel, si placet, curro,—benè quidem pro repenti vel currenti, sed volare non possum: non habeo in me elementa progrediendi [Alternative] surgendi.

Non habeo quantum scio desiderium ullum mundanum; non cupio divitias, potentiam, nomen; contrà, non amo paupertatem, molestias, angustias, incommoda. Timeo infirmam valetudinem, ut qui valetudinem ejusmodi expertus sim; fugio corporis dolorem magis quam olim. Amo mediocritatem vitae, id quod mihi tentatio est; ita tamen, ut sperem quoque, fore ut sine magnâ difficultate possim omnia quae habeo tradere, si Deus jusserit.

Non amo regulam vitae, quanquam per octo decem annos cupivi ut vitam quasi regularem degerem. Amo tranquillitatem, securitatem, vitam cum amicis, cum libris, et sine negotiis actam, Epicuraeam scilicet. Qui status animi, nunquam alienus à me, crevit crescentibus annis.

Quanquam habitum habeo stabilem, omnia referendi ad voluntatem Dei, et cupio perficere Illius voluntatem, et quanquam in actu quoque id ipsum observo revera in rebus majoribus, tamen non actu quaero illius voluntatem in minutioribus. Et etiam in illis majoribus, quanquam quae esset voluntas Ejus saepe enixè petii, actiones tamen meae magis provenerunt ex conscientiâ quadam, me prohibente ne aliàs facerem, ex sensu rectitudinis, ex perceptione illius quod me deceret, et in quo in agendo mihimet ipsi constarem, quàm ex fide et charitate.

Anni ingravescentes hoc quoque in me fecerunt, ut vigorem illum

---

[1] A translation of these notes, written at the Jesuit Retreat House of St Eusebio, where Newman was making a retreat, in view of his approaching ordination, is given in the Appendix to this section. C.S.D.

et vitalem animi impetum, quem quondam habui, nunc non habeam. Quemadmodum membris corporis supervenit rigiditas, ita menti meae et facultatibus ejus abest nunc juvenilis illa agilitas et versatilitas. Moveo tarde et invitè ad agenda bona; quod quidem mihi non parva occasio est molestiarum et laborum jam Catholico; nam sanctissimae consuetudines Ecclesiae, functiones sacrae, opera ad indulgentias obtinendas necessaria, assistentia SS. Sacramenti expositi, ipsa Sacramenti benedictio, mentem meam perturbant, utpote in novo quasi gestu et figurâ positam. Delectant me Missa, Visitatio SS^{mi}, Rosarium, Litaniae, Breviarium; sed quoties multa occurrunt quae agenda sunt mihi, multa, et ea minutiora, (e.g. orationes hae ut obtineantur indulgentiae quaedam, illae ex promisso, aliae pro Novenâ exequenda,) talia memoriam meam opprimunt, animum onerant, distrahunt, propemodum terrent; idque magis quia forsitan scrupulis obnoxius esse soleo. Exemplum sit quod huic tempori opportunum est; maximum habet metum "resolutiones" faciendi.

In omni ferè re amo meam ipsius agendi viam; nolo locum, negotium, in quo sum, mutare, alterius negotium suscipere, ambulare, iter facere, alios visitare, cùm velim domi manere. Minima quaeque mihi labori sunt at sollicitudini. Querulus sum, et timidus, piger, et suspiciosus, repens humi, exigui, demissi, abjecti animi.

Porro non habeo fidem illam practicam et vividam et praesentem, adversus continuam operationem mali spiritûs in corde meo, et illius machinationes, quam debeo habere.

Quando adolescens eram et juvenis, habebam fiduciam et spem in Deo, id est, securè me committebam ejus providentiae, maximam fidem ponebam in efficaciâ precum, in adversis multis semper tranquillâ mente dicebam fore ut me et meos eriperet suo tempore; alios hortabar, eram alacri et hilari animo;—et experiebar multa, ut credebam, (justè quidem, ut spero) responsa facta ad preces meas à Misericordi Deo. Sed, cùm coepi exercere intellectum meum in rebus sacris, et legere et scribere, viginti ante annos et amplius, tùm quanquam quod scripsi ut plurimum verum est et utile, tamen, primùm, fidem meam naturalem et ingenuam perdidi, ita ut nunc multum metuam Sacerdotium, ne non satis reverenter me sim gessurus in re sanctissimâ; deinde, perdidi quoque simplicem meam in verbo Dei fiduciam. Hilaritatem et suavitatem non adhuc perdidi; inter amicos et alios fui affabilis et comis, sed pedetentim evanuit in me illa pristina fiducia in immensâ Dei erga me charitate et in precum

efficacia. Neque vero perdidi intimum meum sensum Praesentiae
Divinae in omni loco, neque bonam conscientiam, et tranquillitatem
animi inde profluentem, sed non considerabam amplius, vel certè
multo minùs quàm antea, orandi consuetudinem non esse solum-
modo, officium praescriptum, sed esse etiam magnum quoddam
talentum et privilegium, quo possumus omnia. Illa subtilis et
delicata vis fidei et spei hebetata est in me usque ad hunc diem.

Quod magis est, per aliquot annos paene in desperationem quan-
dam incidi et tenebrosam mentis statum. Non quod intus non
possim pleno corde dicere "Deus meus et omnia," nam verba haec
trita erant in ore meo, sed habui multa quae me oppresserunt. Ex
spe excidi multis modis. In Ecclesiâ Anglicanâ multos habui obtrecta-
tores; plurima vis calumniarum in me injecta est; quod feceram benè
erga ecclesiam illam, pro malo habitum est fere ab omnibus qui in
eâ auctoritatem habuerunt. Exul factus sum in solitudine, ubi annos
aliquos degi cum amicis quibusdam, neque in illo ipso recessu tutus
ab hominibus qui me curiositate suâ persecuti sunt. Credo equidem
et spero me non idcirco habuisse iracundiam, indignationem, vel
simile aliquod. Namque ex eâ parte sensibilitatem animi non habeo
multam, sed oppressus sum et spem perdidi. Et nunc hilaritas mea,
quae quondam fuit, paene nulla est. Et sentio, acutissimo sensu, me
non esse juvenem, sed optimos meos annos percurrisse, et maereo de
annis praeteritis, et videor mihi ad nullam rem idoneus esse at inutile
lignum.

Tum quando Catholicus fiebam, amisi amicos meos non paucos,
cum alios, mihi charissimos, jam antea morte perdideram.

Amplius;—quando in recessu meo degebam cum aliis quibusdam,
viam vitae quaerens, varia observare soliti sumus, quae Catholicorum
propria sunt, jejunia, meditationes, exercitia sacra, Breviarii usum,
et alia vitae ecclesiasticae, vel potius regularis. Et nunc re-actionem
illam, quam vocant, subii, neque fortem animum habeo ad ea
agenda quae libenter egi in Ecclesiâ Anglicanâ.

Sed et amplius:—explicatu difficile est, et mihimet ipsi mirum, sed
hoc habeo peculiare, quòd in emotione affectuum, sive, sacrorum
sive humanorum, non possunt vires ipsius corporis mei certos
limites transgredi. Languidus semper sum in divinis contemplandis,
quasi quis in ambulando pedes unà colligatos habeat. Vinculum
quoddam super me conjectum est, ut neque in praedicando et
loquendo vehemens, neque in meditando aut orando fervidus,
physicâ tanquam lege, esse valeam.

Hoc insuper. Nunquam possum me retinere fixo animo et intento in materiâ propositâ meditanti, vel in verbis officii diurni. Mens evagatur sine intermissione; et torquetur caput, si mentis aciem in unam rem dirigere aggredior ...

Copy of chief headings of a minute
Journal in detail from Aug 1 to 9
1843

Aug 1.
  1 got up a few minutes after 5 AM
  2 Meditation
  3 at six—breviary office
  4 seven to $\frac{1}{2}$ past—putting on two violin strings
  5 $\frac{1}{2}$ past 7 to 9—correcting proof of Atkinson's Athanasius
  6 at nine—terce
  7   breakfast
  8 walked into Oxford to meet Mr Russell of Maynooth
  9 ten to half past—paying money &c
10 $\frac{1}{2}$ past ten to eleven—read (Anglican) morning prayer to myself.
11 till 20 past one, with Mr Russell.
12 by three got back to Littlemore.
13 after dinner Walker & I played a Sonata of Beethoven in the Schoolroom
14 O. came up & I talked and walked with him till $\frac{1}{2}$ past 8.
15 The evening offices.
16 $\frac{1}{2}$ an hour at Atkinson's Athanasius.
17 11 o'clock P.M. have just said my prayers, & am getting into bed.

Aug. 2
  1 got up a few minutes past five. Prayers & Meditation.
  2 six to $\frac{1}{4}$ past 7. Breviary Office to Terce inclusive
  3 from seven to eleven. At Atkinson's Athanasius.
  4 eleven read service (Anglican) in Church.
  5 then, sext and none
  6 between 12 & 3 went on with the proof of Athanasius, reading letters.
  7 three P.M. read prayers in Church.

8 went back to Athanasius, putting notes.

9 dinner

10 after dinner to Athanasius, and sent off proof.

(at various times   11 then to Life of (Lockhart's or Dalgairns's)
very tired, languid,   St Gilbert for the Series.
drowsy, sleepy all   12 vespers—compline
through these days.)   13 writing letters till eleven, when

14 went to bed

Aug 3.   up at 5.20. Meditation.

2 six—Matins, Lauds &c

3 then till nine—writing letters, & began 3rd vol of (translated) Fleury.

4 eleven—read prayers in Church

5 afterwards, Bowden, who had come up, sat with me for ¾ quarters of an hour.

6 one to three—at breakfast, correcting proof, reading Kaye's Fleury (translated)

7 None.

8 three o'clock—prayers in Church (Anglican service)

9 five. walked to Oxford, visiting at one cottage (Boswell's)

10 dined with Johnson to meet Bowden

11 slept at Oxford—to bed by 12.

Aug. 4.   1 up at 5½ in Oxford—prayers &c

2 read the Papers

3 called on people

4 by ½ past 10 got to Littlemore

5 eleven—service in Church

6 twelve—sext

7 12 to 3. Athanasius

8 none

9 3 o'clock—service in Church

10 till 5, Athanasius

11 till 8 did not do much—read a newspaper. Seager in conversation. put my books to rights.

12 Athanasius

13 Vespers and Compline

14 my prayers &c.

Perceval's Sermons. Palmer's pamphlet. (they felt for Pusey, not for *me*—this was *just*, I know—so I am put aside! this fussed me.) a headache

Aug. 5   rose with a headache
2 a little past 5. meditation
3 six o'clock Breviary office
4 nine o'clock Terce—languid—dreamy—lay down—was refreshed.
5 till eleven, at Athanasius
6 eleven read service in Church
7 twelve—Sext
8 till three at Athanasius. None office
9 three service in Church
10 till five at Athanasius and St Gilbert
11 and after dinner
12 Vespers. compline—read a letter I had from T. Mozley from France.

August 6   1 a bad night. Languid & irritable in head & nerves.
2 lay down some time before the 11 o'clock service.
3 Terce & Sext
4 Holy Communion
5 walked into Oxford
6 afternoon Service at St Mary's—preached. Perhaps some people will be sorry that they never heard me, when I shall have given up St Mary's
7 called on a person
8 back to Littlemore

Aug 7   1 got up at 20 m. past 5. Meditation
2 Breviary office
3 till nine, at Athanasius
4 Terce
5 till eleven at Athanasius.
6 eleven—service in Church
7 twelve—Sext.
8 till three at Athanasius—service in Church
9 None—St John, who is coming for a time, is a great walker—who is to walk with him?

10 till five at Athanasius

11 and after dinner, till St John came—talked with him a good deal.

12 Vespers & compline

Aug. 8   1 Up at ¼ past 5—

2 Six o'clock—office—dreamy

3 till nine at Athanasius—

4 Terce

5 Athanasius—accounts—Whitmore

6 eleven—read morning service in Church

7 Sext

8 at Athanasius. None

9 three o'clock—read service

10 walked with St John, visiting & praying with old H.

11 Vespers & compline.

12 at Athanasius, till I could not keep awake. 'Twas not mere sleepiness—but a sort of collapse of the whole of me—my head falling down &c

August 9 ......

APPENDIX

(Translation of pp. 239-42, Notes of the Retreat before Ordination.)

St Eusebio.   Rome.

April 8-17, 1847.

I have in my mind a wound or cancer, the presence of which prevents me from being a good Oratorian. It cannot be described in a few words, for it is many-sided.

I am in the state of being able to fulfil my duty conscientiously along a prescribed course, but I cannot rise above it to a higher level. I creep along the ground, or even run—well enough for one who creeps or runs, but I cannot fly. I have not in me the elements required for rising or advancing.

So far as I know I do not desire anything of this world; I do not desire riches, power or fame; but on the other hand I do not like poverty, troubles, restrictions, inconveniences. Bad health I fear as one does who has experienced it, and avoid bodily pain more than I used to. I love the mean that lies between riches and poverty, and that is a temptation for me; yet I hope that without great difficulty I should be able to give up all that I have, if God ordered it.

I do not like a rule of life, although for eighteen years I have wished to live a more or less regular life. I like tranquillity, security, a life among friends, and among books, untroubled by business cares —the life of an Epicurean in fact. This state of mind, never strange to me, has grown with the years.

Although I have the fixed habit of referring all things to the will of God, and desire to do His will, and although in practice I really observe this principle in greater matters, yet I do not in practice seek His will in lesser things. And even in those greater matters, although I have often prayed earnestly to do His will, yet my actions have proceeded rather from a kind of conscientiousness which forbade me to act otherwise, from a sense of correctness, from perceiving what became me, and in doing which I should be consistent, than from faith and charity.

Increasing years have deprived me of that vigour and vitality of mind which I once had and now have no more. Just as the limbs become stiff so now my mind and its powers have lost their youthful agility and versatility. I am slow and unready in performing good actions, and this causes me no little trouble and labour, now that I am a Catholic. For the holiest customs of the Church, sacred functions, works necessary for gaining indulgences, assistance at Exposition, and Benediction of the Blessed Sacrament itself, embarrass me like a person acting in a new and unfamiliar rôle. The Mass, visits to the Blessed Sacrament, the Rosary, litanies, the Breviary—all these give me pleasure; but whenever I have to do a number of things, and especially when they are minute (e.g. the prayers necessary for gaining certain indulgences, or other prayers which have been promised, or those for a Novena), they overwhelm my memory, are a weight on my mind, distract and almost terrify me; all the more because I am perhaps liable to be scrupulous. There is an example of this at the present moment:—I have a particular dread of making "resolutions".

In almost everything I like my own way of acting; I do not want to change the place or business in which I find myself, to undertake the affairs of others, to walk, to go on a journey, to visit others, since I prefer to remain at home. I am querulous, timid, lazy, suspicious; I crawl along the ground; feeble, downcast and despondent.

Further, I have not that practical, lively and present faith, against the persistent working and wiles of the evil spirit in my heart, which I ought to have.

When I was growing up, and as a young man, I had confidence and hope in God, i.e. I committed myself without anxiety to His Providence, I had the greatest faith in the efficacy of prayer, in all adversities I used to say calmly that He would deliver me and mine in His own good time. I encouraged others, and was active and joyful; and I believed (rightly, I hope), that I received from the Merciful God many answers to my prayers. But when I began to apply my intellect to sacred subjects, and to read and write, twenty years ago and more, then, although what I wrote was for the most part true and useful, nevertheless, first, I lost my natural and inborn faith, so that now I am much afraid of the priesthood, lest I should behave without due reverence in something so sacred; then too I have lost my simple confidence in the word of God. My joyousness and agreeableness I have not lost; among friends and others I was affable and kind, but gradually my original confidence in God's boundless love for me, and in the efficacy of my prayers has faded away. I have not lost either my intimate sense of the Divine Presence in every place, nor the good conscience and the peace of mind that flows therefrom, but I no longer thought, or at any rate, much less than formerly, that the habit of prayer was not only a prescribed duty but also a great talent and privilege, by which we can do all things. That subtle and delicate vigour of faith has become dulled in me, and remains so to this day.

What is more serious, I have for some years fallen into a kind of despair and a gloomy state of mind. Not that I cannot say interiorly and with my whole heart; "My God and my All", for these words have been constantly on my lips, but I have had many things to oppress me. In a variety of ways I have fallen away from hope. In the Church of England I had many detractors; a mass of calumny was hurled at me; my services towards that Church were misrepresented by almost everyone in authority in it. I became an exile in a solitude, where I spent some years with certain of my friends, but not even in that retreat was I safe from those who pursued me with their curiosity. I believe and hope that I did not on that account give way to anger, indignation, or the like, for in that respect I am not especially sensitive, but I was oppressed and lost hope. And now the cheerfulness I used to have has almost vanished. And I feel acutely that I am no longer young, but that my best years are spent, and I am sad at the thought of the years that have gone by; and I see myself to be fit for nothing, a useless log.

Then on becoming a Catholic I lost not a few of my friends, and that at a time when by death I had lost others most dear to me.

Further;—when I lived in my retreat with certain others, seeking a way of life, we were accustomed to observe many things which are proper to Catholics,—fasts, meditations, retreats, the use of the Breviary, and other practices belonging to the ecclesiastical, or rather to the religious life. And now I undergo a reaction, as they say, and have not the courage to continue those things which I did willingly in the Anglican Church.

But further still;—it is difficult to explain and strange even to myself, but I have this peculiarity, that in the movement of my affections, whether sacred or human, my physical strength cannot go beyond certain limits. I am always languid in the contemplation of divine things, like a man walking with his feet bound together. I am held as it were by a fetter, by a sort of physical law, so that I cannot be forcible in preaching and speaking, nor fervent in praying and meditating.

This besides. I can never keep my mind fixed and intent on the subject proposed for meditation, nor on the words of the daily office. My mind wanders unceasingly; and my head aches if I endeavour to concentrate upon a single subject. ...

December 15, 1859.

Nemo mittens manum suam ad aratrum, et respiciens retro, aptus est regno Dei. I am writing on my knees, and in God's sight. May He be gracious unto me! as years go on, I have less sensible devotion & inward life. I wonder whether it is, or rather whether it is not, so with all men, viewed as apart from the grace of God. The greater part of our devotion in youth, our faith, hope, cheerfulness, perseverance is natural—or, if not natural, it is from a εὐφυΐα which does not resist grace, & requires very little grace to illuminate. The same grace goes much further in youth, as encountering less opposition, that is, in the virtues which I have mentioned. The Greek poet, himself an old man, speaks (in the Chorus of the Oed. Col.) of the unamiable state of the aged. Old men are in soul as stiff, as lean, as bloodless as their bodies, except so far as grace penetrates and softens them. And it requires a flooding of grace to do this. I more and more wonder at *old* saints. St Aloysius or St Francis Xavier or St Carlo, are nothing to St Philip. O Philip gain me some little portion of thy fervour. I live more and more in the past, and in hopes that the past may revive in the future. My God, when shall I learn that I have so parted with the world, that, though I may wish to make friends with it, it will not make friends with me?

When I was young, I thought that with all my heart I gave up the world for Thee. As far as will, purpose, intention go, I think I did. I mean, I deliberately put the world aside. I prayed earnestly that I might not rise to any ecclesiastical dignity. When I was going up for my B. A. examination, I prayed fervently & again & again that I might not gain honors, if they would do me spiritual harm. When I was older and in Anglican orders, I prayed absolutely and without condition against rising in the Church. I put the wish generally into verse above 30 years ago. "Deny me wealth; far, far remove The lure of power or name; Hope thrives in straits, in weakness, Love, and Faith in this world's shame." Nor was this poetry only, but my habitual purpose. I think so, O Lord, but Thou knowest. I knew what I was saying, and how it is Thy way to grant, to fulfil such petitions, and to take men at their word. What could I desire better than that Thou shouldest so take me? Yet I am not at all sure that grace had much to do with my wish. I know perfectly well, and thankfully confess to Thee, O my God, that Thy wonderful grace turned me right round when I was more like a devil than a wicked boy, at the age of fifteen, and gave me what by Thy continual aids I never lost. Thou didst change my heart, and in part my whole mental complexion at that time, and I never should have had the thought of such prayers, as those which I have been speaking of above, but for that great work of thine in my boyhood. Still those prayers were immediately prompted, as I think, in great measure by natural rashness, generosity, cheerfulness, sanguine temperament, and unselfishness, though not, I trust, without Thy grace. I trust they were good and pleasing to Thee—but I much doubt, if I, my present self, just as I am, were set down in those past years, 1820, or 1822, or 1829, if they could be brought back, whether I now should make those good prayers and bold resolves, unless, that is, I had some *vast* and *extraordinary* grant of grace from Thy heavenly treasure-house. And that, I repeat, because I think, as death comes on, his cold breath is felt on soul as on body, and that, viewed naturally, my soul is half dead now, whereas then it was in the freshness and fervour of youth. And this may be the ground of the grave warning of the inspired writer, Memento Creatoris tui in diebus juventutis tuae, antequam veniat tempus afflictionis ... antequam tenebrescat sol &c. And I say the same of my state of mind at a later date, in the year 1834 and following years, when I spoke so much of self-denial, mortification, fasting &c. down to 1845 when I became a Catholic. It is a time past and gone—it relates to a work done and over. Quis mihi tribuat, ut sim juxta menses pristinos, secundum dies, quibus Deus custodiebat me? Quando splendebat lucerna ejus super caput meum, et ad lumen ejus ambulabam *in tenebris*? Sicut fui in diebus adolescentiæ meæ quando secreto Deus erat in tabernaculo meo?

But, O my dear Lord, Thou canst make it otherwise. Time and place are not hindrances to Thee. Thou canst give me grace according to my day. Sicut dies juventutis tuae, (Thou hast said to me in that chapter which has been so dear to me from my youth), ita et senectus tua. Thy hand is not straitened that it cannot save. Domine, opus tuum in medio annorum vivifica illud; in medio annorum notum facies. It is plain that what I feel, Thy servants have from the earliest times felt before me: Job, Moses, and Habacuc felt as I feel thousands of years ago, and I am able to plead with Thee in their never-dying words.

O my God, not as a matter of sentiment, not as a matter of literary exhibition, do I put this down. O rid me of this frightful *cowardice*, for this is at the bottom of all my ills. When I was young, I was bold, because I was ignorant—now I have lost my boldness, because I have had advanced [sic] in experience. I am able to count the cost, better than I did, of being brave for Thy sake, and therefore I shrink from sacrifices. Here is a second reason, over and above the deadness of my soul, why I have so little faith or love in me.

Jan.ʸ 8. 1860.

When I last wrote, I had something to say, but I lost my thread, and got on a different line of thought far away from what I had intended—and now I will recover it, if I can. Circumstances have brought a special temptation upon me of late. I have now been exerting myself, labouring, toiling, ever since I was a Catholic, not I trust *ultimately* for any person on earth, but for God above, but still with a great desire to please those who put me to labour. After the Supreme Judgment of God, I have desired, though in a different order, their praise. But not only have I not got it, but I have been treated, in various ways, only with slight and unkindness. Because I have not pushed myself forward, because I have not dreamed of saying "See what I am doing and have done"—because I have not retailed gossip, flattered great people, and sided with this or that party, I am nobody. I have no friend at Rome, I have laboured in England, to be misrepresented, backbitten, and scorned. I have laboured in Ireland, with a door ever shut in my face. I seem to have had many failures, and what I did well was not understood. I do not think I am saying this in any bitterness.

"Not understood"—this is the point. I have seen great wants which had to be supplied among Catholics, especially as regards education, and of course those who laboured under those wants, did not know their state—& did not see or understand the want at all—or what was the supply of the want, and felt no thankfulness at all, and no consideration towards a person who was doing something towards that supply, but rather thought him restless, or crotchetty, or in some way or other what he should not be. This has naturally made me shrink into myself, or rather it has made me think of turning more to God, if it has not actually turned me. It has made me feel that in the Blessed Sacrament is my great consolation, and that while

I have Him who lives in the Church, the separate members of the Church, my Superiors, though they may claim my obedience, have no claim on my admiration, and offer nothing for my inward trust. I have expressed this feeling, or rather implied it, in one of my Dublin Sermons (preached in 1856). (*Occasional Sermons*, p 64, 65)

p 57 edition 4.

So far well—or not ill—but, it so happens, that, contemporaneously with this neglect on the part of those for whom I laboured, there has been a drawing towards me on the part of Protestants. Those very books and labours of mine, which Catholics did not understand, Protestant[s] did. Moreover, by a coincidence, things I had written years ago, as a Protestant, and the worth or force of which were not understood by Protestants then, are bearing fruit among Protestants now. Hence some sympathy is showing itself towards me on the part of certain persons, who have deliberately beat me down and buried me for the last ten years. And accordingly I have been attracted by that sympathy to desire more of that sympathy, feeling lonely, and fretting under, not so much the coldness towards me, (though that in part), as the ignorance, narrowness of mind, and selfconceit of those, whose faith & virtue & goodness, nevertheless, I at the same time recognised. And thus I certainly am under the temptation of looking out for, if not courting, Protestant praise.

And now I am coming to the meaning of the text with which I began on Decr 15. "No man putting his hand to the plough &c." I *am* tempted to look back. Not so, O Lord, with Thy grace, not so! What I had meant to say then, to ask of Thee then, I ask of Thee now. What a shame that I should fear to ask it. I have asked it often in time past, I think, long before I was a Catholic! Yes, I have referred to it above, as in the words above thirty years ago, "Deny me wealth &c." It has been my *lifelong* prayer, and Thou hast granted it, that I should be set aside in this world. Now then let me make it once again. O Lord, bless what I write and prosper it—let it do much good, let it have much success; but let no praise come to me on that account in my lifetime. Let me go on living, let me die, as I have hitherto lived. Long before I knew St. Philip, I wished "nesciri". Let me more and more learn from Thy grace "sperni", and "spernere me sperni".

Yet one or two things tease me, and, O Lord, help me—and Philip help me.

(1.) Let not the contempt which comes on *me*, injure the future of my *Oratory*—about this I am anxious, though I ought to put it, & do put it simply, into Thy hands, O Lord.

(2.) And again, O teach me (for it is a subject which tries me very much just now, which I have prayed about, & have said Masses about), teach me how to employ myself most profitably, most to Thy glory, in such years as remain to me; for my apparent illsuccess discourages me much. O my God, I seem to have wasted these years that I have been a Catholic. What I wrote as a Protestant has had far greater power, force, meaning, success, than my Catholic works—& this troubles me a great deal—though it is a fresh subject, on which I cannot enter now.

(Nov.ʳ 27. 1866. I write this on the page left blank.)

N. B. A few days after the above was written, viz Janʸ 13. 1860 our Bishop returned from Rome and wished to see me. I was in bed with a bad cold and Ambrose went instead of me. What he told me on his return was of a nature which made me get up at once, though it was late at night, and go to him.

The Bishop had found them at Rome displeased with a passage of an article of mine in the July Rambler (1859) Dr Brown of Newport had brought it before the judgment of Propaganda. The Bishop found it among the books at Propaganda, & translated the passage verbally to Mgr. Barnabò. He (I suppose) took it to the Pope, for the Pope had expressed some concern. Ambrose could not make out the Bp's report of the Pope's words. The Bishop said to Mgr. Barnabo that I had had many disappointments, and that they had irritated or soured me—from Faber &c. &c. especially that I had been disappointed in not having a Bishoprick in 1854! He advised that I should go to Rome, and explain myself, and hinted that I might come back a Bishop! I have got all the *correspondence* together—but I cannot tell whether Ambrose made or not a minute of his (A's) *conversation* with the Bishop. When *I* went to the Bishop, it was to express my great sorrow that I had given the Pope pain.)

Janʸ 21. 1863.

When I wrote my first lines in this book, I meant to have continued similar remarks from time to time; but I found I had a great un-willingness to do so. I have not read what I then wrote since I wrote it, and I recollect nothing about it, except that it had to do with the Rambler. This morning, when I woke, the feeling that I was cumbering the ground came on me so strongly, that I could not get myself to go to my shower-bath. I said, What is the good of trying to preserve or increase strength, when nothing comes of it? what is the good of living for nothing?

I have lately been doing a great deal for my own comfort, but with the real and sincere object of preserving myself in health. Last June year (1861) I suddenly found myself unwell; up to now I have not made out what the matter was. A surgeon, whom I went to in London, said that my nerves were affected, & that was the whole of it. He said I was full of fancies, and owned he did me no good, hardly liking to take my fees; but I was not well, beyond doubt. Well, I went about from place to place for several weeks; then I went for a while to Rednall, then to the Isle of Wight, then to London. After I had been back a while, I could not deny that, not only had my in-disposition gone, but I had received positive good, & was better than I was before I was unwell. So I went to the seaside for bathing for 5 weeks during the last Autumn. And that has done me great good; but it has been a serious expense. Besides this, I have gone the way to hinder the colds I suffer from so much, by papering my room, putting a matting down, putting double windows. And I have put up an excellent shower-bath. Well, it came upon me this morning as I lay in bed, What is the good of all this? what is to come of it? what am I living for? what am I doing for any religious end? Alas, it is my habitual thought, now for years, but circumstances have urged it on me at intervals more than usual of late, and something was told me yesterday which was a clincher.

O how forlorn & dreary has been my course since I have been a Catholic! here has been the contrast—as a Protestant, I felt my religion dreary, but not my life—but, as a Catholic, my life dreary, not my religion. Of course one's earlier years are (humanly speaking) best—and again, events are softened by distance—and I look back on my years at Oxford & Littlemore with tenderness—and it was the time in which I had a remarkable mission—but how am I changed even in look! till the affair of No 90 and my going to Littlemore, I had my mouth half open, and commonly a smile on my face—& from that time onwards my mouth has been closed and contracted, and the muscles are so set now, that I cannot but look grave and forbidding. Even as early as 1847, when I was going through the Vatican with Dalgairns, stopping before a statue of Fate, which was very striking & stern & melancholy, he said, "Who *can* it be like? I know the face so well"—presently he added, "Why, it is you." *Now*, I am so conscious of my own stern look, that I hardly like to see people. It began when I set my face towards Rome; and, since I made the great sacrifice, to which God called me, He has rewarded me in ten thousand ways, O how many! but he has marked my course with almost unintermittent mortification. Few indeed successes has it been His blessed will to give me through life. I doubt whether I can point to any joyful event of this world besides my scholarship at Trinity & my fellowship at Oriel—but since I have been a Catholic, I seem to myself to have had nothing but failure, personally.

How dreary my first year at Maryvale, (I speak differently of this in my letter to H. Wilberforce from Rome)[1] when I was the gaze of so many eyes at Oscott, as if some wild incomprehensible beast, caught by the hunter, and a spectacle for Dr. Wiseman to exhibit to strangers, as himself being the hunter who captured it! I did not realize this at the time except in its discomfort; but also, what I did realize, was the strangeness of ways, habits, religious observances, to which, however, I was urged on to conform without any delicacy towards my feelings. J. B. Morris undertook to lecture me. This has been the way with those who had been Protestants, & who felt themselves (seemingly) on a level with me now. Morris lectured me as the organ of Dr. Wiseman, Dalgairns lectured me still more from France, as the organ of M. Laurent, John Walker lectured me, from the inspiration of Dr. Acqueroni,[2] Capes had lectured us from Prior Park, as put up to it by Dr. Baggs. A smaller fry afterwards presumed to cut at me, and at a later date others, whom just now I cannot call to mind. I was made an humiliation at my minor orders & at the examination for them; and I had to stand at Dr. Wiseman's door waiting for Confession amid the Oscott boys. I did not realize these as indignities at the time, though, as I have said, I felt their dreariness.

[1] Parenthesis added later in pencil, above "first year" etc. C.S.D.
[2] Dr Acqueroni was chaplain to Newman's community at Maryvale, 1846-7. M. Laurent is Canon Lorain of Langres. For the other allusions here and elsewhere see W. Ward, *Life of Cardinal Newman*. C.S.D.

And then when I went to Rome, my first act was a mistake, and a presage and specimen of my after course. Much against my will, as an act of duty, I made a speech over Miss O'Brien [corrected from "Talbot"] at St. Isidore. O, I was a sort of sucking child, just as much knowing what I should say, what I should not say, and saying nothing right, not from want of tact so much as from sheer ignorance. The sermon or oration(!) was the talk of Rome, and the Pope expressed a sort of sorrow for it. And then how dreary (after the happy months, thank God, at Propaganda) how dreary F^r Rossi and St^a Croce, 1847. And then when I came home, at once Faber was upon me, to bully me, humbug me, & make use of me; and, as I committed the blunder at St. Isidore, so, to please Dr. Wiseman, I made the wretched throw off in London, against my will, of the Oratorian Lent-preaching 1848 at Passion-tide,—a blunder & failure, which even now I cannot think of without a raw sensitiveness. Then came the Baron 1849-50.[1] As to what followed in 1851-2, I mean the Achilli matter, it is abnormal (except as regards Wiseman's conduct) in any life, and I do not count it in. When it was over, in Feb^{ry} 1853, I told our people, that depend on it, if God loved us, there were more trials under the horizon, & certainly there were. I do not wonder at trials; trials are our lot here; but what saddens me, is that, as far as one can see, I have *done* so little, *amid* all my trials. My course has been dreary, because, to look back on it, it is so much of a failure.

First in 1853, came my mistake in asking for Dalgairns from the London House; then my going to Ireland, in order to impinge upon Dr. Cullen, while Dalgairns intrigued at home in my absence. Then the great plot of him, Faber &c—and my going to Rome—and the treatment I met at Propaganda. Then the thousand whisperings against me at the London Oratory, which have succeeded in prejudicing the Catholic body to a great extent against me. Then the way the Cardinal treated me both then and in the matter of the Translation of Scripture. Then my taking the Rambler came—I did it, at the wish of the Cardinal and our Bishop, and after as good consideration as I could give—but here again I made a blunder—and then in consequence I got into trouble at Rome. From that time all sorts of suspicions & calumnies, have attended my name. And, since we began the School, have been both increased, and directed against it. Now I

---

[1] A German artist named von Schroeter, and a convert. He was taken in as a guest and then stirred up disaffection in the community. C.S.D.

say again, I am noticing all this opposition and distrust, not on their own account, for St. Philip had them abundantly, but because they have (to all appearance) succeeded in destroying my influence & my usefulness. Persons who would naturally look towards me, converts who would naturally come to me, inquirers who would naturally consult me, are stopped by some light or unkind word said against me. I am passé, in decay; I am untrustworthy; I am strange, odd; I have my own ways & cannot get on with others; something or other is said in disparagement. I am put aside on the ground that I *ought* to be put aside; and thus men make statements of which their very words bring about the fulfilment. Nor is it wonderful that all this slight and scorn reacts upon my own mind. I shrink from a society which is so unjust towards me. I must say, that the converts have behaved to *me* much worse than old Catholics, when they might have had a little gratitude, to say the least.

I should be very ungrateful if I did not bear in mind what God has vouchsafed to do by me. First to introduce the Oratory into England, & to found this Oratory—and therefore I have not mentioned the great trials which we have had inside our walls, by death, secession, & in other ways—for they have been the trials incidental to a new foundation, and have not interfered with its success—secondly to found the London Oratory, which has been the instrument of so much good—thirdly to found the Catholic University—and fourthly to found our Oratory School. This is another matter altogether. They are works of my *name;* what I am speaking of is what belongs to my own person;—things, which I ought to have been especially suited to do, & have not done, not done any one of them.

Rogers the other day asked Ward, Why it was that Catholics understood me so little! i.e. I suppose, why they thought so little of me. And the Saturday Review, writing apropos of my letter to the Globe of last summer, said that I had disappointed friends & enemies, since I had been a Catholic, by doing nothing. The reason is conveyed in the remark of Marshall of Brighton to Fr Ambrose last week; "Why, he has made no converts, as Manning & Faber have." Here is the real secret of my "doing nothing". The only thing of course, which is worth producing, is *fruit*—but with the Cardinal, immediate *show* is fruit, and conversions the *sole* fruit. At Propaganda, conversions, and nothing else, are the proof of doing *any*

thing. Every where with Catholics, to make converts, is doing something; and not to make them, is "doing nothing". And further still,
in the estimate of Propaganda, of the Cardinal, & of Catholics
generally, they must be splendid conversions of great men, noblemen,
learned men, not simply of the poor. It must be recollected that at
Rome they have had visions of the whole of England coming over to
the Church, and that their notion of the instrumentality of this conversion en masse, is the conversion of persons of rank. "Il governo"
is all in all in their ideas. Such an idea is perhaps even conveyed in
our Brief, which sends us to the upper classes. Manning then and
others are great, who live in London, & by their position and influence convert Lords and Ladies. This is what was expected of me.

   But I am altogether different—my objects, my theory of acting,
my powers, go in a different direction, and one not understood or
contemplated at Rome or elsewhere. I never have courted men, but
they have come to me. I wrote in 1829, "Blessings of friends, who to
my door, Unasked, unhoped, have come." And if they did not come
to me, I did not gain them. But, when I became a Catholic, I threw
myself out of the opportunity of their coming to me. I determined,
that it did not become one, who had taken a prominent part against
the Church, to be taking a prominent part against Anglicanism, but
that my place was retirement, which indeed was my nature too.
"I broke my staff"; and the Cardinal did not hinder it. Rather he co-
operated, and I was fixed in Birmingham. But this was not all. To me
conversions were not the first thing, but the edification of Catholics.
So much have I fixed upon the latter as my object, that up to this
time the world persists in saying that I recommend Protestants not to
become Catholics. And, when I have given as my true opinion, that
I am afraid to make hasty converts of educated men, lest they should
not have counted the cost, & should have difficulties after they have
entered the Church, I do but imply the same thing, that the Church
must be prepared for converts, as well as converts prepared for the
Church. How can this be understood at Rome? what do they know
there of the state of English Catholics, of the minds of English
Protestants? what do they know of the antagonism of Protestantism
& Catholicism in England? the Cardinal might know something,
were he not so outsided, so slow to throw himself into other minds,
so sanguine, so controversial & unphilosophic in his attitude of
mind, so desirous to make himself agreeable to authorities at Rome.

And Catholics in England, from their very blindness, cannot see that they are blind. To aim then at improving the condition, the status, of the Catholic body, by a careful survey of their argumentative basis, of their position relatively to the philosophy and the character of the day, by giving them juster views, by enlarging & refining their minds, in one word, by education, is (in their view) more than a superfluity or a hobby, it is an insult. It implies that they are deficient in material points. Now from first to last, education, in this large sense of the word, has been my line, and, over and above the disappointment it has caused as putting conversions comparatively in the background, and the offence it has given by insisting that there was room for improvement among Catholics, it has in two ways seriously annoyed the governing body here and at Rome:—at Rome on the side of the philosophy of polemics—*I* should wish to attempt to meet the great infidel &c. questions of the day, but both Propaganda & the Episcopate, doing nothing themselves, look with extreme jealousy on any one who attempts it, and, giving him no credit for what he does well, come down with severity on any point in which he may have slipped. —And secondly especially at home, because I have set up a school, and so interfered with the vested rights, as they may be called, of this and that College or Seminary. Hence the keen sensitiveness of Dr. Grant & the two Dr. Browns, not to say the Cardinal, and the multitude of slanders which have been spread & are believed, about our boys and our treatment of them. And last of all, since from first to last, these have been the two objects of the Rambler,—to raise the status of Catholics, first by education, secondly by a philosophical basis of argument,—and the Rambler has attempted it injudiciously, intemperately, and erroneously, at least at times, I come in for the odium of all the Rambler's faults, and that the more because for a little while I was the Editor of the Rambler, &, when such, shared in my measure in the imperfections of the preceding & succeeding Editors. The consequence is, that, so far from being thought engaged in any good work, I am simply discouraged and regarded suspiciously by the governing powers as doing an actual harm.

One other circumstance there is, peculiar to the time, to give a special intensity to this feeling of suspicion. At present the Temporal Power is the all important point at Rome—I, thinking that they would be obliged to rely more on reason, a truer defence, than on the sword, if they had it not, am lukewarm on the point; and this luke-warmness [h]as been exaggerated into a supposed complicity with Garibaldi! The Cardinal some years ago said that I had put myself on the shelf. But the position I occupy at the moment is, in his mind, a less harmless one.

(On August 20, 1861, I wrote a letter to a friend, in the first copy of which the following occurred—but I rewrote it, leaving the passage out. "The case has been the same of late. I have felt there were many things to be done, and that God has given me talents to do some of them. I know there are things *in* me, which I have but partially given out; and friends* have said I ought not to die without saying them; but, as sure as I begin to attempt any thing, I am stopped."

* N. B. (Oct 30. 1867.) Dr. Ullathorne especially.)

February 22. 1865.
I have just now looked over what I wrote on Jany 21. 1863. My position of mind now is so different from what it was then, that it would require many words to bring it out. First, I have got hardened against the opposition made to me, and have not the soreness at my ill treatment on the part of certain influential Catholics which I had then—and this simply from the natural effect of time—just as I do not feel that anxiety which I once had that we have no novices—I don't know that this recklessness is a better state of mind than that anxiety. Every year I feel less & less anxiety to please Propaganda, from a feeling that they *cannot* understand England. Next, the two chief persons, whom I felt to be unjust to me, are gone—the Cardinal & Faber. Their place has been taken by Manning and Ward; but somehow, from my never having been brought closely into contact with either of them, as with the Cardinal & Faber, I have not that sense of their cruelty which I felt so much as regards the two last mentioned. Thirdly, in the last year a most wonderful deliverance has been wrought in my favour, by the controversy, of which the upshot was my Apologia. It has been marvellously blest, for, while I have regained, or rather gained, the favour of Protestants, I have received the approbation, in formal addresses, of good part of the English clerical body. They have been highly pleased with me, as doing them a service, and I stand with them, as I never did before. Then again it has pleased Protestants, & of all parties, as much or more. When I wrote those sharp letters, as I did very deliberately, in June 1862, in

consequence of the reports circulated to the effect that I was turning Protestant, I at once brought myself down to my lowest point, as regards popularity, yet by the very force of my descent, I prepared the way for a rebound. It was my lowest point, yet the turning point. When Crawley wrote to remonstrate with me on the part of my Protestant friends, I answered him by showing how unkindly they had treated me for 17 years—so much so that they had no right to remonstrate. This touched Keble. Moreover, it happened just then, that, independent of this, Copeland, having met me accidentally in London, came to see us here, and he spread such a kind report of me, that Keble wrote to me, Rogers visited me (August 30. 1863) and Church proposed to do so. Williams too wished to come and see me —but *he* had never lost sight of me. The kind feeling was growing, when (Copeland accidentally being here) I began the Kingsley controversy, the effect of which I need not enlarge on—I have pleasant proofs of it every day. And thus I am in a totally different position now to what I was in January 1863—and my temptation at this moment is, to value the praise of men too highly, especially of Protestants—and to lose some portion of that sensitiveness towards God's praise, which is so elementary a duty.

On all these accounts, though I still feel keenly the way in which I am kept doing nothing, I am not so much pained at it—both because, by means of my Apologia, I am (as I feel) *indirectly* doing a work, and because its success has put me in spirits to look out for other means of doing good, whether Propaganda cares about them or no. Yet still, it is very singular that the same effective opposition to me does go on, thwarting my attempts to *act*, and what is very singular, "uno avulso non deficit alter"—Faber being taken away, Ward and Manning take his place. Through them, especially Manning, acting on the poor Cardinal (who is to be buried tomorrow) the Oxford scheme has been for the present thwarted—for me probably for good, and this morning I have been signing the agreement by which I sell my land to the University. Bellasis told me that, from what he saw at Rome, he felt that Manning was more set against *my* going to Oxford, than merely against Catholic youths going there. And now I am thrown back again on my do-nothing life here—how marvellous! yet, as I have drawn out above, from habit, from recklessness, and from my late success, my feeling of despondency & irritation seems to have gone.

Octr 30, 1867. What I have written in the foregoing pages, has been written as a sort of relief to my mind; if that were the only reason for writing, I should not write now, for I have no trouble within me to be relieved of. I will put myself under the image of the Patriarch Job, without intending to liken myself to him. He first strenuously resisted the charges of his friends, then he made a long protest of his innocence, & then we read, "The words of Job are ended." Mine are ended too—I have said to Cardinal Barnabò "Viderit Deus." I have lodged my cause with Him—and, while I hope ever by His grace to be obedient, I have now as little desire, as I have hope, to gain the praise of such as him in any thing I shall do henceforth. Faber and others have been too much for me. They have too deeply impressed the minds of authorities at Rome against me, to let the truth about me have fair play while I live; and when one ceases to hope, one ceases to fear. They have done their worst—and, as Almighty God in 1864 cleared up my conduct in the sight of Protestants at the end of twenty years, so as regards my Catholic course, at length, after I am gone hence, Deus viderit! I did not use the words lightly, though they seem to have rested most unfavourably on his mind (C. Barnabò's)—nor do I dream of retracting them. For many years I tried to approve myself to such as him, but it is now more than ten years, that, from failing to do so, I have been gradually weaned from any such expectation or longing. I have recorded the change in the words of my Dublin sermon of Novr 23. 1856, though covertly and only to my own consciousness. "There are those who ... think we mean to spend our devotion upon a human cause, and that we toil for an object of human ambition. They think that we should acknowledge, if crossexamined, that our ultimate purpose was the success of persons and parties, to whom we are bound in honour, or in interest, or in gratitude; and that &c ... They fancy, as the largest concession of their liberality, that we are working *from the design*, generous but still human, *of the praise of earthly superiors*, and that, after all, we are living on the breath, and basking in the smile of man", &c. &c.

And now, alas, I fear that in one sense the iron has entered into my soul. I mean that confidence in any superiors whatever never can blossom again within me. I never shall feel easy with them. I shall (I feel) always think they will be taking some advantage of me—that at length their way will lie across mine, and that my efforts will be displeasing to them. I shall ever be suspicious that they or theirs have secret unkind thoughts of me, and that they deal with me with some arrière pensée. And, as it is my happiness so to be placed as not to have much intercourse with them, therefore, while I hope ever loyally to fulfil their orders, it is my highest gain and most earnest request to them, that they would let me alone—and, since I do not want to initiate any new plan of any kind, that, if they can, they would keep their hands off me. Whether or not they will consent to this is more that I can say, for they seem to wish to ostracize me. But, in saying this, I repeat what I said when I began to write, I am now in a state of quiescence, and fear as little as I hope. And I do not expect this state of mind to be reversed. God forbid I should liken them to the "Scribes and Pharisees"—but still I obey them, as Scribes & Pharisees were to be obeyed, as God's representatives, not from devotion to *them*. Nor does any thing that has happened to me interfere with, rather these external matters have all wonderfully promoted, my inward happiness. I never was in such simply happy circumstances as now, and I do not know how I can fancy I shall continue without some or other real cross. I am my own master—I have my time my own—I am surrounded with comforts & conveniences—I am in easy circumstances, I have no cares, I have good health—I have no pain of mind or body. I enjoy life only too well. The weight of years falls on me as snow, gently tho' surely, but I do not feel it yet. I am surrounded with dear friends—my reputation has been cleared by the Apologia. What can I want but greater gratitude & love towards the Giver of all these good things? There is no state of life I prefer to my own—I would not change my position for that of any one I know— I am simply content—there is nothing I desire—I should be puzzled to know what to ask, if I were free to ask. I should say perhaps that I wished the financial matters of the Oratory & School to be in a better state—but for myself I am as covered with blessings & as full of God's gifts, as is conceivable. And I have nothing to ask for but pardon and grace, & a happy death.

January 29, 1868. Our Lord has said. "Vae cum benedixerint vobis homines." Luc. vi, 26. καλῶς ὑμᾶς εἴπωσι, and I seem to be in this danger as regards the Protestant world. A re-action has set in, nor does one know what will be its limits. Just now, my Verses which I have collected and published, have both stimulated and manifested it. I feel as if a nemesis would come, if I am not careful and am reminded of the ring of Polycrates. Friends & well-wishers out of kindness are writing favorable reviews of my small book, and I am obliged to read out of gratitude what they say of me so generously. I have said "the Protestant world"—but it extends to the great mass of (English speaking) Catholics also; till the Apologia I was thought passé and forgotten. The controversy which occasioned it, and then the Oxford matter and the "Dream of Gerontius", have brought me out, and now I should be hard indeed to please, and very ungrateful to them, and to God, if I did not duly appreciate their thoughts of me.

Then comes the question, what use can I make of these fresh mercies? Not from any supernatural principle, but from mere natural temper, I keep saying, What is the good of all this? what comes of it? Vanitas vanitatum, if it is but empty praise. What use can I make of it? for what is it given me?—And then too on the other hand when I am well thought of, and the world is in good humour with me, I am led to say to myself, "Let well alone; do not hazard by any fresh act the loss of that, which you have been so long without, and found such difficulty, in getting. Enjoy the otium cum dignitate."

"Otium cum dignitate" reminds me of "Otium cum indignitate"; yes, as far as Propaganda goes, and that English party of which Archbp Manning & Ward are the support, I have been dismissed not simply to "inglorious", but to "dishonoured ease"—And this would certainly serve as the ring of Polycrates, did I feel it—but I don't feel it. And, as I had said on some former page, I should be so out of my element if I were without that cold shade on the side of ecclesiastical authority, in which I have dwelt nearly all my life, my eyes would be so dazed, and my limbs so relaxed, were I brought out to bask in the full sun of ecclesiastical favour, that I should not know how to act and should make a fool of myself.

As my Lord had some purpose in letting me be so long forgotten and calumniated, as He has had some purpose in leaving me as regards ecclesiastical authorities under that cloud which He has lately removed from me as regards Catholics and Protestants generally, so now He has some purpose in that late removal—if I could know what it is. Perhaps He wishes me to do nothing new, but He is creating an opportunity for what I have already written to work. Perhaps my duty is, what is only too pleasant, to sit still, do nothing, and enjoy myself. Perhaps my name is to be turned to account as a sanction and outset by which others, who agree with me in opinion, should write and publish instead of me, and thus begin the transmission of views in religious and intellectual matters congenial with my own, to the generation after me.

Ignatius[Ryder]'s second Pamphlet, which has just come, and promises to be very successful, is an instance, actually occurring, of this anticipation. In my Letter to Pusey two years ago, I laid down two subjects for discussion—the prerogatives of our Lady, and their abuse—and those of the Holy See and their abuse. I wished to consider each subject argumentatively, and to ascertain the intellectual view to be taken of each. The former took up so many pages, and the latter subject was so large and intricate, that I published on the subject of the Bl. Virgin, leaving the subject of the Holy See for a separate Pamphlet. When I did so, some anonymous Catholic wrote in a Protestant paper that I was forbidden, or certainly should be forbidden at Rome, did I attempt to write upon my second subject. I meanwhile collected my materials for it. At this moment, viz last September year, Ignatius came to me of his own accord, begging me to write upon it, having heard I had abandoned my notion, confessing his dislike of Ward's tyranny in the Dublin, and offering to do every thing he could in the way of helping me in getting up the subject. When I put off, and almost dismissed the intention from my thoughts, he brought a sketch of an answer of his own; and that was the first copy of his Pamphlet in April last year (1867) after several re-writings, and much anxious thought. When it was found to need further explanation, he got ready a second, published at the beginning of this month, which promises to be quite successful, and to have done a great work in shattering the intolerable dogmatism of the Dublin. It was natural that, though every part of both pamphlets was the work of his own mind, that at first they, or at least the first pamphlet, was attributed to me; to me even certain sentences were attributed, as certainly mine. Gradually this opinion has been set right; still, he has had the advantage of my name, and his Pamphlets have come from this Oratory, & must have had my sanction. Here then is a twofold advantage—to me and to him—he has finished my work, I have introduced him to the Catholic public. And now he is in a position, if he continues what he has so well begun, to uphold truths and views, which I have upheld in my day. This seems to me wonderful, and shows that we are in God's hands, and must be content to do our work day by day, as He puts it before us, without attempting to understand or to anticipate His purposes, and thanking Him for the great mercies He has bestowed on us, and is bestowing.

(Oct. 30. 1870. I am not, and have never been particularly intimate or open-hearted with Ignatius. He is not quite of my sort, and one does not make new friends, when one is old.)

Nov. 30. 1868.

Haec mutatio dexterae Excelsi. I am too old to feel much pleasure or at least to realize that I do—but certainly I have abundantly cause to bless and praise God for the wonderful change that has taken place in men's estimation of me, that is, if I can make that change subservient to any good purpose. An Anglican correspondent writes to me, "You occupy a very unique position in England. There is no other man whose mere word would be more readily taken without the necessity of having it confirmed by any other testimony. I do not know any revolution of public feeling so complete as this."

As far as this is a correct statement, I think the fact arises from the feeling in the public mind that for many, for 20 years, I have been unfairly dealt with. It is a generous feeling desirous of making amends. Thus I account for the great considerateness which the Spectator, the Saturday Review, nay the Pall Mall, and the Anglican Guardian & other Anglican Newspapers show me. But it is showing itself still more in facts—Copeland has lately heard from Rivingtons that the first volume of the new Edition of my Parochial Sermons, published in May, has already, in half a year, sold to the number of 3500 ? copies—and that this number includes an *"extensive* sale" among Dissenters—Another remarkable fact is that Sir F. Doyle, Poetry Professor at Oxford, is paying me the extraordinary compliment of giving a Public Lecture on my "Dream of Gerontius".

Then on the other hand, whereas the Pope directed that I should be asked to go to Rome to take part in preparing matters for the Council, the Catholic Papers, who have not hitherto spoken well of me, say that it has been a special invitation, the first & hitherto only one made to any Priest in England, Scotland, or Ireland, &c. &c.

Per contra—I shall be selling out my newly acquired stock of credit in these Catholic Circles, if I publish this letter on Renouf's pamphlet upon Honorius, as I am thinking of doing.

I have nothing particular to remark on the above—but record it, as I would the risings & fallings of the weatherglass. I am too old not to feel keenly that unless I can do something for God by means of the good words which men give me, such praise is mere chaff, and will be whirled away by the wind some fine morning, leaving nothing behind it.

Another very encouraging fact is, that, in spite of opposition and criticism, Ignatius's Pamphlets certainly have done a work, and have thrown back the ὕβρις ὀρθιᾶν κνωδάλων, the arrogant ipse dixit of various persons who would crush every opinion in theology which is not theirs.

June 25. 1869.
The Providence of God has been wonderful with me all through my life. One thing struck me this morning as an antithesis, which I have often thought of in its details, without observing the contrast they afford. It is this, that my troubles have come from those whom I had aided, and my successes from my opponents. Without me Hawkins would not have been Provost, and he from 1830 to 1843 was my great trial. Without me Golightly would not have come to Oxford, and he was my chief slanderer. Without me J. Mozley would not have been fellow of Magdalen, and he, after showing intimate affection till I became a Catholic, then at once turned round, and began without delay in print (& as I thought with knowledge he otherwise could not have had or used) wrote against me. Without me Faber would not have been a member of the Oratory, and the head of the London Congregation, and he slandered me at Rome & elsewhere, abroad as well as at home. Then on the other hand, whom am I so indebted to as the Heads of Houses, and the Anglican Bishops, and Hawkins & Golightly, when they became my opponents, for having done so much towards making me a Catholic? Of course it was direct "motiva credibilitatis" which convinced me that Catholicism was divine—but how great a suffering was it to part from those I loved! and how much greater would it have been, if the

Bishops & others had, by taking my part, laid me under obligations of gratitude to them, and impressed upon me the φαντασία of their Catholic principles! should I have overcome in the trial?—Then again in the Achilli matter, my opponents by bringing me into a court of law, and entailing on me expenses amounting to near £10,000, nevertheless left me with an overplus of Catholic contributions in my favour to the amount of £3000 and more. And now lately the Archbp of Westminster, W G Ward & others, have succeeded in keeping me out of Oxford, the only place where I could be of service to the Catholic cause; but is it not abundantly for my *private* comfort, for my tranquillity, and for my length of life?

Another thought has come on me, that I have had three great illnesses in my life, and how have they turned out! The first keen, terrible one, when I was a boy of 15, and it made me a Christian—with experiences before and after, awful, and known only to God. My second, not painful, but tedious and shattering was that which I had in 1827 when I was one of the Examining Masters, and it too broke me off from an incipient liberalism—and determined my religious course. The third was in 1833, when I was in Sicily, before the commencement of the Oxford Movement.

I suppose every one has a great deal to say about the Providence of God over him. Every one doubtless is so watched over and tended by Him that at the last day, whether he be saved or not, he will confess that nothing could have been done for him more than had been actually done—and every one will feel his own history as special & singular. Yet I cannot but repeat words which I think I used in a memorandum book of 1820, that among the ordinary mass of men, *no one* has sinned so much, *no one* has been so mercifully treated, as I have; no one has such cause for humiliation, such cause for thanksgiving.

October 30. 1870. How unpleasant it is to read former memoranda —I can't quite tell why. They read affected, unreal, egotistical, petty, fussy. There is much in the above, which I should tear out & burn, if I did as I wished. One writes in particular humours—Perhaps if I looked over it six months hence, I should like what now I don't like. I wonder whether I shall burn it all, when I am going to die. Perhaps I shall leave it for what is valuable in it.

Since I published my Essay on Assent last March, I have meant to make a memorandum on the subject of it. It is the upshot of a very long desire and effort—I don't know the worth of it, but I am happier to have at length done it and got it off my hands. Authors, (or at least I) can as little foretell what their books will be before they are written, as fathers can foretell whether their children will be boys or girls, dark or fair, gentle or fiery, clever or stupid. The book itself I have aimed at writing this twenty years;—& now that it is written I do not quite recognize it for what it was meant to be, though I suppose it is such. I have made more attempts at writing it, than I can enumerate. However, I actually have MS remaining, to prove the following distinct separate beginnings:—

1. June 17. 1846. On St. Thomas's view of faith as "cogitare cum assensu".

2. March 5, 1850. My letters to Dr. Errington about Gerdil, & the enquiries out of which they arose.

3. Feby 1851. "On a view of the conclusion greater and distincter and higher than that of the premisses." This a problem long in my mind, e. g. in University Sermons—go through my attempts historically ... "Against historical religion. 1st. We cannot suppose &c ..." ["]Fluctuations of human opinion ..." "On certainty &c ..."

4. Septr 25. 1851. "A defence of the Catholic Religion."

5. (Without date.) On certainty &c.

6. May & June 1853. Fr. Edward Caswall's notes of my Lectures on Faith and certainty—And my own notes of the same.

7. March 1857. "In festo S. Gregorii" "Opus magnum" (as it was to be).

8. July & Septr 1857. "What God is personally TO US."

9. Jany 1859 & Feby Lectures to Scott &c. on Logic. "Whether religious certitude may be legitimately produced by probable arguments &c" "Whether words stand for ideas or things."

10. 1859-60. Letters to Dr. Meynell—(about Mansell's theory?).

11. Jany 5. 1860. "On the popular, practical, personal evidence for the truth of Revelation."

12. Jan. 12, 1860. "The Evidences of Religion."

13. Jany 1861. "The Holy Trinity in connection with the early Fathers and the Disciplina Arcani."

14. Septr 1. 1861. "I find, my dear—,that you are both interested &c."—"On the senses."

15. Oct.ʳ 12. 1861. At Ventnor. "Schema totius operis &c."

16. Sept.ʳ 22. 1863. Doctrine of the Holy Trinity.

17. December 12. 1863. Doctrine of the Holy Trinity. § 1 begins "The knowledge, which is most intimately our own, and directly personal to us, lies in our experience &c. and so on, what afterwards became "Imaginative and notional apprehension."

18. Aug. 11, 1865. On certitude—intuition—instinct.

These attempts, though some of them close upon others, were, I think, all distinct. They were like attempts to get into a labyrinth, or to find the weak point in the defences of a fortified place. I could not get on, & found myself turned back, utterly baffled. Yet I felt I ought to bring out what my mind saw, but could not grasp, whatever it was worth. I don't say it is worth much, now that it has come out, but I felt as if I did not like to die before I had said it. It may suggest something better and truer than it, to another, though worth little in itself. Thus I went on year after year. At last, when I was up at Glion over the Lake of Geneva, it struck me "You are wrong in beginning with certitude—certitude is only a kind of assent—you should begin with contrasting assent and inference." On that hint I spoke, finding it a key to my own ideas.

August 30. 1874.

I have so depressing a feeling that I have done nothing through my long life—and especially that now I am doing nothing at all. Anglicans indeed rather think more of what I have written than they did, if I may judge from letters I receive—but, as to Catholics, they would not deny that I have done some good service towards bringing Anglicans into the Church, nay am perhaps doing so still; but, as to the great controversies of the day, about the divinity of Christianity &c, they think I am passé—at least this, (perhaps rather,) that I have taken a wrong line in respect to them. At least I think the Jesuits do. They would think my line too free and sceptical, that I made too many admissions &c. On the contrary I *cannot* at all go along with them—and, since they have such enormous influence just now, and are so intolerant in their views, this is pretty much the same as saying that I have not taken, and do not take, what would popularly be called the Catholic line.

I may seem inconsistent or ungrateful to them in this,—that I must grant, that, in spite of their violence against Rosmini, Ubaghs, &c. they have never fallen upon me—the contrary—yet I think they have not felt the same since the Vatican Council & the Grammar of Assent —certainly not, if their sentiments towards me are to be measured and interpreted by my feelings towards them. They certainly seem to me to be too powerful for the health of that Divine Body out of which they grow and which it is their business and duty to subserve.

But then I think—what is this to me? God will provide—He knows what is best. Is He less careful for the Church, less able to defend it than I am? Why need I fash myself about it? What am I? my time is out. I am passé—I may have done something in my day —but I can do nothing now. It is the turn of others. And if things seem done clumsily, my business is, not to criticize, but to have faith in God. The 130th Psalm is the Psalm that suits me—alas! we never read it in the office—Non est exaltatum cor meum, neque &c Neque ambulavi in magnis,—neque in mirabilibus super me—Sicut ablactatus est super matre suâ, ita retributio in animâ meâ. It is enough for me to prepare for death—for, as it would appear, nothing else awaits me—there is nothing else to do.

And He Who has been with me so marvellously all through my life, will not fail me now, I know—though I have no claim upon Him, ... I certainly feel much weaker and less capable [corrected from "more incapable"] than I was—and whether this ἀδυναμία will not rapidly increase upon me, or not, how can I tell? I must give up the thought of the next generation, and think of myself.

October 14. 1874.
I have been startled on considering, that in the last 15 years I have only written two books, the Apologia and the Essay on Assent—of which the former was almost extempore. What have I been doing with my time? though I have never been idle. The last four years or five I have been busy with my reprints—and my Essay on Assent took up four years from 1866 to 1870. Then my smaller publications since 1859, (viz. Occasional Sermons, pp. 75, Letter to Pusey, pp. 140, on Ecce Homo, pp. 36, on St Ignatius, pp. 36, on Anglican Orders &c, pp. 40, on causes of Arianism & on Apollinarianism, pp. 190 and Theodoret, pp. 56) amount to pp. 572, that is, to (at least) a volume

and a half—but these have been mostly done in the course of the last four years, which have already been taken into account—Seven years (from 1859 to 1866) remain, with only the Apologia, done in nine weeks (between April 10 and June 12), and the Letter to Pusey & sermon on Weedall; what was I doing all that time?—First, must be recollected, all through the fifteen years the great number of letters I wrote, whatever be their worth, most of them certainly ephemeral & of no permanent value—next, the time I have given to the School-boys, especially in preparing and editing four Latin Plays for their use;—thirdly, (but I did not begin these till 1864) the time I gave through 1860 to the alterations &c in the Church, which were almost my *occupation*—fourthly my state of health for good part of 1861. Still the fact remains that, whereas before 1859 I wrote almost a book a year, (viz 30 ½ volumes from 1826 to 1859, 33 years) in the last 15, I have written between three and four—though such powers of writing as I may have are not less, to say the least than they were.

This is an unpleasant thought—more than unpleasant. What have I been doing? I have not mentioned above one occupation which has taken a great deal of time, though there is not much to show for it— viz the transcription I have made of my own & my friends' letters. But cui bono?

The cause of my not writing from 1859 to 1864 was my failure with the Rambler. I thought I had got into a scrape, and it became me to be silent. So they thought at Rome, if Mgr. Talbot is to be their spokesman for, referring to the Apologia to Ambrose in 1867, he said of me—"He had ceased writing, and a good riddance—Why did he ever begin again?"—I certainly had myself in 1860 anticipated his view in 1867 of my services to religion. Vid. my remarks above p. 8.[1]

Another reason, closely connected with this, was my habit, or even nature, of not writing & publishing without a *call*. What I have written has been for the most part what may be called official, works done in some office I held or engagement I had made—all my Sermons are such, my Lectures on the Prophetical Office, on Justi-fication, my Essays in the British Critic and translation of St. Athanasius—or has been from some especial call, or invitation, or necessity, or emergency, as my Arians, Anglican difficulties, Apologia

[1] p. 254 above. C.S.D.

or Tales. The Essay on Assent is nearly the only exception. And I *cannot* write without such a stimulus. I feel to myself going out of the way, or impertinent—and I write neither with spirit nor with point. As to the "Assent", I had felt it on my conscience for years, that it would not do to quit the world without doing it. Rightly or wrongly I had ever thought it a duty, as if it was committed to me to do it. I had tried to do it again & again & failed, and though at length I did it, I did it after all with great difficulty—but it was a great relief to me in 1870 to have done it. But to return, this is the real account of my silence from 1859 to 1864—viz. I said to myself "In 14 years (from 1845 to 1859) I have written nine volumes, and have got no thanks for my labour—rather, have been thought inopportune—why should I go on blundering?" On occasion of my Apologia Hope Scott said "Now you have got the ear of the public—take care not to lose it again by your silence."

(Febr. 27. 1876. Curiously enough the foregoing page (about writing not without a call) was written but a few weeks before the call made on me by Gladstone's pamphlets, and my consequent "Letter to the Duke of Norfolk".)

Septr 10. 1876.

I notice the following, lest the subject should turn up when I am gone, and my friends be perplexed how to deal with it.

I have before now said in writing to Cardinals Wiseman & Barnabò, when I considered myself treated with slight and unfairness, "So this is the return made to me for working for the Catholic cause for so many years", i. e. to that effect.—

I feel it still, and ever shall.—but it was not a disappointed ambition which I was then expressing in words, but a scorn and wonder at the *injustice* shown me, and at the demand of toadyism on my part, if I was to get their favour, & the favour of Rome.

I knew perfectly well, when I so wrote, that such language would look like disappointment at having received no promotion, and moreover was the worst way of getting it. But I had no wish to get it, and it was my very consciousness that I never had had such aspiration, nor felt any such disappointment, and was simply careless whether they thought I had or no, that made me thus speak. And at other times of my life also I have used words which, when I used them, I saw could be used against me, but did not care whether they were so used or not, from a clear conscience that it would be a mistaken use of them, if they were. When I wrote to the two Cardinals, I had that strength of conviction that I never had had any motive of secular or ecclesiastical ambition for writing my volumes, which made me not hesitate to denounce, if I may so speak, at the risk of being misunderstood, the *injustice*, for so I felt it, which had been shown towards me. This I did feel very keenly; I was indignant that after all my anxious and not unsuccessful attempts to promote, in my own place and according to my own measure, the Catholic cause, my very first mistake in the Rambler, supposing it one, should have been come down upon, my former services neither having been noticed favorably when they were done, nor telling now as a plea for mercy.

As to my freedom from ambitious views, I don't know that I need defend myself from the imputation of them. Qui s'excuse, s'accuse. But in fact I have from the first presaged that I should get no thanks for what I was doing, (a presage which has only come true in that sense in which I did not care about its being true, and which God's undeserved mercy has falsified or rather reversed in a higher sense, for He has heaped upon me the acknowledgments and the sympathies, for what I have written, of friends & strangers far beyond my deserts—) But as to my presage that I should gain no secular reward for my writings, I have expressed it many times.

1. In 1836 (as I understand Copeland) in a letter which I wrote to Pusey on occasion of the Hampden matter, and which he has, tho' I have not seen it.

2. In 1837 in my letter to the Christian Observer, "Never were such words used on one side, but deeds were on the other. We know our place and our fortunes, to give a witness and to be contemned; to be ill used and to succeed."

3. In 1845 to Cardinal Acton, Apol. pp. 235, 236.

4. In 1850 in a Sermon at St. Chad's, "As to ourselves, the world has long ago done its worst against us. ... We know our place and our fortunes &c."

5. In 1856 in a Sermon at Dublin quoted above at p. 22.[1]
Oct 30 1867

I am dissatisfied with the whole of this book. It is more or less a complaint from one end to the other. But it represents what has been the real state of my mind, and what my Cross has been.

O how light a Cross—think what the Crosses of others are! And think of the compensation, compensation in even this world—I have touched on it in a parenthesis in the foregoing page. I have had, it is true, no recognition in high quarters—but what warm kind letters in private have I had! and how many! and what public acknowledgments! How ungrateful I am, or should I be, if such letters and such notices failed to content me.

Since writing the above I have been made a Cardinal!

[1] p. 262 above. C.S.D.

VI

MEMORANDUM ABOUT MY CONNECTION WITH THE CATHOLIC UNIVERSITY

INTRODUCTION

Newman left two manuscripts of this Memorandum. The first, the rough copy, is dated November 25th, 1870, and was carefully written on the left-hand side of folded sheets of foolscap, the right-hand being used for corrections and additions. It contains matter which Newman later omitted, though some of it found a place in the appendix to be referred to in a moment. The second manuscript is the fair copy, here reproduced, and consists of 172 quarto pages, followed by an appendix, 657 quarto pages of letters or excerpts of letters, to illustrate the story of the Catholic University, all but three of them transcribed by Newman himself. He transferred to this later copy the date, November 25th, on which he had begun his work, and he dates the seventh section in it January 9th, 1873. This later copy is preceded by four pages detailing the contents of papers "belonging to my Rectorship in Dublin", with a note that all were put together on May 31st, 1873. This makes it clear that the Memorandum was written between November 1870 and May 1873.

It will be noticed that Newman sometimes quotes from his contemporary University Journal, 1853-6. This has not been printed here because much of the interesting matter it contains is thus already given, and a good deal of it is taken up with details, which are perhaps chiefly important as proof of Newman's practical ability and powers of organization. It confirms too that impression of his "toughness", which so often emerges for those who study his Irish Campaign. However, if the Journal shows Newman at grips with the difficulties involved in the founding of the Catholic University, the Memorandum represents his considered view, fifteen years later. He saw, for instance, that he had trusted too blindly in the sagacity of Pius IX, who, in spite of great qualities, was, as his most recent Catholic biographers bear witness, not immune from errors of judgment. This led Newman henceforth to regard in a more matter-of-fact and realistic way the practical activities of the Holy See. He noted with the same realism, regretfully but serenely, the causes of his failure in Ireland, and the parts played by those who were in one way or another responsible for it. He considered notwithstanding that his Memorandum might be published at any time, and that there was nothing compromising about it. (See *My Campaign in Ireland*, part i, p. xxxv, 1896.) It was used, of course, by Wilfred Ward in his *Life of Cardinal Newman*, under the name of "Retrospective Notes", and by Father Fergal McGrath, S.J., in his *Newman's University, Idea and Reality*. Father McGrath derived much of his information from Father Henry Tristram, and to this book the reader may be referred for the fullest discussion of the Catholic University.

C. S. D.

Memorandum about my connection with the Catholic University.

Novr 25. 1870.

Section 1.

I first knew Dr. Cullen at Rome in 1847, when he was very civil to me, and took the trouble of being the official theological censor of my four Latin Dissertations then and there published. After he came to Ireland, as Archbishop of Armagh, he showed his recollection of me by asking me to preach in the summer of 1850, at the dedication of a Church in his diocese.

When a University was to be founded for Catholics in Ireland, he wrote to consult me on this subject, being then still Archbishop of Armagh.

Hope, I believe, mention[ed] me to him. On April 15, 1851, he wrote to ask me to advise on the best way of setting about it, and wished me to deliver a set of Lectures in Dublin against Mixed Education.

He called on me in Birmingham on July 6 [8] of that year, and stayed with us till next day. He then went to London, and wrote to me July 13 to ask me to join him there in consultation with Hope, Manning, Monsell, and others. I could not go, as being engaged with my Corn Exchange Lectures. He called on me again on his way back to Ireland, dining with us July 18.

In the conversation he had with me, he proposed to me to be President (Rector) of the proposed University, I replying that, should I be able to serve the undertaking in any way, I should be glad to do so, but I thought that for this end it would be sufficient if I was Prefect of Studies. I believe too, that I felt such an office as the latter would commit me less to an institution which had its seat in another country, and which on that account threatened, if I had the highest post in it, to embarrass my duties to the Birmingham Oratory. A Prefect of Studies might be a temporary office; a Rectorship was almost identified with the University itself, and, while it claimed the whole mind and the continuous presence of its holder, could hardly be resigned without injury to the institution. (Vid. the conclusion of my letter to Dr. Cullen of July 4. 1852.) [?]

On my consulting Hope and F^r. Faber on this point I had the following answers:—

Hope wrote under date of July 24—"I am very clearly of opinion that you should be Rector; not on account of the dignity, though that deserves consideration, but because it is most important in my view that you should be both in name and in fact at the head of the institution. In the discussions which we had with Dr. Cullen, it seemed agreed that the University should be started with[out] statutes, or any formal constitution, and that the Rector and his assistants should govern according to their discretion, until experience had given the data for establishing it in a regular manner. Our whole idea then depends on the *men* who start it, and a great part of it on your being the foremost of them. So do pray be Rector. (sic)."

Father Faber wrote under the same date; "Here we are unanimously in favour of the Rectorship over the Prefecture. 1. because he ought to be the head to do *all* the good he can, and to make the 'necessitas *gravis*' [vid. Reg. Orat. decr. 70] 2. We don't see what he can do as Prefect which he can't do better as Rector: whereas the reverse is not so. 3. His being Prefect won't give that confidence to convert Professors, which his headship would. This seems very important. 4. Would it be well for the Congregation, if the world saw him share his allegiance, short of his being head?—This is what we think, knowing no more than you have told us."

However, I did not at once pledge myself, either to be Rector or Prefect of studies; but became one of a subcommittee of Three, appointed by the Thurles University committee, the other two being Dr. Leahy (afterwards Archbishop of Cashel) and Mr. Myles O'Reilly, with Mr. Allies as Secretary. This Committee was charged with the duty of reporting on the best mode of commencing, on the course of Studies &c. &c.

In consequence of this arrangement Dr. Leahy and Mr. O'Reilly became our guests in the Oratory House in Alcester Street on August 29 [27] of the same year, 1851, bringing with them a list of questions which they had drawn up in Ireland, and intending, after their consultations with me to proceed to our friends in London with the same purpose, and then to return to me for a second conversation; though I don't think this second visit took place. Also, we asked the advice of Mgr de Ram, Dr. Döllinger, Dr. Jerrard of Bristol, and others upon the same list of questions.

I was detained in Birmingham by my Corn Exchange Lectures till the beginning of September; and then by the expedience of waiting till the answers were returned to the questions which we had circulated. However, by the end of the month, September 30, I was able to go over to Ireland, accompanied by Mr. Allies, and directing our course to Thurles, Dr. Leahy's residence, where Mr. O'Reilly met us. Our consultation ended in a Report, which I took to Dr. Cullen at Drogheda, calling on Archbishop Murray, as I passed through Dublin, without seeing him. Then I returned home.

To this Thurles Report Dr. Cullen seems to have given his adhesion, except on a point on which I certainly agreed with him and Hope against Dr. Leahy, viz. that there should be at first no staff of Professors, but that the initial work of the University should be committed to a few, since our start was to be provisional. The Report amended on this point in accordance to the wishes of Dr. Cullen, was brought before the University Committee in Dublin in the course of October, and the decision upon it was deferred till the November meeting.

Another point on which Dr Cullen had expressed an opinion to me in private as early as September 20, was the site of the University. At that date he had written to me as follows:—"There is one point on which I believe the opinion of the people of Ireland is pretty well decided, and it is that the University ought to be at Dublin. I fear no students would go to Thurles; in Dublin on the contrary a great number might be obtained. I was for some time in favour of Thurles, but this consideration is too strong against it." Again, he writes October 28, speaking of the meeting of the University Committee held in that month, "Every one present appeared quite decided that the University should be in Dublin." Of course, there was a prestige on the name of the metropolis; and besides, how could we have had a medical school in a country village, such as Thurles?

On the other hand, Dr. Leahy was for Thurles, where there was a spacious and handsome building ready for our use. So was Mr. Hope, under the notion, I think, that Thurles presented something of a parallel to the situation of Oxford. And there was this difficulty in the way of establishing ourselves at Dublin, that Dr. Murray, the Archbishop, was no friend [of] the undertaking. Moreover, it could not be denied that a metropolis was in itself far from a desirable place for young men. And it was, as feeling this, that some persons, even when Dublin was chosen, advocated our being in the neighbourhood rather than in the city itself. Thus Dr. Cooper thought of

Allhallows; and, after I had left the University (1861), ground was actually bought for the purpose, and a first stone laid there, on the Allhallows side of Dublin.

The University Committee, which had been appointed by the Synod of Thurles, and consisted of certain Bishops and laymen, had deferred, as I have said, their decision upon the Report of the Subcommittee of Three till November; at their meeting in that month, among other things, they passed the following Resolution:—

"November 12. 1851. His Grace the Primate (Dr. Cullen) in the Chair. Resolved that the Very Rev^d. John Henry Newman, D.D. be requested to allow himself to be named the first President of the Catholic University of Ireland, and that his appointment to that office be hereby fixed, subject only to that gentleman's acceptance of the same. (signed) John, Archbp of Tuam."

Dr. Cooper, I suppose as Secretary to the University Committee wrote to me as follows:

"I had the honour to propose you. The Very Rev^d. Dr. O'Brien of Waterford seconded. It was spoken to in terms of warmest approbation by Dr. MacHale amongst others, and passed not only unanimously, but with an acclaim not loud, but most cordial."

Dr. Cullen wrote to me as follows, "I trust you will accept the burden which we are so desirous to place on you. I trust we shall do every thing to conduct matters as you will desire. I will send you tomorrow, or the day after, a copy of the Fundamental Rules which we adopted for the regulation of the University. They are precisely those you agreed to in your Report from Thurles, that the *Summum Imperium* should be in the Bishops, but that the President should have the entire acting discretion. I will write to Dr. Cooper to send you a copy. It was agreed that the President should have a residence &c and £400 per annum. This is not much; but our Funds are as yet not very abundant. No other appointment was made; as the selection of other persons is to be made with the concurrence or on the recommendation of the President."

I accepted the post.

I may remark that I never had a residence found for me; but I suppose it was my own fault. The University House was intended for my residence; but I wished to be independent of it.

Also I observe, that I sent in my resignation on November 12, 1858. Therefore I was Rector for just seven years.

Also, that, though I was appointed Rector in November 1851, I did not commence the University till November 1854.

This loss of three years was a misfortune or a mistake; rather, partly the one, partly the other. Dr. Cullen had made a great effort, and thought it best to wait awhile after making it. He wrote to me, "Mr. Hope is quite for delay, more so even than ourselves; indeed I think a little delay will only do good." It is obvious that the indisposition of Dr. Murray towards the University was a great difficulty. We were holding meetings and coming to practical conclusions in his diocese and episcopal city, he taking no part in them; for myself, I felt I could do nothing, till the Achilli matter was over. Moreover, I had consented to deliver Lectures in Dublin, and on them I was employed during the half year between October 1851, when I returned from Ireland, and May 1852, when I left the Oratory for Ireland Dublin [sic], in order to deliver them.

This accounts for a portion of the time—I will set down all I can recollect about it. At the end of the year 1851, I asked Mr. Manning, then lately received to be my Vice-Rector. This was a post, about which, as I shall presently show, I was specially anxious. He wrote me an affectionate answer, declining my offer on the ground of his unwillingness to take any step which would bias his future, till he had been at Rome, whither he was setting out on November the 3rd.

In February, 1852 there came a letter to Dr. Cullen from Cardinal Fransoni, Prefect of Propaganda, congratulating him on the progress he had made in the establishment of the University. The first topic for satisfaction was the sum of money already collected for it, in consequence of which His Holiness sent indulgences to all who should contribute. The second topic was "Universitatis regimen R.D. Joanni Newman, Superiori Congregationis Oratorii, doctissimo viro et zelantissimo fidei Catholicae administro, fuisse delatum."

Just at this time, February 1852, Dr. Murray, Archbishop of Dublin died. This was an event of great importance, as removing a serious difficulty from our path. In consequence Dr. Cullen was at once translated from Armagh to the metropolitan Archbishoprick. [May 1. 1852].

My lectures commenced on May 10, and ended on June 7. I delivered five on successive Mondays in a room at the Rotunda. Then I stopped. The volume was not finished till the Autumn.

My trial took place June 21-24.

On June 27 I went over again to Ireland with Fr. Ambrose St

John, and was present with him at Dr. Cullen's installation as Archbishop of Dublin on the 29th, and at the great dinner after it. On the
2nd or 3rd of July, we returned to Birmingham, for the opening of
the Synod of Oscott, which took place on the 5th. or 6th. [Wednes-
day July 7.]

I was in Ireland again for a fifth time with Fr Henry Bittleston
from July 30th to about the 13th of August, preaching at Limerick,
and showing myself in various ways; and then, being quite exhausted
and knocked up in mind and body, I went for a week [August 3-
August 10] all by myself to Monsell's empty house at Tervoe. Then
I returned to Birmingham.

After this I made no expedition to Ireland till the beginning of
November 1853, when I went over from Liverpool, where I had
been delivering my Lectures on Turkish history, for two days, in
order to see the house in Stephen's Green, which had lately been
purchased for the purposes of the University, and to give directions
for its adaptation to University and Collegiate purposes.

I should add that Dr. Cullen, in his Pastoral of August 1852, had
introduced me to the Irish world as "one of the most accomplished
scholars and profound divines of the age in which we live, whose
merits are only brought forward more prominently by the persecu-
tions to which he is subjected, and under which he deserves our
sympathy and support." Considering what has happened since,
words like these in the mouth of a person of Dr. Cullen's ecclesiastical connexions sound like irony, or at least provoke on reading
an ironical welcome.

Section 2.

Universities are not brought into existence every day, and the
primary difficulty in originating one, is that commonly they have no
deliberate origination, and, as Oxford, are the slow growth and
random issue of personal and private exertions, or, if erected on set
purpose, they are the work of the State executive. But, in the case of
that to be established in Dublin private men were to dispense with
time and circumstance, and to create it in a day, not only without,
but against the civil Government, and in a population, Catholic
indeed, but indifferent to the undertaking [,] under a Catholic hier-
archy, divided as to its expediency, before a Catholic public viewing
all things in a mere political aspect, and for the sake of a Catholic

gentry both suspicious and hopeless of Episcopal enterprises. And what was an additional difficulty on my own side was my double allegiance. I was bound not to leave England, yet bound to reside in Ireland, and, if my being Rector of the University necessarily involved my presence in Dublin, my absence from my Oratory was the breach of a duty as primary and sacred, as that breach was in the event of evil consequences to our Congregation. The Pope expressed a wish that I should be both in Dublin and Birmingham, but to be in both was to be in neither. There was another obvious difficulty in my case still—I was going to a strange, not to say hostile country—where blunders on my part were not only unavoidable from my ignorance, but of serious consequence, from the existing suspicions and prejudices of those who would be witnesses or the victims of them.

There were two obvious modes of commencing, each with its advantages, and inconveniences, and with its respective advocates. If we followed the course of history and nature, we should commence on a small scale and gradually get into shape and expand; but this was only to sow the seed, whereas we were required to raise a crop, to vaunt it in the faces of the friends of the Queen's Colleges, and to send specimens of our produce to Rome, to be handed round the circle of the Cardinal Prefect of Propaganda. On the other hand, we might begin with a complete staff of officials and a handsome material structure, trusting or hazarding its being filled with students; and then it might turn out in the event that we were in the condition of a carriage, with state coachman and lacquies, but without horses to draw us on. Dr. MacHale was for laying out the £30.000 which had been collected on some one imposing building, which should lodge the whole University, after the model of Trinity College. Most of our friends, I may say, were of this general way of thinking. Dr. Cooper, one of the Secretaries of the University Committee, was for a full staff of Professors; so was, on the whole, Dr. Leahy. Dr. Cullen, on the contrary, feeling the difficulties, agreed with Hope, in the wish of an informal, provisional commencement. Moreover, he was timid, slow as well as gradual in his choice of proceedings; he was for delay, after the Roman fashion, and that from perplexity as well as from principle. I too was for beginning gradually, but any how for beginning, not for dawdling. Dawdling was only losing my time, which was limited, and did not facilitate the work. All that I wanted in the way of show and pretension, was for the Bishops to set me off by some public act, which would be both an advertisement and a sanction of at once my position and of our starting. And, as I have said, feeling how much there was to do, and how little time to do it in, (for I ever limited my Dublin career, in my thoughts and my conversation, to seven years,) I grudged every hour of delay, after that the Achilli matter had ceased to occupy me.

These differences of opinion appear in such letters as the following. After we had drawn up our Report at Thurles and submitted it to Dr. Cullen, Dr. Leahy wrote to me, October 19, 1851,—

"I made a few alterations with Mr. O'Reilly's concurrence, (Having had yours already) to adapt our Report in a few particulars to the Primate's views. One or two little observations (I?) added— that two or more of the subjects to be taught by our Professors and Lecturers might for a time be taught by one person; also, that the *personnel* for the Faculty of Arts needs not to be completed at the outset, because the course of studies being spread over four years, some of the subjects would not come to be treated for some time."

From Dr. Cooper, Febr. 12. 1852. "I don't know if you are aware that the President of Allhallows College, an admirable locality just on the skirts of the city, told me twice in the course of last summer, that he was prepared, at the request of the Bishops, to retire to any other College, such as Thurles, and leave them in possession of Allhallows, say for a period of five years, which would enable our Committee to look for a permanent spot quite at their leisure. ... I would not approve of Stephen's Green, or any site within the city. The distractions of a capital are unfavourable to both the moral and the intellectual training of youth, and the founders of the Middle Age Universities, seem to have thought so too. ... At the same time ours must be as near as possible to the city, to be near the Hospitals."

"No sacrifice," he continued, "or expense should be spared to secure, if at all possible, the services of the first celebrities in Europe, such, for instance, as Döllinger of Munich, if he would come for a few years. We have nothing but character to rest upon."

From Mr. Myles O'Reilly, May 17. 1852: "As a temporary site, there are only two at all eligible, viz. two hotels, Holmes's on the Quays, and Toomey's in Sackville Street. The former the larger, but in bad repair; the latter in good repair, and in a very good situation. It contains one very large coffee room, 8 good sitting rooms, and 37 other good rooms, and a large underground story for kitchen, servants, &c. Other houses could easily be found in the neighbourhood to form temporary mensal Colleges for students and professors.

The best building site is on the Quays opposite the Royal Barracks close to the Park, River, and great southern railway."

From Dr. Cooper, Aug. 1, 1852. "Two things were done at last University meeting; the one to inquire through the Archbishop about the feasibility of getting houses in a desirable position of the city for our first essay,—the second to authorize myself to inquire regarding such men as Döllinger of Munich, who might possibly be induced to come over and take chairs in the University."

Dr. Cooper wrote to me again Octr 10, 1852, thus:—"What is wanted, and what the public looks for, is our list of eminent Professors. Announce such a list of high and well established names, and success is secured. Fall short of this, the University drags on for a few years, a dreary existence, and then expires amid the public contempt. ... It is sovereignly unwise to confine our selection of either officers or professors to priests. The public does not give us priests credit for ability to fit young men for the world, and certain I am that the word and example of a pious layman will always be less suspected and more efficacious with boys than those of an equally pious priest. They have a prejudice that piety is an obliged profession with us,—in fact, our trade."

Again Novr 2 in the same year, he writes: "A word dropped from the Archbishop, which I notice, because it is the third or fourth time I have heard it from him. It is, that it will do to open with four or five Professors, more correctly "three or four." If this be the case the Catholic University would be just a decent boarding school; and the whole thing would be at once crushed beneath the public ridicule ... It is for you to save it from this fate."

I certainly agreed with Dr. Cullen more than with Dr. Cooper, though I knew we must risk something in the way of "supply" to create a "demand". But this difference of views, of which the foregoing letters are but a specimen, did, in my own ignorance of Ireland and the Irish, perplex me: but this I saw clearly, viz. that so marked a difference of views involved a difference of ethical and intellectual character in the holders; and warned me not to commit myself to parties, whom I did not more or less know, as my cooperators and associates; and that the more, when I actually found my correspondents confessing to political views, and to personal feelings against each other. I will illustrate what I mean, by extracts from the letters I received in the course of the same year 1852.

From Dr. Cullen, February 8. "Some ultra-zealous patriots

endeavoured to get up an agitation against every thing English in this country very lately. I was afraid in the beginning that some injury would be done to our University project; but it seems that the good sense of the country was quite opposed to the movement."

From Mr. Ornsby, April 13. "It is perhaps worth while to mention to you, that, happening to say to Mr. Lucas, that you were in doubt whether to stay at H. Wilberforce's, or take a lodging in Dublin, he remarked that he thought the latter would be by far the more prudent course, that he felt quite sure that there was already a strong feeling against the English party, and that any thing which would tend to make it appear a kind of set was being formed, would be liable to be laid hold of, if, as was very likely, an outcry on the subject were raised. Dr. McHale was extremely opposed to Wilberforce's appointment," (to the Secretaryship of the Defence Committee) "and, though you yourself were too remote, as it were, for any jealousy to exist about you, still you would find yourself in a better position in Dublin."

From Mr. H. Wilberforce, April 20th. (James) O'Ferrall thinks that the notion of jealousy against English Catholics is a mere mistake. He said, Pray tell him that no such feeling really exists, as you Englishmen fancy. There are very few really feel it, chiefly Dr. McHale. It is the Dublin Newspapers.

From Dr. A. April 21. "It being my intention to offer myself for such place in the Catholic University as those charged with making its appointments may allot to me, I of course wish to stand well with you, its Head. ... Without violating charity towards others, I intreat you, when you come to consider how far you are likely to receive useful co-operation from this person or that, not to heed, as regards my humble self, the opinion of one particular person in Ireland, with whom you will certainly fall in, who will as certainly tender you advice about all manner of things and persons, and whom I know to be prejudiced against myself. (I think he meant Dr. B.) Having known him in several instances to be not very scrupulous in dealing with others (and that too, when they had no means of setting themselves right with those whose good opinion they valued) I could expect, and do expect, no better treatment at his hands myself."

From Dr. B. April 21. "There is no need of Dr. C's leave for the Lectures, and there is every reason to rejoice that it is so. But, as your intended letter for him is couched in such kind terms, I propose reading it to him, hoping it may exercise a soothing and conciliating effect upon his mind."

From Dr. Cullen, April 25. "I think we shall have no difficulty in getting Mr. Allies appointed Professor; yet I would not counsel him to take any step, as if the matter were finally arranged. We have here a set of Newspaper Editors, and others, who are trying to excite prejudice against every thing English."

Here for the present I make a pause, though I have more letters to quote: illustrative of the fog through which I had to find my way—and illustrative of Dr. B.; illustrative too, I am sorry to say, of the bearing which Dr. Cullen, while really wishing to keep me, had thought most suitable to adopt in his dealings with me. And that is the reason, viz. since we are entering upon a new scene, that I here make a pause.

Section 3.

I was perplexed by my ignorance whom to trust and whom to choose, not only as regards individual Catholics, but as regards the authoritative organ of the Bishops, the University Committee. I had no seat in it, and it was composed of men of whom I knew nothing. I was afraid of important steps being taken by it without me. Advisers of course I needed; but they could not be ready made, they could not be furnished by Bishops unknown to me, as I to them; they must be my own choice, according as I gained experience. I was of no party myself, and did not wish to be advised by party men, nor did I consider ecclesiastics were the best advisers in a great lay undertaking. Also I had a strong apprehension, even as early as the middle of 1852, that I should not be allowed to choose my staff of advisers, for on my parting from Dr. Cullen at Drogheda, I addressed him on July 4th of that year a long and frank letter on the appointment of a Vice-Rector.

Since the need, and the choice of a Vice Rector runs through nearly all my correspondence with Dr. Cullen, and gave a colour and shape to the termination of my Rectorship, it is worth while to note that it was my first as well as my last difficulty.

I said in my above mentioned letter to him, that as to the Professors, "I had no personal interest in their appointment, and did not [care] who they were, so that they were good ones, and creditable to the University, but that it was otherwise" as to those persons who were immediately about me, "who were to help me and to share my responsibilities;—that I must have perfect confidence in them and power over them"—I meant, "the Vice-President, the Deans, the Tutors," answering to Private Tutors at Oxford,—and perhaps the Lecturers; that these were the working body, who would be, at least at first and for a time, the real life of the institution. Then I spoke more distinctly of the Vice President (Vice Rector) as "most intimately near me and involved in my doings and responsibilities." "He takes my place," I said, "when I am absent, and I depend on him simply. It is not enough that I should have full confidence in his zeal, and his desire to act with me; he must see things from the same point of view, as I do. If there is one office, of which I ought to have the absolute appointment, it is this."

At present, however, I said I did not wish to appoint a Vice-Rector, because I knew so little of Ireland; what I wished was, that no appointment should be made, at present. When I knew those out of whom I had to choose, better, then I would appoint. It was not enough to have a man of method, of resource, of business-like habits, of firmness, gentleness and largeness of mind; I wanted "a man who would pull well with me."

I end this letter by insisting on the inexpedience of appointing a Vice-Rector at once. "It might be ruining every thing."

Dr. Cullen never wrote a word to me in answer to this letter. Six weeks passed, and I heard from Dr. Cooper that Dr. Cullen was making inquiries about buildings, and I was anxious lest, as it really did happen in the event, he would fix upon the spot for the University without consulting with me; so on August the 14th. I wrote him a very long statement setting forth my own views on the best mode of starting the University. When I had written it, I had not courage to send it; but instead I wrote him a letter in which I said "I have written you a long letter, so full of details, that I am ashamed to send it. It seems to me, it will only plague your Grace, considering how much your thoughts are employed. And yet I must do so, if any thing is doing in the way of fixing on sites or inquiring about Professors. That is, I fear lest something should be done which *commits* us. When Dr. Cooper spoke to me about it, I thought the difficulty might be got over by my writing to you. Now, when the letter is written, I very much doubt whether you would have time to study it. And therefore I come to the conclusion that it would be well to *do nothing*, till a subcommittee is appointed. It is only the delay of a few weeks."

This projected sub-committee, small—well-chosen, I wished to be the co-operating board with me instead of the "University Committee" of the Synod of Thurles, which had now, as I thought, and as was the recognized fact, all but finished its work and come to a natural end (I think its last act, or almost so was to call me into active service at Dublin at the end of 1853) and the refusal of such a sub-committee steadily to the end by Dr. Cullen was one of the immediate causes of my resignation of the Rectorship. My last difficulties were my first also. There was indeed a sub-committee of Five for financial purposes, appointed by the Committee on Oct 21. 1853 (vid below p. 73)[1] and I have not come to any letter or paper to show that it ever assembled and acted.

My letters then of July 4 and Augst 14 went to the Archbishop at those respective dates—but no answer came from him. A second six weeks passed; and then he simply informed me, as if my letters went for nothing, and with no reference to them, that a helper and associate such as I wanted, in a word a Vice-Rector, had been provided for me in the person of Dr. Taylor, and he intimated a hope that I should consent to the arrangement.

His letter ran as follows:—Oct. 9. "There is a most excellent clergyman here at present, who would, I think, be admirably suited to aid in establishing the University. He was for many years President of (Carlow College?) which he conducted with great success. He is known to almost every one in Ireland, and is beloved by all. He is of most kind and gentlemanlike manners, very humble, and at the same time a most highly instructed ecclesiastic. His name is Dr. Taylor. He would accept the office of Vice-President. No one would co-operate more cheerfully with you. We expect to have a meeting of our Committee before the end of this month, and perhaps this matter may be spoken of there. I would like to have your opinion on it previously."

I have [had] already given my opinion on this subject to Dr Cullen pretty plainly, viz. that I wished to choose the Vice-Rector myself, but not at once, that I might have time to look about me. I felt this of course, yet it was a very invidious thing to reject an amiable and unoffending man. It was just what was done to me in October 1858, shortly before I resigned; the statutes, ratified by the Holy See, gave me the appointment of the Deans, and at that time the Archbishops, Dr. Cullen as much as Dr. Leahy, appointed a new Dean of

[1] p. 302. C.S.D.

St. Patrick's without even consulting me, as he had originally appointed Mr. Flannery himself. The truth is that these Bishops are so accustomed to be absolute that they usurp the rights of others, and rough ride over their wishes & their plans quite innocently, without meaning it, and astonished, not at finding out the fact, but at its being impossible to them. In the difficulty I have described, the priest, I have called Dr. B, came to my relief. The very next day he wrote to me as follows, being an intimate friend of Dr. Cullen's.

From Dr. B. October 10. 1852

"With respect to the gentleman suggested by his Grace for Vice-President, I am sorry to be obliged to gather from His Grace's letter, that his mind is nearly made up on the matter. Mr. Taylor is a very worthy priest, but in my humble judgement not qualified for the high position of first Vice-President of the Catholic University. He was for some time President (of Carlow?) but about 18 months ago he teazed Dr. D. to take him to his Society. Now he is tired of (it) and seeks to quarter himself on the poor Catholic University. Were Mr. Taylor a young man, this unsteadiness of his might not wear so unfavourable an appearance; but at his time of life and on such an important occasion to betray rashness and precipitancy does, to my apprehension, impeach his judgement, though it may be allowed to bear evidence to his piety. Besides, for the years that he has been connected with (the College) I never heard, amid all my opportunities, one word of his talents, either natural or acquired. ... I think it quite premature to name anyone at present to the office. ... His Grace's mention of his amiable manners shows that he is not remarkable for the other equally essential qualities of an educator of our aspiring youth. ... Our amiable good Archbishop is too much influenced by Mr. E. and Dr. D, who desires, I suspect, to effect a comfortable retreat for his late novice."

It is remarkable that the writer of this letter, Dr. B must actually have read the Archbishop's letter which came to me the preceding day to his, for he quotes words of it. I heard from him again on Nov. 2. He said:—"We had a University Meeting the other day. ... The Archbishop introduced the name of Dr. Taylor, as of a fit person for the office of *Secretary* to correspond with you, or (I report truly) perhaps as a *general manager* to look about site, building, furniture &c. &c. Thus it is manifest, that it is not exactly the place that wants Dr. Taylor, but Dr. Taylor and his friends that want the place. ... These friends are Dr. D. and Mr. E. They may be, and doubtless are very amiable, but, if they be equally wise in thus, and from these promptings, filling up University places, I must be the quintessence of a fool."

There is truth in these last remarks, but Dr. Cullen's changing the office and destination of Dr. Taylor might have arisen from some remonstrance of mine in consequence of Dr. B's remarks; and that I did remonstrate, would seem clear from the following letter of Dr. Cullen to me, dated Novr 29.

"I forgot to answer the note, in which you mentioned Dr. Taylor. Your correspondent must have never seen or known him. He is a most kind and amiable gentleman, connected with the most respectable families in Ireland. He is a good man of business, what we want very much in the beginning; and besides, he is a scholar of very respectable acquirements, well versed in Latin, Greek, and the principal modern languages. Moreover, he is well acquainted with all the clergy of Ireland."

In the beginning of 1853, a friend wrote to me, to confirm Dr. Cullen's view of Dr. Taylor, which I am far from denying was the right one. He says "Dr. D. is a wise, well-judging man, discreet man, and will advise you better than any one else. Dr. Taylor is a sensible man. Mr. F. fancied you would not be comfortable with Dr. C. a narrow minded, obstinate man, quite opposed to your views of education, whom nothing but a miracle would convert. Dr. B. is looked upon as so violent a man that he thought your going to him would do harm."

However, whoever was right and whoever was wrong, this great divergence of opinion as to the merits of the Archbishop's surroundings generally and of Dr. Taylor in particular, justified my wish to postpone the appointment of the Vice-Rector. That wish, however, was not to be granted. First Dr. Taylor, then Dr. Leahy were appointed, and both of them, in the intention of the appointment, rather as the Archbishops' representative and as their security and safeguard against me, than as my own helper and backer up.

I am not speaking against Dr. Taylor; I got on well with him, as with Dr. Leahy after him. I will quote a portion of his first letter to me, which is pleasing in the spirit it evidences, and is noticeable as showing that Dr. Cullen quite understood he was going against my wishes in appointing Dr. Taylor to be about me, and yet deliberately appointed him. Dr. Cooper, one of the Secretaries of the University Committee had suddenly died: Dr. Taylor was put into his place, and because Dr. Cooper had been Secretary of the University Committee, it seemed to be desirable to consider Dr. Taylor as Secretary to the University. Nothing can be better than the tone of Dr. Taylor's letter to me, under the circumstances in which he found himself. He says: February 8. 1853,

"Will you allow me to introduce myself to you as one of the Secretaries of the Catholic University, at least *pro tempore*? Though I had once the honour of conversing with you. ... it is not likely that you recollect me; so that I may say I have still to make your acquaintance. ... It cannot be very pleasant for you to receive as an official, immediately under yourself, one who is all but an utter stranger to you. In your new position ... it is, I should think, of the utmost consequence that you have always at hand some one well acquainted with the people and the ways of this country, some Irishman at your side to inform you upon local matters, and to carry out your views as smoothly and effectually as he can. Probably this is your own opinion too. Taking it for granted that you will have some Celt or other to act as your Vice, I shall be happy, if you find yourself able to put up with me. It has been intimated to me that I am intended for that office, but that for the present I am to act as Secretary. ... Yet, much as I relish the idea of being your assistant, I can assure you, dear Dr. Newman, with perfect sincerity, that, if you do not wish to make use of my assistance, I will retire even with alacrity." He ended by saying "Excuse this long tiresome note; one would imagine that I was wanting to show, how *your Secretary* could scribble." "My secretary!" who ever heard of a private Secretary not chosen by his principal?

What he principally did, I think was to act as the Archbishop's secretary, no one's else, and to save the trouble of writing to me. I have no fault to find with him; he was an amiable and modest man, as the Archbishop had said. He remained in his position about a year and a half: Dr. Leahy being placed instead of him in the office of (Vice) Rector by the Synodal meeting of May 1854—or sooner after —I being as before disregarded. Dr. Leahy in a letter dated July 8, 1854, spoke of himself as a sub-rector; and Dr. Taylor in a letter of July 13, in the same year told me his own Bishop had recalled him to undertake parochial duty to his diocese. In a letter to me he wrote a few days after (July 18) he spoke, I think as if I were the cause directly or indirectly of his leaving the University, but I have no reason to suppose he was right in this notion.

Section 4.

There were two things which I had asked of Dr. Cullen, to choose myself the persons with whom I should begin my work, and notably the Vice Rector, and next to be set off on that work at once by some public recognition on the part of the Irish Episcopate. I have shown how he treated my first request; now let us see how he treated my second.

I could not begin without being formally installed in my office, whatever was the way of installation, literal or moral; and I wished to begin at once for various reasons. One was that I was idling my time, being unable to set myself to any other work from the expectation that I might be called off from it at any moment by an order sent to me to proceed at once to Dublin. Again, I intend[ed] to give no more than a limited term of years to the University, and therefore every year was precious. And again, I had a reason of a different kind. Unless I was myself at work, others would do things instead of me. Thus Mr. Bianconi bought the University House without my knowing any thing about it; and officials were appointed without my knowledge; not only Dr. Taylor, but Mr. Flannery, whom Dr. Cullen made "the Dean" of the University, an office which did not come into my list of places, and whom when I found I could not dispense with him, I contrived to accommodate to my own plan of offices, by giving the word "Dean" a different meaning. Dr. Cullen meant these men to advise and to control me, and to be at once his own informants what was doing, and his own secretaries to correspond with me. As Dr. Taylor was intended to give me counsel, so afterwards he was accustomed to say "Ask Mr. Flannery: have a meeting with Mr. Flannery and Dr. Leahy two or three times a week"; and I found Mr. Flannery and Dr. Ford knew of the appointments which were in contemplation by Dr. Cullen, as the appointment of a new Vice Rector in 1857-8, and were able to communicate the tidings, to others, before I had had from Archbishop or any one else any hint or warning on the subject.

It was plain then that, the longer I was kept from Ireland, the more I should find my action anticipated and my work obstruct[ed] by the proceedings of others; and this was in itself a strong reason for my wishing to be set off on my course by the Archbishops.

In my letter to Dr. Cullen of August 14, 1852 I said, as I have already quoted the words, that I could not help intruding upon him, when I was in apprehension that "something might be done to commit us"; "in the way of fixing on sites or inquiring about Professors". All I got in return was the appointment of Dr. Taylor. Accordingly I felt myself at sea; what powers were to be given to me, and what prospects were before me. So, in spite of my having got no answers to my letters of July and August in the foregoing year, I wrote to the Archbishop from Abbotsford, Jan.ʸ 15, 1853, as follows:—

"As the monthly meeting of the University Committee is now approaching, I am led to ask your Grace to consider whether there are not certain points which should be settled by it previously by [to] my coming to Dublin.

"If I am to come after Easter to any purpose, (I do not recollect whether this prospect had been held out to me, or whether I had already proposed it to Dr. Cullen. ... I suspect the latter.) I must be distinctly instructed first what I am to do, and understand the powers I am given for doing it. At present I could do nothing at all, though I were ever so much on the spot, and ever so anxious to make progress, for I have no work committed to me.

"Moreover, I think your Grace will say that there is a reason for deciding *at once*, for I ought to have time to think over my instructions before I come.

"May I then venture on your kindness to represent all this to the Committee, and to beg of them to settle for me such questions as these:—1, whether I am to act with certain others or by myself. 2, if with others, with whom. 3, what objects I am to keep in view and what points to settle. 4, and what degree of weight will attach to the conclusions, to which, whether by myself or with others, I may come;—whether those conclusions are to be final, or whether matter for public deliberation on the part of the Committee."

The time of the meeting came and went, and no answer from Dr. Cullen. So I wrote again on February 3, that is, after an interval of nearly three weeks. I said that "I must urge the Committee of the University to do *something* for me. Had they made a step at the late meeting? I must know *at once* what I had to do, in order to think over it between this and Easter. Again, I must have full powers. I could not act at all, if I were crippled."

I was now in the 16th month of my appointment and nothing was told me when I was to begin or what I was to do. I had written two letters to Dr. Cullen six months before, and two letters now—and could not get, I will not say information, but a reply from him. I can understand he had great difficulties in moving: but I cannot understand his not plainly telling me so. He might have written frankly to me: ["]you won't be wanted for a year to come at least, for we must have a synodal meeting of the Bishops: I really don't know when you will be wanted, and I cannot tell quite what your powers will be. I don't think you should have the appointment of the Vice Rector" &c. &c. But I suppose it is what he had learned at Rome [,—] to act, not to speak—to be peremptory in act, but to keep his counsel; not to commit himself on paper; to treat me, not as an equal, but as one of his subjects.

Certainly he had great difficulties: I should have sympathized with them, if he had told me of them, but even now, I can only conjecture them. As time went on, he seemed hurt that I was not of his party as against Dr. McHale. I wished to be of no party; but I should with the utmost difficulty have kept myself from throwing myself into his more than my sense of propriety and my judgment dictated, if he had opened himself to me. Dr. McHale was really a great trouble to him. He himself was a stranger to Ireland, and the Bishops looked at him on his coming from Rome with the same jealousy and apprehension as the English Bishops had looked on Dr. Wiseman. My personal friends wanted me, because they thought I must sooner or later, to come into collision with "the great Archbishop of the West", as a necessary step to a certain success; and, had Dr. Cullen made himself kind and dear to me, I suppose I should have taken this task off his shoulders. Lucas was the only friend of the Archbishop whom I knew. He it was, I suppose, who had persuaded Dr. MacHale to take part in my nomination, and, had I put myself forward, instead of Dr. Cullen's being in the front (whom Lucas could not stomach) I think Lucas would have mediated between Dr. McHale and me, and would have overcome for me many difficulties—but this is speculation.

At length I heard from Dr. Cullen; not directly, but from Dr. Taylor, in the letter I have already quoted, in which he introduced himself to me. This was on February 8. His letter told me nothing in answer to the questions which I had asked the Archbishop; but he wrote to me again on the 22nd, and then he did communicate something that was to the purpose, and looked towards my being set off on my course, though it would have been more agreeable, if it had come from the Archbishop himself, instead of being communicated for my benefit through "my secretary", and if I had been asked my opinion on the point before he formed his intention. It was this, that the Archbishop proposed that each Bishop should make me his Vicar-General (as had been done in Belgium in the case of the University of Louvain) "for the whole work of organizing the University." Dr. Taylor said that so great an object was worth waiting for; and he added would come over to me at Birmingham to have a conversation with me, if I would let him. He came accordingly.

I have mentioned some reasons why I was desirous there should be no delay in my commencing my operations, and just at this time another matter influenced me, though not so urgent as those which I have mentioned. There was a rumour afloat that Cardinal Wiseman was contemplating my elevation to the Episcopate. This idea I believe he cherished till within a few years of his death, being in those latter years stimulated in that purpose by Dr. Manning. But this time he was under some annoyance at my legal condemnation in the Achilli matter, and wished to make up to me what perhaps he was conscious had come by his own slovenly ways of going on. I had no wish to be a Bishop, and I saw that it would take me from a work for which I considered myself more fitted; so I brought my apprehensions before Dr. Cullen, as an additional argument for despatch in commencing the University. I have not a copy of my letter which I suppose was a short one, but I have a copy of one which I plucked after writing it, perhaps because it was too formal and pretentious on a personal matter, and was a gratuitous display on a matter still hypothetical. It ran as follows:—

"March 2. 1853. Though we are expecting the pleasure of Dr. Taylor's visit so soon, I cannot refrain from writing you a letter on a subject which has been troubling me for the last week.

"I am told on the best authority that the English Bishops are sending in my name to Rome for the see of Nottingham, or the coadjutorship of Liverpool. ... I should have thought it impossible, unless I had heard it on such excellent authority. My friends have protested on the ground of my health, and very likely that protest has been successful."

Then I go on to say, that "to place me in an English see is simply to take me from Ireland". And I continue:—"I feel most deeply and habitually that the office of a Bishop is not suited for me. Some things one is fit for, others one is not fit for. To say I am not a thorough theologian and that I know nothing of Canon law, is obvious; I do not urge what is plain to any one; but more than this, I have not the talent, the energy, the resource, the spirit, the *power* of *ruling* necessary for the high office of a Bishop. This is neither humility nor modesty, but plain commonsense. If I am taken from the University, I am taken from a position where I can do something to an office where I can do little or nothing. I am in a new element. I have never been in power in my life. My mode of influence is quite in another line. And I am sure I should get so oppressed with a sense of my responsibilities and my shortcomings, that I should have my spirit broken. Every instrument is fitted for its own work; a spade, a trowel, a sword, a razor, each has its own use. I trust it will not please them at Rome to throw me away, when they might turn me to account."

It is not wonderful that, on reading it over, I did not send to Dr. Cullen so discursively egotistical, and therefore so impertinent a letter. I quote it here, because it expresses my real sentiments about myself. I suppose in the letter I did send, I merely stated the fact of the intention of Dr. Wiseman.

This letter was written March 2. Dr. Taylor came to the Oratory March 4 and remained till the 7th. I urged him to hasten the movements of the University Committee; and he advised me to write a letter which might be read to the members at their next meeting. Accordingly I wrote on March 7 to the Archbishop to the following effect, though *not* verbatim, as follows:—

"Now that Easter approaches, your Grace may expect to be hearing how I am, and whether I am equal to the great work which lies before me. I am grateful for the rest you have given me, and now I shall be grateful, if you put an end to it, as soon as possible. I am not well, but I do not think I shall be better. I am well enough to begin; and, this being the case, I am of course impatient to do so. Six months at any time of life is a period; therefore the Committee had better make use of me at once, if they wish to do so at all.

"I beg you to consider how absolute and unlimited are the powers you are going to commit to me; and how great the responsibilities they involve. I do not wish to shrink from them, but let me have them while I can bear them.

"While I write, I grieve to hear of Dr. Jerrard's death, whom the Committee has already consulted, and of whose great experience in Academical education I had hoped to avail myself. He was younger than I am.

"Something has lately occurred to suggest an apprehension of a different kind. If I am not soon set to work in Ireland, I may be set to work elsewhere instead.

"You will say I doubt the activity of the Committee. Well, I confess, grateful as I have been for this delay, I think a Committee of whatever kind always finds it easier to do nothing than to put itself in motion. Your Grace will represent all this to the Committee better than I can write it; so I commit the matter to your Grace.

"If we are to commence in the Autumn, every month, every week, is valuable to us. I do not know whether it lies with your Grace to call the Committee together; but I certainly do now wish they would, without any delay, put the undertaking into my hands and let me set to work."

There is something in the tone of this letter I do not understand, and cannot explain. It seems suitable rather to be addressed to Dr. Cullen and [not?] to the Committee. It seems as if I wished to alarm or rouse him.

On March 28, Dr. Taylor wrote to me—"I did think that I would have to tell you, we were in possession of the house, and perhaps in treaty about the land; but all has been at a standstill since my return. ... Until we have the key in the door, I won't believe the opening out at an end.

"The Archbishop wrote to Rome representing that it would be a great blow to the University to make you a Bishop. However, he has no confidence that his letter will be successful, at least very little."

From these last words it appears that my mention of the prospect of my being a Bishop was a mistake, as leading Dr. Cullen to delay till the prospect was removed.

The Committee still did not move. On June 10. Dr. Taylor wrote to me to say, "I hope you are not desponding [of?] the University. ... The Bishops of this Province are after holding a Provincial Synod; and in it the Suffragan Bishops deputed the Archbishop to act for them with you in all that concerns the University. If the other Bishops of Ireland would thus simplify things, we should soon move on briskly. ... We cannot convene a meeting of the Committee until we have the house to assemble in. That will be in about another month."

What a strange excuse! they could not meet except in the new house. Where have they been assembling for the last two years?

The Pastoral of the Synod above mentioned announced that, since "the obstacles which for a time obstructed the agency of the venerable and accomplished scholar who fills the Presidential Chair (of the Cath. Univ^y) have been happily removed, we hope that its doors shall be shortly thrown open."

I suppose the "obstacles" must mean the Achilli trial; I had not been told of any in Ireland.

On June 23, Mr. O'Reilly had a letter from the Committee Room in Dublin to inform him that "the Archbishop did not wish a meeting to be held just now, nor until such time as the deeds transferring 86 Stephen's Green to the Four Archbishops shall have been received from Mr. Bianconi; the most likely time will be from the 15th to the 20th of July."

Mr. O'Reilly, in sending me this announcement on the 24th, observed:—"The great distinctive of our Archbishop is procrastination; and, I need hardly say, we depend on him; as, if he moves slowly, when he does move, he goes right, and others would be pretty certain to go wrong."

On the 18th of August Dr. Taylor wrote me word, that there had been a meeting of the Committee the day before, when it was found that the house was not yet the property of the Archbishops, and it was resolved, since the meeting was small, to secure a full meeting soon, in order to invest me with full powers, and to call me over.

On my asking Dr. Taylor some questions in consequence of this intelligence, he was led to give me on Aug. 23rd a more complete account of what was done at the meeting, that is, of Mr. O'Reilly's notice of a motion, which was to the effect that I should be called over at once, that a subcommittee should be appointed of five persons to assist me in managing the finances, the subcommittee consisting of the Archbishop, Mr. Errington, Mr. O'Ferrall, Mr. O'Reilly, and Dr. Taylor.

Dr. Taylor also told me that he supposed £5000 would be put into my hands for the year's expenses. Moreover, he held out to me the prospect of a seat in the University Committee.

In answering him on August 25, I said that his account of the Sub-committee of Five for financial purposes, quite hits my wishes. I only feared that the power might be left in the hands of the existing (University) committee, whose members were scattered about the country and whose meetings were irregular. I added that I was very averse to being put upon the Committee; I thought it would hamper me, and again that the (University) Committee was too large to be an executive.

At length in October the long contemplated meeting of the Committee took place, the Primate (Dr. Dixon) in the chair, and one other Bishop present. I was called to Ireland "at my earliest convenience"; £2000 was placed in my hands at once, and further sums promised. Also the sub-committee of Finance was appointed; the members being those whom I have mentioned at p. 73.[1] However, I am not aware that that sub-committee ever met. Dr. Taylor in the course of half a year vanished from the scene, and to make Dr. Cullen a member of it, was to guarantee its inaction and inanity.

After this meeting of the University Committee, in which I was called to Ireland, Dr. Taylor and Mr. O'Reilly were very desirous I should go over to Dublin to see the newly purchased University House, before the concluding legal act was taken ratifying the transaction. Accordingly I went over on November 4 from Liverpool, where I was giving Lectures, for twenty hours. Mr. O'Reilly had written on October 25, before I went over, in great spirits at what he had succeeded in doing. "I am more pleased," he said, "than I can express, and look forward with eager anticipation to seeing you in Ireland. The Archbishop will be on his return from France, and you may join him on the road.["]

Section 5.

However, I was not myself so well satisfied as was Mr. O'Reilly. Rather I was disappointed, desponding and sore. The Committee, *magno hiatu*, had done very little. They had called me over to Ireland, but they had done nothing to set me off. What would the public know about a Resolution passed in a private room in Ormond Quay? a Resolution, which was really the act of two men, Mr. O'Reilly and Dr. Taylor. It gave me an excuse for coming, if I wished to come, but I did not wish to come, if the direct act of coming was to proceed from me. I did not wish to obtrude myself on Dublin. I expected to do a favour to others by coming, not to benefit myself. I had written in the following terms to Dr. Taylor, October 23:—

"I thank you very much for your prompt and welcome news &c. &c. ... You do not say, when the Committee expects me; but it will not, I think, be surprised at hearing that I shall not be able to go over till the beginning of January. To tell the truth, I had at length given

[1] p. 302 above. C.S.D.

up the idea of its doing any thing this year, and am giving a course of Lectures at Liverpool &c. &c. ... I have no scruple in this delay, since for so many months I sacrificed all engagements to the prospect of being called over, and did not even allow myself for many weeks even to leave home for a night, thinking I might be summoned.

"This delay (i.e. of going till Jan^y) will have one advantage; I am much disappointed to hear from you that the Provincial Synod of Thurles does *not* allude to the University. A letter of yours in the early part of the year led me to expect it. And the very fact that the Synod of Dublin has mentioned it, makes the omission significant, and moreover suggests the dangerous idea that the University is only to be a *Dublin College*.

"Will you allow me to ask for the text of Friday's Resolution? and for the names of the Bishops who were present at the meeting, as well as of those of the subcommittee?"

It has been seen above that *only one* Bishop was present besides the Primate, Dr. Dixon, who was in fact in this matter nothing more than the proxy of Dr. Cullen.

My feeling was this,—I had now been appointed Rector for two years, and nothing had been done. If for the first of the two, the Achilli trial kept me from Ireland, yet many things might have been done in Ireland, to smooth such difficulties, as were sure to beset me when I did come. For two years, Dr. Cullen had met my earnest applications for information or a settlement of particular points, or the expression of my views and wishes by silence or abrupt acts. He had written to me, I think, once. He did not even correspond with me through a Secretary. He made a stranger to me my Secretary, and obliged me to pick up the crumbs of his words or doings by means of him. The éclat of the (National) Synod of Thurles in 1850 and of the Pope's Brief had passed away. My Lectures in Dublin in May 1852, which Dr. Cullen had sanctioned by his presence, were a flash in the pan. His presence at them had been, I think, the only public recognition of me, since I had been appointed Rector.

If in the coming January I went over to Ireland, as I proposed, I should seem to be acting on my own hook. I should be an Englishman, taking upon himself to teach the Paddies what education was, what a University, and how it was their duty to have one with me for a Rector. I should seem to be carrying, not a great Council's resolve, but a hobby of my own, a propagandist, not an authoritative superior, a convert, without means, looking out for a situation, and finding and feathering a nest from the pockets of the Irish, with an outlay for me and my surroundings to the tune of £5000 *per annum*. That I intended to make a good thing of it, was actually said; and Dr. Cullen himself in the Autumn of 1854, when so many of the Birmingham Fathers were at Dalkey, remarked to me that such a place was a more desirable home than a back street in Birmingham

I felt then that I could not go over to Dublin at all, unless I was distinctly called there by the Irish Episcopate, or in some other formal and public way. I despaired of this being done, and contemplated resignation. I wrote to the Archbishop of Dublin, on Decr 24, begging him, as a preliminary to beginning my operations in Dublin for the opening of the University, publicly to admit me to my duties, suggesting, 1, my taking certain oaths after High Mass and Sermon, or 2, taking them in the University House, with an Inaugural Speech from me, or 3, in any other way.

He did not think fit to answer me, but communicated to Dr. Taylor for my information Decr 28 that nothing public could be done at present; that the Bishops were to be gained over first—besides the University House was not fully ours.

On the receipt of this answer, I drew up a Memorandum for my own guidance, and proceeded to consult some friends what I ought to do.

Memorandum. "Decr 29. 1853. I wish to consider my present position. 1, If I am intrusted with the commencement of the University, *I* am to be the judge what is necessary or not for that object. Now, whether or not it is to be commenced in September, is a further question; but so far I can say distinctly, that, if I am not recognized, and recognized *now*, it will not be commenced *then*, [and further, if it is not commenced *then*,][1] I think it must be postponed till that time year, for there is a serious disadvantage in commencing it except in the Autumn.

"2, I have said, I am not the judge whether it should be commenced next Autumn or next Autumn year; but still I am entirely the judge whether *I* am the person to commence it at the latter date. Now I distinctly say that I cannot undertake it at the latter date, and that, if I am to undertake it at all, then it must commence next Autumn. I have already waited nearly two years and a half, and cannot promise to wait nearly two years more.

---

[1] Newman omitted the words in brackets from the document he was copying. C.S.D.

"3, Now we have brought the matter to a very simple issue:—viz. Unless I am recognized as Rector of the University in the month of January now coming, I resign the office.

"Observe (1) that I must be *recognized*.

"a. that I ought *in some way* to receive a *direct warrant* for commencing is plain from the very circumstance that the Archbishop of Dublin has been so desirous to get me appointed Vicar General of each of the Bishops.

"b. it is necessary from the nature of the case. E.g. supposing I wrote round to the Bishops &c., their simple answer would be, as things stand, "Who in the world are you?" for my name had not yet come before them officially.

"c. Fancy my skulking about Ireland, and acting upon its class[es] in various districts, I being a foreigner, unrecognized by the Bishops, with nothing to say for myself. It would be like an Anglican parson of Oxford going about taking confessions in the Dioceses of Canterbury or Worcester.

"(2) that I must *insist* on being recognized.

"a. I conceive that the reluctance felt to a public recognition is not an accident, but an indication of a misconception of what a University is altogether.

"b. It is a reluctance, not to some particular public act, in my favour, but to my having the power of doing public acts bearing on the University.

"c. A University is a public body, and to set it up is a public act.

"d. Its students, professors, coming from different and often distant parts, & &c. it cannot be set up in a corner.

"e. To consider it not a public institution, is to contemplate a College, not a University.

"f. There are existing reasons for thinking that nothing more is contemplated in some quarters *than* a College.

"g. I have no call to leave England to be the head of a local College.

"h. Thus, accidentally, a public recognition means more than itself: it is the token and instance of a principle, and to insist on it is the way to rid ourselves of a great misconception, to break the ice of a necessary work, and to obviate the chance of a permanent false position.

"(3) that I must insist of [on] being recognized *now*.

"a. For if not now, the time must come for insisting. The sooner the better; else, it is a *clear* lost time. We shall find ourselves where we are, a year hence.

"b. The sooner the better, for the longer the misconception lasts, the more harm it will do.

"c. If we do not insist now, we cannot commence the University next autumn; which throws back the projected commencement, perhaps till next autumn year, that is, ad Graecas Calendas.

"d. I cannot promise for health and strength to do any thing at all, if it is put off.

"e. I have entered on my salary; am I to do nothing for it?

"f. I have engaged Tutors up to £1000 a year, to begin next Autumn; and I am writing abroad for professorial help for the same date. If I am to disappoint these all, I ought to do so at once, & not when they have given up houses & pupils, removed to Dublin &c. &c."

These were my reasons for making at this time a great effort to move the Archbishop of Dublin to take up the execution of the work at once. And accordingly on the day before I had proceeded to appeal in justification or for help & advice to Hope Scott. What I said to him is noted in my University journal thus:—"Decr 28th. "Wrote to Hope, inclosing Dr. Taylor's letter, saying I thought either of carrying my point of being at once recognized or of resigning; that, unless I was recognized *now*, I could not begin next Autumn. On the other hand, I said I felt that if I *did* insist and succeed, I should have all the onus and anxiety of commencing with many of the Bishops dead against me."

Two days after, the 30th, I wrote to Lucas on the same subject; in the beginning of January I wrote to Cardinal Wiseman at Rome. Also on the 30th, keeping apparently my letter back a post or two, I wrote again to Dr. Cullen, pleading for a recognition. I said in my letter that he himself had felt the need of it for me; also, why had he wished me to be Vicar-General of each of the Bishops? "May I not fairly ask leave," I continued, "at the end of two years and a half from the time you first spoke to me on the subject, to do as much as prepare for opening the University Schools? And, when I say I cannot do this without some public sanction on my proceedings, will not you, my dear Lord, who have been so generous and faithful to me all along, will not you be the first (I am sure you will) to say that I must be the judge of this necessity, and no one else, and must do my work in my own way, if I am to do it at all? I do thereby most urgently entreat your Grace to devise some mode of setting me off at once, and to believe that, if I do not prefer my petition in a stronger form, it is because I do not wish to seem to use expressions stronger than the occasion requires."

Hope Scott answered me as follows:—"Bishop Grant and Badeley being with me, I have discussed with them your letter. It is not an easy one to answer, for what we might desire for your own comfort, we cannot wish for Ireland. Indeed, if you were to sever your connexion with the University *now*, the whole scheme would, I suspect, either come to an end, or be so jobbed and bungled as to be worse than useless. You must therefore, if possible, maintain your position, and the only question is, how you can better it.

"Now, an offer to resign (which must mean a threat) might with the apathetic, reluctant majority, appear a favorable opportunity for disposing at once of you and of the University; and the manner of receiving it might be so managed as to make you appear to be in the wrong. Indeed, I think an actual resignation without previous negociation would be the more politic step, *if* the time were come for any decided measure; but this I do not think is yet the case."

He then goes on to say that Bishop Grant tells him I have a plan for founding a Dublin Oratory, & that the Bishop suggests, as he thinks well, that I may, independently of the University project, set about that, of course with Dr. Cullen's leave, give Oratorian lectures, bearing on the University &c. &c.

I did not concur in this suggestion. It is true that I had hoped to found an Oratory in Dublin; it is true also that Dr. Cullen and his friends were so little opposed to it, or rather so favoured it, that they wished and expected the whole Birmingham Oratory to pass over to Dublin and to take possession of the new University house. Of course that never entered into my thoughts, though I think it was one of the supposed baits with which Dr. Cullen thought he was tempting me to undertake the Rectorship. Still I did hope to set up an Oratory in Dublin, and hoped too to find subjects for it there. I was told there were young laymen, lawyers and the like, who were taking or might take a religious turn, and would, from their education and social position, be unfit for Bishops's subjects and suitable for the Oratory. This, however, would have been a work of time, and would rather have been facilitated by my University proceedings than a preparation and introduction to a University. When a University was actually set up, then an Oratory would be its natural attendant, as being what may be called the School of Devotion for its members, supplying confessors & preachers, and forming confraternities and the like among them. Moreover, to have commenced proceedings at Dublin with an Oratory, would have been to impress upon the Dublin public that I had a private and personal end in coming there, not the good of Ireland, a suspicion of which I have already intimated as existing among at least the priests. Nor do I think that Dr. Cullen would have borne an Oratory, when it began to work. Religious orders are understood in Ireland; but not secular priests, living on their patrimonies and in communities independent of the Bishops. Once more, there was an incongruity in Hope Scott's and Bishop Grant's idea of the Fathers of an Oratory being literary and scientific, or in any shape academical Lecturers.

Lucas answered me thus:—"Your letter gave me real pain; and the more so, because I don't know how to answer it. Of course I see only the outside of ecclesiastical affairs, and even less of that than you, I fancy. But, from what I see and hear, it seems to me that, between political and ecclesiastical business, things here are in a strange confusion, which cannot be without its effect on the foundation of the University. It is impossible to guess even at the grounds Dr. Cullen has for the course he takes; but what is clear is that, in almost every thing that is in any way open to dispute, he has broken with those bishops with whom he was supposed originally to act, and has approximated to the other side. Every thing is touched by this, and unsettled. In politics he has abandoned (apparently) the policy which he himself inaugurated at the Aggregate Meeting; joins M. and, whatever his real opinion is, his influence on men's minds is decidedly against us. In the appointment of new Bishops he is *supposed* to exercise an influence, which (not merely in some exceptional cases) is supposed to override the choice of the clergy and the advice of the other bishops completely. And in the University there are jealousies of the same sort, which I am sure impede your work.

"If this were the result exclusively of a struggle against abuses or irregularities, and thus were forced upon him, it would be the more intelligible; but the little experience I have leads me rather to an opposite conclusion. One of the greatest scandals of our times, in reference to public morality, has been the unfortunate connexion of Dr. Browne of Elphin with Sadlier at Sligo and Keogh at Athlone. Dr. McHale has laboured to prevent and correct that scandal, and Dr. Cullen is *understood* to uphold Dr. Brown against the western

Archbishop. Now I believe there is no diocese in Ireland in which there is such frightful pecuniary corruption and immorality among the clergy in connexion with elections as in Elphin. I was thinking of laying before you this whole case with documentary evidence in my possession for your advice, but I thought on further consideration even to lay the case before you might give you embarrassment. It has been remarked, that, since he fell out with Dr. MacHale, on account of these things, Dr. Browne has attended the University Committee, and shown a particular leaning towards Dr. Cullen. Yet Dr. Browne is personally mixed up with the corruption of his diocese, and is indeed on record as a guilty party to the act of bribery which unseated Mr. T. last session. So that, if it be true, as people think, that Dr. Cullen lends any support to Dr. Browne against Dr. McHale, all that is support given to very flagrant immorality and scandal, and— I am sorry to say—even to connexion of the clergy with Ribbon men or Steal-boys. I believe Dr. Cullen has not known a great part of the case, but he has known quite enough &c. ... Fr. James Maher (his uncle) is supposed to have great influence over him; but, while this is *believed*, it is also *known* that Fr. J. Maher was deep in the Carlow election, in support of Sadlier after his abandonment of principle; and I believe that in the late trial he might have been put upon the table by the side of Dempsey with damaging effect. ...

"I do not understand from your letter, exactly from what quarter the difficulty proceeds. The only friendly, i.e. cordial relations I have with Bishops are with Dr. MacHale and Dr. Cantwell, and those who think with them. Does your obstruction proceed from them? If it does, I shall have an opportunity of speaking with them very fully in about a fortnight or three weeks; and if you thought I could do any thing or be of any service, of course it would be to me the greatest honour and the greatest pleasure to do whatever you may wish. I hope I need not say that I should look upon your withdrawal from the University as a literally shocking calamity, and I most sincerely sympathize with the great annoyance you must have endured from the delay and uncertainty of two years, and wish I could do any thing to remove it. ... When Dr. Cooper was alive, I used to pick up stray bits to [of] information, but since his death that source of intelligence is closed. If I may speak with Dr. Cantwell and Dr. MacHale, perhaps it might be of some service. ...

"I take it for granted, though a phrase in your letter might lead to an opposite conclusion, that you will not resign without a full previous intimation of your difficulties, and time given to remove them, with a full knowledge of the consequences they will speedily entail, if not removed. ...

"I almost forgot to mention, that I heard recently a great feeling was excited by an attempt said to have been made by Dr. Cullen to have an important appointment made in connexion with the University, or some important act done, by the lay-members of the Committee outvoting the Bishops. ... The word 'little Pope' is sometimes heard among grave clergymen; and I cannot help thinking you would do well to cultivate as much personal connexion with the other Bishops as possible, not of course siding with any party, but not acting as tho' you thought that to treat with Dr. Cullen was to treat with Dr. MacHale, Dr. Cantwell, Dr. Derry and Dr. MacNally. You speak with just aversion of having to come over in an irresponsible or doubtful position, like Dr. Pusey &c. ... After you have commenced operations, such a position would be simply unendurable, but, to get into a state to commence operations, it seems to me ... that some time spent in what I may call a personal canvass of individual Bishops, might smooth away preliminary difficulties.

"Dear Dr. Newman, I have written many words &c. ... One reason I have for being glad of this occasion of writing to you: it is to beg you to convey to the members of the Birmingham Oratory my deep gratitude for their recent kindness, and the sincere affection which their extraordinary generosity has kindled in my mind ...

"P.S. I do not know what personal interchange of sentiment on the subject of your difficulty you have had with other Bishops, but I cannot help fancying the difficulty is one which letters will *not* remove, but which may be got rid of by personal intercourse, influence, frank and unreserved explanation, *vivâ voce* &c. &c."

There were some good pieces of advice in this letter. I fully entered into the writer's view, that I ought to belong to no party, and in the event carried out the principle of it only too decidedly. Also, it was true that the only way of moving the Bishops was to court them individually. This in the course of a few weeks from the date of his letter I began to do, and partially succeeded in; but Dr. MacHale was rude from the first, and I am a bad hand at forcing myself on unwilling minds. Also, I doubt not the question recurred to me, Are they doing me a favour in sending for me from England, or am I doing them a favour in going? Certainly it was very hard that I should be bound, for no end of my own, to leave my own dear "nidulo" in the Oratory, and plunge into strange quarters in order to wait at Episcopal doors, and to overcome prejudices against myself and the scheme of a University, which was nothing to me, whether they grew in strength or were dissipated. If the Bishops did not want me, they might lump me.

So much for my advisers; next, it so happened, that my letter of December 30th, at last overcame Dr. Cullen. He wrote to me thus, on January 4th of the new year.

"January 4, 1854. I will attend to the wishes expressed in your letter. I do not know, however, in what shape the desired document should be drawn up. It will be necessary to consult some of the Bishops on it. In the meanwhile I would be obliged to you to suggest any thing you think necessary." "Document" hardly expresses on this side of the channel an Episcopal manifestation or function, for which I had asked; however, I accepted his interpretation of my words as nearly as I could, and sent for his consideration copies of several of the Louvain documents which were in my possession. Also he wrote to Propaganda on the subject; but this, why I know not, he did not tell me. Nor do I know what came of his application to that high quarter.

Section 6.

Meanwhile, my interests were exciting attention in the highest quarter of all, and were provoking the interference of the Pope. Cardinal Wiseman, who was full of energy and resource, when he gave his mind to any matter, was then at Rome, and just at this time brought the subject of the University before his Holiness. On the 27th of December, before he received the letter I had addressed to him, he wrote to Dr. Cullen an account of an audience which the Pope had given him, and on the 13th of January, Dr. Taylor had the Archbishop's instructions to send on a copy of it to me. This he did, adding his warm congratulations on the happy event. Dr. Taylor said it "afforded to his Grace the greatest consolation and joy," though it does not appear why he had not himself invoked the intervention of the Holy Father. "He sees the dark cloud, so long hanging over the project, beginning to clear off. He has already written to Rome for authority to convoke the Bishops synodically on the subject, and he expects to have the power very soon, and to convene them in the beginning or course of the Lent. Meanwhile, he hopes you will come over, as soon as business beyond will permit. ... The Archbishop will write to Cardinal Wiseman at once, requesting him to act upon the views which he submits. ... Would it not be well, that you too would write to the Cardinal?"

The Cardinal's letter to Dr. Cullen was as follows:—

"Rome, Decr 27. 1853. Private and confidential. My dear Lord, His Holiness ... has several times spoken to me with the greatest interest, and I may say anxiety, about the University. He desires much to see it commence, and is ready to come forward with his authority to overcome all obstacles. His Holiness thinks indeed that Apostolical Letters should give it its foundation, and has several times repeated, that, if the materials for them were supplied, he will issue them.

"It appears to me, that, if your Grace thinks well ... a preliminary Brief might be issued, approving in general terms the foundation of such an institution in Dublin, confirming Dr. Newman as Rector, giving to such persons as you may name the power to elect Professors, authorizing the beginning with so many Faculties or Classes to be increased, giving the power of conferring degrees, as is done in such and such Colleges and Universities, by way of a temporary rule, and reserving to a future constitution the final approval of rules, regulations &c. 'Vedo' the Pope said to me a few days ago, 'che bisogna che il primo colpo venga del Papa.' If your Grace thinks so too, the thing is done."

To this letter of Dr. Taylor, with the inclosure from the Cardinal to Dr. Cullen, I sent an answer at once, proposing to Dr. Cullen, that I should go at once to Rome myself. My Memorandum in the journal of University matters which I had shortly before this time begun to keep, runs thus:

"January 15 (1854) answered, proposing *I* should go at once to Rome. My reasons are, 1. I fear the Cardinal will do too much, and that we shall have a University set up before we know where we are; at all events that something would be done *different* from what is wanted. 2. I shall be able to leave the matter in Manning's hands then," (who at that time was in Rome,) "but I cannot put it into them without talks with him. 3. I cannot really do any thing in Ireland, till the Brief comes; and now Dr. Cullen presses me to go to Ireland at once, *while* it is coming." (which I did not relish.) "If I don't go to Rome, it won't be done so quickly, meanwhile, I shall have a long kicking my heels and time-wasting in Ireland, when I am so wanted here." (i.e. in Birmingham.) "4. I shall come back from Rome with a prestige, as if I had a blunderbuss in my pocket."

I continue:—

"Jany 19. Letter from Dr. Taylor saying that the Archbishop thought it better I should not go to Rome just now; that he expected a letter from Propaganda, and wished me to be with him when it came. He added, 'He thinks it most probable that the issuing of the Brief, whenever it do[es] take place, will be accompanied by some mark of distinction to yourself as its Rector. To this you could not, for the sake of the University, offer any opposition. That being so, it would appear more appropriate that you should not be on the spot' (at Rome) 'at the time; but should defer your visit until after this first step is taken there, and then go to perfect whatever you might consider still calling for improvement'."

I had been going to Ireland on the 23rd but, as the expected letter from Rome did not arrive, it was agreed that I should delay my crossing till after the Purification.

The Memorandum in my journal runs thus:—

"Jany 23. wrote to Cardinal Wiseman to say that, if there was a brief, it must not do too much: it ought to make me Rector or Vice-Rector, with powers to appoint *Lecturers* (not Professors) with the approbation of the Archbishop for three years:—that we needed 1, on the one hand, an external *manifestation*; 2, on the other the beginning of an inward *formation*; that these were distinct from each other, and that the persons who were Lecturers perhaps would be but temporarily connected with the University; that we needed, not rules but zeal, energy, prudence, in the persons to whom the work was immediately entrusted."

On the 27th Dr. Taylor wrote to me thus:—

"Dr. Cullen has received a letter from Rome, informing him that in a few days a Brief will be issued empowering him to convoke synodically the Bishops of Ireland for the purpose of combining all their forces into one systematic line of action in favour of the University."

As to the Cardinal, before my letter to him of the 23rd reached him at Rome, I received a letter from him on Jany 31, in which he wrote as follows:—

"Rome, Jany 20. 1854. ... It is a delicate thing perhaps for me to learn any thing from *you* about the University," (this I suppose is in answer to my letter of the beginning of January, vid. supr. p. 88[1])

¹ p. 307. C.S.D.

"but it is not so for me to speak about it to the Holy Father for two reasons:—

"First, he has several times spoken to me; and secondly my position is naturally different from what it would be in England. While I am *in curiâ*, no one can consider me merely as an English Bishop, in whom it might be impertinence to meddle in the affairs of another country or Church. As Cardinal, however unworthy, I am bound to assist the Holy See by my advice on any matters proposed to me by it, without reference to country. In fact I am of the Pope's council.

"From the first audience I had of the Holy Father, I did not hesitate to say, that the University would never, could never, be started except by a Pontifical Brief, and that so great a work deserved and required this flowing from the Fountain of jurisdiction. His Holiness said that, if materials were furnished him, he would gladly issue such a high document. He spoke to me again, and agreed in the same conclusion.

"At a third audience I begged to make a suggestion long on my mind, and about which I consulted Archbishop Cullen at Amiens, and obtained his hearty concurrence. Indeed, I had mentioned it in England, I think to H. Wilberforce. It was that His Holiness would graciously please to create you Bishop *in partibus*, which would at once give you a right to sit with the Bishops in all consultations, would raise you above all other officers, professors &c. of the University, and would give dignity to this (?) itself, and to its head. The Holy Father at once assented; I wrote to Dr. Cullen and authorized his Grace to tell you as much as he thought proper.

"Your letter to me came after this:— and your must pardon me, if I communicated it to the Holy Father, of course, in all confidence; for it showed better than any studied narrative could possibly do, the real difficulties of the case. I made my own observations upon it.

"This day I had another audience, in which his Holiness graciously told me, that he has commissioned Mgr. Pacifici (who has been ill since October) yesterday to draw up a Brief, establishing the University, and naming Archbishop Cullen Chancellor; and, smilingly drawing his hands down from each side of his neck to his breast, he added, 'e manderemo a Newman la crocetta, lo faremo Vescovo di Porfirio; o qualchi luogo.' This was spoken in his kindest manner. Of course, Porphyrium was only an *exempli gratia*, as it is filled up. But I thought it might be pleasing to you to have the Pope's own words.

"I trust that the impulse, thus coming from above downwards, will be efficacious. I trust you will keep good heart, and not be discouraged by that opposition, which San Filippo would have considered a good augury in a great and holy work.

"To return to yourself, I will not hurt your feelings by what would be painful to them; but I must add, that I have long wished to do what I have done, even independently of the circumstances which appear to me to *require* it, for it appears to me to end many difficulties, and place things on their right basis. But ever since the Achilli judgment, I have felt that a mark of honour and favour, and an expression of sympathy *from the Church* was requisite, and this seemed to me the proper mode of bestowing it.

"I have only one thing to add, that I request the consolation and honour of conferring on you the proposed dignity, when the proper time shall come.

"Today I have been obtaining the degree of DD for Mr., now Dr. Manning, which the Pope granted with great and manifest pleasure. ...

"I will offer no congratulations as yet. You will use quite your own discretion about this letter.

Yours ever aff^{ly.} in Xt.

(signed) N. Card. Wiseman.

This letter was a great satisfaction to me. I really did think that the Cardinal had hit the right nail on the head, and had effected what would be a real remedy against the difficulties which lay in my way. I wrote to Dr. Grant of Southwark, who congratulated me on the Pope's intention, that I never could have fancied the circumstances would exist such as to lead me to be glad to be made a Bishop; but that so it was, I did feel glad, for I did not see, without some accession of weight to my official position, I could overcome the *inertia* or opposition which existed in Ireland on the project of a University.

The Bishop of Southwark was not the only Bishop who paid me compliments on this occasion. Dr. Ullathorne too, as might be expected, after having made a too eulogistic speech about me on a public occasion at Birmingham, (on which occasion, to the surprise of all present, he called me R^t Rev^d) on my writing to thank him, replied to me in the following terms:—

"Febr. 8. 1854. The announcement in your kind note does not take me by surprise. I had a hint of his Holiness's intention a fortnight since, and it appeared to me that the Episcopacy was the suitable mode of expressing the estimation, which both his Holiness and the Catholic Episcopacy entertain of you. And, whilst the dignity, so conferred as to make the distinction peculiar, will be universally applauded, so it will be useful to the University, and to your own position in reference to that arduous but important undertaking, ... The report of your elevation has been rumoured through England for some time. ...

"I hope that, when you receive your Briefs, some of the brethren will tell me; and, as I suppose that it is the last time I shall ever give you my blessing, I do it very heartily. ...

Your devoted brother in Xt   &c.

On February 12, F^r Stanton of the London Oratory wrote to me a letter beginning thus:—"My dearest Father, We have just heard the certain information of the reports about the Bishoprick. We feel the great propriety of the thing on a thousand grounds, and therefore rejoice heartily at it. I have no doubt it will be greatly for the good of the University. I suppose the consecration will not be at present, as I imagine you have to send your acceptance, and choice of see; and then the Bulls have to be issued. We are all for Ptolemais &c. &c."

Various friends made me costly presents in anticipation of the requirements of a Bishop. The Duke of Norfolk sent me a massive gold chain. Mrs. Bowden a cross and chain of Maltese filagree work. Mr. Hope Scott a morse for a cope, ornamented with his wife's jewels, and Mr. Monsell a cross.

So matters remained for some months. When I went to Ireland I made it known at Limerick and elsewhere that the Holy Father had designated me a Bishop.

Under date of May 1, Dr. Manning wrote to me from London: "I got home last Thursday, and I cannot longer delay writing a few words to give you joy and express my own, at the will of the Holy Father towards you. ... It is the due and fitting end to your long life of work, and fulfils the words of the Chapter in the Office, 'Justum deduxit, et honestavit illum in laboribus, et complevit labores illius'."

On the 3rd. of the same month I preached at the opening of the Church at Stone; and then Dr. Ullathorne treated me as a Bishop, refusing to give me the benediction before the Sermon. Also, as late as June 8, he addressed me a letter which runs as follows:—"My dear Lord, I returned this day from the Continent, and found your kind note. I feel honoured by your proposal to inscribe my name on the books of the Irish University, and of course accept the honour.

One of the first questions I asked on reaching England was about your consecration; but I have [not] yet heard of the where and the when ..."

And later still, on June 18, Lord Shrewsbury wrote to me as follows about the University:—"My dear Lord Bishop elect, ... May I request your Lordship to be so good as to allow my name to be put down as one of its members. ... I suppose your Lordship intends getting a charter to confer degrees, and if any influence I possess with present government might be of use, I put myself entirely at your disposition ... &c. &c.
To the Rt Revd Dr. Newman."

Also Monsell's pectoral cross came to me even later than June 28.

When I saw Dr. Ullathorne first on his return from Rome, between June 8 and 12, he had said "Why are are you not consecrated? it depends on you. You have to name the time &c. &c. I perplexed him by my answer that I had not received the Briefs or any official intelligence of the Pope's intention.

But long before this Dr. Cullen knew that I was not to receive the honour proposed. I judge so from the way in which he commented on the University Brief of March 20. He had sent me word Jany 19 that the Pope most probably would *accompany* the issuing of the Brief by some "mark of distinction" in my favour, and Cardinal Wiseman told him distinctly that that distinction was elevation to the Episcopal dignity. To this I was to offer no *opposition*—But now, showing me the University Brief he pointed out to me the words "Newman, egregiis animi dotibus ornatus &c and said in an awkward and hurried manner, "You see how the Pope speaks of you— *here* is the "distinction".

It was on the 12th. of June that Dr. Manning wrote to me apropos of my formal installation as Rector June 3, in these words:—"I give you joy on the beginning of your great work. On the point affecting yourself, I gathered (!) from the Cardinal that it was thought right to wait till the University had a formal existence. This I suppose will be accomplished already by this inauguration."

I wonder what would have happened if I had refused, as another man might have done, to be installed until I was consecrated.

The Cardinal never wrote to me a single word, or sent any sort of message to me, in explanation of the change of intention about me, till the day of his death. His letter, above transcribed is the beginning and the end of his appearance in this transaction. His concluding words were that he hoped to have the consolation of consecrating me. Nor did Dr. Cullen, nor Dr. Grant, nor Dr. Ullathorne, nor any one else, ever again say one single word on the subject; nor did they make any chance remark by which I have been able to form any idea why that elevation which was thought by Pope, Cardinal, and Arch- bishop so expedient for the University, or at least so settled a point, which was so publicly announced, was suddenly and silently reversed.

My friends for a long time did not realize the fact. In February 1855, Dr. Ullathorne wrote to me, "I cannot make out why certain Prelates should have opposed the Pope's intentions already conveyed to yourself—how it can help the University, or how it accords with so many precedents practised at Rome especially. I of course sub- scribe to the Pope's judgment, though I do not see through it. I suppose it is but a present delay." On my return from Rome in February, 1856, Badeley wrote to me under date of March 25. "I was in some hope that, when the Pope got you at the Vatican, he would take the opportunity to make you a Bishop, before he sent you home. When is this to be?"

Miss Giberne, to my great vexation, one day when she had an audience of the Pope, said without circumlocution, what she had also said to Cardinal Antonelli, "Holy Father, why don't you make F^r Newman a Bishop?" She reported that he looked much confused and took a great deal of snuff.

Dr. Ullathorne referred to the catastrophe once in January 1860. He had just returned from Rome, and reported to F^r Ambrose St John the dissatisfaction of some Roman authorities with an article which I had written in the Rambler of July 1859. He said that he had excused me to Cardinal Barnabò on the ground that I had had a great deal to bear in various ways, and that I had been disappointed in a Bishoprick. This seemed to make an impression on Cardinal Barnabò, for Dr. Ullathorne's report was, that, if I went to Rome and explained matters to the satisfaction of the authorities, there was the prospect of my returning to England a Bishop!

Two particulars I have heard since:—one from Hope Scott, though he gave no authority for his statement, but spoke as if it were commonly known, that Dr. Cullen had stopped proceedings. The other, which came to us on good authority, was to the effect that, not many years ago, Barnabò had said that the intention to make me a Bishop, was all a "hoax".

For myself, I never asked any one a single question from first to last, on the subject first of the delay, and then of the abandonment of the intention. It never occupied my thoughts. The prospect of it faded out of my mind, as the delay was more and more prolonged. I felt that to be a Bishop *there* (in Ireland) would have singularly helped me in my work: but I should never have been able to resign if I had taken such wages. I might have been in Ireland till now. I am ever thankful to St. Philip for having saved me from this. Sic me servavit apollo.

Section 7.

I had been accustomed to believe that, that over and above that attribute of infallibility which attached to the doctrinal decisions of the Holy See, a gift of sagacity had in every age characterized its occupants, so that we might be sure, as experience taught us, without its being a dogma of faith that what the Pope determined was the very measure, or the very policy, expedient for the Church at the time when he determined. This view I have brought out at some length in my "Rise of Universities" first published in the "University Gazette", and in the first lecture, as delivered, on the "Nature and Scope of Universities". I am obliged to say that a sentiment which history has impressed upon me, and impresses still, has been very considerably weakened as far as the present Pope is concerned, by the experience of the result of the policy which his chosen Counsellors had led him to pursue. I cannot help thinking in particular, that, if he had known more of the state of things in Ireland, he would not have taken up the quarrel about the higher education which his predecessor left him, and, if he could not religiously have found a way of recognizing the Queen's Colleges, then at least he would have abstained from decreeing [?] a Catholic University. I was a poor innocent as regards the actual state of things in Ireland when I went there, and did not care to think about it, for I relied on the word of the Pope, but from the event I am led to think it not rash to say that I knew as much about Ireland as he did.

I shall merely refer to some of the Pope's acts in furtherance of the University scheme, and thence refer to some of the testimonies in contrast to them which encountered me, when in February 1854 I at length went over to set the scheme in motion.

First in 1850, five years after the Parliamentary decision about the Queen's Colleges, the Synod of Thurles was held as a National

Synod, and by the influence of Pope Pius, and, it is said, with a bare majority of votes, the foundation of a Catholic University for Ireland was determined on. The decree of the Synod to this effect was confirmed with the other decrees in 1851; it was again confirmed in 1852; and contemporaneously with the second confirmation, viz on March 25, 1852, a Brief was issued with the purpose of stirring up the Bishops to greater activity than they had hitherto shown. It seems to have been issued apropos of Dr. Murray's the Archbishop of Dublin's death, which took place in the foregoing month; and it quotes the severe words which had been addressed to him from Rome for his direct disapproval of the attempt to establish a University, a disapproval so undisguised, that it could hardly have been commenced in Dublin during his life time.

This Brief, after a reference to the historical loyalty of the Irish Church to the Holy See, proceeds to animadvert sharply upon the Bishops for their party differences. It quotes St. Gregory's words, "Summopere necesse est, ut per caritatem semper uniti atque constricti, et nunquam interrupti per discordiam, inveniamur &c", and then applies the lesson to them, "Intimo nostri cordis affectu vos alloquimur, monemus, hortamur, et obsecramus, ut arctissimo inter vos caritatis foedere quotidie magis devincti, atque obstricti ... magis in dies sitis unanimes, ac perfecti in eodem sensu et in eadem sententiâ, et solliciti servare unitatem spiritûs in vinculo pacis." Not only ought they to be at peace among themselves, but "nobis persuasissimum est, vos nihil potius unquam habituros, quàm usque magis ejusmodi concordiam, non solum inter vos fovere, verùm etiam cum aliis, Venerabilibus Fratribus Angliae praesertim, et Scotiae Antistitibus, majorem in modum tueri atque augere."

Then the Brief proceeds, as an admonition to those who were backward among the Bishops in their zeal against the Queen's Colleges, to quote the Pope's words to the late Archbishop Murray in the preceding November, three months before his death, on occasion of a memorial on the subject addressed by the Archbishop and some other Bishops in the September, before it, or 1851? [Sept. 11. 1850]. They ran as follows:—

"Quod autem attinet ad Reginae Collegia, de quibus in commemoratis tuis litteris loqueris, pro certo habe, nobis pergratum fuisse, scire, te, Venerabilis Frater, post decreta, ab hac Apostolicâ sede de tanti momenti negotio edita, promptissimo animo decretis ipsis parere declarasse: ac persuasum habemus, te, non solùm decreta ipsa sollicitè esse executurum, verum etiam omni cura, contentione, et zelo curaturum ut illi antistites, quorum litteras die 11 Septembris superiori anno datas, atque à te quoque subscriptas accepimus, obsequio, venerentur, et omni charitate [alacritate] sedulo adimpleant."

And then the Brief exhorts the Bishops to spare no pains in carrying out as quickly as possible the project of a Catholic University.

This Brief had been issued just two years before the Brief of 1854, under cover of which I passed over to Ireland; to that Brief then, viz. of March 20, 1854, being the fourth formal act [to] which the Holy See had committed itself for the establishment of a University, I now proceed. It had been announced as imminent in the previous December, and contained, as I have already quoted from [it] me, a most gracious eulogy on me. It observed that two years had passed since his former brief, yet no step had been taken in advance towards the foundation of the University, and it orders the Bishops to hold within three months a Synodal meeting under the Presidency of Dr. Cullen, who had succeeded Dr. Murray as Archbishop of Dublin, with a view to opening the new Institution without any delay.

Though it is going out of my way, I am led to notice one or two peculiarities of this Brief.

One is that, though the Bishops had already elected me, the Pope says "*Volumus* ut idem Presbyter ejusdem Universitatis curam et regimen suscipiat, eique *velut Rector* praesit." This certainly is as if the Pope appointed me—but if really he had put down on me his hand, how was it that I was able to leave without his distinct permission?

Next, I remark that in this Brief the Pope several times, calls the University a "Lyceum"; and, in his letter to Dr. Cullen which accompanied it, he calls it a "Gymnasium". I do not know whether these words limit or modify the idea of a University: one would hardly suppose they were substituted for "University" without a reason.

And again the Pope exhorts the Bishops to make "divina nostra religio *tamquam anima* totius litterariae institutionis" in the University; that is, *the form*. "Omnes disciplinae" are to go forward in the most *strict league* with religion, that is, with the assumption of Catholic doctrine in their *intrinsic* treatment: and the Professors are directly to mould "totis viribus", "the youth to piety and virtue, and to ground them in literature and science in conformity with the

Church's teaching". I wrote on a different idea my "Discourses on University Education" in 1852, vid especially the original 5th Discourse.

The Synodal Meeting enjoined in the above Brief was held in Dublin, May 18, 1854 and following days—when the Fundamental Statutes of the University were passed, including the formal appointment of myself as Rector and Dr. Leahy as Sub Rector.

And now let us turn to the other side of the picture, and observe what the feeling of the Irish Catholics was on the subject of a University.

I got from Birmingham to Dublin on February 7, 1854. When I got there Dr. Cullen was away. The day after my arrival I called on Fr. Curtis, the Provincial, I think, of the Jesuits, or at least the Superior of the House in Gardiner Street. He was a man of great character and experience. I have this notice of my visit in my University Journal:—

"Febr. 8. Called on Fr. Curtis, who said 'On the experience of thirty years, that 1 the class of youths *did not exist* in Ireland, who would come to the University; that the middle class was too poor; that the gentleman class wished a degree for their sons, and sent them to Trinity College: and the upper class, who were few, sent their sons to English Universities &c; that many went abroad, e.g. to Belgium, until 17 or 18. 2. that there were no youths to fill evening classes (for show) in Dublin, unless I looked to the persons who frequented concerts &c. &c., men, women, and children.' Part of this was said in answer to my own anticipation, that there would be a class of students answering to the day-pupils of King's College, London. Also, there would be the class who frequent Mechanics Institutes, and, who as being Catholics, would require some guidance in the midst of a Protestant population. Fr. Curtis ended by saying 'My advice to you is this, to go to the Archbishop and say, Don't attempt the University—give up the idea.'"

This was the greeting from the first ecclesiastic I called upon, when, in consequence of the summons of the Committee in October, 1853, I found I was able to go over to Dublin.

Then as to Maynooth, the President, Dr. Kenehan, was distinctly cold towards the project of a University, while Dr. Russell, under date of July 2 wrote to me "I explained to you, when we last met, how I myself have felt the subject of the University, and how despondently I have looked on the prospects."

What Dr. Ryan said a few days after F^r Curtis, the following extract from my Journal will show:—

"Febr^y 24-27. The Bishop of Limerick very strong against the possibility of the University answering. However he has consented to have his name put down [in] the Book, on condition ... that he should [not?] be supposed to prophecy any thing but failure."

And two years and a half afterwards he sent me a message by Fr. Flanagan, "You will never do any good with the University till you put yourself in connexion with the Head of the Empire."

Dr. Murray I never saw, and he was now gone—but he still spoke in such men as these. We must take as you [things as they?] are: when a certain country is to be operated on, the opinions or judgments which are then expressed may be true or false, but they are facts, and must be treated as facts—for they are materials which have to be used as instruments or subjects. Men like Dr. Murray and Dr. Russell, were of the most cultivated class in Ireland—as Fr. Curtis was among the most experienced. Of course as good Catholics such men would not be slow to do all that they could do for any object on which the Holy Father had set his heart—but they had an omen of failure damping all their endeavours, if any of them were called to take part in the University.

The same must be said as regards the lawyers who were the natural and the actual allies of the class of ecclesiastics which I have been speaking of. Lucas had written me word in October 1851 of the objections which Mr. Thomas O'Hagan, now Lord Chancellor, made to the scheme of a University, and among them the opinions of the leading bishops, who had acted with the lawyers in the days of O'Connell, are prominent. "A fundamental" he says, "on the side of Trinity College against a Catholic University is the historical feeling. For years under Dr. Doyle, mixed schools, that is, equal rights in education, were the cry. A Bishop said the other day, Where is the line of demarcation to be drawn? how can separate education be carried on completely? When people are mixed and society is mixed, education must be mixed." These feelings I found to be in full possession of educated minds in 1854. At that time I had a conversation with Mr. Thomas O'Hagan, and on June 27 he wrote to me in answer. He says:—

"On Saturday or Sunday I spoke to several of our leading men," on the circuit? he writes from Longford—"and I think I may say that the suggestions which I ventured to make in our hurried conversation did not unfairly represent the condition of feeling and opinion, which is, to some extent to be encountered in its regard. Many Irish Catholics ... apprehend that the simple inscription of their names on its books might be taken to imply the abandonment of their opinions, and a compromise of their consistency."

In like manner Mr. Monsell writes me word September 5, that he send[s] me a "disheartening letter from Mr. Fitzgerald", (now Judge). Mr. Butler of Limerick, Oct. 14. says that Serjeant, now Judge, O'Brien has "been endeavouring to induce some members of the bar, who have scruples in the matter to go together in body and give their adhesion."

The feelings of the lawyers were shared by the country-gentleman, and that on various grounds, some of which I give instances of. "I applied to Lords Kenmare, Castleross and Fingall," writes Monsell on July 13, "to give their names to the University, and was surprised to find that they objected to do so. I think their names of great importance."

And I have a memorandum of March 1., thus: "Mr. Errington called. He said that Mr. James O'Ferrall had a more desponding view than ever of the University, from things which came out in the Maynooth commissions." I suppose, clerical jobs. "He thought there was simply no demand for it. He told me last November," I continue, "that the Catholic party had been obliged to move, in order to oppose the Queen's Colleges. Perhaps many will content themselves with their failures, looking on the project of a University merely as something negative." If this use of me was what called me to Ireland, viz. to be flung at the heads of the advocates of Queen's Colleges, and not to introduce a positive policy, this might be a great object, but a very different one from that which filled my own mind.

Mr. James O'Ferrall, who, as well as Mr. Errington, was a kind friend to me all the time that I was in Ireland, wrote to me about clerical jobs at the end of the year [December 17, 1854], bringing out the feeling which operated so much among the Catholic gentry against the University, that they were not allowed their just place in the institution. He writes thus on the subject of a money secretary:— "I know nothing of the Rev. Mr. M[ullen] but from my experience I do not consider clergymen much suited for such an office, nor that office suitable to them ... I fear, and I know such fears generally exist, that the tendency is to make the University a close borough of clergymen and a clerical college, which was neither the intention nor the wish of those who have encountered much obloquy in trying to establish it."

Again he says "I regretted the appointment of Dr. Leahy as Vice-President, I think a lay man would be more acceptable to the laity.

His brother, Mr. More O'Ferrall, had written May 5 to Mr. James O'F. "I concur with Dr. Newman that it is desirable to connect a large portion of the Catholic body with the new University, but there is some difficulty in deciding on the course most likely to effect this object. The Protestant party will endeavour to raise a cry, in which many Catholics are disposed to join, that the new University is got up [with] the purposing of placing Catholic education entirely in the hands of the clergy, and for the exclusion of the laity from all interference. I should have no objection to have my name among the number (given), provided it was taken as a recognition of the right of the laity to a voice in the management of the University."

In some of these passages allusion is made to the list of honorary members of the University, principally laymen from Ireland or elsewhere, I was trying to form—the plan was not viewed without jealousy by Dr. Cullen, and at Rome they gave it no countenance.

And here I might go to speak of the opposition made by the party antagonistic to the classes on whose sentiments I have been dwelling, viz Dr. McHale and Connaught and the Nationalists; but I have already mentioned them in the letter which I quoted of Lucas's written at the end of 1853.

So much for the leaders of the people. As to the masses of the population, from whom the contributions were to come, they of course knew nothing at all of the matter; had no direct interest and took no interest in any of the proceedings, and made their offerings when, and would make them while, they were told to do so by their Bishops, but no longer.

The letters I have given of course are only specimens of the state of opinion in Ireland generally in the years 1850-1854 on the prospect of a University; and they certainly do seem to show that to plan its establishment was to attempt an impossibility.

Jany 9. 1873.

Section 8.

I will briefly state what were the main points on which Dr. Cullen complained of me, and I of Dr. Cullen.

First from the first he quarrelled with my partial residence at Dublin. He thought, that, with the exception of a fair annual holiday, I ought to be at my post all through the year. He did not recognise I had duties elsewhere. He thought I ought to give them up. So ingrained this idea was in his mind, that, when our Congregation, in refusing to continue my leave of absence, pointedly limited their refusal to an absence such as had been "for the last three years", opening the doors to negociation for a residence not so strict as mine had been, he did not avail himself of it—and, when I directly called Dr. Leahy's attention to this middle way, proposing a residence for some weeks during each Term, he said it might be tried as an experiment for one year. And, when nothing in consequence came of this proposal, and I remained on, without taking any salary, till a successor was appointed, suddenly he, and Dr. Leahy with him, abruptly called me into residence, which was the immediate cause of my resignation. I do not say he was not right in wishing for a Rector who had no duties elsewhere; but, if that was his judgment, he ought not have asked me to be Rector—but I think he fancied that the superior attractions of the Rectorship would lead to my separating from the Oratory—, and, if not, to my bringing over the whole Oratory to Dublin.

I think this difficulty was a continual fret to him—and accounted, to his judgment, for whatever went amiss in the University.

But what I think was the real serious cause of distance, jealousy, distrust, & disapproval, as regards me & my doings, what [was?] the desire I had to make the laity a substantive power in the University. Here I was reprehensible in two respects.

First, I wished the gentry whose sons were to be taught by us to have the financial matters of the institution in their hands. The trustees of the property must, I knew, be ecclesiastics—but what I felt about was the expenditure. And in two ways—I thought that they had a right to the management of the current accounts, because else these accounts would not be kept in order at all—there would be no auditing—and no knowledge what was spent—it would be, as I expressed it, in my first report, like putting one's hands into a bag— All the time I was there I in vain repeatedly assailed Dr. Cullen on the necessity of a Finance Committee—& this was a great source of suspicion, of irritation to him. It made me indignant to find how little there seemed to be of responsibility in the expenditure. I did not choose to act in this way—it was laying me, a foreigner, open to imputations—years afterwards the question might arise, how had I spent the money—but it was contrary to the tradition and taste of the Irish ecclesiastics—and I am told that this shun-day habit has gone on [to] this day—and that sums, no one knows how great have been squandered away (I was told in one matter £10,000 with nothing to show for it) and no account drawn up or record taken of it.

I believe[d] laymen would put an end to this and therefore I wished the account to be in lay hands. Moreover I thought that such an arrangement would conciliate the laity and would interest them in the University more than anything else. They were treated like good little boys—were told to shut their eyes and open their mouths, and take what we give [sic] to them—and this they did not relish.

But a cause of offence to Dr. Cullen, far greater than my desire of a lay Finance Committee, was my countenance of those whom he considered young Irelanders, and generally nationalists—and to these he added a very different party, the friends of Lucas, up to the Archbishop of Tuam. I never of course would give up Lucas as a friend. I differed from him, but I thought him an honest good man— Dr. Cullen's treatment of him at Rome is too painful for me to talk of. As soon as the Archbishop thought I was on what may be called speaking terms with him, he grew cold towards me, then warned me against him, and I of course would not be warned.

But again there was a knot of men who in 1848 had been quasi rebels—they were clever men and had cooled down most of them. I did not care much for their political opinions—Dr. Moriarty introduced them to me, and I made them Professors. They are the ablest men who had belonged to the University—such as Professor O'Curry —and Professor Sullivan. I can never be sorry for asking their assistance—not to take them would have been preposterous—There you had good men, Irishmen, did Dr. Cullen wish Irish? had he not warned me against English and Scotch? If I did not take men made ready to my hand, desirable on their own accounts, desirable because their fellows were not to be found, I must put up, if not with English and Scotch, with incapable priests—is this what Dr. Cullen wanted?

He, however, seems to have been in a great alarm, what was coming next. I saw a great deal of Mr. Pigot, now dead, the Chief Baron's son—he talked like a republican—but he was full of views and a clever man. I had a thought of giving [him] a law Professorship—or I did. Dr. Cullen brought down with him to me, an excellent man the Archbishop of Halifax, Dr. Walsh?, to dissuade me by telling me things against Mr. Pigot. I have forgotten every word he said. It made no impression on me—I dared say he had said and done a number of wild things—he was a fanatic even then—but I did not see that therefore I should separate myself from him. But Dr. Cullen always compared young Ireland to young Italy—and with the most intense expression of words and countenance assured me they never came right—never—he knew them from his experience of Rome.

I cannot pursue these things at this distance of time—but the consequence was that Dr. Cullen became alienated from me, and from an early date either did not write to me, or, if ever he did, wrote by a secretary.

So much on his side of the question—now as to what I would say in objection to him.

In truth I have already suggested what I have to say—but I must say for myself that my reasons for separating myself from the University were far broader than any of a personal nature.

Or course, I was very much offended with Dr. Cullen. I could not act because I could not get him to say yes or no to questions which I asked him, and if I acted without asking, then I displeased him.

I begged him to substitute persons for himself to whom I might go, if it was inconvenient to him to converse or to correspond with me. It was one of those conditions I made as preliminary to my continuing in the Rectorship—but I got no answer beyond that of an incomprehensible silence. I could not go on in such a state of things, and therefore I confess that my relations towards Dr. Cullen had much to do with my leaving.

But there were those more direct and serious difficulties in my remaining which our Fathers put forth in their Letter in answer to the Three Archbishops. All that sad quarrel with the London House was owing to Fr Dalgairns thinking he might do what he pleased in my absence. It was an unfortunate coincidence of untoward events—but so it was that my residence here was absolutely necessary to the welfare of this Oratory, and this is the very thing, as I have said, which Dr. Cullen would not grant.

This was the main cause of my leaving then, that I could not give to the University that continuous preference which Dr. Cullen wished. His own conduct was a subordinate reason. There was a third still, though it was not of primary influence, still it had a force in reconciling me to my step. It was the fact, which had by this time become so plain, that English Catholics felt no interest at all in the

University scheme & had no intention to make use of it, should it get into shape. I had gone to Ireland on the express understanding that it was an English as well as an Irish University, and the Irish had done all in their power to make it an Irish University and nothing else. And further, I say, the English Catholics had given it up. It had begun a very little time, when Dr. Ullathorne told me, as if a matter in which he acquiesced, that "the English gentlemen would never send their sons to it."

Now it happened at the end of the year 1857, that Dr. Cullen expressed regret that the Professors did not make greater use of the Newspaper Press in bringing the University before the public, and I urged Mr. Ornsby and others to turn their thoughts to the subject. They were willing, and the only question was how to do it. It occurred to me that it would be well to begin some controversy about the University—so, telling no one but Mr. H Wilberforce, the Editor, I inserted in the Weekly Register a very bitter letter signed "Q in the corner". Ornsby replied and I wrote as many as four short letters; but to my disgust I found I was beating him. But what it brought out clearly was the English sentiment. No[t] a word came in advocacy of the University from any English College or centre, and Q's letters were, without disavowal of the sentiments which they contained, attributed generally to this or that English priest. I tried to make it up to the University by writing leading articles for four weeks in its defence; but what came home clearly to me was, that I was spending my life in the service of those who had not the claim upon me which my own countrymen had: that, in the decline of life, I was throwing myself out of that sphere of action and those connexions which I had been forming for myself so many years. All work is good, but what special claim had a University exclusively Irish upon my time?

Section 9.

I have made a memorandum of my visits to Ireland up to November 1853, above Section I, pp. 1-17. I will now continue it.

The next was, as I have said p. 137,[1] when I went to prepare for the opening of the University, on Febr^y 7, 1854. When I went to deliver my Lectures in 1852, I had a lodging in the neighbourhood of Rutland Square; but I soon moved as a boarder into Dr. Quinn's

[1] p. 323. C.S.D.

school in Harcourt Street. I kept my room there through 1853, and returned to it now. In the Autumn of 1854, when the University began, I began to rent, and removed into, Miss Segrave's house in Harcourt Street. This I rented on till, I think, the summer of 1859, it being inhabited after my departure by Scratton, Scott, Anderdon and Penny, with some young men.

On my getting to Dublin in February 1854, my first business was to put into execution Lucas's advice to me about visiting the Bishops. With the assistance of Bradshaw I drew out the scheme of a tour which would comprehend them all, though I did not communicate my intention further than to be a little in advance of my actual progress in the announcements I sent to them. I wished besides making their acquaintance to learn something of the state of the colleges and schools and to beat up for Professors and Scholars. I have still a portion of my projected itinerary. I was to start on Friday the 17th from Dublin for Thurles, thence to Kilkenny, Carlow, Waterford, Cork, and Killarney. This was to take a week. From Killarney I was to start on Friday the 24 for Limerick—thence to Galway by coach—thence to Athenry, Tuam, and Loughrea. From Galway in succession to Athlone, Mullingar, Navan, Drogheda, which I was to reach by the next Friday March 3. Thence I was to proceed to Newry, Belfast, Balmena, Coleraine, and Londonderry.

It was the worst winter that the country had had since 1814; and I had been laid up, as early as the foregoing November with one of those bad colds which began with me at Littlemore, and did not lose hold of me till about the year 1864. A second winter came on in February, and a second severe cold,—and, when I started from Dublin it was snowing hard. I directed my course to Kilkenny in consequence; and it was on Saturday the 18th.

It was extravagant to think of such a round of visits at that season, however seasonable the weather: but the weather was extraordinary. I was soon stopped short in my course. I got to Kilkenny in time for dinner at the Bishop's Dr. Walshe, and went on at night to the College at Carlow. There I remained over the Sunday, calling on the Bishop, Dr. Hely. On Monday morning the 20th I left for Dr. Foran's at Waterford, the Bishop of the place. I remained there Monday and Tuesday, and in the evening of the 21st went off to Cork, to the Vincentians. On the 22nd I was called on by the Bishop, Dr. Delany, who lived, I think, in the neighbourhood. Thence I went to Thurles, and was the guest of the Archbishop, Dr. Slattery, dining with Dr. Leahy at the College to meet a large party of priests. On the 24th I went to Limerick, to the Bishop's, Dr. Ryan, with whom I remained till Monday the 27th.

I had now seen six Bishops, and my progress was stopped. My cold had got worse and worse. I got very weak—and from Limerick my next step was a long coach journey to Galway. Nor was this all: I had neither food nor sleep: I could not sleep upon the featherbedded curtained fourposters, and I could not eat the coarse and bleeding mutton which was the ordinary dinner, and I created remark of course, do what I would, by going without it. With the prospect of a long coach journey and Dr. MacHale at the end of it, and the certainty of the same entertainment, coming all upon my indisposition, I felt it would be imprudent and useless to attempt more than I had done, and on the 27th I returned to Dublin.

I had visited six Bishops—I had met Dr. Denver of Belfast at Dr. Cullen's the evening before I set out. I had called at the Bishop of Killaloe's at Nenagh in 1852. Dr. Dixon I knew since the Synod of Oscott in 1852. In the course of the next few months several Bishops called on me in Harcourt Street, and I think I saw all of them or all the rest at Maynooth in June.

I was in Ireland from February 7 to July 3, with visits to England from March 20 to April 22 for Easter, from May 1 to May 5, when I went over expressly to preach at the opening of the Stone Convent Church—and May 23 to June 3, when, after keeping St. Philip's day, I went a round of visits, in behalf of the University to London, St. Edmund's, and Ushaw.

Immediately on my return to Dublin, on Whitsunday June 4, I was formally installed Rector of the University in Marlborough Street Church, & took the oath to Pope Pius's Creed.

On the 8th the University Gazette began, dating from June 1. It was at this time formally announced that the Schools in Philosophy & Letters would open on Nov 3, St Malachi's day. I returned to England July 4.

I remained in England from July 4 to September 5, when I crossed to Ireland—while at home I was engaged, as when I got across, with writing articles for the University Gazette.

I remained in Ireland from September 5 till at least Decr 8, and as I think till Decr 22.

I returned to Dublin on January 12 or 13, 1855. On February 4 I went to England and remained till the 10th, when I returned to

Ireland. There I remained till April 3, when I went to Birmingham for Easter, till the 16th, when I returned. On May 31 I crossed to Birmingham for St. Philip's day, returning to Dublin on June 9, where I remained to July 20. Then I went to B^m for the Vacation.

About the 18th of October 1855 I left Birmingham for Dublin, where I remained, except running over to London between November 20th and 23rd, till, I think, December 19. I did not return to Dublin till February 18 of the New year (1856) going with F^r A. St John to Rome in the interval.

Then I remained in Dublin from February 18 till May 18.

On May 1, the University Church was opened.

I was in Birmingham from May 19 to May 31, when I returned to Dublin.

The Bishops' Synodal Meeting was on June 20. I was up before them on June 26.

I went off to England on July 20 and remained there till October 24.

From Oct 24. (1856) to November 23 I was in Dublin. Then I went to England till Decr 10. From Decr 11 till the 23rd. I was in Dublin.

I was in England from Decr 23 till Jany 7 of the new year (1857) when I went to Ireland. I crossed back on the 26th remaining in England till February 12. And being in Dublin till March 9. On March 16th I crossed again for Dublin, and crossed back to Birmingham on April 3. Back again to Ireland on April 28. On May the 24th I went to England—and on June the 4th I returned to Dublin. On June 9th I crossed back to England and went back to Dublin on the 18th where I remained till July 18 when I went away for the vacation.

I remained in Birmingham from July 18, 1857 to October 29. I remained in Dublin till Novr 19. and returned to Birmingham, having given up residence in Dublin.

Once more I went there, viz from October 24 to November 4. 1858.

As far as I can calculate, I have crossed the St. George's Channel 56 times in the service of the University.

INDEX